THE RIGHT'S FIRST AMENDMENT

Stanford Studies in Law and Politics
Edited by Keith J. Bybee

THE RIGHT'S FIRST AMENDMENT

The Politics of Free Speech & the
Return of Conservative Libertarianism

Wayne Batchis

STANFORD LAW BOOKS
An Imprint of Stanford University Press
Stanford, California

Stanford University Press
Stanford, California

Printed in the United States of America on acid-free, archival-quality paper

Library of Congress Cataloging-in-Publication Data

Batchis, Wayne, 1974- author.
   The right's First Amendment : the politics of free speech and the return of conservative libertarianism / Wayne Batchis.
      pages cm -- (Stanford studies in law and politics)
   Includes bibliographical references and index.
   ISBN 978-0-8047-9606-4 (cloth : alk. paper) --
   ISBN 978-0-8047-9800-6 (pbk. : alk. paper) --
   ISBN 978-0-8047-9801-3 (electronic)
   1. Freedom of speech--United States. 2. United States. Constitution. 1st Amendment.
3. Political correctness--United States. 4. Constitutional law--United States. 5. Judicial process--United States. 6. Conservatism--United States. 7. Libertarianism--United States. I. Title. II. Series: Stanford studies in law and politics.
   KF4772.B38 2016
   342.7308'53--dc23

                         2015033514

Typeset by Bruce Lundquist in 10/14 Minion

Table of Contents

Preface

It doesn't take a political scientist to see that America is politically polarized. "Blue states" and "red states" have become the ubiquitous shorthand for a seemingly irreconcilable ideological gulf that has poisoned the well of collegiality, compromise, and accomplishment in Congress and in American politics generally. It likewise doesn't take a legal scholar to see that the U.S. Supreme Court has fed this intractable divide with repeated 5–4 decisions partitioned along sharp ideological lines. The media's obsessive focus on 5–4 opinions paints a portrait of judicial decision making that all too often resembles, not a rule of law, but a rule of raw, partisan majoritarianism.

This narrative, although simplified for public consumption, is not completely lacking in merit. Today, ideological alignment on the Court is correlated with the political party of the president who appointed the justice to an unprecedented historical extent.[1] There is unquestionably a relationship between ideology and Supreme Court decision making, and many political scientists applaud this acknowledgment; indeed, many have actively focused the public eye on this relationship.[2]

I have a background in two traditions. I am both a political scientist and a legal scholar. I believe there is much more to the story. I believe that legal interpretation matters—and it matters in a way that is inherently distinct from politics. Law and politics, in other words, should be understood as neither purely dichotomous nor nihilistically conflated. The balance lies somewhere in between; and in my view, there is perhaps no better illustration of this messy truth than in the politics and jurisprudence of free speech—consecrated in the very first of America's twenty-seven constitutional amendments.

Why the First Amendment? Free speech is enraging. It is degrading. It is frightening and shocking. Free speech means having one's most cherished beliefs dragged through the proverbial mud. It means that self-esteem, cultural pride, and national honor will be trampled; deeply held social norms will be callously flouted. For the political right and left, free speech is an open-ended and empowering tool for one's ideological adversaries. It is also—for good reason—a freedom that is among the most sacred and zealously guarded keystones of America's civic religion.

In the abstract, free speech is lionized. In practical, everyday life, it can manifest as ugly, painful, humiliating, and arguably damaging to American security and democracy. One might presume, then, that freedom of speech—with its profound ability to either aid or wound "both" political camps—would be an example of an ideologically neutral constitutional principle that is truly above politics. This, however, is not the case. Particular constitutional rights can be favored or disfavored by the right or left respectively at different periods in political history—and the First Amendment is no exception.

This study explores the interplay between political ideology and constitutional principle. The relationship, as I try to convey, is not a simple one. It is rife with nuance. It is the kind of nuance that might make purists—if such purists indeed exist—in both the "law is law" camp and the "law is politics" camp moderately uncomfortable. I believe that such discomfort is entirely healthy. The line between constitutional principle and ideology is both blurry and essential to the framers' design. In my view, denying the relationship between political ideology and constitutional interpretation would be naïve; but, even worse, denying there is an important and very real distinction between the two would be a democratic (with a small "d") suicide pact.

The story of this study is not neat and tidy. Many will eagerly poke holes in the broad conclusion that the political right in the United States has moved in a speech-protective direction, pointing to the many exceptions to this thesis, both on and off the Court. As I willingly concede, qualitative and quantitative assessments of the contemporary relationship between conservatism and free-speech values run the gamut. In part, this is due to the fact that the very meaning of "free speech" is contested. How can one be said to be pro–free speech if what one supports is, to one's detractors, not "speech" at all? Being pro–free speech might mean supporting a right to spend money, advertise Viagra, engage in sexually explicit performance art, exclude homosexuals from an association, burn draft cards, or burn crosses—and many, on both sides of the political spectrum, simply deny that the First Amendment has any relationship to these actions. The *principle* of free speech, in other words, cannot be separated from the *meaning* of free speech. One man's freedom of speech may, to another, have nothing whatsoever to do with speech.

Furthermore, and perhaps even more confounding, what are we to make of a situation where two purported free-speech interests are pitted *against each other*? Is the advocate for a dissenting shareholder's free-speech right *not* to be forced to speak any less pro–free speech than the advocate of unlimited corporate spending on campaign speech that disregards such shareholder dissent? How about the shopping mall owner who seeks to exercise her First Amendment right to convey a message of unbridled free-market capitalism by excluding Occupy Wall Street protestors, who themselves seek to freely express their views on mall property? Who gets to claim the prize? Who gets the gold medal for free-speech advocacy? To what extent might one's answer turn on one's political worldview?

Truly understanding the relationship between constitutional interpretation and political ideology—particularly with regard to the First Amendment—demands so much more than a mere crunching of judicial voting data, a favorite pastime of many political scientists. And it also quite clearly calls for looking far beyond the pure doctrinal analysis found in court opinions, a central focus of many legal scholars. In short, it's complicated. The relationship is nonetheless a real one—one with very real implications for American society and indeed for democracy itself.

.   .   .

In the recent past, a robust freedom of speech has been understood to be a core value of contemporary liberalism—and perceived to be antithetical to modern conservatism. Being aggressively pro–free speech was as comfortably associated with American political liberalism as being pro-choice, pro–affirmative action, or pro–gun control. Particularly during the heyday of the Warren Court, opinions protecting the right to freely express controversial, distasteful, or ostensibly immoral ideas were derided by conservatives and hailed by liberals. Contemporary liberalism seemed to consistently stand on the side of the First Amendment, even when the short-term costs were perceived to be relatively high. Political and jurisprudential conservatives, in contrast, saw a

First Amendment that was less of an absolute—a guarantee that could be balanced more comfortably against the democratic needs of civility and morality in some areas or evaded entirely in others.

With little notice, this political dynamic has been shaken to the core. Today, a critical mass of conservatives both on and off the Supreme Court are much more willing than they have been in the past to agree with their liberal counterparts that speech is deserving of First Amendment protection. In many instances, political liberals find themselves on the opposite end of the spectrum, advocating a narrower First Amendment. At the same time, the First Amendment has become an affirmative tool for advancing mainstream conservative policy objectives. A conservative legal movement has gained influence and has increasingly advocated a First Amendment approach to combating what it characterizes as liberal political correctness on college campuses. Conservatives on the Court have used the First Amendment to ensure greater corporate representation in American politics by allowing unlimited corporate spending on campaign speech. The Court has advanced conservative moral views—and curtailed minority representation—by utilizing the First Amendment's nontextual "right of the association" to strike down laws aimed at preventing organizations such as the Boy Scouts from discriminating against homosexuals.

Constitutional principles do not live in political isolation; politicians, pundits, commentators, and ideologically inclined scholars have adopted entrenched, passionate, and influential positions on constitutional meaning. This study brings together a close examination of the evolving political and ideological perspective on free speech with a fine-grained analysis of the shifting doctrinal and jurisprudential approach taken by the conservative members of the Supreme Court. On the political side, I anchor the study in an examination of the preeminent conservative publication, *National Review*. Its sixty-year history tells the story of modern American conservatism and reveals a fascinating shift in the way political conservatives have come to view the expressive rights guaranteed in the First Amendment. I show how the constitutional freedom of speech now carries a much more complex and nuanced political identity. In the process, I explore the ways in which this has, or has not, translated into doctrinal change on the Court.

Once acknowledged, these broader jurisprudential and political trends raise important questions. Does this shift represent a genuine and principled change in conservative philosophy regarding the role of the First Amendment in representative democracy? In the alternative, might we explain this trend, at least in part, as a results-oriented political expedient? How do ideologically inspired goals affect legal doctrine, and vice versa? And perhaps most importantly, what do these changes suggest for the future of First Amendment interpretation?

As with any project this size, I have by necessity made hard choices as to its scope. This is not a treatise on the First Amendment, and economy required that many important and interesting First Amendment cases simply could not be discussed while others receive only brief treatment. This is also primarily a book about ideas. There is a rich backstory to the intriguing interplay of ideology and doctrine on and off the Court: the world of conservative legal advocacy. The rise of the conservative legal movement is a fascinating and consequential tale, one deserving of its own book-length treatment. And indeed, there have been a number of excellent scholarly books on the subject in recent years. I tread only lightly on this subject.

The Introduction broaches the topic by taking a broad look at the relationship between conservatism and free speech over time—both on and off the high court. I then set the stage by exploring the earliest Supreme Court First Amendment decisions, most of which focused on the rights of communists and other dissident political minorities. Chapter 1 begins by exploring the concept of political conservatism. I look at the contents of the influential publication *National Review*, a longstanding barometer of mainstream conservative political thought, and assess its evolving view of free speech. In Chapter 2 I contemplate the contrasting approaches to understanding judicial decision making taken by political science and legal scholarship. I ask what it means to explore the First Amendment from a political perspective and why it is a useful and important exercise. I examine the lack of consensus, scholarly or otherwise, regarding the relationship between free-speech values and conservative politics and propose a new way forward—one that draws on both political science and legal models of judicial decision making.

In Chapters 3 and 4, I examine what I refer to as the political correctness backlash. In Chapter 3 I show how the conservative war on perceived political correctness, particularly on university campuses, would come to define the political landscape in the late 1980s and 1990s and would help *redefine* the conservative perspective on free speech and expression. I explore the popular anti-PC literature; the high-profile controversies at schools such as Yale, Dartmouth, and the University of Pennsylvania; and the speech-code policies that ultimately led to a conservative embrace of the First Amendment. Chapter 4 turns its attention to the judiciary's entrance into the political correctness debate, examining a number of Supreme Court decisions in depth and looking to the legal mobilization the debate inspired.

Chapters 5 and 6 focus on another significant inspiration for the evolving conservative view on the First Amendment: the rise of free-market conservatism and commercial speech. Chapter 5 focuses on the 1970s and 1980s, a period in which the conservative perspective on free speech in the commercial context was in a state of flux and a time when the Supreme Court radically remade its commercial speech doctrine. Chapter 6 moves us into the present, showing how the conservative view on commercial speech has solidified and how even traditional conservatives who had been inclined to reject broad free-speech rights moved in a speech-protective direction.

Finally, in Chapter 7 I approach the topic from a different angle. This chapter is a case study in what can go wrong in First Amendment interpretation, particularly when ideology acts as an impetus for doctrinal change. I critically examine the freedom of associational speech, a doctrine that reached its apogee in the 2010 decision *Citizens United v. FEC*. The chapter closely traces the politically liberal roots of the Supreme Court's freedom of association jurisprudence and critiques the way it was ultimately utilized by conservatives in *Citizens United*.

Acknowledgments

I am deeply grateful for all of those who have helped make this project possible. I count myself as remarkably fortunate to have landed in an academic department comprised of, quite simply, great people. I am particularly indebted to our department chair, Gretchen Bauer, whose inspiring leadership will be dearly missed as she steps down after many years of ably guiding the Department of Political Science and International Relations at the University of Delaware. I also offer heartfelt thanks to my colleague and mentor Leslie Goldstein, an inspiring scholar who offered not just valuable substantive assistance with this project but who helped make my success in academia possible. Others in my department (although this is far from an exhaustive list) who have offered their time, insight, and moral support include Alice Ba, Phil Jones, James Magee, Claire Rasmussen, and Matthew Weinert.

I am thankful for the helpful comments I received on portions of this book presented at a number of academic conferences including the Midwest Political Science Association, the Law and Society Association, and the Mid-Atlantic Law and Society Association. I received valuable feedback from many participants including Tabatha Abu El-Haj, William Blake, Michael Combs, Jason Schulman, and Gerry Turkel. I am especially grateful to the organizers and participants of the Loyola University Chicago School of Law Constitutional Law Colloquium, who welcomed me with open arms—one of few political scientists in a sea of law professors—to participate in what has become the intellectual highlight of my year. There I benefited greatly from thoughtful commentary, insightful conversations, and general inspiration relating to several chapters in this book from many brilliant legal minds, including William Araiza, Josh Blackman, Paul Gowder, Robert Knowles, Genevieve Lakier, Kyle Langvardt, Steven Morrison, Derek Muller, Helen Norton, Juan Perea, Joseph Tomain, Alexander Tsesis, and Rebecca Zietlow.

I am grateful for the fine research assistance of Jeremy Maerling, Scott Oliva, Matt Talmo, and Sean Shirali. I thank the diligent editorial staff of the *N.Y.U. Review of Law and Social Change* who worked so tirelessly on what would become Chapter 7 of this book, including among others Patrick Clark, Benjamin Cady, and Jonathan Fayer.

I am especially indebted to the enthusiasm, support, and hard work of those at Stanford University Press, including Keith Bybee, the series editor of Stanford Studies in Law and Politics, Michelle Lipinski, Nora Spiegel, Emily Smith, and Jennifer Gordon. I also thank the two anonymous reviewers who provided remarkably thorough and insightful commentary.

Above all, I would be remiss if I did not thank the most important people in my life—my family: my mother, Camille Batchis, for instilling in me her unrelenting curiosity; my father, George Batchis, for his endless support and thoughtful guidance; my two beautiful children Griffin and Sadie; and my wife, Leah Snyder Batchis, whose passion, drive, compassion, and intellect will always be my inspiration.

Introduction

The Right's First Amendment

In 1990 *National Review* published a piece by Robert Bork critically reviewing the Supreme Court's previous term. Bork's essay could not have better captured the transitional conservative tenor of the times. He positioned himself not in a manner that was consistently for or against broad free-speech rights, but instead as one who was willing to come to very different conclusions depending upon the issue at stake. He admonished the Court for its decision in *United States v. Eichman*, which, consistent with *Texas v. Johnson*, struck down a federal law protecting the American flag. According to Bork, the Court's majority failed to see that "no idea was being suppressed but merely a particularly offensive mode of expression."[1] Yet, at the same time that he brusquely dismissed the possibility that publicly desecrating a flag should constitute a protected form of expression, he rushed to condemn a Michigan campaign finance law that the Court upheld in *Austin v. Michigan Chamber of Commerce*, a law that to Bork "barred political speech, speech that is at the center of First Amendment protection."[2]

On the question of flag burning, Bork was playing the part of the moralistic conservative; on the issue of corporate speech, he cast himself as a libertarian conservative. On one hand, Bork told us that it should be permissible to prevent a "mode of expression" to make a political statement if it is "particularly offensive."[3] On the other hand, Bork asserted that legally prohibiting corporations from exerting influence over political campaigns was "flatly inconsistent with the idea, central to the First Amendment, that the right to speak is especially important when ideas expressed are not shared, or are even hated, by the majority."[4] In the campaign finance context, Bork bemoaned the *Austin* Court's holding "that government may act so that disfavored political views are disadvantaged in public debate," yet, just one page prior, he admonished the Court for doing the precise opposite: striking down a law that penalized a particular method (burning an American flag) of expressing a certain disfavored political view. Yes, different facts garner different results. However, as we shall see, this split personality on display in the pages of *National Review* was more than just an example of a case-by-case fact-intensive analysis by a respected conservative jurist and constitutional scholar: It was emblematic of a much broader splintering among political conservatives on First Amendment matters.

This fracture would ultimately, and largely, heal—but the relationship between political conservatism and free-speech values would not look the same. Public polling on subversive advocacy confirms the shift in conservative sentiment. In the 1970s, only 51.8 percent of self-identified conservatives would have allowed a speech by a person who advocated doing away with elections and letting the military run the country.[5] The number jumped to 70.3 percent in the years from 2010 to 2014.[6] William F. Buckley and other moralistic conservatives of the Red Scare and Cold War era, deeply suspicious of free-speech proponents, would be replaced by a new generation of conservative libertarians who would harken back on First Amendment matters to a long-forgotten period of conservatism. In turn, moralistic conservatives would themselves come to appreciate the libertarian position on free expression, in many cases adopting it as their own. From the 1970s to 2010–2014, conservatives who would allow speech against churches and religion would jump from 62.6 to 77.2 percent.[7]

The Conservative and Liberal Justices: A Brief First Amendment Snapshot

Let's return to the 1970s, a time in the not-so-distant past when Supreme Court decisions helped cement the perception that jurisprudential conservatives largely rejected a broad reading of the First Amendment. In 1971, ideological dichotomy in First Amendment thinking was attested to by Robert Bork in a controversial *Indiana Law Journal* article that would come back to haunt him as a failed nominee to the U.S. Supreme Court sixteen years later. In *Miller v. California* and *Paris Adult Theatre v. Slaton*—landmark companion obscenity cases argued just a year after Bork penned his article—the Court split right down the middle, with the ideological divide much in evidence.

Richard Nixon had been elected president just a few years before these cases were considered. His election occurred at what would prove to be the final days of the liberal Warren Court, and it was readily apparent that this new conservative president saw it as his mission to alter the ideological tenor of the Court. As Nixon insider John Dean observed, "More than any other president since Franklin D. Roosevelt, [Nixon] worked hard to mold the Court to his personal liking . . . making conservative appointments."[8] Perhaps unsurprisingly, four of the five justices who comprised the majority opinion upholding the obscenity exception to the First Amendment were recent Nixon appointees: Warren Burger, William Rehnquist, Lewis Powell, and Harry Blackman. Three of the four dissenters were vestigial stalwarts from the liberal Warren Court: William Douglas, Thurgood Marshall, and William Brennan.

Granted, the majority opinion in *Miller* by no means went as far in circumscribing First Amendment protection as Robert Bork proposed in his 1971 article. Unlike Bork's view, which would have narrowly limited protected speech to overtly political expression, the majority in *Miller v. California* was clear that the First Amendment protected "serious literary, artistic" and "scientific expression."[9] Why the contrast between Bork's position and the view of the conservative wing of the Court? Perhaps this was simply a difference in *degree* of conservatism rather than *kind*. The Court, as a consequence of the Nixon appointments, was clearly moving in a rightward direction. However, jurisprudential philosophy—like ideology—operates on a continuum rather than being strictly dichotomous. So, one way of understanding the Court's obscenity decisions of the early 1970s is that the Court was emerging as conservative on certain First Amendment matters—yet it was still quite a bit *less* conservative than the philosophy articulated by Robert Bork.

However, this assessment may not tell the whole story. It is also important to note that Bork, *in his capacity as an academic* writing a scholarly article, had much greater latitude in outlining his ideal vision of legal doctrine. This is also true of a judge writing *outside* of the context of a formal case or controversy. Judges qua judges, at least in theory, are constrained by precedent. Thus, even a legal decision that lays out a new doctrinal test—as the Court did in *Miller*—will be informed by previous case law. By the time of *Miller* and *Paris Adult Theatre*, the Court's "obscenity" jurisprudence, as a categorical exception to First Amendment protection, was considerably confused.[10] These two companion cases offered a needed opportunity to clarify and perhaps even reformulate the Court's preexisting doctrine on the subject.[11] The

Court had not directly addressed the contentious issue since 1957, when it determined that obscenity was "not within the protection intended for speech and press."[12] The doctrinal uncertainty after this point lay in finding an appropriate, workable, and consistent definition of obscenity. The Court's task, operating under the limiting principle of *stare decisis* and the canon of judicial decision making that circumscribed its role to the constitutional issue at hand, was to determine the nature and breadth of the unprotected category of obscenity—not to enlarge the unprotected class of speech well beyond obscenity as Bork would presumably have preferred. Thus, it is hard to even say that the majority opinion necessarily reflects a less-conservative (and more speech-protective) ideological perspective than the one promoted by Robert Bork. It could simply illuminate the distinction between judges, acting as judges, and other political actors.

The dissenting Justice Douglas—who was at the time the most liberal member of the Court[13]—remained consistent by simply maintaining his original objection to the very idea that "obscenity is not expression protected by the First Amendment."[14] Dissenting Justices Brennan, Stewart, and Marshall took a different approach, rejecting the majority's conclusions for more nuanced reasons. Brennan argued that the majority's holding could not "bring stability to this area of law without jeopardizing fundamental First Amendment values."[15] He explained that since first declaring obscenity unprotected, the Court had been "manifestly unable to describe it in advance except by reference to concepts so elusive that they fail to distinguish clearly between protected and unprotected speech."[16] Thus, to Brennan, there was something inherently unworkable about allowing a constitutional right to turn upon a nebulous and seemingly subjective concept such as obscenity.

Brennan's reversal from his prior position upholding the obscenity exception was guided by an acute sensitivity to free speech. To Brennan—who next to Douglas was the most liberal member of the Court that term[17]—the potential that obscenity restrictions might ultimately inhibit other speech was fatal. In contrast with Judge Bork, Brennan and his fellow dissenters presumed that literature—even the nonpolitical variety—must be protected by the First Amendment. These dissenters feared that the new doctrinal formulation, in part defining obscenity as material that lacks "serious literary value," would invite censorship of sexually oriented but socially valuable literature simply because some do not believe is it "serious" *enough.*[18] This is a concern that is consistent with the politically liberal ideal that elevates the freedom of, and tolerance for, unpopular or eccentric individuals and ideas over the value of promoting more limited moral conceptions of community.

Unlike the dissenters, the five most conservative justices[19] felt comfortable excluding an entire category of expression—obscenity—from the ambit of the First Amendment. They relied upon philosophical concerns traditionally adopted by moralistic conservatism. The majority opinion in *Paris Adult Theatre v. Slaton* highlighted obscenity's "corrupting"[20] impact, stressed "the social interest in order and morality,"[21] and twice cited the prominent neoconservative Irving Kristol to support its conclusions.[22] They emphasized the centrality of *local* "tastes and attitudes" and tailored their doctrinal test to accommodate regional tradition over national "imposed uniformity."[23] Even in light of the literal command of the First Amendment, the traditionally conservative concerns of law and order and public morality were to override the claim that "individual 'free will' must govern."[24] They stressed that "a sensitive, key relationship of human existence, central to family life, community welfare, and the development of human personality, can be debased and distorted by crass commercial exploitation of sex."[25]

As this illustration suggests, forty years ago, both on and off the Court, the alignment between conservative political ideology and the First Amendment's protection of free speech and expression was relatively clear. As a general matter, conservatives were much less speech protective. For conservatives, concern for tradition, family, and morality trumped individual expressive freedom. As we shall discuss, social scientists who have studied the relationship between ideology and judging have consistently relied upon this assumption, repeatedly associating support for increased regulation of expression with conservatism.[26]

However, much would change in the ensuing decades. We need only look to the Court's most recent First Amendment decisions to get a taste of the striking transformation. In 2011, it was Justice Antonin Scalia, perhaps the most evocative political symbol of jurisprudential conservatism on today's Supreme Court, who wrote the majority opinion striking down a morality-imbued California law on First Amendment grounds.[27] The law prohibiting the sale or rental of violent video games was designed as an "aid to parental authority."[28] With little equivocation, Scalia explained that "[l]ike the protected books, plays, and movies that preceded them, video games communicate ideas—and even social messages—through many familiar devices . . . and [t]hat suffices to confer First Amendment protection."[29] Scalia made a brief and loose concession to the view famously articulated by Robert Bork, admitting that "[t]he Free Speech Clause exists principally to protect discourse on public matters."[30] However, he just as quickly dispelled the notion that the Court was in a position to parse political speech from nonpolitical speech and protect only the former. He cautioned, "we have long recognized that it is difficult to distinguish politics from entertainment, and dangerous to try. . . . What is one man's amusement, teaches another's doctrine."[31] Scalia was effectively summoning the spirit of liberal icon Oliver Wendell Holmes, Jr. A half century ago, such a starkly relativistic admission would have been assumed without hesitation to be the product of a politically liberal mind, yet such sentiments—at least when discussing freedom of speech—are increasingly uttered by conservative jurists and commentators.

Scalia's majority opinion might have come as a surprise to those familiar with his jurisprudence. Scalia consistently ranks as among the most conservative justices on the high court and has become well known for rhetorically powerful opinions with a signature emphasis on tradition and morality. Here, California ostensibly sought to reinforce parental control over the moral development of children in the state, certainly a value with a longstanding historical pedigree. In *Brown*, however, Scalia defined tradition narrowly—not in the broader sense of parental control over children but in terms of the very specific restriction here sought. Scalia pulled "tradition" from his jurisprudential arsenal—not as a way of defending the conservative notion that parents should have the broadest possible leeway in shaping the moral development of their children, but as a way of rejecting this legislatively devised tool. It is difficult to quarrel with the illustrative examples of violent children's literature Scalia provided, including particularly disturbing and vivid images drawn from Grimm's fairy tales.[32] Scalia opined that "California's argument would fare better if there were a longstanding tradition in this country of specially restricting children's access to depictions of violence, but there is none."[33] It is striking that Scalia drew upon the interpretive tool of "tradition," frequently utilized to arrive at more conservative judicial outcomes, to disserve a quintessentially conservative political goal, combating moral degradation in society by enhancing authority of parents over their children.

Defending this moralistic position proved to be a lonely task. Only one of the five conservative justices dissented. Justice Thomas stood firm, but alone, for the proposition that speech directed at children is an unprotected category of First Amendment expression. He explained:

the founding generation believed parents had absolute authority over their minor children and expected parents to use authority to direct the proper development of their children. It would be absurd to suggest that such a society understood "the freedom of speech" to include a right to speak to minors . . . without going through the minors' parents.[34]

While two other conservatives on the Court refused to sign onto the majority opinion penned by Scalia and joined by Justice Kennedy, it is notable that these two justices, Alito and Roberts, concurred. Both were unwilling to join the path forged by Thomas. Instead, the two justices appointed by President George W. Bush struck a middle ground, agreeing that the California law was unconstitutional, but only because of the inadequate specificity of the law's terminology.[35] The concurrence implied that much material that might fall within California's definition of a "violent video game" is still protected by the First Amendment and that the statute might have passed constitutional muster "if it targeted a narrower class of graphic depictions."[36] Thus, they left open the possibility that, to minors, certain objectionable violent material might be unprotected.

Nevertheless, the litany of "vagueness" problems associated with the statute identified by the concurrence does not leave one feeling optimistic about the possibility of a satisfactorily drawn law. While Alito and Roberts were more cautious than Scalia, and thus unwilling to foreclose the possibility of a constitutional law limiting access to violent video games by minors, their view was in many respects reminiscent of Justice Brennan's dissent in Miller, acknowledging the practical difficulties of moral line-drawing when it comes to the First Amendment. They noted, for example, that "the prevalence of violent depictions in children's literature and entertainment creates numerous opportunities for reasonable people to disagree about which depictions may excite 'deviant' or 'morbid' impulses."[37] Although such an observation may be eminently reasonable, this is again a concession to relativism that might strike many as the very opposite of conservatism. In short, where there is a conflict between conservative principles on the First Amendment, the conservatives on the Court do not appear to be unified as to which model of conservatism should inform their jurisprudence—moralistic conservatism or libertarian conservatism—but increasingly they seem to have moved toward the latter. As we shall see throughout this study, other examples of this phenomenon abound.

In two additional recent First Amendment cases, it was Justice Alito who stood alone as the sole dissenter against a unified Court willing to reject laws that impinge on free expression. Strikingly, other than his single dissenting voice, the conservatives and liberals on the Court appeared to act in harmony. This relative tranquility existed in factual settings rife with heated issues of morality politics that might have in the past resulted in a distinct ideological divide. In *United States v. Stevens*, the Court struck down on overbreadth grounds a federal law criminalizing "the commercial creation, sale, or possession of certain depictions of animal cruelty."[38] In *Snyder v. Phelps*, the Court concluded that the First Amendment barred recovery in tort for intentional infliction of emotional distress imposed upon relatives attending a funeral for a veteran killed in the line of duty.[39] Picketers from the Westboro Baptist Church, who stood outside of the funeral grounds, held an array of incendiary signs suggesting that dead U.S. soldiers had been punished by God for America's tolerance of sinful behavior.[40]

At first glance the *Stevens* holding might appear utterly predictable from a purely political perspective. The Court majority expressed concern that the law intended to target the market for cruel, fetishistic "crush videos" (depicting the torture and death of innocent animals) would in fact reach much further, having the unintended consequence of potentially criminalizing popular "hunting television programs, videos, and Web sites."[41] The powerful politically conservative National Rifle Association filed an amicus curiae brief articulating this concern.[42] Seen as a contest between hunting enthusiasts and animal rights activists, it might be unsurprising that four of the five conservatives on the Court aligned themselves with the former. However, here the conservatives acted in lockstep with the liberals on the Court, who might be expected to have greater sympathies for the animal rights movement. On the surface it would appear to be Justice Alito in dissent, who ironically struck the most ideologically "liberal" chord on the Court. He made a plea for compassion—what moral foundations theory would identify as the "care" foundation—and sounded the alarm of cold commerce. He vehemently objected that the majority struck "down in its entirety a valuable statute . . . that was enacted not to suppress speech, but to prevent horrific acts of animal cruelty—in particular, the creation and commercial exploitation of 'crush videos,' a form of depraved entertainment that has no social value."[43]

Viewed in another way, however, Justice Alito's position is very much in line with traditional moralistic conservatism on the Court. As I shall argue later, this form of moralistic conservatism—a view that frequently ran unapologetically counter to free-market conservatism—was prevalent in the past, as exemplified by Justice Rehnquist's position in numerous commercial speech cases discussed in Chapters 5 and 6. What is striking is that today Justice Alito finds himself in a distinct minority among his conservative brethren. Just a few decades earlier his brand of moralistic and commonsense conservatism on the First Amendment was the norm. Under this view, when the Court is in the position of balancing law enforcement and individual rights, the benefit of the doubt should be given to those responsible for maintaining law and order. This is true even where, and perhaps especially where, the "individual" rights at stake are the rights of actors seeking commercial gain. Justice Alito was persuaded by Congress' argument that, in this instance, effective law enforcement against criminal acts of animal cruelty could not occur without targeting commercial trade in the videos depicting the illegal acts.[44] In Alito's dissent, we see clearly how moralistic conservatism may be at odds with libertarian and free-market conservatism. Alito understands this statute to be a law enforcement tool. If there has been one theme that consistently divides political liberals and political conservatives in America, it is the extent to which individual liberties may be sacrificed in order to achieve more effective criminal prosecution.

In *Snyder*, Alito is once again the outlier. Again, Alito stands up for principles that are traditionally "conservative" yet remarkably distinct from today's conservative norms of First Amendment interpretation. Contrary to the view of the unified majority, Alito would allow for recovery in tort for the "severe and lasting emotional injury" that resulted from the Westboro picketers.[45] On its face, this emphasis would appear to draw upon the moral foundation of "care." But Alito's concern reached deeply into values of "loyalty," "authority," and "sanctity"—foundations deeply associated with political conservatism in America.[46] Throughout his dissent, Alito emphasized the nature of the interests at stake: respect for family, country, ceremony, and military heroism. He emphasized the sacred nature of funerals, thus entitling them to a special level of protection.[47] To Alito, the case involved one of the most traditionally rooted of moral entitlements: "the right of any parent who experiences such an incalculable loss: to bury his son in peace."[48]

So what does all of this suggest? Do First Amendment cases from the very recent past imply that tying free speech principles to ideology is an anachronistic and futile enterprise—that there is simply no longer a relationship between conservatism and freedom of expression? Have political liberals and political conservatives both on and off the Court, with some exceptions, simply coalesced on this issue? While *Brown, Stevens,* and *Snyder* might lead one to the conclusion that conservative justices have moved away from the conservatism of Robert Bork—and perhaps joined hand-in-hand with the left on First Amendment issues—other very recent decisions reveal that the divide remains as distinct and volatile as ever. As we shall see in Chapter 7, at times this divide takes a very different form. The 2010 decision in *Citizens United* is one example of an ideological 5–4 formation where it was the liberal justices who uniformly supported speech regulation and the conservative majority who stood firmly opposed. The case has been described by one of the foremost constitutional scholars as the *very first* Supreme Court case in which an ostensible victory for First Amendment rights was decided in such a manner.[49] Not only was the traditional ideological alignment precisely reversed, but external political criticism of the supposedly pro–free-speech opinion came almost exclusively from the political left.[50]

Nevertheless, some legal scholars arguably saw this coming—and some saw movement with regard to First Amendment issues on both the right *and* the left. Almost fifteen years before *Citizens United* was decided, David M. Rabban detailed an emerging shift among legal intellectuals on the left away from the traditionally coveted liberal ideal of a broadly construed freedom of speech.[51] Rabban described this change of heart among liberals—a shift we explore in Chapter 3—as "the most striking development in First Amendment analysis in the generation since Brandenburg."[52] During the liberal heyday of First Amendment lionization, the intended beneficiary of pro–First Amendment activism was the disempowered individual—a fact that made such cases more sympathetic to liberalism, even if their message of dissent was otherwise not favorable to the left.[53] Today, however, a number of liberal scholars feel that the First Amendment is being utilized as the Due Process Clause of the Fourteenth Amendment was (ab)used a century ago—as constitutional support for inequality.[54] In order to combat this Lochnerization of the First Amendment, one prominent liberal scholar, Cass Sunstein, has proposed what he calls "a New Deal for speech," which would mirror the constitutional repudiation of laissez-faire economics that began in the late 1930s.[55]

There is, of course, a straightforward, cynical explanation for the decision in *Citizens United*—both the alignment on the Court and the political critique. By promoting the interests of the wealthy—that is, the ability of large corporations to influence elections—*Citizens United* served instrumental goals. By striking down campaign finance regulations that limited corporate expenditures on supposed campaign "speech," the practical interests of the Republican Party were being served. Indeed, a recent study does reveal some correlation between conservative justices' willingness to uphold free-speech rights and the ideological conservatism of the speakers at issue.[56] As Frederick Schauer concluded in 1993—looking at previous campaign finance decisions and the manner in which "the First Amendment banner"[57] was held high by those with great wealth—"the affinity between economic libertarians, most of whom vote Republican, and the principle of free speech may be less startling than it has recently seemed."[58]

However, the instrumentalist explanation, one that cynically views the Court as political—not merely in the sense that it adopts ideologically aligned decisions but in that its decisions reflect the desire for raw political advantage for the home team—is not the only way to understand *Citizens United* as political. On principled grounds, the decision is consistent with free-market and libertarian conservatism. Kathleen Sullivan attempts to explain the puzzling "flip-flop" of liberalism and conservatism in *Citizens United* as reflective of two differing visions of free speech: "free-speech-as-equality" on the left and "free-speech-as-liberty" on the right.[59] In Sullivan's view, cases where liberals and conservatives have been united on First Amendment issues, resulting in the series of unexpectedly harmonious holdings discussed above, are circumstances where these two visions of the First Amendment overlap.[60]

From this are we to conclude that conservatives are the new, and emerging, champions of First Amendment freedoms, while liberals are all too willing to compromise these values where they conflict with equality concerns? Not quite. One problem with this thesis is that in some areas traditional assumptions do still hold—with liberals remaining more speech protective and conservatives less so. I critique Sullivan's thesis more extensively in Chapter 7. Relatively recent decisions—although increasingly rare—such as *Garcetti v. Ceballos*,[61] *Morse v. Frederick*,[62] and *Holder v. Humanitarian Law Project*[63]—still exhibit the traditional liberal/pro–free speech, conservative/pro–speech-regulation alignment. However, the conservative majority opinions in such decisions tend to be quite self-conscious and narrowly drawn—not at all resembling the First Amendment minimalism of, for example, Robert Bork.

The Early Years: Communism, Communism, and More Communism

The early history of the Supreme Court's free-speech jurisprudence is well worn. It began, most lamentably, with over a century of silence—a period in which "courts would not distinguish themselves in the defense of First Amendment values."[64] With the onset of the twentieth century came a story of defeat and resilience for the First Amendment, a display of jurisprudential heroism and

tenacity by team Holmes–Brandeis, and one of the most important and principled demonstrations of how even the greatest of judicial minds may change.

Justice Holmes famously affirmed his alliance with the left in his powerful and enduring *Lochner v. New York* dissent. Holmes would initially show a
similar restraint, preferring legislative deference to judicial command, in the
field of free expression. *Lochner* was, of course, a decision that would come to
define for an entire generation what it meant to be a politically conservative
jurist. The *Lochner* era, which ran from approximately 1905 to 1934, was marked
by conservative judicial activism.[65] During this period the Supreme Court
frequently invalidated progressive economic regulations. Judicial inaction, or
procedural conservatism, came to be associated with political liberalism. If the
State of New York deemed it appropriate to limit the working hours of bakers,
the progressive voices on the Court argued that it was not for the judiciary to
interfere. Supreme Court justices were not in the position to determine the
wisdom of economic theory undergirding a particular policy. As Holmes explained in *Lochner*, "I do not conceive that to be my duty, because I strongly
believe that my agreement or disagreement has nothing to do with the right of
a majority to embody their opinions in law."[66]

It is with this backdrop, one in which procedural activism was aligned with
political conservatism, that the Court first took up the power of the government to penalize free expression. Yet, by the early twentieth century, the apparent support for judicial intervention among conservatives when it came
to economic matters, so evident in *Lochner*, was not visible in other "non-
economic" areas of law. Having left behind the libertarian views dominant in
the Victorian era, mainstream conservatives did not advocate constitutional
protection for words that were believed to risk disturbing the peace or social
order; and, of course, conservatives of this period were particularly hostile to
"dangerous" propaganda disseminated by communists or anarchists.[67] Indeed,
several conservative members of the Supreme Court, including Chief Justice
White, had expressed—off the bench—the view that political anarchists posed
a genuine danger to American democracy.[68] Historian Richard Polenberg described the conservative Court tenor of the times:

> Holmes and Brandeis excepted, the Justices' belief in property rights was
> matched only by their fear of radicalism, and their view of the First Amend-
> ment was summed up by [Chief Justice] White's comment that freedom of
> speech was "subject to the restraints which separate right from wrong-doing."[69]

Progressives of the era, on the other hand, were informed by their deep disapproval of the way the courts repeatedly overturned a wide range of liberal social reforms. Observing the devastating impact conservative judicial activism had in holding back critical social advances such as minimum wage and maximum hours laws, progressives tended to look with suspicion on individual rights-based judicial invalidations.[70] For most mainstream progressives, this suspicion of judicial intervention extended to potential First Amendment claims.[71]

By the time the Supreme Court faced its first major challenge to a piece of legislation on First Amendment grounds, the predisposition of all jurists to favor deference to the political branches—progressives and conservatives alike—was heightened by one additional factor: the fog of war. The Court has a controversial but undeniable history of judicial nonintervention—what some critics might call "abdications of duty"—during times of war and national insecurity. Whether it be the retrospective approval of President Lincoln's unilateral blockade of ports under authority provided by a "war" that had been yet to be declared by Congress,[72] or the Court's infamous sanctioning of the country's most notorious mass human rights violation since the abolition of slavery in *Korematsu v. United States*,[73] the Court has been deeply reluctant to interfere with the political branches in wartime, even in the face of deeply questionable behavior. Incursions into free speech were no different. Almost a half century of Supreme Court jurisprudence—beginning in 1919, the year the Court first began to seriously address free-speech claims—was marked by such reticence. Volumes of the *Supreme Court Reporter* were peppered with examples of judicial inaction in cases where government, in the name of national security, had attempted to quiet dissenting speech.

Fighting in World War I had just ended a matter of months before *Schenck v. United States*[74] was decided. This was a period in which more than 2,000 individuals were prosecuted and 1,000 were convicted under the Espionage Act of 1917 and the Sedition Act of 1918 for protesting America's involvement.[75] The wartime hands-off judicial impulse was palpable. Justice Holmes conceded that "in many places and in ordinary times" the words in a socialist anti-war leaflet would have constituted protected speech, but the "the character of every act depends upon the circumstances in which it is done."[76] History would eventually judge these words in the Court's seminal *Schenck v. United States* as a dubious justification for a deeply regrettable holding. However, by upholding the conviction in *Schenck*, Justice Holmes, widely understood to be a hero of the progressive era, was simply acting in accord with the tenor of the political moment, a time of war in which neither political pole seemed particularly concerned about the freedom of speech.

Viewed with a broader lens, the content of Holmes's unanimous opinion in *Schenck* in fact marked a sharp departure from a pronouncement on free speech he had made just a dozen years earlier; the decision's logic implicitly repudiated the view he expressed in *Patterson v. Colorado,* in which he had suggested that the First Amendment merely prohibits prior restraints.[77] While the outcome of *Schenck* may have been regressive by today's standards, the language that followed Holmes's concession about wartime jurisprudence contained words that would come to frame First Amendment thinking for generations to come.

First, Holmes made clear that the First Amendment is not an absolute. In determining where its boundaries lie, context is paramount; the Amendment did not protect "falsely shouting fire in a crowded theatre and causing a panic," Holmes famously proclaimed.[78] Second, deprivation of a constitutional right should not be taken lightly, and it should only be subject to punishment where a threshold of harm is surpassed. To be suppressed, words must "create a clear and present danger that they will bring about the substantive evils that Congress has a right to prevent."[79]

To critics, like Holmes's contemporary Judge Learned Hand, the "clear and present danger" test was flawed. Hand—who two years earlier had engineered his own attempt at a doctrinal solution to the vexing problem of "dangerous" speech in *Masses Publishing Co. v. Patten*—thought Holmes's test opened the door to subjectivity and argued that it would instead be preferable to focus on the objective meaning of the words spoken.[80] Holmes, who exchanged a series of letters with his friend Learned Hand on the subject, initially responded quizzically to Hand's argument, professing that he didn't "quite get" his point.[81] However, in less than a year, Holmes dramatically transformed his position on free speech; he crafted, in the form of a dissent in *Abrams v. United States,* one of the most influential arguments for free speech ever written.[82] And while Holmes largely maintained his reputation as a strong advocate of judicial restraint, in the field of First Amendment law he would cleanly abandon this posture. His transformation on the First Amendment also marked the beginning of a transformation for political liberals generally, who, formerly equating judicial activism with conservative antiregulatory economic theory, began to see the value of a bold judiciary willing to strike down laws that interfered with free speech. By the time Holmes read his *Abrams* dissent from the bench, "it caused a sensation. Conservatives denounced it as dangerous and extreme.

Progressives hailed it as a monument to liberty. And the future of free speech was forever changed."[83]

By staking out a position somewhere in between absolutism and the First Amendment avoidance that had effectively reigned since the amendment was first ratified, Holmes was laying the foundation for a framework that would ultimately prove to be quite speech protective. As it stood, the "clear and present danger" standard had not seemed to offer a great deal of protection, at least judged by the draconian outcomes for Charles Schenck and many others, including socialist presidential candidate Eugene Debs,[84] whose prosecutions under the Espionage Act of 1917 did not trigger judicial relief. The "clear and present danger" test was subject to varying interpretation, and until additional flesh was put on its bones, it was uncertain what it would ultimately mean in practice. By one interpretation, the "clear and present danger" test was really just a call for balancing, in which a court simply weighs a range of factors to determine whether protecting particular speech is appropriate. The question is a matter "of proximity and degree" Holmes told us in *Schenck*.[85] The initial malleability of the test, however, set the stage for Holmes's bold move toward a more demanding First Amendment standard. In his *Abrams* dissent, Holmes articulated a much more aggressive, speech-protective vision of what is required for expression to constitute a proscribable "clear and present danger" under the First Amendment. The Court would eventually abandon the "balancing test" approach insinuated by *Schenck*.

Holmes's *Abrams* dissent was a masterwork of judicial draftsmanship. The case addressed two leaflets criticizing American military intervention in the burgeoning Russian Revolution that garnered multiple charges under the Espionage Act. Holmes began his opinion with mildly qualified language. He conceded that by advocating a strike by those working in ammunition factories as a response to America's involvement in Russia, the defendants were ultimately supporting the "curtailment of production of things necessary to the prosecution" of the ongoing war with Germany.[86] Holmes noted, however, that under the Espionage Act a defendant must *intend* to "hinder the United States in the prosecution of that war" and that here such intent was clearly lacking.[87] The leaflets, in other words, were not directed at aiding America's wartime enemy but at supporting Russian revolutionaries.

Holmes began by explaining—in soporific prose that would inspire glazed eyes on even the most eager law student—that it may be "obvious to the actor, that the consequences will follow, and he may be liable for it even if he regrets it, but he does not do the act with intent to produce it unless the aim to produce it is the proximate motive of the specific act."[88] Declaring that a statute must be read in a "strict and accurate sense," Holmes concluded that the Court majority was wrong to understand the law to apply to indirect consequences of speech. Holmes's professorial statutory argument picked up some momentum with his trenchant observation of the "absurd" possibility that "a patriot"—who successfully advocated for the curtailment of government spending because he believed that we were "wasting money on aeroplanes"—could be prosecuted under the majority's logic if an American war effort was even indirectly hindered.[89] Nonetheless, up to this point, the dissent read as a relatively inconsequential disagreement about statutory interpretation.

Had Holmes stopped with this question, his *Abrams* dissent would have been forgotten long ago. Holmes, however, was just getting warmed up. He decided to take on the First Amendment question as well but was fully aware that doing so would risk appearing inconsistent; so, as he moved on to what he called "the more important aspect of this case," he qualified his discussion with the insistent disclaimer that his opinions in the three First Amendment cases earlier in the year—*Schenck, Frohwerk,* and *Debs*—"were rightfully decided."[90] He reiterated his claim that the right of a government to punish speech "is greater in time of war than in time of peace."[91] He asserted, quite modestly, that "Congress certainly cannot forbid all effort to change the mind of the country," seeming to accept a default rule that the government may "forbid" many if not most such efforts.[92] He minimized the significance of this "surreptitious publishing of a silly leaflet by an unknown man," implicitly suggesting that the more persuasive and compelling the expression, the less likely it would be entitled to protection.[93]

At first glance this might seem to be a perverse inversion of the marketplace metaphor, one that would permit removing from the shelves only the most enticing products. Yet, as his dissent moves toward its crescendo, it becomes increasingly difficult to believe that Holmes remained convinced by his own words. It was as if a grand Socratic dialogue was playing out in the justice's mind, and Holmes was persuading himself—at the same time that he was making an argument to his readers—that the First Amendment must mean more. Then, almost abruptly, his rhetoric transformed from qualified to unequivocal. "In this case" Holmes proclaimed, "sentences of twenty years imprisonment have been imposed for the publishing of two leaflets that I believe the defendants had as much right to publish as the Government has to publish the Constitution of the United States now vainly invoked by them."[94]

Holmes reserved his most potent argument for the final paragraph. He stepped into the shoes of a hypothetical leader who, confident in the correctness of his goals, had the "perfectly logical" instinct to "sweep away all opposition"[95] by persecuting opinions that might thwart his laudable intentions. Indeed, permitting such speech, Holmes opined, might be thought an indicator of weakness, perhaps painting a portrait of a leader wracked by self-doubt. The words that follow betray Holmes's reputation as a cynic; he expressed hope that man would move beyond his baser instincts. In this uncharacteristically optimistic plea to rise above partisan interests, Holmes envisioned that

> when men have realized that time has upset many fighting faiths, they may come to believe even more than they believe the very foundations of their own conduct that the ultimate good desired is better reached by free trade in ideas—that the best test of truth is the power of the thought to get itself accepted in the competition of the market, and that truth is the only ground upon which their wishes safely can be carried out. That at any rate is the theory of our Constitution.[96]

His words demand humility from those most unaccustomed to self-doubt. They are implored to acknowledge that even many of the most deeply embedded certainties, over time, have proven uncertain. Indeed, just under the surface, Holmes was arguably himself in the very process of taking this very advice, amending his view on free speech after extensive dialogues with influential friends and colleagues such as Learned Hand, Zechariah Chafee, and Harold Laski.[97]

Underlying his eloquent words was a profound indictment of a key tenet of much political conservatism: moral certitude. However, his indictment may have been deceptive, and somewhat easy to miss, because he couched his argument in the language of "truth." How can a Constitution that prioritizes "truth" be said to degrade moral certitude? For Holmes, the First Amendment's approach to truth was more about *journey* than it was about *destination*. It was an end without end, a vision of truth that was inherently progressive. It does not rest. The search for truth requires constant motion. Indeed, the most significant threat to truth was the stasis advocated by those who were so foolishly confident that they had achieved it. This search-in-perpetuity is facilitated by the First Amendment of the United States Constitution.

Moralistic conservatives, however, had much more to dislike in Holmes's dissent than his "theory of our Constitution."[98] Holmes tied his understanding of the First Amendment to an inherently relativistic philosophy. "Life," like the First Amendment, "is an experiment. Every year if not every day we have to wager our salvation upon some prophecy based upon imperfect knowledge."[99] As we shall see, while such a perspective might appeal to a sensibility held by free-market conservatives, who, for example, celebrate so-called creative destruction in the economy, moral certitude—certainly not a relativistic embrace of the unfamiliar—defines moralistic conservatism. Indeed, Holmes remains a favorite whipping boy for moralistic conservatives to this day. Holding him responsible for alleged pathologies engrained in American jurisprudence, one contemporary *National Review* commentator caustically characterized Holmes's philosophy:

> Morality, he felt, has nothing to do with the law; it amounts to no more than a state of mind. There are no objective standards for determining right and wrong. . . . Following in Holmes's footsteps, a long line of progressive jurists have broken with . . . the very notion that human beings are creatures of a certain type, with transcendent purposes that do not change over time.[100]

Moral psychology points to the "blinding" impact of morality. When social conventions become sanctified, they become shrouded in a cloak of necessity that is rarely questioned—indeed, the very act of questioning is sometimes deemed immoral.[101] Examples may be found in forms of patriotism that characterize as disloyal those who question the tenets of an established political system or in the puritanical sexual mores that cause one to "know" obscenity when "one sees it." According to Jonathan Haidt, from an evolutionary perspective, the "blinding" effect carries significant advantages. It binds groups together and helps them succeed and outcompete other groups. "Irrational beliefs can sometimes help the group function more rationally, particularly when those beliefs rest upon the Sanctity foundation. Sacredness binds people together, and then blinds them to the arbitrariness of the practice."[102]

The Holmesian vision of the First Amendment, in contrast, demands an acknowledgment that even our most deeply held "fighting faiths" in time may prove fleeting. Rationality, and the steadfast belief in intellectual progress, requires such humility; and to Holmes, this was the cornerstone of the First Amendment. Indeed, as Holmes's repeated dissents during the Red Scare of the post–World War I period grew increasingly defiant, he held little back and drove home this theme with raw candor. In *Gitlow v. New York*, for example, Holmes no longer felt the need to couch his defense of free speech in a soothing *Abrams*-like reassurance that the persecuted speech was merely a "silly leaflet" that presented little chance of having an impact. Holmes conceded that a "Left Wing Manifesto" laden with incendiary revolutionary language—and the target of a New York law against so-called criminal anarchy at issue in *Gitlow*—"had no chance of starting a present conflagration."[103]

But strikingly, Holmes would go on to cavalierly suggest—as if confronting a dare—that *if* the ideas expressed by this movement *did* have the ultimate result of undoing our democracy as we know it, so be it:

> Every idea is an incitement. It offers itself for belief and if believed it is acted on unless some other belief outweighs it. . . . If in the long run the beliefs expressed in proletarian dictatorship are destined to be accepted by the dominant forces of the community, the only meaning of free speech is that they should be given their chance and have their way.[104]

Such an approach is fundamentally at odds with unbending faith in the sacred, unquestioning respect for authority, and unwavering loyalty to country that define moralistic conservatism.

It is true that Holmes's jurisprudence is generally viewed quite favorably by the left, particularly because it aligned neatly with the political goals of the New Deal era.[105] *National Review* proclaimed that "Holmes set forth the essence of progressivism as a legal theory."[106] However, not all of Holmes's decisions were held in high esteem by political liberals. As a humanitarian, Holmes's deficits could at times shock the conscience—the most notorious example being his majority opinion in *Buck v. Bell*, in which he upheld, in stunningly cold language, a legal regime of compulsory sterilization for the mentally disabled.[107] In correspondence, Holmes once infamously explained that he saw "no reason for attributing to man a significance different in kind from that which belongs to a baboon or to a grain of sand."[108] Holmes had the capacity to repel not only moralistic conservatives' sacred views about mankind, but liberal and progressive perspectives that prioritized human compassion, what moral psychology refers to as the harm/care foundation.[109] Holmes, however, in his tenacious quest to reform First Amendment doctrine, had an ally, and this partner-in-crime's liberal bona-fides were beyond question.

Louis Brandeis was affectionately known as "the people's attorney." After making a name for himself as a highly successful Gilded Age courtroom advocate, Brandeis chose to leave the profit-oriented side of his profession behind, joining other progressives to mitigate the harsh realities of the industrial revolution.[110] Brandeis would grow to be a harsh critic of the allegiances between the legal profession and large corporations, calling on other lawyers to represent the interests of the people and becoming one of the first attorneys to do work in the public interest without charging a fee.[111] Brandeis was the sole justice joining Holmes's famous *Abrams* dissent and would try his own hand at writing a dissenting First Amendment opinion for the duo the following year in *Schaefer v. United States.*[112]

Like the *Abrams* dissent, Brandeis initially struck a cautious tone, focusing much of his disagreement on statutory fit rather than First Amendment principle. The *Schaefer* case involved charges under the Espionage Act against two German-language newspapers based in Philadelphia. Brandeis closely scrutinized the claim that one of the newspapers had—in republishing articles from newspapers abroad, with certain minor errors—"willfully convey[ed] false reports and statements with intent to promote the success of the enemies of the United States."[113] On the First Amendment question, Brandeis reiterated that the "clear and present danger" standard, first articulated in *Schenck*, was the appropriate rule. At the same time, he quietly ratcheted-up the speech protectiveness of the test, citing not only the Court's own precedent but Zechariah Chafee's influential *Harvard Law Review* article "Freedom of Speech in War Time."[114] Brandeis closed on a cautionary note, arguing that allowing the prosecution of "impotent expressions of editorial opinion" would necessarily "discourage criticism" of government policy and noting that "intolerant" majorities moved by "passion or by fear" would continue to "stamp as disloyal opinions with which it disagrees."[115] Brandeis, however, was just getting started. His magnum opus of First Amendment advocacy would come seven years later, when he penned the concurrence in *Whitney v. California.*

The *Whitney* concurrence is notable not merely for its impassioned argument for a robust freedom of expression, but also for the underlying ideological justifications provided for this position. With unparalleled rhetorical force, Brandeis tied free-speech values to progressivism and at the same time castigated the ideologically conservative impulses that would call for a cramped vision of the First Amendment. The First Amendment welcomes change. Brandeis famously exclaimed: "Those who won our independence by revolution were not cowards. They did not fear political change. They did not exalt order at the cost of liberty."[116] They were, in Brandeis's mind, no conservatives.

To Brandeis, the conservative compulsion to favor stability, predictability, and order was anathema to the First Amendment. The same held true for the moralistic conservative impulse to fear the unknown. "Men feared witches and burnt women,"[117] Brandeis proclaimed. "It is the function of speech to free men from the bondage of irrational fear."[118] And Brandeis did not limit his critique of conservatism to the moralists. For good measure, he subtly took on *Lochner–* era free-market conservatives as well, asserting that even property rights must take a backseat to free expression. "The fact that speech is likely to result in some violence or in destruction of property is not enough to justify its suppression."[119] In other words, economic liberty, as any progressive of the time would quite certainly have agreed, was a relatively low priority.

National Review Takes Aim

The dichotomy between liberal and conservative approaches to free speech, and the predicable posture in which their respective ideological camps would align, would remain relatively fixed for several decades following *Whitney*. Conservative skepticism over First Amendment claims rose to the surface in a number of early opinion pieces in *National Review*, addressing the liberal reaction (both on and off the Supreme Court) to Red Scare–era attempts to confront the threat posed by communism.

In 1962 M. Stanton Evans expressed dismay that the struggle against communism had even been framed as a First Amendment issue in the first place.[120] He lamented that

> [f]or years, the Communists have attempted to palm themselves off as simply another political party—a plucky band of heretics whose rights of disagreement are protected by the First Amendment. They have attempted to shape the national debate over subversion in terms of "free speech"—an effort in which they have received considerable help, not only from Liberals, but from some conservatives.[121]

To Evans, if dominant public opinion began to see the battle over communism as a question of free political expression—even if there was agreement that such rights must to some extent be curtailed—the communists would effectively score a victory. Such acknowledgment would move "the argument to the terrain they have chosen."[122] To Evans the First Amendment was a dangerous distraction.

> This threat has nothing to do with "the content of the political program" of the Communist Party. It has nothing to do with the permissible limits of free speech, with heresy or with dissent. It has everything to do with the fact that the real function of the Communist Party is to subvert the interest of the United

States, and to advance the interest of the Soviet Union. And there is no clause in the Constitution guaranteeing that pastime to anyone.[123]

In an earlier piece Evans had bemoaned the way liberals in America "have clung with bulldog tenacity to the First Amendment" throughout a protracted period in which the country faced the challenge of "Communist subversion."[124] He was deeply troubled by the view that "no matter how repulsive or politically dangerous a man's political beliefs, one does not, thanks to the First Amendment, interfere with them."[125] It is worth noting that while Evans reserved the heft of his ire for liberalism, he begrudgingly acknowledged that there were strains of conservatives who held onto a libertarian perspective.[126]

In 1957, Forrest Davis wrote a scathing critique of the Court's opinion in *Watkins v. United States.*[127] There the Court confronted a First Amendment claim by labor organizer John Watkins who refused to answer select questions by a subcommittee of the Committee on Un-American Activities regarding individuals who were allegedly past members of the Communist Party.[128] Although it would significantly backpedal from its decision just two years later,[129] the Supreme Court agreed with Watkins, concluding that "[a]buses of the investigative process may imperceptibly lead to abridgment of protected freedoms. And when . . . forced revelations concern matters that are unorthodox, unpopular, or even hateful to the general public, the reaction in the life of the witness may be disastrous."[130]

To Davis, the *Watkins* decision "precipitated a Constitutional crisis long in the making," one that pits the Supreme Court against vital congressional powers.[131] At the same time, "[t]he only visible beneficiary of the Court's solicitude for the Communist cause is that cause itself."[132] According to Davis,

> The Warren-Black-Douglas axis on the Court lies, in my judgment, under the nihilistic blight of fashionable Liberalism. Intellectually inadequate, the Justices of the childish Left mistake the liberty of the citizen for the franchise of the Soviet subversionist. It pains me to say this, but I fear that we have a dumb core of the Court.[133]

Davis's assessment of the expansive "liberal" view of the First Amendment was not one of mere respectful disagreement: It was a challenge of the very intellectual integrity of its perspective.

The early views presented in *National Review* were not necessarily hostile to First Amendment principles generally. However, the recurring perception was that these principles were being applied without reasonable limitation and without an appreciation of the dangers posed by communism. Thus, in 1961, the magazine exclaimed that a 5–4 Supreme Court decision recognizing "that there *is* a Communist conspiracy is good news for those who have maintained that a general dedication to free speech need not commit a free society to making available to its enemies the instruments of its own destruction."[134] At the same time, the editorial expressed distress that "[f]our members of the Court appear incapable of assessing evidence which could inconvenience their simplistic commitment to the idea that all political 'movements' are more or less equal, and deserving, each one equally, of the immunities of the First Amendment."[135]

The editorial did purportedly accept that the First Amendment generally protected political speech and expression, and that the speech at issue comfortably fell within this category. In fact, the anticommunist Smith Act was in the editor's judgment "very dubiously constitutional."[136] Why then did the editorial express such strenuous support for the law? "[B]ecause the Bill of Rights simply did not anticipate something like the Communist Party when it proscribed legislation that would hinder free speech."[137] In other words, the urgent need to address the issue of communism and "outlaw the Communist Party and all its maneuverings" justified divergence from otherwise applicable First Amendment principles.[138]

This logic is striking for at least two reasons. First, unlike contemporary jurisprudential conservatives who celebrate "originalism"—generally defined as maintaining a strict adherence to the original meaning of the text—the perspective here calls for "a constitutional clarification" that would acknowledge modern realities.[139] This method of constitutional interpretation is more akin to—and sometimes derided as—a "living Constitution" approach. Second, it emphasizes consequences over principle. The editorial complains that the "open society paradigm, described by John Stuart Mill and festooned by the free-society rhetoric of one hundred years, is lodged so deeply in the Liberal mentality as to have totally bureaucratized its capacity for urgently necessary creative thought. Still, realities must be dealt with."[140] This focus would appear to conflict with the sine qua non of one of today's most influential conservative jurisprudential icons, Supreme Court Justice Antonin Scalia, who repeatedly asserts that looking to consequences in constitutional interpretation should be avoided, because it "invite[s] subjectivity."[141] The 1961 editorial goes as far as to propose that we "rethink the theory of the open society as defended by our Victorian theorists . . . to accommodate reality."[142] This theme recurs repeatedly in

National Review opinion pieces that address liberalism, the First Amendment, and the threat posed by communism.

Some early critiques simply disagree with liberal claims that a legitimate First Amendment issue is even present. For example, in a highly critical review of a book enumerating the alleged "misdeeds" of the House Committee on Un-American Activities, M. Stanton Evans takes issue with the claim that inquiries by the committee regarding matters of political belief—where the consequence of such exposure is social disgrace—are prohibited by the First Amendment.[143] Evans derides this claim as "absurdly defective. It is simply a special plea for political cowards—for those who do not have the courage to stand by their 'beliefs.'"[144] Indeed, to Evans the very notion that a communist affiliation should be placed in the ordinary category of "political belief" is dubious. He suggests that the author's "plaint about 'exposure' and his demand for 'privacy' add up to a right never before claimed by even the most ardent advocates of 'civil liberties': the right to envelop treason in secrecy."[145]

The conservative movement was struggling with its selective move away from Victorian-era conservative libertarianism. American conservatism, as reflected in the pages of *National Review*, exposed the inevitable tension between an idealization of small, noninvasive government and a narrow First Amendment that *invited* government intrusion. In a 1962 piece defending the House Committee on Un-American Activities, William F. Buckley began with the seemingly speech-friendly premise that "[l]ots of ideas are despicable, but those of us who favor limited government want to let despicable ideas be disciplined by the market place."[146] Yet, he went on to proclaim that not all "despicable" ideas are created equal. Buckley saw justification for relaxing this market-based premise where the facts merited it. Thus, instead of waiting patiently for the market to sort truth from falsity, the government may step in and "discipline" ideas, where, for example, the target of an investigation "was actively attempting to influence American foreign policy in behalf of a foreign dictatorship, and doing so by use of intrigue, false propaganda, and espionage and subversion."[147]

At times, the view that free-speech rights should be *highly qualified* was even more blatantly explicated. In 1962 Willmoore Kendall agreed

> that in a certain kind of community, where people have in some sense contracted with one another to conduct their affairs by freedom-of-speech procedures, I should to some extent on principle say there is a presumption in favor of freedom of speech; and I have said that for *me* the United States is such a community.

> But you will notice that I stashed into my aircraft a great many verbal parachutes that would enable me, if and when that seemed advisable, to bail out.[148]

These "bail outs" include the fact that Congress is constitutionally empowered to do many things, including promoting the general welfare, and that acting on this power may require "impairing freedom of speech."[149] Kendall appeared untroubled that other interests will often trump free-speech claims. Indeed, he cited a poll that purportedly revealed that two-thirds of Americans would enthusiastically prevent a communist or atheist from speaking in their community, from teaching at a local school, or from including their book in the collection of a local library.[150]

Kendall begrudgingly admitted that "[t]emperamentally, I happen to be a man who in any given situation would always favor letting everybody have his 'say.'"[151] Yet, he went on to argue "that the classic attempt to defend freedom of speech as a compelling principle, applicable to all communities, that is, Mill's famous *Essay on Liberty*, is a piece of bad political philosophy, and one that has done great harm."[152] The view seems to be that free speech is fine, as long as we continue to want it. Of course, such an understanding of freedom of expression—one that is merely a majoritarian choice subject to the fickle winds of public opinion—would offer little protection to the individual who is most in need of a First Amendment shield: the unpopular speaker.

1 Conservatism, the First Amendment, and *National Review*

What is "conservatism?" As foundational components of the contemporary political lexicon, the word "conservative" and its purported polar opposite "liberal" are bandied about with reckless abandon. In the rough and tumble of everyday American politics, these terms may be used to validate one's policy preferences, to denigrate another's, or merely to represent one's preferred political team. In the United States, there is, of course, no mainstream political party that adopts these words as their own—there is no Liberal Party or Conservative Party per se as in many countries throughout the world—but there might as well be. For even as the two major parties continue to evolve and adapt to their changing constituencies, today the Democratic Party is generally characterized as liberal and the Republican Party is understood to be conservative. By extension, many members of the judiciary, appointed by these very party politicians, must endure these labels as well, even when such labels are unwelcome.

The word "conservative" does, of course, have a core meaning. The *American Heritage Dictionary* defines conservative as "favoring traditional views and values; tending to oppose change. Traditional or restrained in style. Moderate; cautious."[1] However, it also offers these definitions: "Of or relating to the political philosophy of conservatism. Belonging to a conservative party, group, or movement."[2] Thus, when a judge is identified as conservative, it may suggest that her decisions convey a greater degree of respect for tradition, restraint, and caution than is the norm for judges in her class—the median judge. However, use of the identifier "conservative" might also merely indicate that that particular judge is aligned with the Republican Party, that she was nominated by a Republican president, or that her judicial decision making is perceived to be tainted by an ideological bias.

One thing is clear: Conservatism is not monolithic. Political conservatives, just like liberals, do not always see eye-to-eye. As already alluded to, there are readily identifiable tensions that exist among conservatives, the most familiar being the sometimes-contradictory emphasis on economic freedom lauded by free-market conservatives and deeply rooted tradition celebrated by moralistic conservatives. These two ideological camps largely defined the conservative landscape in the years following World War II, a period that marked the emergence of a coherent conservative movement in America.[3] These two strains of conservative thinking do not necessarily conflict—and may indeed be complementary. David Brooks recounted how when he joined the staff of *National Review* in 1984, "the magazine, and the conservative movement, was a *fusion* of [these] two different mentalities."[4] Although Brooks argued that the "traditional conservative" is "less familiar now," he described how these two strains of thinking could in fact support each other. "The economic conservatives were in charge of daring ventures that produced economic growth. The traditionalists were in charge of establishing the secure base—a society in which families are intact, self-discipline is the rule, children are secure and government provides a subtle hand."[5]

Certainly, conservatism today may be broken down into more than just two ideological camps, and the subtle differences can have profound implications for the First Amendment. The awkward but politically beneficial "fusion" of traditional conservatism (what I will refer to as *moralistic conservatism*) and economic conservatism (heretofore referred to as *free-market conservatism*) would promote a breed of conservatives that would come to accept a bright line between the two types of individual freedoms. Some freedoms—those curtailed by economic regulations—were deserving of a fierce defense against overzealous government; other individual freedoms—curtailed by moralistic regulations intended to ensure the endurance of traditional societal values— *demanded interference* from the very same government.

Frank S. Meyer, who joined forces with William F. Buckley as an editor at *National Review* during its early days, is an example of a thinker and scholar who found this bright line to be essential. While accepting free-market conservatism, Meyer rejected the outright libertarianism of Ayn Rand and believed that economic freedom needed to be grounded in a stable social order.[6] Conservative intellectuals like Meyer saw the need for balance, noting in 1969 a danger from "untrammeled libertarianism, which tends as directly to anarchy and nihilism as unchecked traditionalism tends to authoritarianism."[7] However, Meyer's nuanced view—accepting a selective, and tempered, incorporation of both individual freedom and moralistic restraint—stood in sharp contrast with that of other thinkers who were deeply uncomfortable with the bifurcation of liberty. One of the most notable objectors was the deeply influential economist, F. A. Hayek.[8] Hayek's classical liberalism, with its emphasis on expansive individual liberty, fits quite well with today's free-market conservatism but would not countenance the restraints on individual liberty that typically accompany moralistic conservatism.

However, many conservatives—particularly those who wanted to facilitate the emergence of a vital and potent conservative movement in America—were eager to cast a broader net. They observed the pragmatic benefits of joining free-market ideals with moralistic ones. And the success of the efforts of Buckley, Meyer, and others in doing so cannot be denied. They fused a movement that has been credited for the Barry Goldwater presidential campaign and, ultimately, the presidency of Ronald Reagan.[9] Yet fissures in this marriage of convenience remain.

The Voice of Conservatism in the United States: *National Review*

One approach to understanding conservative political opinion *outside* of the Court is to look to media sources most likely to reflect the contemporaneous sentiment of political conservatives. Perhaps no other source of opinion stands as prominently as a barometer of mainstream American conservative political thought than *National Review*. The publication describes itself as "America's most widely read and influential magazine . . . for Republican/conservative news, commentary and opinion."[10] It is widely "recognized as the intellectual fountainhead of modern conservatism."[11] Political scientist Ken Kersch, who has utilized the publication to assess the development of conservative constitutional thought, characterizes it as "postwar conservatism's premier magazine," one that "proved crucial in cultivating intellectual talent and in disseminating conservative political ideas."[12] From its inception, the magazine effectively sought to consolidate the disparate—and at times conflicting—strains of thought of the right. Blending humor and penetrating commentary, *National Review* provided a single stream of conservative opinion, not merely for the intellectual elite, but for a new generation of middle-class suburbanites, many of whom served in World War II.[13] It helped build the conservative coalition we know today "by giving audience to the views of traditionalists, libertarians, anti-Communists and neoconservatives."[14] Because the magazine's influence spans six decades—first published in 1955—it is a particularly incisive indicator, not only of where current mainstream conservative opinion on free-speech matters lies, but how such opinion has evolved through time.

Such change came into high relief in 2001. Two articles in *National Review*, separated by just two months, were authored by two respective editors-in-chief—one young, one old. They presented starkly different visions of the First Amendment. The latter piece was penned by the iconic *National Review* founder William F. Buckley, Jr., who "[m]ore than anyone else, . . . has come to embody conservatism itself."[15] "He"—according the younger editor—"made the term 'conservative' respectable."[16] In his article, Buckley derided those who would question the constitutionality of the political spending limits in the most recent round of proposed campaign finance reform.[17] He cuttingly aligned First Amendment challenges to the legislation with "[o]ddball interpretations of the Constitution [that] are the licensed property of constitutional ultramontanists, the kind of people who grew up on the mother's milk of the American Civil Liberties Union."[18] While Buckley implicitly expressed support for those who sought to "fight back" against a surfeit of government regulation, he opined, "in this case, the weapon being used by opponents of McCain-Feingold is a view of the First Amendment's protections that is historically disreputable."[19]

Strikingly, just two months earlier, the current editor of *National Review*, Richard Lowry, wrote a piece sharply critical of Republican Senator John McCain and his campaign finance reform legislation.[20] Lowry, unlike Buckley, exhibited no signs of reluctance when it came to the First Amendment arguments against the law.[21] Lowry pointed to the "constitutional vulnerability of McCain's efforts" and argued that "[a]s the net of regulations gets wider and wider, the First Amendment problems become starker and starker."[22] These two pieces were written almost ten years before the Supreme Court's *Citizens United* decision; today there could be little doubt as to which position—Mr. Buckley's or Mr. Lowry's—is a better snapshot of mainstream conservative thinking about the relationship between campaign finance restrictions and the First Amendment. The view that campaign finance regulations conflict with the First Amendment has become conservative conventional wisdom.[23]

One might be tempted to view campaign finance reform as just an anomalous exception to the otherwise prevalent conservative norm adopting a narrow conception of the First Amendment. Lowry himself has acknowledged that American conservatives are not always an entirely cohesive and coherent group. He explains: "We live in a time of intraconservative fights. People ask, 'Are you a neoconservative, a paleoconservative?' The appropriate answer . . . is, 'I'm a Bill Buckley conservative.'"[24] However, on the First Amendment, this appeared not to be the case. Indeed, as we shall see, constitutional objection to campaign finance reform is not just a tale of an idiosyncratic few who dared to diverge from the conservative mainstream. Nor is it a tale of a single-issue shift within the domain of expressive freedom that anomalously strays from an otherwise narrow vision. The contrast between Buckley and Lowry is emblematic of a much larger ideological shift in constitutional meaning. When Rich Lowry took over as editor of *National Review* in 1997, he was a youthful 29 years old and only the third to fill Buckley's shoes.[25] His broader vision of the First Amendment represents a perspective that is increasingly the status quo among conservative thinkers. Lowry's view reflects a changing of the guard when it comes to the conservative political perspective on the First Amendment—one that runs parallel with changes taking place among the conservative wing of the Supreme Court.

Examining the six-decade history of *National Review*—focusing exclusively on articles substantively addressing free-speech rights—we see a striking pattern. Over this time period there has been a consistent, but gradual, decline in the ratio of pro–speech-regulation articles to pro–free-speech articles.[26] In the first decade of publication, between the years 1955–1964, 73 percent of such articles expressed a pro–speech-regulation sentiment,[27] between 1965 and 1974 the number was 58 percent,[28] while during the periods from 1975 to 1984[29] and 1985 to 1994[30] pro–free-speech and pro–speech-regulation articles reached an equilibrium of 50 percent each. The period from 1995 to 2004 saw a decline of the percentage of pro–speech-regulation articles to 40 percent,[31] and from 2005 to 2014 the percentage has fallen dramatically to just 13 percent.[32]

The results reveal a steady shift among conservative thinkers and commentators away from a narrow understanding of free speech and toward a more expansive one. Indeed, in the nearly six decades of *National Review* publication, the ratio of pro–free-speech to pro–speech-regulation articles has performed a spectacular flip. The percentage of pro–free-speech articles from the magazine's inception to the most recent decade examined has increased a stunning 60 percentage points, from 27 percent to 87 percent. These figures support the conclusion that mainstream conservative political opinion concerning the meaning of the First Amendment has changed substantially in the past half century (Figure 1).

PERCENTAGE OF *NATIONAL REVIEW* FIRST AMENDMENT–RELATED ARTICLES THAT ARE PRO–SPEECH REGULATION

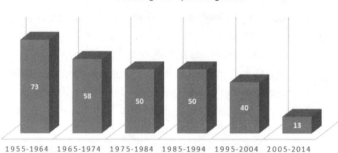

■ Percentage Pro–Speech Regulation

1955-1964	1965-1974	1975-1984	1985-1994	1995-2004	2005-2014
73	58	50	50	40	13

FIGURE 1. Percentage of *National Review* articles expressing a clear point of view on free speech or the First Amendment that were pro–speech regulation. Bars show the percentage of free speech–related articles in *National Review* that are pro–speech regulation.

A Conservative Typology

Although far from an exhaustive list, for purposes of this study I have identified four strains of conservatism that appear to exert significant influence in guiding conservative convictions with regard to the First Amendment: moralistic conservatism, libertarian conservatism, free-market conservatism, and commonsense conservatism. This typology is not an attempt to capture a holistic portrait of any individual conservative thinker or group of thinkers; it merely seeks to distill and identify some of the most relevant core beliefs and recurrent themes that underlie the politically conservative approach to the First Amendment.

For the purposes of this study, I have defined *moralistic conservatism* as an ideology that places legal primacy on the promotion and maintenance of the three moral values of loyalty, patriotism, and sanctity. According to moral foundations theory, these values represent three of the (at least) six psychological systems that make up the foundation of morality for cultures across the globe.[33] As moral psychologist Jonathan Haidt explains, these three moralities "show the biggest and most consistent partisan differences. Liberals are ambivalent about these foundations at best, whereas social conservatives embrace them."[34] The other three moral foundations—care, liberty, and fairness—more commonly cross ideological boundaries and are therefore, for our purposes, not appropriately classified as a part of a uniquely conservative moralism.

Moralistic conservatism may advocate balancing away freedom of expression where such freedom is seen as an impediment to achieving morally important goals. An example of this approach might be found in certain "indecency" cases in which slim majorities of the Supreme Court have at times been willing to uphold restrictions on distasteful speech where the countervailing interests are deemed sufficient.[35] They might likewise support the view that entire categories of immoral expression do not fall within the ambit of the First Amendment—as the Court has concluded in the area of so-called obscene speech.

Libertarian conservatives were the primary advocates of free speech in the late nineteenth century.[36] Yet, for them, freedom of expression was just

> one aspect of the personal liberty "to be free in the enjoyment of all faculties." Courts were expected to protect this freedom as part of their obligation to prevent untrammeled majorities from violating individual rights. [Thus, they] did not separate the system of free expression and the system of private property.[37]

From the perspective of moral foundations theory, the most influential psychological system for political libertarians is, not surprisingly, liberty. Both liberals and conservatives generally share a concern for liberty as a moral foundation, but the liberties emphasized can be quite different.[38]

> American liberals tend to be most concerned about the rights of certain vulnerable groups (e.g. racial minorities, children, animals), and they look to government to defend the weak against oppression by the strong. Conservatives, in contrast, hold more traditional ideas of liberty as the right to be left alone.[39]

Because moralistic conservatives may advocate morality-based government regulation, the liberty strain of conservatism can be difficult to square with moralistic conservatism. In contrast, moralistic conservatism can often work hand-in-hand with free-market conservatism, where the emphasis on liberty may be limited to the economic sphere.

Free-market conservatism might be considered a subset of libertarian conservatism, incorporating many of its key philosophical principles, but not all. Free-market conservatism does not generally concern itself with freedoms outside of the economic realm, whereas libertarian conservatism extends the freedom ethic to many other aspects of social life, including free expression. Free-market conservatives are not necessarily hostile to broad expressive rights, but they may be, particularly if their views are also moralistic in orientation. Moralistic and free-market conservatism might come into conflict, however, where an expressive product brought to market is thought to be immoral—for example, sexually explicit literature or commercial speech selling abortion services.[40] Free-market conservatives are often particularly pro–free speech when the expression at issue is directly relevant to the market economy. Thus, a free-market conservative may be more likely to argue that commercial speech—"speech which 'does no more than propose a commercial transaction'"[41]—which historically has been accorded less than full protection by the Supreme Court,[42] should instead be fully protected. As discussed in Chapter 7, a free-market conservative might likewise strongly support a decision such as *Citizens United* that empowered business corporations by providing them a "free-speech" right to spend treasury funds on political campaigns.[43]

Finally, I have identified what I call *commonsense conservatism*. Quite simply, this is the view that freedom of speech should not be treated as an unassailable principle—it should be tempered by "commonsense" considerations. Commonsense conservatism is not necessarily tethered to a particular morality; it simply rejects the view that First Amendment principle should trump practicality. It might be exemplified by President George W. Bush's admission that he doesn't "do nuance."[44] If it appears from prior experience and "gut reaction" that freedom of speech in a particular setting will impose additional risks to our nation's security, create disorder in the public square, or simply defy readily identifiable social norms, a commonsense conservative is willing to accept reduced expressive freedom. It rejects the notion that we should adhere to First Amendment principle when there are significant costs in doing so and where such costs are readily apparent to the average person. In this respect, the strain of thinking I call commonsense conservatism has much in common with the interpretive "costs and benefits" approach some scholars refer to as "prudentialism."[45]

Reliance on common sense is arguably inherently conservative: It suggests that we should accept the straightforward lessons of the past, that tradition is *traditional* for a reason. Trusting in common sense is trusting that what seems to have worked in the past will work in the future. Common sense is also suspicious of the *uncommon*. It rejects the politically liberal premise that one should continually strive to challenge one's own perspective, to scrutinize what appears to be "obviously true." To a commonsense conservative, this type of liberal thinking—with its incessant emphasis on tolerance and open-mindedness—is, at its worst, a recipe for nihilism and inaction.

Indeed, to a commonsense conservative, willful resistance to common sense may be downright dangerous; it may plant the seeds of one's own destruction. Contrast the view of famously absolutist Justice Black, who conceded that "a governmental policy of unfettered communication of ideas does entail dangers"[46] but that "the benefits derived from free expression were worth the risk."[47] Commonsense conservatism would reject this conclusion, exemplified by the many conservatives who chastised the left for defending the First Amendment rights of communists during the Red Scare. For them, the bar for testing whether costs are sufficiently high to justify reducing First Amendment protection is set relatively low.

Ideology and the First Amendment— The Historic Alignments

What does conservatism have to say about the free-speech principles derived from the First Amendment? Is the speech clause "tilted," in Frederick Schauer's words,[48] such that conservatives are predisposed to construe it narrowly and liberals prone to a broad interpretation? Is the freedom of speech an inherently liberal value or an inherently conservative one—or neither?

The longstanding affiliation between broad, expansive, and sometimes even absolutist notions of free-speech rights with political liberalism in America has deep roots—dating back to the period in which the Supreme Court first seriously engaged with the First Amendment almost a century ago. In the early twentieth century, progressive civil libertarians, in response to a conservative Supreme Court that would deliver repeated blows to free-speech values, took the reins of the First Amendment. Zechariah Chafee, foreshadowing the liberal retort to the Red-fearing arguments that would fill the pages of *National Review* in the 1950s and 1960s, asserted in 1928 that it was innately human to believe that "what one dislikes" necessarily poses a threat to "the social order."[49] The First Amendment was needed to guard against elected legislators who "cannot be trusted to discriminate between dangerous and harmless ideas."[50] In 1931 Chafee praised those justices with the courage to strike down restrictions on expression and—distinguishing his view from the libertarian conservatives of the previous century—extended plaudits to concomitant judicial votes to sustain economic regulations.[51] This was a recognition that the conservative Supreme

Court of the *Lochner* era, a Court that would again and again demonstrate its hostility toward government intervention into the economic sphere, in no way resembled the antigovernment purity of an earlier era. For the conservatives that dominated the political landscape—and the courts—in the early twentieth century, the cause of freedom was generally limited to the economic realm.

This period also marked the emergence of the American Civil Liberties Union (or ACLU). As a well-known progressive legal organization, the ACLU came to embody First Amendment values in the public mind. An organization with a core mission of aggressively defending free expression, the ACLU rapidly rose to prominence in the early twentieth century. It "was born in response to the massive suppression of freedom of speech and the press by the government during World War I."[52] Many of the founders of the organization had been, prior to the war, active progressives involved in other traditionally "liberal" concerns such as fostering "harmonious community."[53] With its early pedigree as an organization "led by labor radicals and socialists,"[54] there was little doubt that this legal advocacy organization was from its inception firmly affiliated with the left in America. Its existence and prominence is further illustration of the historic alignment between robust free-speech advocacy and liberalism.

Outside legal groups can have a significant impact on the politics of constitutional interpretation. Political scientist Steven Teles refers to politically motivated, law-oriented public-interest groups, along with other individuals and organizations in the legal profession and law schools, as liberal or conservative "legal networks."[55] The ACLU might be said to be one of the earliest entrants, and most significant players, in the liberal legal network. It figured prominently in the earliest crop of First Amendment cases to come before the U.S. Supreme Court. In 1925 it was an ACLU attorney who, in front of the Supreme Court, unsuccessfully defended Benjamin Gitlow, "a member of the Left Wing Section of the Socialist Party."[56]

This ideological alignment carried forward well into the modern political era. As late as the 1988 presidential election, candidate George H. W. Bush repeatedly and pejoratively cast about the phrase "card-carrying member of the ACLU" to derogate his Democratic opponent Michael Dukakis as a "Massachusetts liberal."[57] There was little question that associating a Democratic opponent with the "liberalism" of the ACLU's aggressive free-speech advocacy was a political attack of the first order, intended to sully the reputation of this candidate and disfavorably distinguish him from the respectable conservatism of the Republican candidate.

In the world of political science, the relationship between conservatism and a narrow reading of the Free Speech Clause of the First Amendment had, until recently, largely gone unquestioned.[58] As discussed in the next chapter, political scientists who study judicial decision making equate pro–First Amendment holdings—that is, decisions that strike down governmental regulations on free-expression grounds—with a liberal political ideology.[59] Quantitative social science demands dichotomous variables capable of being empirically tested. The underlying assumption of political science has been that "support for First Amendment freedoms is one of the, if not *the*, defining features of a 'liberal' judge, a 'liberal' case outcome, or a 'liberal' vote."[60] In the converse, a narrow reading of the types of expression protected by the First Amendment—and holdings that reject constitutional challenges to speech regulation—have been presumed to be ideologically "conservative."[61] While many have questioned the extent to which the essence of judicial decision making can realistically be boiled down to a simple, dichotomous ideological label, until recently there has been little reason to doubt the presumed relationship between conservatism and the First Amendment. Both on the Court and off—in the body of Supreme Court decisions, the prognostications among the political classes, and the baseline assumptions of social scientists—American conservatism has been much more comfortable with a limited conception of the First Amendment.

To place the liberal perspective of the First Amendment championed by the ACLU in high relief, we might once again revisit the views of the late Robert Bork. As a preeminent scholar, professor at Yale Law School, and judge on the prestigious Court of Appeals for the District of Columbia, there could perhaps be no better representative of legal conservatism than Robert Bork. Appeals Court Judge Richard Posner, well known as a political conservative himself, referred to Bork as an "ultraconservative."[62] Bork was, at the same time, no stranger to divisive partisan controversy. In addition to being a prolific and provocative writer and thinker, he was Solicitor General under Nixon and Ford and was responsible for carrying out the "Saturday Night Massacre" against Watergate Special Prosecutor Archibald Cox.

Most infamously, Bork became a political lightning rod after being selected by President Ronald Reagan as a nominee to the Supreme Court—a nomination that ultimately concluded in one of the most spectacular and dramatic rejections in the Court's history. Conservatives sympathetic to Bork's plight might characterize Bork's failure to attain a seat on the high court as a tale of martyrdom—an unjustified and shameful partisan tarring and feathering of one of the country's most respected jurists.[63] Others clearly disagree, feeling that it was Bork's extremist ideology that ultimately—and rightfully—led to his downfall.[64] Either way, it is widely accepted that the dramatic and aggressive campaign against his appointment irrevocably altered the confirmation process of U.S. Supreme Court justices going forward.[65]

Bork's understanding of what the Constitution protected differed markedly from his liberal opponents. The harsh condemnation of Bork by liberal Democrats was relentless, the capstone being Senator Edward Kennedy's rhetorical portrait of "Robert Bork's America" as "a land in which women would be forced into back-alley abortions, blacks would sit at segregated lunch counters, rogue police could break down citizens' doors in midnight raids, schoolchildren could not be taught about evolution," and most relevant here, "writers and artists could be censored at the whim of the government."[66] Bork was one of only three Supreme Court nominees to be actively opposed by the ACLU.[67] That the organization would find itself at odds with then Judge Bork's nomination by Ronald Reagan in 1987 is hardly surprising when one briefly examines Bork's First Amendment scholarship. His previously mentioned 1971 *Indiana Law Journal* article—a significant focus during his confirmation hearings in front of the Senate Judiciary Committee—expressly sided with the 1925 *Gitlow* majority rejecting First Amendment protection for the publication of a "Left Wing Manifesto."[68] This put Bork at odds with the widely celebrated Holmes dissent in *Gitlow*, as well as the ACLU position.

Consistent with his view on many subjects, Bork's approach to the First Amendment was framed by the *political* battles that swelled outside the rarefied world of judicial interpretation. There can be no doubt that his was a *conservative* view, one aligned with particular partisan political forces. His approach to constitutional interpretation reflected and overtly touted this alliance, as well as the belief that there were inherently *conservative* and inherently *liberal* ways of understanding the Constitution. As he lamented in 1990, "Due to decades of left-liberal dominance on the Supreme Court, moral relativism and untrammeled individualism are built into Court-created first amendment doctrine."[69]

Upon his passing in 2012, long-time *New York Times* Supreme Court reporter Linda Greenhouse characterized Bork as a "tragic figure."[70] He died with a deeply embedded sense of victimhood remaining from his failed Supreme Court nomination, yet, according to Greenhouse, was unable to grasp the truly substantive reasons his appointment faltered.[71] Ironically, as we shall see in Chapter 3, it was this very notion of conservative victimhood—the belief that conservative voices were being silenced on college campuses—that would ultimately lead mainstream conservatives to reject Bork's views on the First Amendment.

The Conservative Libertarian Legacy
and the Ideological Bifurcation of Individual Liberty

It would be a mistake to assume that the same political dichotomy observed by quantitative political science and by Robert Bork—necessarily equating political liberalism with a robust reading of the First Amendment and political conservatism with a more narrow conception—had been, or would be, forever fixed in time. Indeed, political scientist and legal scholar Mark A. Graber has pointed out that well before the Supreme Court took up the issue of free speech almost a century ago it was political conservatives who were, in fact, more likely to champion free speech.[72]

Granted, prior to World War I, the issue of free expression was not terribly salient among the general public, nor the political elite.[73] The long stretch of time between the Sedition Act of 1798 and the Espionage Act of 1917 marked a period of relative quiescence for free-speech rights, a time in which suppression of speech and expression was largely off of the national radar. However, to the extent that this freedom *was* addressed during this period, it was typically conservatives who made their voices heard. Conservative libertarians of the Gilded Age defended free speech, not due to a primary concern for this particular liberty but as a part of a larger philosophical aversion to governmental power.[74] Libertarian conservatives of the late nineteenth century were focused primarily upon freedom of contract and property. Yet, these same laissez-faire principles that were said to justify a hands-off approach by government were also to be applied with vigor to other individual freedoms—including free speech.[75]

Graber contends that this conservative view of a robust First Amendment is, for the most part, forgotten.[76] In his words, "the conservative libertarian tradition did not merely end; it largely vanished."[77] In its place were political conservatives who ardently held on to their views with regard to the ideal of limited government and individual freedom in the economic realm, but who gradually shed the belief that this ideal should extend as vigorously to the sphere of free expression. When the question of speech suppression rose to the surface during World War I, it was a new generation of thinkers and activists that took on the free-speech mantle, led by Zechariah Chafee.[78] No longer was freedom of speech tethered to economic freedoms. Indeed, Graber argues that Chafee sought not only to do away with the philosophical and political link between economic and expressive freedoms, but to effectively rewrite the history of First Amendment advocacy. Chafee's highly influential scholarship wiped the slate clean, establishing an entirely new edifice upon which to rest a structural defense of free-speech rights, while barely acknowledging the existence of a conservative libertarian tradition.[79] The result has been a still-pervasive "myth" that there is, and always has been, just a "single libertarian tradition" in defense of free speech—a leftwing civil libertarianism that does not incorporate economic freedom.[80] The vestiges of this narrative can still be felt in the sphere of contemporary politics.

The ideological bifurcation of individual freedom lives on. It is still common for today's mainstream political conservatives to speak with an almost religious zeal of minimizing government intrusion into the economic affairs of individuals, yet eagerly and passionately seek greater governmental intervention where morality or national security is implicated. The converse is likewise familiar: American liberals who vehemently oppose governmental intervention into personal freedoms, yet unapologetically embrace the imposition of an extensive regulatory regime that circumscribes the freedom of individual economic decision making. This bifurcation has created a rhetorical opportunity for both political camps: the repeated accusation that one's political adversaries are hypocrites, wholeheartedly embracing the principle of "individual freedom" only when it suits their tastes.[81]

In *National Review*'s first year, the magazine published an article addressing this very theme. Frank S. Meyer critically described what he saw as a troublingly inconsistent academic left—thoroughly comfortable curtailing the property rights guaranteed by the Fifth and Fourteenth Amendments, while asserting that the rights derived from the First Amendment were to be treated as "preferred rights."[82] This line of argument was of course made possible by the bifurcated view of "individual freedom" adopted by the ideological political poles in America. It was an equal opportunity political slight—and it appeared again and again among conservative critiques of liberal antiregulatory views on the First Amendment.

Meyer's seminal 1956 piece was also a convenient vehicle for critiquing the liberal tendency to discount the importance of economic liberty. Here Meyer did not expressly argue against a broad conception of the First Amendment. The villain was instead a group of liberal political scientists who abused their ivory tower vantage, either denying "immutable principles as the basis of jurisprudence" in a "bog of moral relativism" or using "specious . . . scientific concepts of objectivity which underlie that sociological jurisprudence that seems to be replacing legal positivism."[83] According to this latter view,

> Since we all believe in democracy and since the political scientists can tell us that without the guarantees of the First Amendment "the community does not achieve that wise and representative quality in its judgments which is the heart of self-government," the First Amendment has a "preferred status" denied to other Constitutional Guarantees.[84]

Economic and property rights do not receive due respect.

At times, the charges of liberal hypocrisy were multilayered. M. Stanton Evans opined in 1960 that liberal consecration of "the First Amendment has always seemed to me to be slightly suspect, particularly in view of its votaries' notable distaste for the rest of the Constitution."[85] Evans went on to argue that "that Liberalism's concern for 'free speech,' constitutionally guaranteed, extends only so far as do the common interests of the Left, and not an inch beyond."[86] What was the evidence for this charge? Proposed civil rights legislation favored by liberals would make it a crime to willfully obstruct federal desegregation orders. Because "threatening communications" would be prohibited by the legislation, a mere "newspaper editorial" would potentially be considered "a criminal act"—for example, a piece that warns a politician of defeat at the polls unless he supports massive resistance against integration.[87] According to Evans, liberals did not appear at all concerned about this potential threat to free speech: "Thus did freedom of opinion go glimmering in the Senate—without a single Liberal coming forward to say that, however repulsive or potentially dangerous the views of the South may be, we cannot tamper with the sacred right of dissent."[88]

The emphasis here was not on the correctness of the argument in favor of robust First Amendment rights; it was on the left's purported failure to apply its own fervor for free speech with consistency. Two years later, the magazine took a swipe at liberal First Amendment champion Hugo Black. It disapprovingly noted that the Court had recently offered free-speech protection against charges of libel or slander, characterizing the decision as "the last preposterous length to which the free-speech absolutists are willing to take the First Amendment."[89] It then acerbically noted "that Justice Black takes a highly *non-absolutist* view of the Ninth and Tenth Amendments. In fact he absolutely ignores them."[90]

As we shall see, the longstanding bifurcation of individual liberty by ideological partisans on the right opened an opportunity for today's libertarian conservatives to split with moralistic conservatives and argue that true consistency requires individual freedom in all spheres. Effectively, they would be arguing that conservatives should return to the "vanished" tradition of conservative libertarianism of the late nineteenth century.[91]

2 The Political Science of
Judicial Decision Making

Many—including prominent political scientists—assume that what quietly happens on the Court is largely a mirror image of what happens off of it: conservative Republican-appointed justices and liberal Democratic-appointed justices voting in predictable ideological blocs that mimic rough-and-tumble ideological divides "on the outside." There is, of course, *some* truth to this characterization. However, things are not quite as simple as they appear. The Court, after all, is *a court* and operates under a very different set of rules than the political branches. The relationship between ideology and legal doctrine is, to put it mildly, nuanced. This chapter explores the way in which scholars, and in particular political scientists, seek to understand judicial decision making.

The freedoms of speech, press, assembly (and their associated freedoms) can take many forms. These various manifestations are often loaded with political meaning. As any student of the First Amendment quickly becomes aware, First Amendment freedoms can be said to apply in a vast array of contexts, each instance offering opportunities to inflame political passion on both sides of the proverbial aisle. On the micro-level, fact-sensitive applications of the First Amendment can invoke the most contentious political and ideological loyalties. A conservative advocate of the pro-life position might, for example, passionately defend the First Amendment right of anti-abortion protestors to stand in close proximity to an abortion clinic,[1] yet with comparable vigor reject the claim that doctors have a free-speech right to present abortion as a viable option to their patients.[2] However, a broadly construed freedom of speech is also a value in itself, a principle independent of any particular application. It would be a mistake to conclude that the relationship between political ideology and constitutional principle is confined to the case-specific instances in which a robust reading of the First Amendment either supports or harms preexisting ideological commitments.

Approaching the First Amendment from a political perspective is thus bound to be fraught with challenge. Constitutional principles interact with political passions in a complex and unpredictable manner; political ideologies play out on more than one level simultaneously. Yet, none of this keeps scholars from attempting to understand, and generalize about, the relationship between free-speech ideals and political ideology. Today the waters are muddy—and a debate has emerged as to the contours of this relationship. Many scholars, thinkers, and advocates have portrayed the conservative Roberts Court as highly speech protective, some even concluding that it is the most pro–First Amendment Supreme Court in American history.[3] As discussed in the Introduction, a recent string of highly publicized controversial decisions—in which many of the Court's most conservative members voted to strike down federal and state laws as violations of the First Amendment—has helped solidify this impression.[4] Other scholars emphasize that in the field of campaign finance reform legislation, the traditional political alignment on the Court has completely flipped on its head, with the conservatives in favor of a robust First Amendment and the liberals advancing a more narrow vision.[5] Some, however, disagree with the characterization of the conservative Roberts Court as uniquely pro–free speech, pointing to quantitative data showing that overall the Roberts Court decided in favor of the First Amendment in a smaller percentage of cases than the Rehnquist, Burger, or Warren Courts.[6]

Most recently, a study by prominent political scientists advanced what was framed as a third alternative to the two dominant narratives.[7] These scholars instead posit that justices across the ideological spectrum are "opportunistic free speechers" and find "that the justices are much less apt to protect expression rights when the expresser is from the opposing ideological team."[8] However, as any scholar of First Amendment doctrine would immediately recognize, the "hard" free-speech cases the Supreme Court confronts typically involve innumerable factors and remarkable complexity—all which must be weighed and thrown into the jurisprudential mix.

It would be thoroughly surprising *if there were not* some positive correlation (over what is, of course, a large pool of cases) between the ideological worldview of the particular justice deciding a case and the ideological associa-tion with the unique factual interests involved. Indeed, we would presumably see some such correlation in most if not all areas of Court jurisprudence. After all, it is the job of courts to apply *judgment,* and ideology to some extent colors judgment. This is particularly true where precedent is thin and where inevi-table judicial discretion in interpreting highly contestable concepts—such as "equality," "liberty," and, yes, even "speech"—is vast. Perhaps it is dubious to claim that it is even possible to disaggregate the constitutional principle from "other" interests a court weighs when it issues a constitutional decision. In some circumstances they may be said to be distinct, but in others they are in-extricably intertwined.

Values and Value Conflicts: A Burning Flag

The ultimate symbol of loyalty to country—of courage and sacrifice, of shared principle and patriotic solidarity—was on fire. Conservative passions were in-flamed over the contention that burning an American flag constituted protected speech. This issue entered the political limelight immediately following the 1989 Supreme Court 5–4 decision in *Texas v. Johnson,* striking down a conviction, under Texas law, of desecrating an American flag.[9] The reaction on the right was swift, with conservative politicians and pundits lining up in lockstep outrage to condemn using the First Amendment to protect an act that many saw as an intolerable slight on American patriotism. The action on the Court, however, was a different matter. Of the Court's four conservative Republican appointees, two—Scalia and Kennedy—voted with the majority to strike down the law.

The incendiary ideological issue of flag burning was the ultimate political drama. For some it was the quintessential story of good versus evil. Patriotism has long been at the heart of the conservative political worldview. The expres-sive interests of political subversives who cavalierly flout loyalty to country were not merely a low priority among conservatives; historically, even the men-tion of such concerns would elicit outright hostility. And indeed conservative public opinion held fast to this longstanding posture. Eighty-four percent of self-identified conservatives supported a constitutional amendment making it illegal to destroy the flag for political reasons.[10] Yet, the conservatives on the *Texas v. Johnson* Court told a different story. They were not nearly as united in spirit as one might have expected.

One way of explaining this divergence among conservatives on versus off the Court is that as an elite institution, the Supreme Court was in the vanguard.

Popular constitutionalist scholars such as Barry Friedman assert that although the Court rarely strays too far from popular opinion, it is often a catalyst for public debate,[11] issuing decisions that can be slightly ahead of the public opinion curve. Mainstream conservatives of the late 1980s and early 1990s were increasingly, but selectively, singing the praises of a broadly construed First Amendment. This was particularly apparent when the rights of sympathetic defendants were at the center of the controversy, for example, as we shall see in the next chapter: student activists taking on the perceived scourge of liberal political correctness on a college campus. Understandably, principled adherence to an abstract right comes much easier when applying that right results in an outcome that conforms to one's political beliefs. This newfound enthusiasm decidedly did *not* extend to anti-American protestors burning an American flag.[12] Presumably, this principled view must be deeply embedded before partisans would willingly accept the application of that principle in a context where the consequences would be deeply distasteful.

To many conservatives, preventing governments from protecting sacred symbols threatened important values—and these values easily outweighed the importance of free expression. William F. Buckley's perspective on the flag-burning issue harkened back to the arguments justifying Red Scare–era communist suppression. Although he acknowledged that "[t]he creep in Dallas who, in 1984, burned the flag chanting, 'America, the red, white, and blue, we spit on you,' certainly did not threaten the 'safety' of the Republic," Thomas Jefferson opined "that we are free to ignore challenges to our liberties [only] *for so long as we are confident that they will not prevail.*"[13] Conceding that this particular act of flag burning did not put American safety at risk, Buckley maintained that allowing the violation of America's "monuments, in which its higher thoughts are enshrined"[14] would have deleterious cumulative effect. Patriotism, in other words, is not just an abstract value; it is a practical necessity. Thus, Buckley concluded that "[i]t is correct for a society as a matter of prudence to guard its banner against desecration, and to do so is also an act of dignity. And the maintenance of national dignity is essential to the maintenance of the national morale."[15]

Approaches to Understanding Judicial Decision Making

Let's begin under the premise that constitutional principles are real and that they have value in themselves. They are not merely empty vessels waiting to be filled by political opportunists. At the same time, however, certain constitu-

tional principles, by their nature, are more likely to appeal to those with particular political ideologies and less likely to appeal to others. Liberals may be
may be more inclined to celebrate the equality concepts rooted in the Equal
Protection Clause and defendants' rights principles of the Due Process Clause,
while conservatives might be drawn to the protection of property rights found
in the Takings Clause or notions of executive power in times of war articulated
in Article II. Frederick Schauer has referred to these types of rules as "tilted,"
which he defines as having "some substantive political or ideological incidence
(whether by design, by intrinsic theoretical affinity, or by effect—or by some
combination of these) in one direction or another."[16]

Other constitutional principles, however, might have less obvious partisan
appeal in either direction and may encourage exercises in political fill-in-the
blank. To a conservative, the guarantee of "liberty," for example, might ideally represent a laissez-faire freedom to contract whereas, to a liberal, it might
provide a license to pursue private sexual desires without government interference. Yet, for true believers—representing what political scientists would call
the "legal model" of judicial decision making[17]—the Constitution is more than
just a grab bag of ideological treats for partisans or an exercise in ideologically
inspired creativity. As a baseline, I accept that constitutional principles retain
their own inherent significance—even in cases where ideology and constitutional interpretation clearly overlap. In exploring the First Amendment's relationship with conservatism, my approach is to strike a delicate balance, with
the goal of avoiding the polar pitfalls of studying constitutional politics: political naïveté on one end and constitutional nihilism on the other. Examining the
relationship between ideology and constitutional principle need not be a stark
choice between the foolhardy or the unduly cynical.

There are, of course, many ways to conceptualize and explain judicial decision making.[18] Political scientists and legal scholars traditionally view judging in
very different ways.[19] The former frequently view ideology as central to explaining judicial outcomes, while the latter tend to understand judging as a product of legal reasoning, precedent, and doctrine.[20] In recent years there has been
some effort to bridge this gap.[21] However, many still see these two views of judging as fundamentally at odds with one another—and unable to be reconciled.

If political scientists are correct that judging is fundamentally a political act,
the dispiriting implication is that legal scholars and judges devote their career
to nothing but a trivial exercise in studying and employing high-concept window dressing.[22] According to some political scientists, legal scholars perpetuate

a "myth" that legal reasoning is an objective enterprise and not the resolutely political behavior that social scientists, armed with their quantitative tools, are able to identify.[23] To such scholars, typically identified as "attitudinalists," law-as-mythmaking is evident from three simple facts: First, various courts and judges reach different conclusions with regard to the same case; second, appellate decisions often contain dissents; and third, it is not uncommon for membership changes among the judges or justices on a particular court to change judicial outcomes.[24] Essentially, the premise that judges preside over a "rule of man, not of law" guides the attitudinalists' research agenda. This foundation facilitates methodologically sophisticated—but theoretically simplistic—quantitative studies that utilize a straightforward liberal/conservative measure of political ideology to explain judicial decision making.

Although this study utilizes the scholarship of quantitative political scientists such as Lee Epstein, Jeffrey Segal, Harold Spaeth, and Andrew D. Martin, this is *not* a quantitative study. The attitudinal model of understanding judicial decision making has been influential among political scientists—and for good reason. It can be a very powerful tool for understanding, in macro-perspective, the relationship between political ideology and court behavior. The two scholars most frequently associated with this approach describe it thusly:

> The attitudinal model represents a melding together of concepts from legal realism, political science, psychology, and economics. The model holds that the Supreme Court decides disputes in light of facts of the case vis-à-vis the ideological attitudes and values of the justices. Simply put, Rehnquist votes the way he does because he is extremely conservative; Marshall voted the way he did because he was extremely liberal.[25]

Unfortunately, for purposes of this study, such an approach simply begs the most important questions. While the attitudinal model may be helpful when examining the relationship between First Amendment judicial decision making and broader commitments to a conservative ideology, it tells us nothing about how, why, or if the relationship between political conservatism and free-speech values has changed over time. As Barry Friedman and Andrew Martin point out, "many political science studies overlook the dynamism of the common law."[26] Indeed, even what we identify as "free-speech values" is arguably in constant motion, evolving (or devolving) along with society. As technology alters the way we receive and communicate ideas, the landscape of idea transmission changes shape. In just twenty years, what it even means "to speak" has arguably changed dramatically—consider the ubiquity of the Internet and social networking. How differing ideological factions within society—which are themselves in a constant state of flux and reinvention—come to value and understand differing forms of "speech" is a dynamic process.

The attitudinal model—by its very nature—is also terribly deficient at detecting, analyzing, and conceptualizing jurisprudential nuance. As Segal and Spaeth concede, "[a] model is a simplified representation of reality; it does not constitute reality itself."[27] By design, the data-driven approach of many political scientists requires that judicial decisions be boiled down to their dichotomous essence—a decision is either "liberal" or "conservative." There is no room for subtlety, no room for ambiguity. Within the scope of the attitudinalist project, this makes perfect sense: "Useful models ignore idiosyncratic factors and highlight instead variables that explain a high percentage of the behavior in question."[28] Nonetheless, judicial decision making can often turn on idiosyncratic factors. Indeed, it might be argued that the hardest cases are thoroughly idiosyncratic. So too is the process by which judicial actors, implicitly or explicitly, reconcile their political and ideological values and commitments with their constitutional values and commitments. This is particularly true of First Amendment free-speech jurisprudence. As we shall see, the assumption that a pro–free-speech decision or posture is inherently politically conservative or liberal is fundamentally contestable and has shifted in political time.

Underlying attitudinalist research, not unlike the legal realists of an earlier era, is a rather cynical approach to understanding the judicial mission. Three leading attitudinal scholars sum up their view of judicial power in this way:

> [W]e have given judges the authority to play God with regard to the life, liberty, and property of those who appear before them. . . . Such autotheistic power ought not be vested in mere mortals. But because American society has chosen to allow it to be, we have devised myths to sustain and rationalize such an awesome exercise of power.[29]

The people, in other words, are not mere victims of an overreaching judiciary; they have aided and abetted the judicial power-grab. And to the attitudinalists, the implications are dire: "Judicial mythology blunts criticism and insulates judges from the hue and cry that permeates governmental action (and nonaction), thereby enabling judges to do as they wish, obligated to none but themselves."[30] With the public and legal community willfully blind to the unpleasant truth that raw politics, not principled legal interpretation, explains judicial decisions, it becomes the task of political science to tear off the judicial mask, to expose the inherently political and chronically deceptive nature of the judicial process.

Suffice it to say, it is not just legal scholars and members of the legal bar who take issue with this glum perspective. Today it is increasingly common to find political scientists who question a starkly dichotomous, either/or view that pits the so-called legal model directly against the political model. Lawrence Baum argues that "the breadth and complexity of judicial motivations limit the value of the standard dichotomous framework for explanation."[31] A growing cohort of political scientists rejects the quantitative dogma that may be traced to the field's "behavioral revolution" of the 1960s, taking instead a broader view of law and politics.[32] Thomas Keck has keenly observed that the "[t]he 'legal' ideas that influence the justices . . . are derived in large part from ongoing debates in the broader political system, and the 'political' interests that pressure the Court are often constituted by legal categories created by the justices themselves."[33]

The relationship between politics and legal decision making, in other words, it not illegitimate; it is inevitable. It is also much more multifaceted and multi-directional than some political scientists suggest. Law and politics are, at the same time, *distinct* and *intimately intertwined*. Judicial legitimacy is all about managing this apparent paradox. Many political scientists now realize that there is a middle ground. Acknowledgment, exploration, analysis, and assessment of the *political* attributes and ramifications of judicial decision making can harmoniously coexist with doctrinal analysis. Indeed, they complement each other.

Mark Graber has suggested that if social science is to ever fully explain judicial behavior, it must incorporate normative considerations about what constitutes good law.[34] To Lawrence Baum, any attempt to precisely disaggregate the relative extent to which policy preferences versus legal analysis influences judicial decision making is doomed to fail.[35] "The fundamental reason is that legal and policy considerations are intertwined in the process through which judges make their choices."[36]

Conceding that politics plays a role in jurisprudence reflexively may make a small number of doctrinally pure legal scholars uncomfortable. Certainly, scholars with more legalistic inclinations may be uneasy referring to judicial "policy preferences" rather than "judicial philosophy." However, the message from an increasing array of mainstream political scientists and legal scholars is clear: The fact that the personal beliefs of judges impact judicial decisions—independent of ostensibly "pure" legalistic influences—is not necessary problematic. Granted, such influence may be normatively troubling where, for example, a judge opportunistically disregards the substance of a particular law or precedent in order to advance instrumentalist goals. However, under ordinary circumstances, ideology is not subversive of law. The fact that, as attitudinalists point out, courts can come to differing conclusions shows us only that the judicial enterprise is a *human* enterprise, not a *mechanistic* one.

The framers opted for a constitution that, in the words of the great Chief Justice Marshall, did not "partake of the prolixity of a legal code."[37] It did not specify with precision the breadth and depth of the rights the First Amendment protects. This, however, does not mean that all of the gaps are being filled by thoroughly politicized judicial behavior without regard to "the law." Indeed, in *McCulloch v. Maryland,* the chief justice went on to argue that a constitution of excessive detail "could scarcely be embraced by the human mind. It would probably never be understood by the public."[38] Marshall understood that filling in the "great outlines" marked by the Constitution meant utilizing the evolving complexity of human understanding. With complexity in human understanding comes diversity in human understanding. The fact that a political conservative justice might find Court A's interpretation of the First Amendment more persuasive, whereas a liberal justice might believe Court B's to be "better," in no way impugns the legitimacy of the legal judgments being made. That reasonable—even brilliant—minds disagree, in other words, is hardly a basis for equating legal analysis with political subterfuge.

As a subfield of political science, today the study of law and politics takes a diversity of forms. Much political science scholarship is not only complementary to the "legal model" of understanding judicial behavior, it overlaps with the approach taken by legal scholars—incorporating the exploration of doctrinal developments within particular areas of constitutional law.[39] Typically, however, when political science engages doctrinal analysis, it does so with a broader lens than does legal scholarship. This is the case, for example, with historical institutionalism, an approach within political science that has "recovered an interest in constitutional ideas and historical development and wedded it to the post-behaviorist concern with political action and the broader political system."[40]

According to Rogers Smith, public law scholars who questioned the dominance and value of behaviorism first began to make their voices heard in the late 1980s, identifying as "new institutionalists" initially but eventually settling on "historical institutionalism."[41] To these scholars, jurisprudential doctrine is not, as attitudinalists would claim, just smoke and mirrors. Attitudinalists have critiqued the major premises of historical institutionalism as "not far from the traditional legal model."[42] However, to historical institutionalists, doctrine must be taken seriously. As credible legal interpretation, doctrine provides institutional authority to judges and courts, providing them with "real power to affect political results."[43] Contrary to the attitudinalist view, historical institutionalists see judges as constrained by the very doctrines they create. Yet, they do not shy away from the view that doctrines may, at the same time, be "expressions of broader political ideologies."[44] Influential political scientist Gerald Rosenberg has argued that the First Amendment acts as "'a forum for substantive arguments about the cultural definitions of liberty' and its relation to equality."[45] In the chapters that follow in this study, I bring together historical institutionalism, doctrinal analysis, and, yes, attitudinalist scholarship to explore the relationship between political ideology and the First Amendment.

Beyond the sometimes startlingly deep divide between these approaches to explaining judicial decision making, there are also less-contestable relationships between the political world and the legal world. Politics matters. Regardless of the extent to which *legal actors* do or do not act for political reasons, it is clear that political actors external to the courts *react* to legal actors.[46] Citizens may *react* politically to legal decision making by taking stronger positions on ideological issues either consistent with or in opposition to a court holding.[47] Public opinion polls have revealed that approval or disapproval of Supreme Court performance is often evaluated in partisan terms.[48] Liberal and conservative members of the public, in other words, are more or less prone to judge the Court favorably depending upon its perceived ideological leanings.[49] Political party platforms often incorporate a range of interpretive stances on the Constitution, whether it be the position held by the Republican Party that voluntary prayer in public schools is constitutional under the Establishment and Free Exercise clauses of the First Amendment or that affirmative action is unconstitutional under the Fourteenth Amendment.[50] Political operatives may take such positions preemptively in order to make their view clear *before* the high court has decided the issue definitively, or candidates and elected officials may *react* to holdings once they are decided by incorporating their distaste or approval of particular Court decisions into their political platform or agenda.[51] It is clear that these reactions will often have much to do with political ideology—and how a particular decision is ultimately spun for public consumption.

Controversial Supreme Court decisions that are perceived to be conservative and believed to be a consequence of conservative political appointments to the court—such as *Citizens United v. FEC,* discussed in depth in Chapter 7—galvanize political forces.[52] Such decisions shape how liberal and conservative politicians, pundits, and citizens talk about the courts, conceive of the courts' role, and attempt to influence them in the future. In other words, court decisions have exogenous political import, regardless of the extent to which politics is or is not endogenous to courts.[53] And most would likely agree that this relationship between political ideology and court behavior necessarily flows in both directions. Even scholars with the most idealized notions of what judges do once they are judges understand that these very same members of the bench once had a pre-judge existence—and that the route to earning that black robe is inherently political. Thus, the political realm not only *reacts* to politically controversial decisions, it must, following these *reactions,* continue to determine the composition of the courts. Court membership is invariably informed by ideological political perceptions—whether judges are elected as they often are at the state level or appointed by elected politicians at the federal level.[54]

As we shall see, within the broad ideological category of "conservatism" there is significant variance. Political ideals are in some sense relativistic; not only do they shift in political time, but their very definition is subject to change. One political and social era's vision of an ideal conservative might be another's vision of moderation. Since 2008 and the advent of the Tea Party wing of the Republican Party, politicians formerly understood to be solidly conservative have been pejoratively rebranded as moderate RINOs (Republicans in Name Only) by their adversaries and primaried out of office. Policies that were initiated and widely celebrated by one era's conservatives may be castigated as unduly liberal by the next.[55]

Such relativity is evident both on and off the court. Is Justice Antonin Scalia an ideal judicial conservative or does Justice Anthony Kennedy fit the bill? The answer might very much depend upon the de jour definition of conservatism and the accumulation of reactions by the political establishment to the justices' various votes during their respective tenures on the Court. Both justices arguably bring to their judging conservative values—but these values are not always in harmony with one another or with the ever-shifting ideological ideals cultivated in the political world.

Thus, this study seeks to acknowledge the complex multidirectional relationship between political ideology and constitutional jurisprudence, as well as the fact that political ideologies themselves are to some extent in flux. What often goes unacknowledged both in the realm of political science and legal scholarship is the subtle way in which jurisprudence itself can spur ideological change, and, in the converse, the way politically charged ideological concerns of the day can be agents of jurisprudential change. Although it was the liberal Warren Court that cemented a principled speech-protective approach to the First Amendment in the 1960s, it would only be a matter of time before the Court would be confronted with applications of free expression that would be seen as serving conservative political interests. Many such cases would be brought to the fore by entrepreneurial conservative legal organizations. The right to propagate commercial speech discussed in Chapters 5 and 6, for example, is a freedom that typically confers benefits on the business community—a traditionally conservative constituency. Freedom of commercial speech provides businesses with greater opportunity to market their services or wares without governmental interference. Thus, applying the freedom of speech—a jurisprudential principle long associated with political liberalism—to commercial speech establishes an alignment between the First Amendment advocacy and the ideological and practical interests of conservatism: laissez-faire economics.

Just how might conservatives resolve the understandable desire to apply a constitutional principle associated with liberalism to advance a conservative ideological concern? There are two obvious possibilities. The first narrative is purely instrumental:

> *The constitutional principle of uninhibited free speech, cultivated and nurtured by liberalism, is suddenly found to be useful to conservatives. Political conservatives see an opportunity to co-opt liberal constitutional principles for their own advantage and shamelessly take it. They do so despite the fact that it requires them to support a position on constitutional interpretation—broad speech protection— that in other settings where liberal interests were served they firmly opposed.*

The second narrative focuses on legal principle:

> *Those conservatives who support broad commercial free speech either (a) see a principled way of distinguishing other contexts in which they believe that constitutionally guaranteed free expression is rightfully narrower or (b) genuinely see the light and feel honestly compelled to change their perspective on an issue of constitutional principle for reasons that are unrelated to their political and ideological interests.*

There is, however, a third option for understanding this situation, one that takes into consideration the messiness and complexity of the relationship between constitutional principle and political ideology. This third option acknowledges that both the first and second explanation may be at play, at different times, and in different ways. The third option understands that what might initially be inspired by some degree of political instrumentalism—what I refer to as an "ideological nudge"—might ultimately lead to insight and changed perspective about constitutional principle, and vice versa.

In other words, once this conservative sees the advantages a broader interpretation of the First Amendment might have for the free market, she might be inspired to make a principled adjustment in her understanding of how the Constitution should be interpreted. This change might, in turn, gradually alter the way she conceptualizes what is instrumentally beneficial as a conservative. Once she accepts the premise that freedom of expression is a fundamental good in the free-market context, she might gradually begin to see such freedom as a conservative value—even outside of the free-market context. Reasoning by analogy, a fundamental component of legal reasoning, might in fact encourage this progression. In short, the ideological implications of jurisprudence—and the interactions between doctrine and politics—matter.

Shifting Conservatism on the Court— The Conclusions and Deficiencies of Political Science

Although the perception that aggressive First Amendment advocacy is politically "liberal" lives on,[56] ideological alignments on the Court have become substantially muddled. As political scientists Lee Epstein and Jeffrey Segal conclude, even though the academy has been slow to acknowledge this shift, a "commitment to First Amendment values is no longer a lodestar of liberalism."[57]

In a study of First Amendment decisions between 1994 and 2002, legal scholar Eugene Volokh likewise confirmed the counterintuitive discontinuity between ideology and the free speech values.[58] He not only found that alignment between conservative ideology and what he terms "free speech minimalism" no longer held, but he found that a number of conservative members on the Court had stronger records of "free speech maximalism" than their liberal colleagues.[59] Some legal scholars began to observe this unexpected shift as early as the 1990s.[60] It may thus be surprising that there has been so little in-depth exploration, or even acknowledgement, of this changing dynamic and its relationship to the political world outside of the judiciary. However, reticence might be in part a product of the somewhat slow-moving nature of this change. Even Kathleen Sullivan, who was one of the first to note this trend back in 1992, expressed surprise at the unprecedented extent to which traditional alignments were reversed, both inside and outside the Court, in the *Citizens United* decision in 2010.[61]

A Case Study in Attitudinal Analysis

In 2006 Epstein and Segal attempted to better understand the First Amendment dynamic on the high court by customizing the attitudinal model to account for ideological tensions built into free-speech decisions.[62] Their attempt to do so, however, raised many additional questions and served to illuminate the perilous—and sometimes dubious—task of boiling down highly complex and lengthy First Amendment decisions to a simplistic "liberal" or "conservative" moniker. The Supreme Court Database, on which they and many other political scientists rely, utilizes a coding scheme that provides enormous room for discretion by those making the coding decisions.

For example, according to the codebook, a First Amendment decision is to be coded "liberal" where it "represents . . . support for individual rights."[63] Under this scheme one might quickly conclude that although *Citizens United*—discussed in greater detail in Chapter 7—was a speech-protective decision, it was in fact *not* a liberal one because it upheld a *corporation's*, not an *individual's*, right to free speech. And this might seem to be a satisfying conclusion—after all, *Citizens United* was a 5–4 decision in which the five "conservative" judges joined together to issue their holding. However, a cursory reading of the substance of the decision itself would reveal that to the majority, matters were not quite this simple. On one hand, it is certainly true that the majority struck down the McCain–Feingold campaign finance law provisions restricting corporate political spending because of the way this "silences entities."[64] On the other hand, it is also true that to the majority, their decision supported an *individual's* right; that *individual* just happened to be the *listener*.

To the Court, the campaign finance law violated the First Amendment because it "deprived the public of the right and privilege to determine for itself what speech and speakers are worthy of consideration."[65] So for coding purposes, whether the holding supports "individual rights" is perhaps less clear than it at first appeared. Is this holding *primarily* about "the rights" of individual members of the public or the rights of corporate entities? The coder must make this debatable judgment call.

Then there is the inconvenient fact that *Citizens United*'s holding addressed not merely *corporations'* First Amendment rights, but *unions'* as well.[66] The Supreme Court Database codebook requires that with regard to "issues pertaining to unions and economic activity," a pro-union outcome is to be coded as liberal while a pro-business outcome is to be coded as conservative.[67] Under this scheme, the *Citizens United* holding could once again be considered either liberal or conservative—and it is up to the coder to make the call. As legal scholar Carolyn Shapiro has incisively observed, "rather than illuminate the workings of the Supreme Court, some empirical findings may reflect the way the Database [codes] information."[68]

To deal with the ambiguity of multiple-issue Court decisions, the Supreme Court Database separately codes each issue such that a holding might be liberal on one issue but conservative on another.[69] The overall direction of the decision is then determined by the case's "primary issue."[70] This scheme allows for the coding of multiple issues, all of which are maintained in the database. However, the need to decide what is, or is not, the primary issue in a case once again raises concerns about coder discretion. The possibility of multiple issues complicates the task of assessing ideological voting on First Amendment cases because, quite simply, many First Amendment cases involve more than just a First Amendment issue, and in many such instances the First Amendment issue is not deemed by the coder to be the primary issue.

In their 2006 study, Epstein and Segal cite *Boy Scouts v. Dale* as an example of just such a case. In *Dale*, discussed in Chapter 7, the Court struck down on First Amendment grounds a New Jersey public accommodations law that would have prohibited the Boy Scouts from discriminating on the basis of sexual orientation.[71] The decision was coded as *both* a civil rights case and a First Amendment case.[72] For purposes of the former, the holding was deemed conservative (anti–civil rights) while on the latter issue it was labeled liberal (pro–free speech).[73] Because the primary issue of the case was determined to be the civil-rights issue and not the free-speech issue, the Supreme Court Database considered the decision to be conservative.[74]

From the perspective of the "legal model"—as political scientists sometimes characterize the approach of mainstream legal scholarship and jurisprudence—the very fact that a coder must choose a so-called primary issue is deeply problematic. Legal decision-makers are on a regular basis required to resolve an array of intricately intertwined issues. Within the ambit of a single case, judges are tasked not only with untangling the many internal tensions and contradictions that may exist among the various issues, but with identifying or denying the existence of such issues in the first place. Indeed, learning to "find issues"—and concomitantly developing an appreciation for the fundamental contestability of each issue's relevance—is one of the first skills a first-year law student must acquire. To suggest that a coder should somehow divine a "primary issue" using his or her common sense thus might strike legal scholars as somewhat fanciful. "'Primary' in what sense?," a legal thinker would likely ask. Would the fact that a certain issue in a particularly high-profile court decision receives especially heavy media attention make that issue "primary"? What if politicians or scholars find the issue particularly salient? Is this enough for "primary" status? Or, does the "primary" identifier turn on how frequently an issue is singled out by future courts? There is no way to know. Indeed, it is hard to escape the conclusion that making such a determination will inherently be influenced by the coder's own sensibilities and assumptions about what contextual factors are or are not important.

Nevertheless, as discussed earlier, the attitudinalist's data-driven approach to understanding judicial decision making is not about becoming "immers[ed] in detail."[75] Attitudinalists flatly reject the detail-oriented—one might even say nuance-centric—case study approach of the legal model. Attitudinalist scholars openly acknowledge that rejecting the case study method does have its drawbacks, but they argue that the trade-offs are well worth the explanatory benefits. As Segal and Spaeth explain, "[u]seful models ignore idiosyncratic factors and highlight instead variables that explain a high percentage of the behavior in question. Because models simplify reality, we cannot judge them as true or false."[76]

The Epstein and Segal 2006 study of the Court's free-speech jurisprudence examined all 506 of the Supreme Court's First Amendment decisions between the years of 1953 and 2004. However, in order to answer the question they set out to investigate—whether the relationship between liberalism and speech-protective decisions was on the wane—it was clear that they had to tweak their model. Under their modified approach, all cases with a First Amendment issue were coded as if that issue were the "primary" one.[77] Upon making this coding adjustment, their findings indicate that indeed a shift had occurred. A return to libertarian conservatism was apparent from the votes of a number of the contemporary conservative justices. From their study, we learn that conservative Justice Kennedy has voted in favor of free speech in a greater proportion of cases than liberal Justices Ginsburg and Breyer, and he is almost as friendly to First Amendment values as the liberal Stevens and Souter.[78] Over this time, sharply conservative Justice Thomas also voted in a more speech-protective fashion than Justice Breyer, as well as in a more pro–First Amendment direction than the Democratically-appointed moderate conservative Justice White.[79] Chief Justice Rehnquist's voting record, in contrast, reveals that he is something of a pre-libertarian, shift-in-time conservative when it comes to the First Amendment; his proportion of pro–First Amendment decisions is among the lowest of all of the justices who served during this period.[80] Rehnquist's role as a conservative holdout is explored in depth in Chapters 5 and 6.

Epstein and Segal, however, appear to be unsatisfied with the results they garner from their modified coding scheme. Instead of merely focusing on the 506 cases as a single category of First Amendment decisions, they tell us that these cases may be divided into two classes: "pure" disputes and "value-conflict" cases.[81] They explain that the former "by and large, do not require the Justices to weigh First Amendment guarantees against any other constitutional or political value," while the latter do.[82] These scholars do not explain precisely why they chose to draw this supposed distinction. One might surmise that they felt the understandable urge to reinject some of the complexity they extracted when they altered their coding scheme to convert all multiple-issue cases into decisions "primarily" addressing the First Amendment. In other words, if they could "purify" their data by segregating the messy nuanced cases from the crystal-clear First Amendment cases, their unadulterated data might better expose what is truly happening.

To Epstein and Segal's credit, they acknowledge in a footnote that "[s]everal colleagues . . . have suggested to us that the distinction between pure and value-conflict cases may be one without meaning because in all disputes a competing interest exists."[83] It is difficult not to agree with this critique; and indeed, Epstein and Segal themselves concede this point, but they retort that to them, "the question is one of degree."[84] Yet here we run up against the very same problematic methodological issues discussed above—that is, that Epstein and Segal's judgment regarding this question of "degree" is subjective, just as the inherent discretion required of their coders to assess whether a particular decision is "pro-individual" or "primarily" about "civil rights" is subjective. The risk that this subjectivity substantially and systemically adulterates the results of their analysis is hardly trivial.

We are told that over the entire universe of cases examined—covering more than half a century—"the more liberal the Court, the more likely it is to rule in favor of a party alleging an abridgement of First Amendment liberties."[85] At the same time, however, the scholars report that this relationship "either disappears or reverses when we focus exclusively on the eighty-nine 'value conflict' cases."[86] Should this be considered a revealing and consequential finding? Because value-conflict cases have apparently become much more common in recent decades, does this tell us something critically important about the evolving psyche of the conservative and liberal justices? Does it provide a predictive methodology, one that uses social science to boil judicial behavior down to its essence? Or, on the other hand, does it tell us little more than that these scholars hold certain preconceived notions of what it means for there to be a "value conflict?"

Unfortunately, the distinction made by Epstein and Segal between value-conflict and non–value-conflict cases simply serves to highlight the inherent subjectivity of all line-drawing—whether inked by a judge or a political scientist. The remarkable fact that the scholars cite *Texas v. Johnson* as an "easy" example of a "pure" case where there is no value conflict is illustrative.[87] As we saw, to many observers and participants in the case, the value conflict in *Johnson* could not have been more clear; it just happened to be a *conservative* value conflict. Perhaps to Epstein and Segal the value conflict inherent in *Dale*—where First Amendment values conflicted with equality concerns for homosexuals— was a "degree" more significant than the value conflict in *Johnson*—which pitted free-expression interests inherent in burning an American flag against deeply held values of patriotism and even national self-preservation (as far-fetched as this may sound to some liberals). Perhaps Epstein and Segal did not see the latter as a conflict at all. However, a regular reader of *National Review*— as well as the dissenters in *Johnson*—would likely disagree.

In defending the relative merits of their quantitative approach, attitudinalists argue that the legal model is deficient because it is not scientifically "testable."[88] Segal and Spaeth explain that "if precedents exist on both sides of a case, a legal model based on precedent so long as the judges followed one precedent or another would not be falsifiable."[89] However, there is little reason to believe that in this respect the choice of a judge to utilize a particular precedent is unlike the judgment calls of coders who must answer "questions of degree" in the process converting complex jurisprudence into crude binary data. If we truly seek to understand the relationship between conservatism and the First Amendment, political science must seek to understand conservatism *and* First Amendment values. Otherwise, one's analysis risks taking on a tautological hue. In other words, is this just a case of liberal academics handpicking cases *they* perceive to involve an internal value conflict, and then, after rigorous statistical analysis concluding that "[l]iberal justices are conflicted in cases that involve conflicting liberal values"?

The broad correlations between judicial voting behavior and ideology are worthy of observation—indeed, I refer to these broad correlations throughout this study. However, particularly in an area as historically rich and politically loaded as the First Amendment, a qualitative analysis in line with the work of historical intuitionalists and legal scholars offers insight that simply may not be achieved through quantitative study. First Amendment law is too complex, too subtle, and too intertwined with evolving political and social movements to justify simply applying our own gloss to what we observe and treating this gloss as raw data. We *must address nuance.* And to do this, we need not reject the conclusion that ideology and politics have some bearing on the decisions judges make. But nor do we need to artificially flatten judicial behavior. As political scientist Keith Bybee has argued, just because "[i]mpartial, logically ordered principles do not wholly explain or motivate [judicial] conduct . . . does not mean that these principles are disposable window dressing."[90]

First Amendment Opportunism

Since the early to mid-twentieth century, when the Supreme Court first began to take seriously the free-speech guarantee in the First Amendment, its doctrine has evolved much like common-law jurisprudence. As David A. Strauss has pointed out, the "central features of First Amendment law were hammered out . . . in fits and starts, in a series of judicial decisions and extrajudicial developments."[91]

With each new precedent establishing a new area in which free expression was deemed to apply, the field of protected speech has broadened. Libel law in 1964, for example, went from being an area of tort law within the province of the states, with few if any restraints imposed by the Constitution, to an area in which a defamatory falsehood against a public official was considered protected speech unless it was shown to be made with "actual malice."[92] Three years later, this First Amendment protection was expanded to include public figures.[93] As I show in Chapter 7, freedom of association, a non-textual right that was said to be derivative of the Free Speech Clause, has gone from largely nonexistent prior to the Supreme Court's 1927 decision in *Whitney v. California*,[94] to a right that provided protection under narrow factually bound circumstances in 1958,[95] to a full-fledged expressive right granted to associations *qua associations* in 2010.[96] The doctrinal bar is not static. It rises or falls as the Court's First Amendment jurisprudence evolves. While the Court has certainly at times chosen to narrow particular fields of speech protection, on the whole the last half century has been a story of expansion rather than contraction.

Thus, to contrast the current Court's treatment of its First Amendment docket with the Court's past rulings does not necessarily shed much light on the overall relative trajectory of the Court's jurisprudence and may in fact tell a false tale. As the bar is nudged further and further north by advocates we might identify as First Amendment opportunists,[97] the Court must inevitably attach limits to the scope of First Amendment protection. If there were no reasonable limits on the applicability of the First Amendment, its guarantees could be used for arguably absurd and socially counterproductive ends. A crime involving even the most insignificant expressive component—a bank robber, for example, expressing her critique of the global financial system through a brazenly violent act—could be said to be immune from prosecution. Even the great so-called First Amendment absolutist Justice Hugo Black was of the view that free speech quite simply does not apply in certain domains—for example, on privately owned property[98] or where government-owned land is not a public forum.[99]

Certainly, First Amendment opportunists have an incentive to push the envelope. As Frederick Shauer has argued, "the First Amendment is frequently called on to do a job for which it is poorly designed. The job frequently gets done but, as with driving a nail with a pipe wrench, the job gets done poorly and the tool is damaged in the process."[100] The appropriate boundaries are, of course, subject to great debate—Schauer would place commercial speech, nude dancing, and campaign finance into the ill-fitted "opportunistic" category,[101] judgments with which many reasonable minds certainly may disagree. However, to say that a modern Court denying a bank robber First Amendment immunity would constitute evidence of a less speech-protective posture, because such a denial might be contrasted with the protection the Court afforded to a political leafleter in an earlier jurisprudential era, is to establish a false and misleading dichotomy. Line-drawing is inevitable, but as the doctrinal portrait continues to expand and take shape over time, the lines the Court is asked to draw become qualitatively different.

Truly understanding the relationship between conservatism and the First Amendment thus requires more than merely looking to quantitative data. And the data that exist are far from conclusive. Some studies directly rebut the growing belief that the conservative Roberts Court is highly speech protective—

pointing to the fact that, overall, the current Court has been less likely to find a free-speech violation than prior Courts.[102] One study noted that between 2006 and 2011 the Roberts Court supported a free-speech claim in 34.48 percent of its First Amendment decisions, whereas between 1953 and 2004, the Supreme Court agreed with such claims 53.95 percent of the time.[103]

However, such data may be more likely to distort than to enlighten. By selectively shining a light only on Court holdings or raw judicial votes, data-driven studies bypass—and risk mischaracterizing—the substantive content of the Court's written opinions. They also ignore the nature of the evolving universe of First Amendment cases from which the Court chooses—or is asked—to review. When the Court interprets the Constitution such that the scope of the First Amendment expands, the number of potential First Amendment cases also expands, sometimes dramatically. Thus, for example, a reduced percentage of pro–free-speech decisions might simply reflect a larger denominator, courtesy of the Court's own speech-protective precedents. We see an example of this kind of doctrinal expansion in Chapter 7. In sum, explaining Supreme Court decision making through the aggregation of quantitative data does not tell the whole story. Such studies have pointed in a number of seemingly contradictory directions, resulting in inconsistent assessments of the relationship between contemporary conservatism and free speech.

A qualitative exploration of the Court's evolving First Amendment jurisprudence and the corresponding exogenous conservative political commentary reveals a significant shift toward a more speech-protective posture, one that may be obscured if one were limited to quantitative data. The only way to truly understand this changing First Amendment ideological landscape is to disaggregate the phenomenon—looking both inside and outside the Court. In the following four chapters, the study identifies and examines moments in jurisprudential history in which the formerly clear ideological correlation between the pro–speech-regulation position of political conservatism and anti–speech regulation of political liberalism began to ambiguate.

J. M. Balkin refers to this phenomenon as "ideological drift." He suggests "that legal ideas and symbols will change their political valence as they are used over and over again in new contexts. This description envisions an idea or symbol changing its political significance over time while its content is held constant."[104] This concept is concededly something of a thought experiment; in truth, there are no such constants. The meaning of "free speech," as well as the meanings of "conservatism" and "liberalism," is to some extent a moving target.

"Free speech" might today, for example, be defined such that it includes computer code composed entirely of ones and zeros—a notion that would have been laughable a few decades ago. A classically liberal "libertarian" presidential candidate might be more likely to be defined as "conservative" in 2012 or 2016 than that same candidate would have been in 2004, prior to the advent of the Tea Party movement. Yet, words still have meanings. And these meanings have consequences.

Identifying and understanding the changing relationship between ideology and constitutional principle remains a task of great significance from the standpoint of legal theory, political theory, practical on-the-ground politics, and legal decision making. The following four chapters of this study focus on two ideological turning points, or constitutional fissures, that reshaped the constitutional politics of free speech. These fissures obscured the relationship between conservatism and the First Amendment such that it is no longer the vision of ideological clarity it was when Robert Bork penned his infamous 1971 law review article. The first, which I focus on in Chapters 3 and 4, I call the political correctness backlash. It began in the early 1990s and was marked on the Supreme Court most notably by the decision *R.A.V. v. City of St. Paul.*[105] The other constitutional fissure, explored in Chapters 5 and 6, is the advent of commercial speech protection, what might be seen more broadly as the monetization of speech. This period began roughly in the mid-1970s when the Supreme Court started to radically remake its commercial speech doctrine in *Virginia State Board of Pharmacy v. Virginia Citizens Consumer Council.*[106] This study looks at these two turning points both endogenously—as illustrated through Supreme Court decisions—and exogenously—though political reaction and actions among the political class.

3 Political Correctness and the Rise of the Conservative Victim

In a 1986 editorial, *National Review* noted with alarm that "Yale sophomore Wayne Dick received a draconian sentence of two years' probation for putting up posters satirizing Yale's 'Gay/Lesbian Awareness Days.'"[1] The concern rose above mere ideological disagreement over the moral issue of homosexuality and its acceptance in society. The editorial asserted in bold terms that

> the case involves what Margaret Anne Gallagher has called . . . the "tyranny of pity." In this syndrome, supposed victims acquire exceptional power—and implicitly, the alleged victimizers become the *true* victims. In the Wayne Dick case, the tyranny of pity enabled Yale homosexuals to abrogate not only Dick's constitutional rights but Yale's own contractual obligations to its students.[2]

In other words, through the conservative lens, liberal academic administrators— by imposing ostensibly pro-tolerance policies on college campuses across the country—were in fact creating a new class of victims on the right, suppressing conservatives and their ideas. The short 1986 editorial was a preview of a consequential battle in constitutional politics that would soon come to dominate America's national conversation.

The term "politically correct" did not become widely used until the late 1980s and early 1990s. Its widespread use reflected a perception that conservatives, particularly students and faculty in the academic setting, were being muzzled. The anti–political correctness movement—whether one believes it was rooted in cynical political opportunism or a genuine and legitimate pattern of grievances—helped *redefine* the conservative approach to free speech. It was a key constitutional fissure that would transform First Amendment politics. The conservative war on perceived political correctness, particularly on university campuses, would come to define the political landscape.

By the early 1990s, concern over supposed political correctness on college campuses had reached a fever pitch. A number of influential books, including Allan Bloom's *The Closing of the American Mind: How Higher Education Has Failed Democracy and Impoverished the Souls of Today's Students* and Dinesh D'Souza's *Illiberal Education: The Politics of Race and Sex on Campus*, made the case—as the titles of their books suggest—that an oppressive cadre of liberal thought-police had taken the reins of American higher education. One critic of the PC movement argued that what began "as an effort to diminish racism and sexism has turned into an orgy of Orwellian Newspeak."[3] To opponents the dangers of political correctness reached far beyond the attempt to tinker with the American lexicon, often crossing into overt *punishment* for disfavored ideas. An influential book by Alan Charles Kors and Harvey A. Silverglate infused critique with language borrowed from the left, deriding the "shadow university" as a place that "hands students a moral agenda upon arrival, subjects them to mandatory political reeducation, sends them to sensitivity training, submerges their individuality in official group identity, intrudes upon private conscience, treats them with scandalous inequality, and, when it chooses, suspends or expels them."[4]

The media in the 1990s was saturated with comedic stories highlighting the ostensible absurdity of politically correct zealotry.[5] Indeed, stories about political correctness ran a close second to the war during America's military intervention in the Gulf.[6] This attempt to portray those who dwell in the ivory tower as consumed by foolish oversensitivity, divorced from the true concerns of everyday Americans, clearly had resonance—and there was little question that such oversensitivity was by and large equated with liberalism. However, the PC indictment had become so pervasive in the mainstream media that even some liberal commentators joined in, adopting aspects of the critique as their own.[7]

Contrarians professed that something nefarious was afoot. To the skeptics, despite the populist appeal of the PC critique, the portrayal of a militant and unrelenting movement was much more "straw man" than "genuine phenomenon." In other words, the battle *against* the battle *for* political correctness was largely a clever and well-orchestrated bit of political theater—not a legitimate debate; it was nothing but "a *harangue*—a politically motivated, brilliantly

publicized conservative attack on progressive ideas in academia."[8] Undoubtedly, there was opportunistic behavior by conservatives who cherry-picked
colorful—and not necessarily representative—examples of political correctness run amok to drive home their point. Nevertheless, weighty fundamental ideas rested just under this veneer—ideas about tradition versus progress,
meritocracy versus egalitarianism, hierarchy versus equality.[9] And regardless of
how one characterizes the controversy, one thing is clear: The PC indictment
drove conservatives toward the First Amendment with an urgency, intensity,
and enthusiasm that was perhaps unparalleled in American history.

Coopting the arguments of one's adversaries is a political strategy with
a rich pedigree; and there can be little doubt that raising the "liberal" First
Amendment flag was a shrewd move by conservatives eager to give liberals a
dose of their own medicine. Whether or not reliance on the First Amendment
represented a political calculation or a genuine turn among conservatives toward free-speech values, it was clear that freedom of speech was becoming a
conservative rallying cry against the perceived tactics of the left—tactics that
ostensibly sought to diminish white male traditionalism in favor of multicultural relativism. Conservatives criticized everything from affirmative action
and minority outreach on campus, to the addition of Women's or African
American Studies departments, to the alteration of "great books" curricula to
include literature by "non-traditional" authors.[10] Harnessing the anti-PC rhetoric, a supporter of these programs could "be stereotyped as a humorless tool
of prepackaged political ideology and an enemy of free speech to boot."[11] Aim-
ing free-speech claims at the "politically correct" university infused conservative protestations with an air of legitimacy. And indeed, many of the challenged
PC policies that were proliferating across the country, including campus speech
codes and limited free-speech zones, did implicate the First Amendment—so
much so that even many liberals expressed alarm.[12]

Ironically, conservative enthusiasm for the First Amendment in this setting
was growing so strong that it was utilized rhetorically even where the Constitution itself was inapplicable. *National Review* editorials addressing incidents
at *private*, not *state*, universities hinted, without much elaboration, at a First
Amendment defense against leftist suppression on college campuses.[13] However, it is a central tenet of constitutional law—a principle referred to as the
"state action doctrine"—that the Constitution generally restrains only *governmental* actors and would not apply to *private* Ivy League universities. A 1988
letter to the editor of *National Review* by David D. Boaz of the Cato Institute

incisively pointed to this fallacy.[14] A 1988 *National Review* editorial sympatheti-
cally described the plight of three Dartmouth College students who "received
draconian sentences for participating in a brief and nonviolent confrontation with a black music teacher."[15] The three penalized students were editors
of the famously conservative *Dartmouth Review*. The editorial speculated that
the college seemed "to have been trying to crush an independently incorporated newspaper—a First Amendment Issue."[16]

Boaz, however, normally an ally, was quick to criticize the magazine's newfound role as guardian of free speech. He argued, consistent with the libertarian
conservatism one would expect from the avowedly libertarian Cato Institute,
that "[f]reedom and diversity are best served not when every university is required to have the same rules but when private institutions are free to set different standards and offer different environments. Then consumers have wider
choices."[17] So *National Review*, in the past hardly an outspoken proponent of
robust First Amendment rights, did not just reference the First Amendment;
it enthusiastically cited it in instances in which it clearly was not applicable
and where, strikingly, in order to remedy the supposed infringement on free
speech, government would have to impose its will on *private* institutions. The
magazine was, in other words, so intent on critiquing the "plague" of political
correctness that it revealed an implicit willingness to sacrifice—at least in this
context—free-market conservatism. As Boaz suggested, the free-market approach would clearly prioritize competition and the ability of private institutions to operate on their own terms.

What was emerging was a new reality—one in which, to conservative ears,
First Amendment advocacy was no longer synonymous with the left. Indeed,
just as today references to Second Amendment rights have become a catch
phrase—a sort of mantra, uttered in response to any alleged action that might
in any way be perceived to curtail access to guns, regardless of whether there is
truly a viable constitutional claim—the First Amendment was becoming a new
mantra on the right against victimization by the liberal establishment.

First Amendment scholars like Kenneth Karst had long pointed out that
typically "it is outsiders who have to invoke the first amendment."[18] Now the
tables had turned. The perception that conservatives were "outsiders," particularly on college campuses, began to gain currency, and with this sprung a
renewed appreciation of free expression. No doubt baggage remained—baggage from a recent past in which the links between political liberalism and
free-speech ideals were strong. Yet, by the early 1990s a rather stunning shift

was occurring. Conservatives increasingly saw themselves as defenders of free speech; and the liberals who were associated with university decision making were being cast not merely as, at times, mildly inconsistent on First Amendment issues, but as the outright enemies of free expression.

Hate Speech

In 1989 a *National Review* editorial issued a warning: "Colleges and universities across the country are passing regulations that prohibit 'offensive' language or behavior relative to race, gender, or, as they say nowadays, 'sexual orientation.' . . . [T]he spirit of censorship is abroad in academia."[19] By the close of the 1980s, 60 percent of all colleges and universities in America had enacted some form of hate-speech code.[20] "Hate speech" is generally defined as speech that is harmful or offensive to racial minorities, religious groups, or other historically disempowered minorities.[21] And it was this approach to this category of expression that was perhaps most responsible for the growing perception that modern liberalism was veering far from the civil libertarian tradition of the Warren Court era. In the early 1990s, over 450 editorials in the popular press addressed the issue of hate-speech codes on college campuses.[22] And while concern over hate speech was by no means limited to the verdant confines of college campuses, many of the most volatile debates about the propriety of punishing hate speech were centered in the academic world, where many scholars and administrators increasingly advocated a more aggressive approach to bigoted speech.

Many conservatives saw in the speech codes that sought to eradicate hate speech not merely a misguided route to achieving an unalloyed "social good" but a self-serving political agenda. The debate played out on several fields simultaneously, from scholarly academic journals to popular culture. Conservative scholar and jurist Charles Fried skewered the scholarly defense of speech codes, while implicitly acknowledging the way the debate over political correctness seemed to bleed from one forum to another. "The sophistries used to defend the various campus speech codes have made intellectuals and academia the deserved butt of public ridicule. The PC jokes may not be very subtle, but they capture something that really is there."[23] Kors and Silverglate argued that "[s]peech codes, prohibiting speech that 'offends,' protect ideologically or politically favored groups, and, what is more important, insulate these groups' self-appointed spokesmen and spokeswomen from criticism and even from the need to participate in debate."[24]

In 1993, another Ivy League institution got its opportunity to bask in the limelight of conservative ire. This incident provoked widespread national attention and to many was a watershed moment, bringing needed attention to the wave of pervasive PC-overreach that dominated college campuses. It began one night in Philadelphia, when a white University of Pennsylvania undergraduate student—hard at work on a paper for his English class—was disturbed by loud singing and chanting outside his dorm room window. He shouted to the merrymakers below, requesting that they "please keep quiet."[25] After twenty minutes passed and the noise did not abate, the Israeli-born student once again approached his window. This time he yelled, "Shut up, you water buffalo. If you're looking for a party, there's a zoo a mile from here."[26] The university charged the student under Penn's hate-speech code, accusing him of racial harassment and threatening him with expulsion—the offending revelers were five black sorority sisters. The alleged harasser sued Penn for emotional distress; as it turned out, the term "water buffalo" was a translation of the Hebrew slang word "behemah," which means foolish or obnoxious person.[27] The ultimate result was a settlement in which the university admitted no wrongdoing,[28] but the incident brought intensive national scrutiny to the issue of college speech codes. In response to the outcry, Penn publicly committed to reworking its racial harassment policy. The interim university president described the task as "balance[ing] two important principles—the right to free speech and the right to be left alone—while promoting civility within the university community."[29]

The Hate-Speech Critique
and the Early Days of *National Review*

There was an irony in the political alignments of the political correctness wars of the late 1980s and 1990s. In the past, it had been moralistic conservatives who were most likely to *support* speech-suppressive policies at universities. In the 1950s and 1960s, when the dominant threats on college campuses were perceived to be communist infiltration and unbridled hedonism, it was political conservatives who rallied behind the attempt to tamp down on harmful expression.[30] The period of the late 1960s and early 1970s also marked a move from a conservative focus on the ostensible threat of communist infiltration to concern over vociferous generational and racial tensions that were increasingly apparent, particularly on the streets of America's cities. Student protestors, civil rights activists, and countercultural hippies began to edge out communists as the most popular perceived threat to civil society. Frank S. Meyer had warned that protesting university students are "the mass army of a coherent, ideologically motivated attack upon the tradition and the structure of our civilization and our Republic."[31]

Thus, even as some conservatives instinctually began to revert to ideals of conservative libertarianism as the communist threat began to fade in salience, other perceived threats had filled in the gap and continued to justify a narrow reading of the First Amendment. In 1970, Meyer explained the need for continued vigilance:

> Although the elitists who today in America are attempting to thwart constitutional process and impose their ideological control on the country are not organized in the conspiratorial, paramilitary fashion of the Communist and fascist totalitarians, their endeavor is functionally similar, And, as with their totalitarian predecessors, the responsibility for bringing them to heel before it is too late rests with the constituted authorities.[32]

According to Meyer, mass demonstrations, which at the time occurred with some frequency, were nothing short of "mob intimidation." Since intimidation of this form "threatens the rights of all to live in a free society," Meyer reasoned that First Amendment rights may be justifiably limited.[33]

The following year Meyer once again compared the strategies and tactics used by protestors to those of Nazi Germany. In fact, Meyer went as far as to argue that "[i]n one respect, indeed, the generation of the Sixties and Seventies, and their adult gurus, are more despicable then their Nazi and Communist predecessors. These at least made no bones about their dedication to the duty and necessity of open violence to bring down civilized government."[34] To Meyer, even nonviolent "mass street action," a common approach to achieving social change during the civil rights era, was parallel to the tactics of Weimar Germany, because it is "designed to intimidate constitutional government."[35] Here Meyer was even more blunt in his conclusion that such protestors should be afforded no protection by the First Amendment: "[M]anifestations [of mass action], even when they proclaim their 'nonviolence,' is neither freedom of speech in any reasonable interpretation of that phrase, nor peaceable assembly to petition the government for redress. It is universally intimidatory in character."[36] Because he saw no constitutional obstacle, Meyer proposed that legislation be passed to curtail protests in public places. He argued that "[i]t may be necessary not only to protect governmental bodies themselves from mass intimidation, but to forbid such use of the streets and public places altogether."[37]

In a 1968 review of a book entitled *The Second Civil War*, Richmond Crinkley addressed some prospective solutions to the rampant "civil discord" of the era. One was to simply declare that mass protests are themselves not free speech protected by the First Amendment.[38] This was another instance in which commonsense conservatism would seem to trump consistency of principle. To Crinkley, the "march, the protest, the vigil, mass picketing, sit-ins and sleep-ins, corporal inundation—all these means of 'protest' move towards the anarchy of riot."[39] Where the relevant problem is disorder on the streets, the problem must be addressed directly—by establishing order. "There are too many men-in-the-mass for the law to be able to protect either the groups or the property which they damage, and therefore man-in-the-mass must cease to exist as a form of political expression."[40] The straightforward solution, according to Crinkley, was that "the modern 'demonstrative' extension of the right of assembly must be shelved."[41]

Granted, for Crinkley, things were not quite this simple. He acknowledged the need for a free exchange of ideas and suggested an alternative in the form of mass communication—such as the "phone-in radio show."[42] Alternatives promised to "not only replace the wailing, incoherent mob, but give voice to its individual members."[43] Of course, as the Supreme Court itself has acknowledged, the medium often *does* matter when it comes to free speech;[44] a message that can be effectively conveyed in one manner may be all but impossible to convey as effectively in another. Yet, here we see an unapologetic assertion that certain forms of expression are, quite simply, more valuable, and thus more deserving, of First Amendment respect. What is to be the fate of "the man whose ideology depends upon group frenzy?"[45] He, the author blithely concludes, may be sacrificed in favor of more important interests.[46] In other words, there is a distinction between the respectable individual and the unruly crowd. Individual rights should be protected, but only to the extent that the individual asserting those rights does so in a respectable and responsible manner. Such an approach would again, to some, represent a win for common sense over blind adherence to principle.

Sometimes, what was criticized was not the First Amendment itself, the breadth of its interpretation, or the supposed ideal of free expression that it stood for, but the adverse secondary effects of the "First Amendment lifestyle." The recurring critique against the academy in the early era of *National Review* often revolved around the propensity of universities to promote relativistic thinking, to actively encourage the questioning of that which is presumed to be true. As we shall see, the substance of the critique would change substantially in the 1980s and 1990s. Indeed, one might even assert that with regard to free speech, conservatives would come to adopt the very opposite posture, claiming that views were being wrongfully shut out of the academy—and those views just happened to be their own. The older critique was on full view in a piece written in 1968, in which William F. Buckley reflected upon his 1962 college "sojourn" to the University of Texas:

> So much time has been given over in our recent intellectual past to pounding home the necessity for freedom of speech, to celebrating the value of dissent, to singing the praises of academic freedom, that the impression is given that what they have most to look forward to is the process of flux, or the changes that dissent and academic freedom will ring in. If, out of piety for the First Amendment, we end up encouraging man to use his freedom to cultivate and evangelize whatever is his belief—Communism, say—we are actually very close to saying that our own disbelief in Communism is less strong than our belief that Communism should have continuing opportunity to win over a majority.[47]

In other words, even if the First Amendment was itself not problematic, First Amendment values may be, particularly when they result in "nihilis[m]" and "doctrinal egalitarianism."[48] Embracing the ethos that all ideas should be tested in the marketplace and that through such a rigorous and uncompromising process the best—or "most true"—ideas shall emerge meant letting go of certitude. It meant that nothing was out of bounds. Buckley cautioned, "If man is to be encouraged to exercise his freedom to deny the bases of American life, the bases of American life are presumptively suspect."[49]

What was Buckley ultimately suggesting here? To borrow a contemporary conservative pejorative, Buckley's argument seemed to sanction a sort of "nanny state" for the life of the mind. The natural implications that follow from his argument are hard to ignore. To prevent this tarnishing of American ideals, presumably some governmental authority should have license to step in and curtail the plague of "doctrinal egalitarianism" by imposing controls over speech on university campuses. This is precisely the cause so passionately embraced by many of today's conservative activists, yet they are on the very opposite side of the free-speech equation—adamantly arguing against oppressive hate-speech codes and the like. One struggles to imagine how thinkers such as Meyer, Crinkley, and Buckley would have reacted to *Snyder v. Phelps*, in which only one of the five conservative Republican appointees dissented from the

majority decision upholding immunity from civil liability for protestors holding highly inflammatory rallies outside of funerals for fallen soldiers.[50]

The Hate-Speech Critique and the Early Court Decisions

In the 1960s, the time these authors filled the pages of *National Review* with
conservative justifications for narrowing First Amendment protections, a similar dynamic could be observed among the justices on the Supreme Court; the
justices split along ideological lines on the role of the First Amendment in con-
straining attempts to limit free expression on college campuses. In the 1967 decision *Keyishian v. Board of Regents*, the Court fractured in a 5–4 alignment in
which the five most liberal justices at the time[51] voted to strike down a New York
law on First Amendment grounds.[52] The four most conservative justices on the
liberal Warren Court—Clark, Harlan, Stewart, and White—dissented. The law
required that faculty members at state universities sign a certificate attesting
that they were not communists.[53] It also required that faculty be removed "for
'treasonable or seditious' utterances."[54] The majority opinion striking down the
law was penned by "liberal lion" William Brennan and emphasized the essential
role of free speech in the educational setting:[55]

> Our Nation is deeply committed to safeguarding academic freedom, which is of
> transcendent value to all of us and not merely to the teachers concerned. That
> freedom is therefore a special concern of the First Amendment, which does not
> tolerate laws that cast a pall of orthodoxy over the classroom.[56]

The Court's most liberal members made clear that the exchange of ideas
was uniquely central to the academic mission—one in which the marketplace
metaphor was distinctively apropos. According to Brennan, vague terms such as
"seditious" and "treasonable" left much room for interpretation, providing faculty with little clarity as to where the line between acceptable and unacceptable
utterances lay.[57] Upholding this law would have pushed us one step closer to an
academic landscape drained of its vitality, an idea marketplace constrained by
draconian rules governing what may be discussed or taught in the classroom
or on campus. The natural instinct for self-preservation would suggest that it
would only be the rare "bold teacher who would not stray as far as possible
from utterances or acts that might jeopardize his living" under this law.[58]

For the liberals on the *Keyishian* Court, the overbreadth principle com-
manded overturning the New York law.[59] Overbreadth is a doctrine that is distinctively speech protective but has proven to be quite controversial.[60] On its

face, the doctrine violates the classical mode of constitutional adjudication—and traditional notions of judicial restraint—in which a law is only to be struck down if it is found to violate the Constitution "as applied" to the narrowly construed facts at hand. The overbreadth doctrine allows the judiciary to go further than this, permitting a Court to strike down aspects of a law that will not directly impact the parties themselves. The enlargement of judicial power is considered to be appropriate in the First Amendment context because overly broad statutes create uncertainty as to whether or not particular speech might be included within the ambit of the law. As a result, the logic runs, such a law has the potential to chill speech by creating a climate of fear. In a setting in which one cannot be certain whether or not expressing oneself will result in adverse consequences, many, it is presumed, will simply refrain from taking the risk.[61]

Not only did the liberal justices on the Court pepper their opinion with grand rhetoric about the centrality of the First Amendment in academia, but the majority went out of its way to strike down aspects of the law that did not even apply to the appellant faculty members.[62] The more conservative dissenters lamented the unjustifiable "death blow" the majority imposed on the New York law, concluding that "[n]o court has ever reached out so far to destroy so much with so little."[63]

It is striking that just over forty years later, in what was perhaps the most controversial and politically impactful First Amendment decision of the modern era, it would be the five most conservative justices on the *Citizens United* Court who would be widely criticized for aggressively seeking out an issue that was not initially presented to it in order to strike down one of the fundamental tenets of the McCain–Feingold campaign finance law. Of course, this ideological role reversal has not been limited to the campaign finance setting. As mentioned previously, particularly in the academic setting, conservatives by and large find themselves on *the very opposite side* of the free-speech equation.

Nevertheless, in the mid- to late 1960s conservatives remained deeply skeptical of what they referred to as the open society paradigm. Consider a 1967 *National Review* editorial commenting on the decision in *Keyishian*. The editorial was critical not only of the decision itself, but of a "consistent pattern" of First Amendment opinions "the Court has been handing down for a decade."[64] This pattern was troubling because of its vision "of society and the citizen within society."[65] The editorial emphasized that when it comes to morality, social cohesion, and national security, governmental regulation is sometimes a practical necessity. Echoing James Madison, it reasoned that while the open society conception advocated by broadly protective First Amendment jurisprudence "would be ideal for a society of angels," we are not such.[66] In *Federalist* No. 51, Madison famously pointed to the inconvenient fact that men are not "angels." He was arguing for a system of checks and balances—and extolling the proposed Constitution's ability to both "enable the government to control the governed; and in the next place oblige it to control itself."[67] We cannot be sure where Madison would have stood in this particular context. However, there is little doubt on which side of the equation *National Review* stood in 1967.

The editorial argued that government power was needed as a sort of social glue: Government restrictions, by limiting what ideas may be held by those who were tasked with teaching the younger generation, prevented amoral social anomie while at the same time keeping us safe. The piece described in stark terms the "breathtaking" alternative vision propounded by the Supreme Court's First Amendment decisions:

> The citizens function only as isolated atoms in external relationships with one another. No objective claim of discipline or responsibility is recognized. Each citizen may believe and say whatever he thinks or feels about anything—war, revolution, perversion, crime, God, morality—and may associate himself freely with others who believe and say as he does.[68]

It was a vision that was antithetical to traditionally conservative notions of patriotism and duty that place country and honor over the exhalation of "the self." Broadly construed, First Amendment freedoms were conceived as a license for narcissistic pleasure-seeking, permission to shed all vestiges of self-restraint that might have, in a previous era, constrained crude selfishness.

The First Amendment protagonist "may advocate Communism, sodomy, anarchy, fascism or slavery; he not only can exempt himself by pleading a personal belief, from all obligations to defend his society but can urge others to join in his refusal."[69] Alarm regarding the national security implications of such a view were largely interchangeable with issues of personal morality. Not only may this protagonist associate with those who might wish to overthrow American democracy as we know it, but "[h]e may write, publish, read, and distribute to whomever he wishes, any sort of pornography."[70] What did this overarching free-speech philosophy suggest for civil society? The editorial sneeringly surmised that under this worldview, "Society is to be held together, it must be presumed, by the free and utterly unfettered choice of each individual, without any coercion, pressure or reminder from any law, from government or from any objective social source."[71] Applied to the free-market economy, the editors would have presumably cheered such a vision. But ideological bifurcation over individual rights among conservatives still dominated—and when it came to individual freedom to violate social mores, the libertarian ethic remained largely in hiding.

To the conservative dissenters on the *Keyishian* Court, the majority had "by its broadside swept away one of the most precious rights, namely, the right of self-preservation."[72] It is worth positing that today, if one were to replace the words "self-preservation" with the words "human dignity," many liberal jurists, scholars, or commentators would find themselves in agreement with the conservatives. As we shall see, a sizable group of contemporary political liberals express a very similar sentiment—a willingness to balance away free speech—with speech codes that attempt to stamp out racial and gender-based intolerance. Indeed, one merely needs to recall Penn's reaction to the water buffalo scandal, in which the university's president framed the central challenge in reworking its speech-code policy as a fundamental need to "balance" free speech against "the right to be left alone"—a balance that was ostensibly needed to encourage "civility within the university community."[73]

It is tempting to explain away what would seem to be a dramatic change in perspective among political conservatives when it comes to free expression in academia as a mere reflection of the contending interests that need to be balanced. When it was national security—the danger of communist subversion—conservatives were quite comfortable balancing away free-speech values. However, in the modern era, where the culture of political correctness purportedly saturates academia and where the perceived threat is racial and other kinds of insensitivity, the scales shift. The conservative view seems to be that we must remain steadfast and vigilant against any potential incursion on First Amendment freedoms. For those who decry the politicization of the judiciary, this might appear to be just another instance of unprincipled hypocrisy in which the First Amendment values are a convenient pretext for promoting other political interests—constitutional principles be damned. It is free-speech instrumentalism of the first order—and both ends of the political spectrum are equally guilty.

The Supreme Court's history of hate-speech jurisprudence, however, suggests otherwise. Fifteen years before *Keyishian*, in what was arguably the Court's first hate-speech decision—before hate speech was even called hate speech— the Court's more conservative members were on the same page as many of today's liberals, agreeing that expressive freedom may be justifiably balanced away to allow racist speech to be penalized. Although the ideological lines in *Beauharnais v. Illinois* were not quite as cleanly drawn as in *Keyishian*—where all the justices voting to strike down the law on First Amendment grounds were more liberal than the four dissenting justices—sharp ideological correlations were in evidence. The two most liberal justices on the Court, Douglas and Black, voted to strike down on First Amendment grounds Beauharnais's conviction for publishing a racist leaflet, and the Court's two most conservative members, Vinson and Minton, voted with the majority to uphold it.[74] Martin-Quinn scores, averaged for the justices on the majority (Burton, Clark, Frankfurter, Minton, and Vinson), came out at a conservative 1.013, well to the right of the median justice score for that term of 0.455.[75] The dissenters (Black, Douglas, Jackson, and Reed) averaged a liberal -0.317.[76]

Joseph Beauharnais presided over an organization called the White Circle League of America. In early 1950 he distributed literature expressing alarm that white neighborhoods in Chicago faced black "encroachment, harassment and invasion."[77] The leaflet implored "self respecting white people" throughout the city to unite, proclaiming that "[i]f persuasion and the need to prevent the white race from becoming mongrelized by the negro will not unite us, then the aggressions . . . rapes, robberies, knives, guns and marijuana of the negro, surely will."[78] Under Illinois law, it was a criminal offense to distribute a publication that "portrays depravity, criminality, unchastity, or lack of virtue of a class of citizens, of any race" and as a result exposes them "to contempt, derision, or obloquy."[79] Beauharnais was convicted but argued that the law violated his freedom of speech and press.[80] The slim conservative majority on the Court ultimately upheld the law, not because it deemed the expression to be hate speech, but under the tenuous and now roundly rejected theory that such speech constituted a form of "group libel."[81] While the decision in *Beauharnais* has not been directly overruled, the Court's libel jurisprudence in the intervening years—including cases such as the celebrated *New York Times v. Sullivan*[82]—has largely discredited its reasoning.[83]

It is quite certain that the Court's precedents would preclude a similar ruling today and that the changed tenor of modern political conservatism would likewise suggest a far different holding in the hands of contemporary conservatives. The majority opinion in *Beauharnais* nonetheless reflects a number of traditionally conservative political themes. Frankfurter's opinion, for example, emphasizes the value of judicial modesty. The view that the Court should generally defer to the judgment of the legislature—and avoid whenever possible interfering with the decisions made by democratically elected bodies—would become a familiar staple of Frankfurter's jurisprudence.[84] Such judicial minimalism is on its face fundamentally conservative. As moral psychology has observed, conservatives generally "have a stronger preference for things that are familiar, stable, and predictable."[85] And not only did the approach taken by the *Beauharnais* majority prioritize the status quo over judicially imposed change, but it held local problem solving to be preferable to the centralized power of the Supreme Court. Frankfurter reasoned that "[o]nly those lacking responsible humility will have a confident solution for problems as intractable as the frictions attributable to differences of race, color or religion. This being so, it would be out of bounds for the judiciary to deny the legislature a choice of policy."[86] Without question, this brand of *procedural* conservatism has had a long and storied association with *political* conservatism, most evidently since the perceived judicial "activism" of the Warren Court.

However, to a previous generation of jurists, procedural conservatism had precisely the opposite connotation. During the New Deal era, it was the political liberals who argued for procedural conservatism, lambasting the willingness of conservative opponents of the New Deal on the Court to strike down regulatory legislation on both the federal and state level because it purportedly violated substantive due process. Indeed, Frankfurter was a member of this generation, an FDR appointee who held fast to his "liberal" procedural conservatism well beyond the time in which it was in vogue to do so. As a result, Frankfurter looked more and more politically conservative as political time marched along. Justice Douglas, in contrast, wrote a dissent in *Beauharnais* that directly addressed this conundrum—justifying an approach that to some conservative critics was emblematic of hypocrisy, inconsistency, and results-oriented judging. Douglas suggested that while the Court may have learned its lesson and appropriately reversed its prior tendency to assert "judicial supremacy" to strike down laws on the basis of the "vague contours of the Due Process Clause," the Court should not show the same reticence when it comes to laws that violate the First Amendment.[87]

To the liberal Douglas, the First Amendment was distinct, its language clear and unequivocal. "Free speech, free press, free exercise of religion are placed separate and apart; they are above and beyond the police power; they are not subject to regulation in the manner of factories, slums, apartment houses, production of oil, and the like."[88] There are reasons to be skeptical of Justice Douglas's attempt to make a principled distinction between those settings in which "judicial activism" is or is not appropriate. One simply need consider that as the would-be author of *Griswold v. Connecticut* the following decade, he would arguably be responsible for reinvigorating the concept of substantive due process in the realm of personal privacy.

Nonetheless, the Court's history is arguably riddled with examples of liberal *and* conservative flip-flops on the sinfulness of judicial activism—turning, of course, upon the context. We see a similar trend today, as conservatives—who pounded the drum of judicial modesty ever since Earl Warren took the helm at the high court—now find themselves in the majority. While many of these conservatives may still cling to the language of judicial modesty, on the contemporary Court a new judicial activism has unquestionably taken hold, one in which the conservative justices appear increasingly eager and willing to discard recent precedents and overturn legislation. There are, however, in addition to the Court's conservative procedural posture, other indicia of political conservatism in the *Beauharnais* majority opinion.

One might initially imagine that the moral foundations of a decision upholding a state's right to enforce a law against racist group defamation would draw most heavily on moral principles resonant with political liberals, such as the "harm/care" and "fairness" foundations. It might seem self-evident that allowing Illinois to stand up for historically subjugated minorities fits well with the traditionally liberal "human concern about caring, nurturing, and protecting vulnerable individuals from harm."[89] Certainly, framing Beauharnais's divisive words as group libel would seem, on its face, to reflect a sensitivity by the Court to the harm imposed on the targeted racial groups—a harm inflicted by the defendant's noxious accusations that an entire class of citizens is to be feared and despised due to its propensity for violence, aggression, and illicit drug use.[90] And indeed, the Court's majority does concede that a legislature may reasonably "believe that a man's job and his educational opportunities and the dignity accorded him may depend as much on the reputation of the racial and religious group to which he willy-nilly belongs, as on his own merits."[91] After all, the majority reasoned, these are claims that have been made by "social scientists."[92]

However, recall that it was the *conservative* majority, not the liberal dissenters, who made these arguments. It is telling that mainstream political liberals of the era immediately following the *Beauharnais* decision did not, and would not (until the 1980s and 1990s), show any signs of endorsing a speech-suppressive approach to achieving their political goals—even where the speech at issue ran directly counter to liberal egalitarian ideals. The preeminent constitutional scholar Harry Kalven made this point with pride in 1965, pointing to the refusal of the civil rights movement to advance its goals through the use of group libel laws.[93] A closer analysis of the language of the majority opinion *does* reveal the deeply conservative foundations of the decision. While the conservative *Beauharnais* majority did in a sense acknowledge the "liberal" moral harm principle, it did so in a highly qualified manner. Considering the nature of the harm involved, the *Beauharnais* majority seemed to have consciously minimized the care principle as a guiding foundation for its decision.

In contrast to the restrained tone the Court struck when addressing "compassion" and "harm" justifications for its holding, the conservative majority repeatedly and enthusiastically emphasized moral foundations resonant with political conservatism. First, we might observe the majority's tone. The Court's language quoted above took as a baseline that all individuals should be judged on their "merits"—and that the "willy-nilly" fact of one's "racial or religious group" has the potential to distort this assessment. To the conservative members of the Court majority, combating racial libel was much more about letting America's meritocracy shine through than it was about feeling the pain of minorities who were wrongfully maligned.

Second, in ceding authority to the state of Illinois, the Court emphasized what moral psychology would refer to as the "authority/respect" foundation.[94] In modern political parlance this might be understood as the "law and order" strain of conservatism. Addressing racial strife, the Court suggested, is first and foremost a police power. If the Court were to deny state authorities the power to address this issue effectively, social disorder might be the result. The majority tells us that disseminating falsehoods about racial groups "tend powerfully to obstruct the manifold adjustments required for free, ordered life."[95] The Court recounted an extensive bloody history of murderous and riotous behavior inspired by racial animus, suggesting that aggressive and assertive social control may be a necessity.[96] In other words, this was an instance in which those in authority must be permitted to act on a "sound discretion, applied to the exigencies of the state as they arise."[97] Just as in the field of criminal justice generally, conservatism has been much more comfortable ceding power to respected authority figures who are given the task of tamping down social deviance and civil disorder. As moral psychologists have long understood, "Conservatives have traditionally taken a more pessimistic view of human nature, believing that people are inherently selfish and imperfectible [and that they] need the constraints of authority, institutions, and traditions to live civilly with each other."[98]

Justice Black, second only to Justice Douglas on the 1951 term's scale of liberalism, immediately called attention to this instinctual trust in authority in the majority opinion. In his dissent, he skewered what he saw as an authoritarian mindset, pointing to the lamentable consequences that have been known to result from placing too much confidence in elected leaders. "The motives behind the state law may have been to do good. But the same can be said about most laws making opinions punishable as crimes. History indicates that urges to do good have led to the burning of books and even the burning of 'witches.'"[99]

A conservative vision is more likely to emphasize the importance of obedience and conformity, hierarchy and rule adherence. Conservatives are generally much more comfortable placing trust in those at the top of the hierarchy, even where there is a risk that their power will at times be abused. Frankfurter conveyed this philosophy succinctly, arguing that "[e]very power may be abused, but the possibility of abuse is a poor reason for denying Illinois the power to adopt measures against criminal libels sanctioned by centuries of Anglo-American law."[100] Notably, the anomalous conservative dissenter, Justice Reed, adopted none of Black's language and instead dissented on narrow grounds. Reed expressed absolute comfort with the state's power to criminalize so-called group libel; he simply believed the statute's language was unacceptably vague.[101]

If we fast-forward to 1975, we see hints of things to come in a *National Review* editorial critical of colleges that deterred unpopular—read "conservative"— speakers from appearing on campus.[102] The editorial began by mirroring the prevailing conservative First Amendment view—a highly constrained one. It offered a harsh condemnation of the liberal interpretation of the First Amendment, observing that "[f]or all the highfalutin cant, it is never made clear in what sense freedom of speech is a 'right.'"[103] A "promiscuous invocation" of the right, we were told, was questionable both because the original amendment was only intended to limit the *federal* government and because the language of the amendment should only be understood to include the original meaning of "free speech," that is, what was considered free at the time of ratification. The editorial took a swipe at Justice Holmes's view that "the best test of truth is the power of thought to get itself accepted in the competition of the market," calling this dictum "dubious."[104]

In the final three paragraphs, however, the focus shifted away from a conservative critique of "liberal" First Amendment interpretation. Here the critique moved instead to the clever and subtle way "liberal academics and pundits" manage to justify curtailing free speech when it is perceived that the speaker "presumably can say nothing to promote 'necessary social and political change.'"[105] The editorial decried the way liberals might divert attention from "the right of the audience" and instead focus on the fee the conservative speaker would receive in exchange for appearing on campus. The liberals would assert that while freedom of speech may apply, there was no right to a "fat fee."[106] The editors hypothesized that these same liberals would have had a very different interpretation had the speaker been endowed with a favored viewpoint.

National Review returned to the issue of controversial college campus speakers the following year in a sardonic critique of West Virginia University's decision to allow student activity fees to fund the appearance of Harry Reems, a star of the 1970s low-budget, sexually explicit sleeper hit *Deep Throat*.[107] Notably, there was no direct rebuke of a First Amendment interpretation that would protect such a lecture, only an underlying snicker directed toward the "worshippers at the altar of absolute free speech" so common on college campuses.[108] Although in the mid-1970s the magazine was not yet on the pro–free-speech-in-light-of-oppressive-political-correctness-on-college-campuses bandwagon, it was sending an early signal. This was the beginning of conservatives crying foul on First Amendment grounds. Soon it would be conservatives who were the victims of suppression. The editorial concludes: "The lesson . . . is this. All of us have the right to speak. Especially some of us."[109]

A Conservative Reversal

By 1988, the contrast with *Beauharnais* could not have been more stark. Outside of the hallowed courtroom, in a *National Review* piece tellingly entitled "Liberalism Versus Free Speech," Wilcomb E. Washburn portrayed liberals as the oppressors and conservatives as the oppressed.[110] The four-page article, taken from a speech made to Dartmouth alumni, was a thorough rebuke of the school's policies. It begins by pointing out one of the most foundational and inevitable dilemmas faced by advocates of free expression, one that was at the heart of the *Beauharnais* decision: "Defenders of free speech will concede that they face a real difficulty when this freedom is abused to incite hatred, violence, or racial or religious intolerance."[111] Washburn acknowledged that there were real trade-offs at stake. One may not merely disagree with particular speech; that speech may cause genuine harm. First Amendment principles bump up against real-world consequences. Speech-protective Supreme Court doctrine has generally addressed this dilemma with fact-dependent categorical line-drawing—rather than with a flexible balancing test. Only when a danger is clear and present, for example, may the law sanction speech that incites violence—and only the facts tell us whether or not the likelihood of harm is so immediate that it may meet the threshold of "imminence" required by the Court.[112]

However, this ever-present difficulty of gauging harm and determining whether such harm justifies diverging from free-speech protection might in fact be the easier part of the First Amendment equation. The more difficult challenge might be determining what is or is not harmful in the first place. Many disagree on this question, as Washburn was quick to point out. The challenge of reaching agreement is compounded by the fact that those making the assessment come with their own ideologically tinted glasses. The conservative trust of the forces of law and order so vividly on display in *Beauharnais* shifts to distrust when power is in the hands of a suspect liberal institution. Thus, although Washburn claimed to agree with the liberal college president that "harassment, racism, and intolerance have no place at Dartmouth," to the conservative author these sentiments "apply more appropriately to those [the president] is defending than to those he is attacking."[113]

In the Dartmouth controversy, the alleged perpetrators of hate speech were conservative students who approached a black professor after class. They sought comments on a controversial article the student-run *Dartmouth Review* had published transcribing a lecture he had given in class—a lecture that included ample helpings of vulgar language. To Washburn, it was the professor whose words and actions were harmful, not the students. The students posed their questions with an appropriate level of respect, according to Washburn's telling—for example, "repeatedly addressing Professor Cole as 'Sir'"—while the professor, in contrast, "physically assaulted" and "verbally abused" the students.[114] Nevertheless, it was the students who were subject to disciplinary proceedings by the college, not the professor.

The inconvenient reality is that the "true" meaning of a particular verbal exchange is, to a large extent, inherently subjective. Even if a precise record of the words spoken is provided after the fact, parties may remain wedded to very different narratives of what transpired. Whether one perceives words exchanged to constitute a form of verbal abuse or principled assertiveness may simply boil down to conversational style. This relativism was famously captured by Justice Harlan's celebrated—and by some, castigated—observation that "one man's vulgarity is another's lyric."[115] In this sense, humility might be said to be the guiding principle of the First Amendment.

However, whenever one ideological perspective dominates a particular setting, whether it be on the tranquil quad of a liberal college campus or among the solemn dark pews of a conservative Baptist church, this insight can get lost—if it was ever there to begin with. Washburn reasoned:

> Inevitably, members of an intellectual community will strongly hold views that contradict equally strongly held views of other members of that community. People who are hurt by strong expressions of disagreement belong not in a university but in a Trappist monastery. Conservatives, long in the minority, understand this. It would seem the Left does not—at least, not when its convictions are the ones under attack.[116]

Washburn cited French philosopher Julien Benda, who referred to this phenomenon as "'the treason of the intellectuals': they betrayed their obligation to the *process* of free inquiry, which is at the heart of liberal education, in order to advance their political, religious, or other interests."[117]

In the past, the right had few qualms painting liberals as lost in a nihilistic haze of moral relativism—dangerously permissive and open-minded—while conservatives remained properly grounded in fundamental, unchanging moral principles. Washburn inverts this traditional critique: "It is, I think, safe to generalize: Intolerance on campus today is almost exclusively a product of the Left. *All* the speakers silenced by protestors on American campuses in recent years have been conservatives."[118] To describe this pattern of injustice, Washburn coopts the language and arguments of the left—calling for "tolerance," "diversity," and even "affirmative action."[119] He laments: "It is sad to see the self-righteousness of the college administration in dealing with intellectual diversity."[120] Strikingly, when addressing the dearth of conservative faculty members on college campuses, he suggests that "[a]ffirmative action is [a] promising avenue. Alumni might 'demand' that Dartmouth institute an affirmative action plan to recruit more conservative professors until Dartmouth achieves statistical equality with the general population of the country."[121]

Washburn concluded with a damning critique of the state of higher education:

> It seems irrefutable that the American university, once a bastion of free inquiry and defense of the unpopular idea, is now interested in exploring and defending only *certain* ideas. It has countenanced, in the words of Education Secretary William Bennett, the "tactics of intimidation" and allowed those with a particular political agenda to determine university policy "not through force of argument, but through bullying, threatening, and name calling."[122]

The reflexive trust for authority on display in *Beauharnais* had vanished; abuse of power in academia had become a central concern. At the same time, conservatives mischievously delighted that two values traditionally held dear to the left—equality and free expression—seemed at impending war with each other. A 1989 *National Review* editorial characterized this tension as "an ironic confrontation between the academic fascists and their cousins, the First Amendment absolutists. If a lawsuit along these lines ever makes it to the Supreme Court—which it surely will—sit back and enjoy the fun."[123]

By the 1990s, the political culture wars were in full swing—as was a bipolar approach to the First Amendment among political conservatives. The right was focused on moral degeneration in American society—and the twin perpetrators were imagined to be a shameless media and entertainment elite selling sex and violence and an academic elite selling social relativism and tolerance. This moralistic conservative sentiment—promoted by, among others, a politically influential religious right—was simultaneously sending two very different First Amendment signals. On one hand, claims that graphic depictions of sex and violence were deserving of First Amendment protection were venomously criticized. On the other hand, enforced political correctness—such as speech codes that attempted to limit and penalize speech that overtly rejected the liberal ethic of tolerance on college campuses and other politically liberal enclaves—was portrayed as an intolerable affront to free speech.

The Scholarly Debate

As the debate over political correctness heated up on the pages of publications like *National Review*, a parallel discussion was occurring both in the legal academy and in the courts. The scholarly battle played out, and continues to play out, primarily as intramural combat among competing sects of the political liberal establishment. Representing an emerging position on the left that increasingly argued for a narrower conception of free expression in service of promoting racial and gender equality were scholars falling within the disciplines of critical legal theory, critical race theory, and critical feminism. In the late 1980s and early 1990s, scholars such as Charles R. Lawrence, III, Richard Delgado, Mari Matsuda, and Catharine MacKinnon justified reduced speech protection by emphasizing, often in the form of intimate narrative, the profound toll hateful expression could take on political minorities and the historically disadvantaged. On the other side of the ledger were liberal scholars such as Kenneth L. Karst and Nadine Strossen, who held fast to the civil libertarian tradition, maintaining their dedication to a broad First Amendment protection even while expressing deep concern and acknowledgment of the plight of racial and other minorities. Adhering to the spirit of Holmes/Brandeis and Warren Court liberalism on the First Amendment, these thinkers would not countenance an independent categorical exception for hate speech.

However, for critical theorists, addressing and penalizing hate speech was not merely permissible under the First Amendment, it was a moral, ethical, and perhaps even legal responsibility. To Lawrence the mandate of a landmark decision such a *Brown v. Board of Education* extended well beyond merely ensuring equal, non-segregated education for black children; it also prohibited sending messages of racial inferiority.[124] Lawrence posited that "[w]henever we decide that racist hate speech must be tolerated because of the importance of tolerating unpopular speech we ask blacks and other subordinated groups to bear a burden for the good of society. . . . This amounts to white domination, pure and simple."[125] In a heavily cited 1990 law review article, Lawrence took "traditional civil libertarians" to task for their speech-protective stance, arguing that the ACLU-type liberals who were quick to protest speech codes were rarely found speaking up against racist voices.[126] For Lawrence, this insensitivity was part and parcel of the typical civil libertarian view, a position that looked down on—as a form of "private censorship"—attempts to shame racist speech out of existence through counterdemonstrations and other means.[127]

Even where the censorship comes directly from the government, Lawrence was convinced that the costs of suppressing hate speech were minimal to nonexistent. This was because hate speech, to Lawrence, was comparable to the low-value "fighting words" category of speech, already deemed unprotected by the Supreme Court.[128] Like fighting words, hate speech could be understood as a verbal assault, "like receiving a slap in the face," that made little if any contribution to the marketplace of ideas.[129] As we shall see in the next chapter, just two years later, the Supreme Court would draw critical attention to this thesis, finding fault not in the claim that there may be some overlap between hateful speech and fighting words, but rather that the fit would often be tenuous. Prohibiting hate speech may ban *too much* speech, potentially including expression that does not have the attributes of fighting words, or *too little*, leaving many fighting words unsanctioned based on the government's preferred viewpoint.[130]

Nonetheless, the stage was being set for a showdown between contending liberal voices on the First Amendment, and the message that was increasingly being sent by critical theorists was: "You're either with us, or against us."

According to Lawrence, when the ACLU steps up to challenge campus speech codes like the one at the University of Michigan, "non-white students feel abandoned."[131] Indeed, Lawrence implicitly suggested that the civil libertarian left was sleeping with the enemy—thwarting the effort to move toward greater racial equality by giving moral ammunition to conservatives. He cautioned his brethren on the left that if they respond to minority "students' pleas for protection [from hate speech] by accusing them of seeking to silence all who disagree with them, we paint the harassing bigot as a martyred defender of democracy."[132] In other words, the ACLU was unwittingly feeding the powerful conservative narrative that it was those on the right who were the new victims, particularly on college campuses across the country. "Pick a side," the Crits seemed to be suggesting. Either the "abstractions of first amendment theory"[133] will win—shunting aside efforts to further racial justice—or the countervailing constitutional principle of equality will act as a reasonable counterbalance—allowing for some seemingly modest restraints on expression to address the real and significant harms inflicted by hateful speech.

There seemed to be growing agreement among critical theorists that there was little middle ground between themselves and ACLU liberals. Critical theorist Richard Delgado, in an influential 1991 article in the *Northwestern Law Review*, agreed that there was a sharp dichotomy between equality and freedom.[134] To confront the insidious harm of hate speech, which to Delgado was "like water dripping on sandstone," fundamental premises of much First Amendment doctrine would have to be upended.[135] Under established doctrinal principles, a danger must be *clear* and *present*, not *gradual* and *accumulative*. When harm may be judged cumulatively—the way the federal government's commerce power was famously determined to include anything that affects commerce, even if only in the aggregate—it becomes much easier to justify restrictions on speech. It was a standard that was reminiscent of the group libel principles articulated in *Beauharnais* and quite unlike the more speech-protective tests that have developed since that time. To Delgado, the freedom to use hate speech perpetuated a socially constructed stigma of inferiority and denied "equal personhood" to those minorities harmed.[136]

To many civil libertarians, however, the approach taken by the Delgado and other critical theorists would open a Pandora's box.[137] If the Court were to move in their direction under a belief that the First Amendment must be balanced against the equal protection principles, would there be any room for a limiting principle? What, in other words, would be left of the First Amendment? In an endless number of spheres, speech ultimately affects attitudes and behaviors and might thus be said to foster inequality. Delgado's retort was that "race—like gender and a few other characteristics—is different . . . judges easily could differentiate speech which subordinates blacks, for example, from that which disparages factory owners."[138] Civil libertarians, however, questioned the underlying premise that this was a contest between dichotomous constitutional principles—freedom of speech and equal protection—and that this contest was a zero sum game. Civil libertarians saw these two ideals—long considered to be pillars of political liberalism in America—as complementary.

Although it may appear counterintuitive, civil libertarians argued that tolerance of the intolerant—at least when it comes to the constitutional freedom of expression—ultimately produced greater tolerance, and thus, greater equality. In response to the call for an expanded use of the "fighting words" doctrine, Nadine Strossen, law professor and former president of the ACLU, pointed out that although calls for a narrower First Amendment may initially be motivated by a desire to shield racial minorities from harm, broader regulatory leeway has in reality meant that these very same classes of individuals have themselves become targets of prosecution for their own purported use of fighting words.[139] And not only may expanded exceptions to the Free Speech Clause be used against the very minorities the reforms seek to assist, but racist speakers who *are* censored may be glorified as a result; many psychological studies have revealed that forbidden speech, by virtue of being forbidden, becomes all the more appealing.[140]

Civil libertarians argued that hate-speech laws might hinder the kind of open dialogue that ultimately serves to reduce discrimination and enhance intergroup understanding.[141] Prohibiting hateful speech might deprive individuals—and society as a whole—of the valuable, albeit painful, knowledge that racism and other forms of group hatred exist and must be confronted. With the true nature and magnitude of group hatred driven underground, there may be reduced opportunity to persuade the intolerant to consider the merits of tolerance, to identify and understand hatred's origins, and to ultimately slow its growth. Indeed, many civil libertarians asserted that free expression was no less than an "essential" ingredient for a thriving "multicultural nation."[142] Modifying constitutional principle for politically instrumentalist purposes, in other words, may backfire.

Many conservative intellectuals shared the civil libertarian opposition to the critical theorists' narrow vision of the First Amendment. Charles Fried, conservative Harvard Law professor and Solicitor General under President

Ronald Reagan, proclaimed with dismay in 1992 that "the great liberal ideal of free expression is under attack."[143] In the same breath that Fried critically dissected the arguments of Catharine MacKinnon and other scholars on the First Amendment–narrowing left, the free-speech views of traditional moralistic conservative Robert Bork were tossed into the fire as well.[144] It was clear from Fried's brief reference to Bork that he believed the conservative stalwart to have succumbed to similar failings as the liberal Crits: specifically, "ignor[ing] the special route by which speech attains its effect."[145]

Nevertheless, despite the fact that an increasing number of scholars on the right shared the civil libertarian distaste for the critical theorists' approach, and even at times extended their critique to conservative scholars who in the recent past had been much more willing to see speech suppressed, the motivation for the conservative position was typically quite distinct. While ACLU-styled liberals contended that free speech will more often than not enhance equality, and that the Crits were simply mistaken that expressive freedom and equality are in tension, the conservative critique was more likely to respond with a curt "So what?" To political conservatives, not only is societal "inequality of results" at times completely justified, such inequality might indeed constitute a societal good—a way of separating the wheat from the chaff. Indeed, "acceptance of inequality" has been identified by moral psychology as one of the core elements of conservative ideology.[146]

Thus Fried was utterly unsympathetic, for example, to the openly acknowledged intent of Stanford University to impose an "asymmetrical" speech code on its campus that would mitigate the civil libertarian fear that such codes might be used against the very minorities they were intended to protect.[147] Invective used by those in the majority (or those deemed empowered) against those in the minority (or those deemed disempowered) would be sanctionable—for example, if a male, white, or heterosexual student castigated a female, black, or homosexual student. However, under the Stanford code, the reverse would not be true—minorities and the disempowered "can use all the words they have at their disposal."[148] Fried condemned the proffered notion that such asymmetry should be *accepted* under the same logic that *Plessy v. Ferguson*'s separate-but-equal doctrine was *rejected*. Fried implied that, to the contrary, it was a policy of symmetry that would be most consistent with the celebrated *Plessy* dissent and its emphasis on colorblindness.[149]

Although the design of the Stanford code would certainly raise concerns for the civil libertarian left, Fried did not express the kind of sensitivity toward equality that typically accompanied the liberal critique. Instead the concern was primarily one of governmental overreach, albeit in this case through a perceived abuse of power by an analogous "government-like" private university. Just like the libertarian conservatives of the late nineteenth century, and Justice Holmes in the early twentieth, Fried carried the principles of free-market conservatism into the realm of free expression, proclaiming "that adult persons should be free to come to whatever opinions of which they may be convinced."[150]

To conservatives like Fried, unsurprisingly, government regulation was quite simply a bad idea—from both a policy perspective and from the view of core constitutional principles. However, Fried went further, impugning not merely the intellectual justifications of speech codes, but what he saw as one of the underlying motives behind such regulatory regimes. By selectively targeting only certain disfavored ideas, "the proponents of these codes scorn the idea of content neutrality. The ban is an exercise of power. It shows who is boss. Thus the holders of noxious ideas are suppressed and the rest of the community is impressed and intimidated by this display of political might."[151]

4 The Courts and the
Political Correctness Indictment

R.A.V. v. St. Paul

Perhaps no case better encapsulates the Supreme Court's response to the spirit of the times explored in the previous chapter as the 1992 decision *R.A.V. v. St. Paul.*[1] The case was the Court's first major confrontation with anti–hate-speech legislation since *Beauharnais*, and as we have seen, much had changed in the intervening years. It was authored by the famously conservative Antonin Scalia yet seemed on its face to provide a dramatic victory for First Amendment values. The Court ultimately struck down the St. Paul Bias-Motivated Crime Ordinance, a law that made it a crime to "place on public or private property a symbol" such as a "burning cross or Nazi swastika" where the perpetrator "knows or has reasonable grounds to know" that it will cause "anger, alarm or resentment in others on the basis of race, color, creed, religion or gender."[2] However, the Court achieved its speech-protective result by offering up a Byzantine doctrinal test that left many scratching their head. Indeed, it would not be an exaggeration to claim that R.A.V. stands as one of the most notably complex and confounding First Amendment cases decided by the Court to date.

Concededly, the body of First Amendment law had grown remarkably extensive and multilayered in the years since the Court first began to seriously confront the issue of free speech—and since considering the Court's first hate-speech case, *Beauharnais v. Illinois.* The result has been a sometimes perplexing patchwork of doctrinal categories and concepts that have the potential to overlap and interact in various and unpredictable ways. And one might argue that the facts of *R.A.V.* presented just such a perfect storm: an instance in which the Court could not avoid the consequences of its creation, what some have derided as an unduly complex and incoherent body of First Amendment doctrine. One might posit that *R.A.V.* quite simply demanded that the Court confront this complexity head-on and come up with a new doctrinal synthesis that would adequately address the troubling intersection of concepts to which the case gave rise. However, a close analysis of both the decision itself, the alignment of the various justices, and the broader ideological and political context would suggest that this assessment is wrong.

Like *Beauharnais*, *R.A.V.* is an example of a case that might provide a profoundly deceptive impression if one were to simply look at its outcome alone. Although a political scientist focusing purely on judicial voting behavior might see a decision in which the liberal and conservative members of the Court were remarkably united—the justices unanimously concluded that the St. Paul ordinance was unconstitutional—a close reading of the various opinions reveals a stark contrast in judicial philosophy and in how the various justices would go about reaching this outcome.

But let's begin with the breakdown of opinions. The five justices who joined the majority opinion ranked as the most conservative justices according to their Martin-Quinn scores for the 1991 October term—Thomas, Scalia, Rehnquist, Kennedy, and Souter, respectively, in the order of their conservatism score.[3] It might be noted that Justice Souter, just appointed in 1991 by the Republican President George H. W. Bush, was himself something of an outlier. Souter would move rapidly away from his initial voting pattern when first appointed in 1990 as a relatively conservative justice—considerably to the right of the median justice in that year—to become among the most liberal justices on the Court by the time he retired in 2009.[4] Two "moderate" justices—White and O'Connor—closest numerically to the median justice score that term, along with the liberal Justice Blackmun, filed a concurring opinion that was sharply critical of the majority's reasoning. And Justice Stevens, the most liberal justice at the time, joined in part by White and Blackmun, wrote an additional concurrence, presenting a third theory as to why the law at issue should be declared unconstitutional.

Before getting into the substance of the opinions themselves, let's pull back for a moment and imagine how things might, hypothetically, have looked from the vantage point of a conservative justice. Envision a conservative member of the highest court in the land in 1992—one who reads *National Review* and other mainstream conservative publications on a regular basis and one who is aware and concerned on a personal level about what seems to be a genuine crisis in higher education and even in American society at large instigated by the pervasive and powerful fad of political correctness. But let's assume that this hypothetical justice still holds on to the vestiges of moralistic conservatism—à la Robert Bork—believing a narrow construction of the First Amendment is appropriate in many contexts. At the same time, however, assume that this jurist sees himself as a principled judge who takes seriously his obligation to interpret the law objectively and without recourse to political views. How might this array of attributes influence this justice's decision making? How might this justice reconcile these impulses? What kind of opinion might we predict would flow from this hypothetical justice?

The answer is an opinion that just might look quite a bit like the one handed down by the majority in *R.A.V.*—one that crafts an entirely new theory of First Amendment law yet attempts to be as true as possible to the Court's precedents. This judge would craft a precedent that allows for the striking down of troubling laws promoted by ideological adversaries yet provides future Courts with an "out" to avoid opening the floodgates of free-speech permissiveness where the justice might want them to remain shut. In other words, perhaps the *R.A.V.* opinion, while well intentioned, truly reflects Justice Blackmun's "fear that the Court has been distracted from its proper mission by the temptation to decide the issue over 'politically correct speech' and 'cultural diversity.'"[5]

The complexity of *R.A.V. v. St. Paul* may be attributed to the confluence of at least four potentially applicable doctrines developed over time by the Court to address First Amendment claims: overbreadth, the categorical "low-value" speech approach, content discrimination, and secondary effects. The petitioner who challenged the law relied on the overbreadth doctrine, arguing that the St. Paul ordinance reached beyond unprotected "fighting words" and had the effect of impermissibly prohibiting constitutionally protected speech.[6] In other words, although "fighting words"—words that "by their very utterance inflict injury or tend to incite an immediate breach of the peace"[7]—have been considered an unprotected low-value category of speech since the Court declared this to be so in the 1942 decision *Chaplinsky v. New Hampshire*, the Bias-Motivated Crime Ordinance was drafted in an overly broad fashion, covering more than mere "fighting words." The Minnesota Supreme Court, however, interpreted the ordinance narrowly such that it would not extend beyond *Chaplinsky's* definition of "fighting words."[8] The U.S. Supreme Court majority in *R.A.V.* both accepted the Minnesota court's "judicial gloss" on the ordinance's meaning and refused to narrow "the scope of the *Chaplinsky* formulation" as the petitioner requested.[9] Instead, the majority opted to strike down the ordinance on the novel theory that it was impermissible to make a content or viewpoint-based distinction even within a proscribable category of speech like "fighting words."[10] Scalia opined that the reason the Court long ago decided on a categorical approach to free speech was to allow certain narrow types of expression—such as obscenity and defamation—to be regulated *because* of their uniquely objectionable content, not so that these categories "may be made the vehicles for content discrimination unrelated to their distinctively proscribable content."[11]

It is difficult to avoid the conclusion that the five-justice majority, composed of the Court's most conservative justices, saw this St. Paul ordinance through the lens, not only of their political ideology but of the political outrage de jour—political correctness run amok. The message here is not difficult to decode. The implication was that St. Paul disingenuously used the "fighting words" doctrine as a "vehicle" for furthering its politically correct agenda, and this agenda was "unrelated" to the reasons "fighting words" have been considered an unprotected category of speech. Indeed, this interpretive conclusion was written into the very complex doctrine the majority crafted.

The majority was well aware that it would be untenable to simply prohibit all content-based distinctions within a proscribable category of speech. The Court understood that legislatures—as policymakers, problem-solvers, and consensus-seekers—would at times necessarily find themselves in the position of picking, choosing, and regulating particular expression on the basis of content: for example, "obscenity" that is deemed the most offensive, "threats" that are deemed the most injurious, or "fighting words" that are deemed to be the most provocative of violence. In other words, a simple rule prohibiting content-based distinctions within an unprotected category of speech across the board would not do. After all, why shouldn't a legislature have the discretion to ban only the most noxious obscenity, rather than being required to make an all-or-nothing decision? The majority realized the practical necessity of some content discrimination—and perhaps also the jurisprudential desirability from a conservative perspective of favoring local legislative discretion over judicial fiat. Thus, the majority felt compelled to carve out an exception to the exception to the exception to the First Amendment. It runs as follows: Otherwise proscribable speech (the categorical exception to the First Amendment) is not proscribable if it is restricted on the basis of its content (the exception to that categorical exception) *unless* "the basis for the content discrimination consists entirely of the very reason the entire class of speech at issue is proscribable"[12] (the exception to the exception to the exception).

Under this framework, there are at least two ways to understand what St. Paul was attempting to achieve with its Bias-Motivated Crime Ordinance. The first is the conservative majority's approach to framing the ordinance, as a way not of targeting the most "vicious or severe" invective but as a way of punishing speech concerning one of a number of discrete "disfavored topics"—specifically racial, religious, or gender-based hate speech.[13] Under this view, and consistent with the majority opinion's newly devised doctrinal test, the ordinance is constitutionally impermissible, because it makes a content-based distinction that is unrelated to the "very reason" the class of speech is proscribable—in this case because it provokes violence. However, there is an equally tenable interpretation that would result in the very opposite conclusion. Indeed, this is precisely what Justice Stevens argued in his concurrence.[14] Under this view, St. Paul was using its judgment to target precisely those types of "fighting words" that, in its judgment, were most likely to provoke violence. Considering the historically divisive nature of issues of race, religion, and gender, this would hardly appear to be a far-fetched interpretation. Indeed, as Stevens opined, "that harms caused by racial, religious, and gender-based invective are qualitatively different from that caused by other "fighting words"—seems to me eminently reasonable and realistic."[15]

If this new doctrinal test is so potentially problematic, why did the five members of the majority insist on taking this route? One, of course, cannot read the minds of these preeminent justices. Perhaps, quite simply, to the five justices it *seemed* clear that the ordinance, and the arguments defending it, were a transparent and cynical attempt to manipulate existing First Amendment doctrine to further a political agenda—and the majority was intent on calling out this behavior for what it was. Perhaps, in doing so, the majority did not want to throw the baby out with the bathwater, by, for example, simply doing away with the "fighting words" exception entirely—a category that some have criticized as anachronistic and increasingly irrelevant.[16] One might likewise surmise that the majority feared that accepting the overbreadth argument made by the petitioner would mean casting doubt on an authoritative interpretation of the ordinance by a proximately appropriate judicial body—the Minnesota Supreme Court—and it was not willing to do this. The precedent such an approach would set might conceivably make it more likely that a growing number of laws would be struck down on overbreadth grounds, even where such laws are construed narrowly. This is a result that might be understandably distasteful to "law and order" conservatives who look favorably on granting local legislatures broad discretion to address issues of social disorder.

Nevertheless, it is hard to imagine that the majority was unaware of the weakness endemic to its new doctrinal creation: the fact that determining whether or not a content-based law falls within its exception to the exception to the exception inherently involves policy judgment. Determinations that certain threats are more threatening than others, and therefore may be targeted based on their content, or that some obscenity is especially obscene and may thus be singled out, are inherently legislative in nature. Under the majority's complex test, courts are required to second-guess local legislatures. A Court may be put in the position of reasoning that "you, *legislature,* may profess to have banned obscene depictions of bestiality because your community believes it is the most repugnant form of obscenity, but we, *the Court,* interpret your choice as a mere reflection of your animal-rights agenda." Could one even distinguish between, for example, the conclusion that a local culture that happens to have an especially high degree of compassion for animals and, therefore, consistent with the First Amendment, finds bestiality to be the most loathsome form of obscenity, and the determination that that very same community's choice to punish only certain obscenity based on its animal-related content unconstitutionally imposes "special prohibitions on those speakers who express views on disfavored subjects"?[17]

However, from an instrumental perspective the benefits of the majority's approach are clear. The ideological wars over political correctness were, at the time, deeply felt, and this complex three-tier exception allowed the majority to strike back against a liberal "sensitivity" agenda that was increasingly seen as imposing a "tyranny of pity"[18] on conservatives. While I would not suggest that the conservatives on the majority in *R.A.V.* were consciously politicizing their judicial decision, their opinion was unquestionably laced with the politically conservative righteous indignation of the times. At every turn, the underlying message seemed to suggest that conservatives who did not conform to narrow liberal notions of sensitivity are the "new victims."

Scalia highlights such potential injustice by putting forth arguably far-fetched hypotheticals that ostensibly revealed how, under the St. Paul ordinance, those with a liberal viewpoint were attempting to socially engineer the marketplace of ideas—artificially disadvantaging some and advantaging others. He posits that under this law "'fighting words' that do not themselves invoke race, color, creed, religion, or gender—aspersions upon a person's mother, for example—would seemingly be usable *ad libitum* in the placards of those arguing *in favor* of racial, color, etc., tolerance and equality, but could not be used by those speakers' opponents."[19] And, indeed, perhaps this hypothetical captures how many conservatives felt at the time, as if they were being neutered by laws and speech codes that effectively disallowed them to fight back against deeply personal attacks; that when they spoke out against a liberal agenda supporting affirmative action and multiculturalism, they were labeled as hatemongers and castigated as second-tier citizens who were unworthy of sharing the First Amendment stage on equal terms. It is hard to see Scalia's provocative choice for his hypothetical of insults of one's mother as mere coincidence; this was, indeed, personal—and this time, it was the conservatives for whom "the personal was political."

At times, the majority opinion took on an almost ahistorical quality, presenting a striking contrast with the baseline assumptions undergirding the conservative perspective in *Beauharnais*. In that decision, the fact that the individual character of minorities—by exclusive virtue of their racial status—was frequently and unjustly under assault seemed beyond question; and the resulting distortion, the Court seemed to suggest, would detract attention from where it belonged: on individual merit.[20] However, the *R.A.V.* majority reversed this logic. To Scalia, St. Paul's rejection of "group hatred" itself reflected a "majority preference"—one that under the First Amendment "must be expressed in some fashion other than silencing speech on the basis of its own content."[21] The assessment of the ordinance in *R.A.V.*, in other words, did not appear to be situated in the same historical reality as the Court in *Beauharnais*: one that acknowledged the deep and abiding legacy of discrimination against minorities in the United States and the continuing quest for equality that has in many respects shaped the country's laws and character.

Yes, the *R.A.V.* Court conceded that ensuring "basic human rights" is "compelling," but it went on to characterize the St. Paul ordinance as emblematic of that "city's council's *special* hostility" toward certain "particular biases."[22] It was as if the ordinance that would penalize cross burnings reflected just one quirky point of view among many, merely a "disfavored topic" and "viewpoint"[23] no different from any other. Scalia charged that the "politicians of St. Paul are entitled to express that hostility [to particular biases]—but not through the means of imposing unique limitations upon speakers who (however benightedly) disagree."[24] Of course, expressions of racial, religious, or gender-based animus are not the equal of other expressive biases. Indeed, many respected scholars have argued that they are *sui generis*.[25] Even for those who believe that any purported qualitative difference still does not generally justify differential First Amendment treatment, under the Court's doctrinal rubric, the unique content-based character of particular types of expressive insults *does matter*— here where it would be especially likely to provoke a fight.

The *R.A.V.* majority could have avoided this confusion, and ultimately come to a much more speech-protective conclusion, had it simply decided to do away with the "fighting words" exception to the First Amendment entirely. At minimum, it could have narrowed the scope of the "fighting words" doctrine, as had been suggested by the petitioner.[26] Considering the fact that the Court had not upheld a "fighting words" conviction since the doctrine was first articulated in 1942,[27] it would not have been surprising had the Court moved in this direction.[28]

However, *R.A.V.* is illustrative of the peculiar results the intersection of politics and jurisprudence can garner. Few would see equivalence between the kinds of policies that were frequently the target of anti–political correctness conservatives, such as broadly drawn speech codes that apply to a vast array of intentional and unintentional verbal insensitivities, and a law punishing the burning of a cross, like the one in St. Paul. And the *R.A.V.* Court does not directly draw this analogy. Yet, the comparison seems to lie just under the surface. It was as if in the Court's mind it was fighting the war against political correctness—but awkwardly found itself at the wrong battle. The unfortunate result, as Justice White sees it, is that "by characterizing fighting words as a form of 'debate,' the majority legitimates hate speech as a form of public discussion."[29]

As we shall see, as the times changed and the wounds from the perceived conservative victimization grew less raw, the sensitivities of the conservative justices would also change; just over a decade after *R.A.V.* some of the very same justices who joined the majority opinion would strike a very different chord in response to a very similar law in Virginia. Surely, significant shifts in ideological identity do not occur overnight. Like most social and political movement, change occurs in fits and starts.

The Conservative Political Perspective in the *R.A.V.* Era

At the same time that this shift was occurring on the Court, the perception by conservatives that they were the true advocates of free speech continued to gain currency in *National Review*. Yet, even as the speech-protective libertarian conservatism was becoming increasingly prominent, the narrower view of the First Amendment traditionally advocated by moralistic conservatives lived on. In 1992, for example, *National Review* published remarks made by Academy Award–winning actor and conservative activist Charlton Heston, at a Time Warner shareholders meeting. With the Los Angeles riots fresh in Americans' minds, Heston issued a scathing indictment of a media conglomerate's decision to continue to market the controversial Ice-T rap album *Body Count.*[30] Heston was particularly critical of the company's repeated reliance upon "the artist's creative freedom" and "the First Amendment"[31] when justifying its decision not to pull the album from circulation.

A private company, of course, is not subject to the strictures of the First Amendment absent some "state action."[32] However, as we saw earlier it is not uncommon for the boundaries of legal principles to be blurred when the discussion occurs in the political, not legal, realm. In the political world, legal principles, such as those represented by the First Amendment, readily morph into broad philosophical ideals divorced from their legal application. While it may have been doubtful that there was truly a *legal* First Amendment issue at stake, there was certainly a political and ideological one. And Heston made clear on which side of that debate he fell. He emphasized "that the right to free speech is not without limits, both public and private."[33] To Heston, there was no doubt that such limits applied here: "Supreme Court Justice Holmes said it: Free speech does not include the right to yell "Fire!" in a crowded theater. The lyrics of "Cop Killer" go a lot further than that. They celebrate the murder of police officers."[34] To any legal scholar familiar with the Court's "clear and present danger" or "true threats" doctrines, it would be abundantly clear that Heston was mistaken— restrictions that may be permissible where speech creates an imminent danger or true threat are not permitted where illegal behavior is merely "celebrated."[35]

Nevertheless, Heston's message regarding the First Amendment, flawed as it may have been, was that free speech should be construed narrowly. Where free speech is pitted against immorality and risk of harm, First Amendment values should defer. After recounting in great detail some of the highly offensive lyrics at issue, Heston scolds the company's CEO for defending material not "out of principle, but out of greed. Mr. Levin, I ask you to stop selling *Body Count.* Donate the money you have made from it to the families of murdered police officers. In the name of decency, sir."[36]

This moralistic conservative vision raises traditional concerns about not merely preventing harm, but doing so where this harm is inflicted on a figure of authority. Although, as a moral principle, compassion is more readily associated with political liberalism, as psychologist Jonathan Haidt explains, it is particularly resonant for moralistic conservatives in particular settings: "[C]onservative caring . . . is aimed not at animals or at people in other countries but at those who've sacrificed for the group. It is not universalist; it is more local, and blended with loyalty."[37] Thus, Heston's perspective fits well within the conservative tradition. At the same time, however, Heston's brand of moralistic conservatism would seem to reject a conservative free-market vision, in which the "greed" of a corporate executive might be understood as a social "good." Here the free-market economy fulfills the demand for a morally questionable product—something Heston does not countenance. As we shall see in the following two chapters, this is the same clash of conservatisms—free-market conservatism versus moralistic conservatism—that has played out on the Court in the commercial speech arena.

It is also striking that less than one year after *National Review* published Heston's commentary arguing *for* a narrow First Amendment construction in the name of morality, it published a piece arguing *against* a narrow First Amendment construction in the name of morality. This article entitled "PC in LA," so close in time to the Heston piece, was a paean to First Amendment freedom—issuing a dire warning about the threat to expressive freedom posed by liberal colleges and universities. It would seem that where the morality at issue was "politically correct" concern over "sexual harassment" propagated by "campus feminists," instead of the opposition to repellent lyrics in rap music celebrating the assassination of police officers, the First Amendment balance should result in a very different outcome.[38] Ironically, one of the examples the article's author Linda Seebach provides to evince "that academic freedom is in great danger" involves a lawsuit "against California State University in Northridge, where a chapter of Zeta Beta Tau was suspended for 14 months for distributing a party flier that mentioned a racially and sexually offensive song."[39] It is clearly difficult to reconcile Seebach's perspective with Heston's. However, the point here is not to impugn *National Review* for inconsistency. *National Review* serves as an outlet for a range of conservative perspectives; there is no reason to expect just one monolithic conservative voice.

Nevertheless, what this inconsistency does reveal is a struggle within conservatism to come to terms with how the moral principles it holds dear are to be reconciled with the First Amendment. Was the First Amendment to be a mere political instrument—one that might be cavalierly minimized where moral issues close to conservatives' hearts are threatened but maximized where the purported moral threats relate only to issues of concern to their political adversaries? If this was true in the political sphere, was it also true in the legal sphere, where the principle of *stare decisis* theoretically demands consistency? Over the years, on the pages of *National Review* conservatives had repeatedly made similar accusations against political liberals, arguing that their thinking on the First Amendment is riddled with hypocrisy. In the midst of conservatism's own internal struggle between moralism and libertarianism in the early 1990s, conservatives continued to emphasize First Amendment incongruity on the left. In addition to speech codes on college campuses and other restrictions ostensibly rooted in liberal political correctness, conservatives drew attention to increasingly assertive arguments for suppressing pornography made by feminists on the left such as Catharine MacKinnon and Andrea Dworkin.[40]

The politically skillful rhetorical balancing act required to both condemn anti-pornography feminism while simultaneously defending anti-pornography moralistic conservatism was on full display in Roger Scruton's scathing 1993 review of MacKinnon's polemic, *Only Words*.[41] Scruton's ultimate point is not that conservatism is consistent on the First Amendment while liberalism is not, but rather that both camps are inconsistent; however, only the liberal inconsistency is flawed. Scruton laments,

> [T]oday the United States is perhaps the only country in the civilized world where quite reasonable opinions about matters of the greatest importance— such as race and sexuality—cannot be expressed without risk of legal or disciplinary action. And it is one of the few countries where access to pornography of a kind that beggars all description, save that bestowed on it by Miss MacKinnon is regarded as a constitutional right.[42]

Scruton attributed the ubiquity of pornography in America to "liberal" judicial "activism" with regard to the First Amendment. At the same time, judicial forces victimize conservatives and subvert the First Amendment, by characterizing their opinions as not speech but as "discrimination."[43] Scruton readily admitted that he agreed with MacKinnon that pornography should be unprotected by the First Amendment. However, Scruton implied that MacKinnon's desire to suppress pornography was rooted not in legitimate concern over "the abolition of shame, modesty, hesitation, and innocence" but instead in "misandry."[44] According to Scruton, MacKinnon and other feminists conveyed a "hatred of men that knows no bounds."[45] And this hatred was being played out on college campuses across the country, where speech codes carried out this feminist worldview. Thus, to Scruton and other like-minded conservatives, it was completely appropriate to conclude that the First Amendment must be selective as to what expression is or is not to be protected. However, in making the distinction between protected and unprotected speech, it is conservative common sense and morality that should prevail.

Scruton thus ultimately suggests that "we are all political instrumentalists when it comes to the First Amendment." Those on the right have their chosen moralistic justifications for reduced expressive rights, just as have those on the left. Perhaps this is a more honest approach. After all, it is arguably quite disingenuous for ideologues on either side of the political spectrum to emphatically point left or right crying "hypocrisy," when they themselves share a highly selective approach to First Amendment interpretation. In attempting to better understand the relationship between conservatism and the First Amendment, it would seem that the issue of whether one political "side" is more or less hypocritical than the other is of dubious consequence. As mentioned earlier, both ideological sides have an incentive to make this charge against the other. Many such allegations are likely much more about rhetorically bludgeoning one's political opponent than they are about making a substantive argument supporting one's own position on First Amendment interpretation. A more important question to ask is whether the freedom of speech enshrined in the First Amendment was *itself* becoming a prominent conservative value.

In the 1990s there was no question that political and judicial voices on the right were increasingly advocating a bold and protective First Amendment stance. On the other hand, moralistic conservative voices, such as Heston and Scruton, continued to sing the praises of First Amendment minimalism. Commentators, such as *National Review* editor John O'Sullivan, persisted in gleefully mocking the view, for example, that nude dancing should be considered a form of speech protected by the First Amendment.[46] O'Sullivan impugned the political motives of liberal free-speech advocacy by claiming that "Democrats and the Left have wrapped themselves in the First Amendment whenever something like pornography or flag-burning was at issue."[47]

Throughout the decade, the magazine continued to take swipes at one of its most prominent liberal adversaries, the ACLU, for its excessive, common sense–defying allegiance to free speech. In 1995 Maggie Gallagher painted this derisive caricature of the view of the then-president of the ACLU: "In Nadine Strossen's America any attempt to exercise taste, prudence, or (ACLU forbid!)

moral judgment in sexual matters is frightening evidence of the omnipresent sex 'repression' that First Amendment fighters like her are only just holding at bay."[48] At the same time, Gallagher threw a bone to the growing contingent of anti–political correctness conservatives who are more apt to embrace First Amendment maximalism in the liberal enclave of the academy. She conceded: "Strossen makes some just and penetrating observations about the absurdity of the current sexual-harassment and date-rape panic, especially on college campuses."[49] Nevertheless, it would seem that to Ms. Gallagher, the ACLU's idealized view of principled First Amendment application was one that defied the common sense, morally attainable objectives that might be achieved through reasonable speech regulation: "The goal in regulating pornography ought to be . . . modest: to find ways to prevent private vice from becoming the prevailing public standard of virtue."[50]

The internal ambivalence about how conservatives should approach arguments regarding First Amendment limitations on government was reaching something of a tipping point. Even opinion pieces that argued for the traditionally conservative narrow First Amendment position seemed unable to resist the temptation to make concessions to the more speech-protective counterpoint. A 1999 editorial entitled "That's Entertainment" began with the unequivocal assertion that the Constitution's framers intentionally chose to protect "speech" not "expression."[51] It is the spurious belief that these two concepts are one and the same that has empowered those in "the entertainment industry," among others, to argue that nude dancing, flag burning, and "works of art" are protected by the First Amendment.[52] The editorial lamented the tendency of First Amendment advocates to make dubious slippery slope arguments: "If pressed, they use the Bard as a human shield: Restrict *Natural Born Killers*, and Shakespeare will be next."[53]

Yet, the editorial goes on to criticize both Democratic President Bill Clinton and "some Republicans" for their efforts to address violence marketed to children—for example, the suggestion that moviemakers be held "liable if their products encourage disturbed minds to commit crime."[54] Legislation in this area is "inappropriate" argued *National Review.* "The worst defects of our popular entertainments—just for starters, their coarseness, nihilism, and stupidity—are amenable neither to measurement by social science nor correction by law."[55] Although in this case the magazine did not rely on a full-throated First Amendment position to argue for a hands-off government, the plea of the editorial was clear: Conservative factions should unify in favor of a libertarian vision. In an attempt to soothe moralistic conservatives, the editorial argued that the "objection to federal action here is not only a libertarian one. Traditionalists, too, should be suspicious of edicts from the central government."[56] This was also about federalism, the editorial claimed, and moralistic (that is, "traditional") conservatives have a stake in ensuring that localities and states, not the federal government, remain the primary arbiters of morality.

In the new millennium, the political benefits of overtly embracing the First Amendment, or critically pointing to a liberal willingness to bypass free speech, were readily apparent. The sense that, as a conservative, staking out such a position might be embarking on dangerous political territory was looking more and more like a distant memory. Take, for example, a piece written by a young Matthew Continetti in 2002.[57] Continetti, then a senior at Columbia University who would become a respected and influential conservative commentator, published a blistering essay on Lee Bollinger, then the president of his university. Continetti's piece suggested that this liberal university president had committed a litany of offenses against conscientious conservatism, one of which implicated the First Amendment.[58] This charge, however, was quite unlike the types of critiques that had been laid on colleges' doorsteps during the 1960s, discussed in the previous chapter, when universities were perceived by conservatives as unduly permissive bastions of hedonism. Continetti's ire was instead focused on the bogeyman of oppressive political correctness.

Bollinger's offense was failing to speak out against a speech code at the University of Michigan, where he had been the dean of the law school. And, according to Continetti, not only had Bollinger failed to act against the speech code that was ultimately determined to be unconstitutional by a federal court, but he disingenuously claimed to have been opposed to the code from the beginning, when in fact he had expressed a clear willingness to balance away free speech where "civility and discourse" were at stake.[59] Making matters worse, Continetti explained, Bollinger was a First Amendment scholar. For our purposes, it is notable that Continetti introduced this bit of biographical information by describing how, as "the author of several books on free speech [Bollinger] argued before the Senate" against Robert Bork's nomination to the Supreme Court.[60] He had criticized the candidate by asserting that Bork's "interpretation of the First Amendment could lead to an eventual rollback of legal precedent."[61]

One way to understand Continetti's critique of Bollinger is that it is just one more instance of the right charging the left with hypocrisy. As we have seen, this recurring theme goes something like this: The left only adheres to its free-speech values when it is politically expedient; as well as casting doubts on liberal politics and argumentation generally, this shows us that the entire "liberal" contention that First Amendment values are imperative and untouchable is dubious. This, however, was not the argument Continetti was making. Instead, Continetti seemed to be drawing a clear contrast between the policies promoted by someone like Bollinger—who had "a history of associating the good of his students with whatever leftish cause is currently garnering national attention," such as sacrificing the First Amendment at the altar of racial offense avoidance—and conservatives, who worry that "college students face a future bereft of important principles like freedom of speech."[62]

Any ambivalence or equivocation about the claim that conservatives were the *true* guardians of the First Amendment had slipped away. Any discussion of how this new vision of conservatism, as the guarantor "of important principles like freedom of speech," fit with or *did not fit with* the views of a conservative icon like Robert Bork was notably absent. Continetti did not argue that Bollinger's critique of Bork's First Amendment position was wrong, right, or simply no longer applicable. The silence was deafening. The suggestion seemed to be that conservatism had left the likes of Robert Bork behind—in favor of conservative libertarianism.

A Campus Speech Code Reaches the Judiciary: *Doe v. University of Michigan*

The more-than-a-decade-old Michigan case to which Continetti referred, while merely a federal district court decision, proved highly significant for all First Amendment stakeholders. While the facts of the Supreme Court's *R.A.V.* opinion did not unfold on a college campus, we might say that *Doe v. University of Michigan*[63] set the stage for *R.A.V.*, helping frame a local ordinance that in other times might have appeared to be an uncontroversial attempt to combat dangerous racism as an example of liberal political correctness run amok.

The 1989 decision, penned by U.S. District Judge Avern Cohn, a 1979 appointee of Democratic president Jimmy Carter, was the first to apply First Amendment free-speech principles to a hate-speech regulation at a university.[64] And the outcome was perhaps aided by the fact that, unlike *R.A.V.*, *Doe* did not invoke cross burnings or other unambiguously noxious racist expression. Rather, at the center of *Doe* was a plaintiff who, as a graduate student in psychology, specialized in an academic field that included theories believed by some to have sexist or racist overtones.[65] No doubt, biopsychology, which purports to examine the biological bases for individual difference in mental abilities and personality, sparked sharp controversy, implicitly recalling the troubling legacy of eugenics. Within the field, certain theories correlate innate attributes of intellect and personality with one's race or gender. Although the plaintiff had not been directly sanctioned under the university's speech code, he argued that under the codified terms of Michigan's speech policy, merely discussing the controversial theories he was studying might result in punitive consequences.[66] As a result, he asserted, his freedom to openly discuss certain ideas had been impermissibly chilled.[67]

The decision striking down the Michigan speech code as unconstitutional shined a bright light—not just on the benefits a robust First Amendment might have for conservatives trapped in the liberal universe of higher education but on the increasingly evident First Amendment fissures within contemporary political liberalism. Representing the aggrieved University of Michigan student who went by the pseudonym John Doe was that symbolic figurehead of American liberalism, the ACLU. Here, however, victory for the ACLU represented defeat for liberal college administrators who increasingly saw, and acted upon, a perceived need to restrict racist and sexist expression on campus in order to protect victimized students.[68] The decision was striking on a number of levels, one of which was the way it exposed the shift in thinking on the First Amendment among those in the liberal establishment. As with the subtle movement away from the Warren Court–era *Brandenburg* decision—in which the liberals on the Court were once unequivocal and united on free expression even in the face of viciously bigoted words, but gradually softened their commitment in future decades—Judge Cohn draws attention to the university's shift away from its own speech-protective "Statement on Freedom of Speech and Artistic Expression."[69] There, the university's formal policy stated in no uncertain terms that believing "some opinion [to be] pernicious, false, or in any other way detestable cannot be grounds for its suppression."[70]

Yet, just eleven years after this statement was formalized in 1977, those who drafted the University's speech code could not have adopted a more strikingly different posture, firmly conveying that "speech need only be offensive to be sanctionable."[71] Indeed, feelings in favor of the speech code apparently ran so strong that the university attorney who researched the law and helped draft the policy advocated outright defiance of existing First Amendment doctrine. He suggested prior to its enactment that the code should move forward *despite* the likelihood that much of the speech it would be sanctioning was constitutionally protected.[72] In a memorandum, he advised that the university look beyond constitutional concerns and not "be frustrated by the reluctance of the courts and common law to recognize the personal damage that is caused by discriminatory speech, nor should our policy attempt to conform to traditional methods of identifying harmful speech."[73]

The result was a policy that was, at least as drafted, broad indeed. It called for disciplining students who engaged in

[a]ny behavior, verbal or physical, that stigmatizes or victimizes an individual on the basis of race, ethnicity, religion, sex, sexual orientation . . . [and h]as the purpose or reasonably foreseeable effect of interfering with an individual's academic efforts . . . or [c]reates an intimidating, hostile or demeaning environment for educational pursuits.[74]

According to an interpretive guide to the policy, issued shortly after the policy was promulgated, a hypothetical male student who makes a remark in class such as "Women just aren't as good in this field as men" would be subject to university sanctions.[75] While many would rightfully be offended by such an assertion, a student like Doe may wish to discuss theories of biological difference but be inclined to censor his own speech for fear of facing punitive sanction.

We might consider that just a few years after the *Doe* decision the incendiary book *The Bell Curve*, by conservative political scientist Charles Murray and psychologist Richard Herrnstein, caused a political firestorm. It argued in one chapter, most controversially, that some races are inherently intellectually inferior to others.[76] The book received an enormous amount of media coverage, including front-cover stories in *Newsweek* and the *New York Times Magazine* and segments on public affairs programs such as *Nightline,* the *MacNeil/Lehrer NewsHour,* the *McLaughlin Group,* and *Charlie Rose.*[77]

Many conservatives embraced the thesis and interpreted the controversy surrounding the book's release as illustrative of misguided liberal thinking. In a 1994 *National Review* opinion piece, Ernest Van den Haag opined that the data in the book demonstrated empirically what many conservatives have long emphasized: "[M]eritocracy is becoming reality."[78] In other words, the controversy over *The Bell Curve* was perhaps less a product of the arguably tangential portions of the book dealing with race and more about what it had to say about the liberal egalitarian orthodoxy. Van den Haag explains: "Liberals believed that, once opportunity was equal outcomes would become equal too: They thought unequal outcomes were due largely to unequal opportunities. However,

Herrnstein and Murray show conclusively that inequalities won't disappear."[79] *The Bell Curve* and the notion that there may be inheritable differences in IQ speaks to the conservative respect for hierarchy and authority and a distaste for the liberal desire to use government to produce equality of outcome.

It is thus instructive that the *Doe* case, decided a mere five years before *The Bell Curve* controversy roiled the nation, addressed the rights of a student who studied similar theories of biological difference and feared punitive sanctions if he were to voice the central tenets of these theories. The tension that broke out on the University of Michigan campus over a hate-speech code was not about the right of cross-burners or skinheads to assertively voice their bigoted messages; it was about conservative students feeling victimized by a liberal orthodoxy that sought to shut down conservative ideas by branding them with the "hate speech" label. The sage advice of liberal hero Oliver Wendell Holmes, that "we should be eternally vigilant against attempts to check the expression of opinions that we loathe,"[80] resonated with the right. The words of the liberal "people's attorney" Louis Brandeis in his famous *Whitney* concurrence were also remarkably apropos. Brandeis proclaimed that the framers, "[b]elieving in the power of reason as applied through public discussion, eschewed silence coerced by law."[81] In response to a campus power structure asserting that even the mere acknowledgement of ideas that demean or degrade a student's capabilities on the basis of her race or sex impose an unacceptable stigma, a conservative might respond by citing Brandeis's doctrinal First Amendment tenet: "If there be time to expose through discussion the falsehood and fallacies, to avert the evil by the process of education, the remedy to be applied is more speech, not enforced silence. Only an emergency can justify repression."[82]

Interestingly, Judge Cohn opted to reach back much further than the wisdom of Holmes and Brandeis to support his holding that the university's speech code was an unconstitutional abridgement of speech and expression. In 1868, it was the conservative Thomas Cooley's enduring treatise on constitutional law that forcefully advocated a robust reading of the First Amendment—arguing that, on balance, the costs involved in government attempts to quash discussion of even the most "immoderate" ideas are simply too high to justify potential benefits that are too low.[83] In other words, Judge Cohn, a Democratic appointee, looked to one of the most prominent intellectual proponents of libertarian conservatism of the late nineteenth century to justify what just a couple of decades earlier would have been perceived as an unequivocally liberal

holding; but, as applied, it benefited conservatives who increasingly felt oppressed by liberal dogma on university campuses across the country.

Conservative Ambivalence on the High Court:
Virginia v. Black

Although libertarian conservatism had clearly reemerged as an energized voice
in modern conservatism, one that was increasingly willing to zealously take
up the First Amendment cause, this robust free-speech view had still not arrived at a point of consensus among political conservatives—the way, perhaps,
we might say that mainstream liberalism during the Warren Court era had
reached widespread agreement about First Amendment issues. On the Supreme
Court, this lack of consensus was strikingly on display in 2003, with the case of
Virginia v. Black—a decision that might be viewed as a sequel to its seminal
hate-speech decision, *R.A.V. v. St. Paul*. While a majority of the Court in *Black*
would insist that its decision was consistent with *R.A.V.*, many others, both on
and off the Court, would strongly disagree.[84] Indeed, the Supreme Court of
Virginia, which had heard the case before it arrived at the U.S. Supreme Court's
doorstep, had determined that the Virginia cross-burning statute was unconstitutional under the rationale of *R.A.V.*[85] Cross burning is a form of symbolic
expression, the Virginia court had reasoned, and a law targeting this particular expressive act "discriminates on the basis of content and viewpoint."[86] This
seemed like a straightforward application of *R.A.V.* Although the Virginia
law sought to prohibit cross burnings under what looked like a different rationale—that the message constitutes a "true threat" rather than a form of
"fighting words"—Virginia, like St. Paul, was cherry-picking particular expression on the basis of its content, something *R.A.V.* purportedly forbade. There
was no reason to believe that the category of low-value speech from which a
governmental body makes a content-based distinction—"true threats" versus
"fighting words"—should make a difference in the constitutional calculus. Yet
somehow it did—or *something* did. For although a plurality in *Black* ultimately
struck down the statute on narrow overbreadth grounds, the opinion stated in
unequivocal terms that a law making it a felony to burn a cross with the intent
to intimidate may be constitutional.[87]

Thus, it appeared that just eleven years after the Court's contentious, complex, but seemingly definitive statement on anti–hate-speech laws and the constitutional infirmities of political correctness, the Court was taking a second
look, and once again nudging open the *Beauharnais*-door that it had seemed

to so firmly shut after *R.A.V.* One scholar characterized *Black* as nothing short of "a fundamental doctrinal shift with respect to cross burning."[88] It was all the more stunning in that a largely stable bench marked the period between the two cases; only two justices—Blackmun and White—were replaced over this time. If seven of the nine justices on the Court at the time of *Virginia v. Black* had been on the Court when *R.A.V.* was decided, what might explain this sharp doctrinal turn? More importantly, was this a left-hand turn or a turn to the right?

The alignment in *Virginia v. Black*, quite unlike *R.A.V.*, was all over the ideological map. The plurality opinion that would have upheld the Virginia law but for a provision specifying that cross burning "shall be prima facie evidence of an intent to intimidate"[89] was drafted by the moderately conservative Justice O'Connor (with a .230 Martin-Quinn score) but joined by the conservative Chief Justice Rehnquist (1.226), the liberal Justice Breyer (−1.341), as well as the most liberal member of the Court at the time, Justice Stevens (scoring a −2.455).[90] Justice Scalia, who ranked as the second-most conservative justice on the Court that term (3.184),[91] largely agreed with the plurality, except that he would not have struck down the statute based on the prima facie evidence provision.[92] Justice Thomas, the most conservative justice (4.048),[93] would have upheld the Virginia statute on the grounds that it "prohibits only conduct, not expression."[94] Only three justices in *Black* signed on to the speech-protective position that would not only have struck down the law, as the plurality did, but would have done so on the grounds that the law made an impermissible content-based distinction that, like *R.A.V.*, was not subject to an exception. This trio of justices included the liberal justices Souter (−1.517) and Ginsburg (−1.694) and the moderately conservative Kennedy (.868).[95]

What should one make of the fact that the ideological alignments that were so visible in First Amendment cases like *Beauharnais*, *Keyishian*, and *R.A.V.* seem to have completely broken down in *Black*? Might this suggest that the justices were quite simply doing their jobs, looking beyond politics and ideology and deciding on the basis of legal principle? Or, on the contrary, does this represent a victory for politicization? Perhaps, as one scholar opined, *Black* represented a "triumph of the crits."[96] As discussed, critical race theorists had for years been arguing for a more flexible free-speech doctrine, one that would account for historical context while paying greater heed to structural inequalities.[97] Is it possible that members of the Court were swayed, not by a convincing jurisprudential distinction between the facts of *R.A.V.* and *Black*, but by the ongoing exogenous influence of scholars and political thinkers who emphasized equality over expressive freedom? Or, perhaps this case is just an outlier—a decision that is not emblematic of any larger doctrinal or ideological trend. After all, cases, just like the justices themselves, are idiosyncratic creatures prone to unpredictability. No one theory has been able to fully explain judicial decision making, just as no one theory has succeeded in capturing all of the complexity involved in human decision making generally. The contours of this decision are worthy of exploration.

The difference in tone and content in the analysis of *Black* and *R.A.V.* could not be more striking. In *Black,* history is placed in the foreground. The *Black* plurality took pains to recount in great detail the historical origins of cross burnings in the United States, as well as this expressive act's inextricable relationship with the Ku Klux Klan's reign of terror.[98] Justice Thomas, in his impassioned and highly personal dissent, painted an even more vivid description of the disturbing historical associations of cross burning.[99] Indeed, Thomas, as an African American who grew up impoverished in the segregated rural South, was not shy about alluding to his own intimate understanding of the reality of racialized terrorism in the United States. Thomas began his dissent by observing that "[i]n every culture, certain things acquire meaning well beyond what outsiders can comprehend";[100] cross burning is one such example. For Thomas, this meaning is so deeply embedded that the act of burning a cross should be understood purely as "a tool for the intimidation and harassment of racial minorities."[101] The historical association of this act with terrorism convinced Thomas that this Virginia law did not restrict expression at all, and because it only prohibited conduct there was "no need to analyze it under any of our First Amendment tests."[102]

Yet, just eleven years earlier in *R.A.V. v. St. Paul,* historical explication of cross burnings was completely lacking, as was any in-depth discussion of the harm imposed.[103] Justice Thomas joined the *R.A.V.* majority striking down the anti–cross-burning ordinance, but opted not to write separately. Concededly, the Court in *R.A.V.* analyzed the law under a different categorical rubric, and one might argue that the historical associations of cross burnings with "fighting words" are less compelling than those with "true threats." Yet, certainly the same historical quality that makes "burning a cross a particularly virulent form of intimidation,"[104] as the *Black* plurality concluded, could make it as well "a particularly virulent form of physical provocation."

Meaning, however, is not derived in a vacuum. The Court's choice to focus on the history of cross burnings in *Black* was just that—a choice. Contextual factors must be considered to assess whether a particular content-based distinction falls within *R.A.V.*'s three-tiered exception—that is, whether the reason for the distinction within the category of speech directly relates to the "very reason" the class of speech is proscribable in the first place. The *R.A.V.* Court's choice *not* to focus on history as a contextual variable was also a choice to see the St. Paul ordinance primarily through the lens of the contemporaneous political debate over political correctness.

The Court saw a different law in 1992 than they saw in 2003. Although, in retrospect, these two laws might look quite similar, when a Court decides a case, it does so within the sociopolitical context of the times. In 1992 the ordinance was the faddish product of liberal academic dogma. In 2003 the law addressed an indisputable history of race-based terrorism. The Court's decision to focus on sharply different contextual factors in *Black* than it had in *R.A.V.* might have been abetted by the fact that the former arose in Virginia, a jurisdiction firmly associated with a history of Jim Crow segregation and government-sanctioned racism, while the latter was an ordinance passed in a liberal northern city without such a history. The respective decisions were each situated in their own political time and geographic space, and as a consequence of these very different contexts the Virginia law was perceived to have a legitimate motive, whereas the Minnesota ordinance was not.

The difference might also be attributable to, as Guy-Uriel Charles has argued, the "epistemic authority" of Justice Thomas.[105] Quite simply, Justice Thomas was uniquely positioned to speak on this subject from a position of experiential authority. In a manner that was dramatically uncharacteristic for a justice who goes many years without speaking during oral arguments, Thomas made his voice heard. He asked incisive questions during oral arguments and lent his own deeply personal experience to his dissenting opinion. And all of this came from one who was known to be fiercely critical of the liberal politically correct agenda—giving Thomas all the more credibility. "When Justice Thomas maintains that the cross is unlike any other symbol in our society, he cannot be dismissed simply as a purveyor of political correctness, as were the critical race theorists and St. Paul in *R.A.V.*"[106] This confluence of factors safely removed the Virginia law from the taint of politically correct politics—a taint that could not be scrubbed away from the St. Paul ordinance.

It may seem that liberal proponents of anti–hate-speech legislation won the day with *Virginia v. Black*. And some liberal scholars in the legal realist or critical legal studies camps have argued that this was a victory of their own doing—

that their ideas have migrated beyond the legal academy and penetrated the Supreme Court. Alexander Tsesis asserts that these "efforts over the years have influenced academics and practitioners."[107] To Tsesis, *Virginia v. Black* is a prime example; it "shifted the jurisprudence on hate speech away from the virtually absolute rejection of cross burning legislation in *R.A.V. v. St. Paul* to a more critical perspective, which [critical legal scholars] Delgado and Stefancic advocate."[108] However, there is significant reason to question the assessment of *Black*, advanced by critical legal scholars, that portrays it as a broad reevaluation (or reconsideration) of the Supreme Court's approach to hate speech. Political liberals are still quite divided over this issue, and many prominent civil libertarian voices, such as former ACLU president Nadine Strossen, maintain strong opposition to hate-speech regulations on First Amendment grounds.[109] These are voices the critical legal scholars refer to as the "moderate left."[110] And viewed narrowly, *Black* simply addressed a category of speech, that, while perhaps under-theorized, has long been believed to be unprotected by the First Amendment: so-called true threats.[111]

Furthermore, if we read the opinions in *Black* closely, and in the context of jurisprudential ideological history, we notice less a dominance of ideals emanating from critical legal theorists and more the pervasive conservative ideological impulses that have long been resistant to robust speech protection. Some of the same conservative rationales utilized in *Beauharnais*—moral foundations that celebrate order through authority and respect—did not simply vanish into the ether and were once again prominent in *Black*. Once freed from the prominent countervailing pressure to reject supposed liberal dogma, many of the Court's conservatives revert to a conservative view that applauds authoritarian governmental power—specifically, where a state needs a robust police power to manage social disorder. Thus, Thomas emphasized that a burning cross is not merely "a signal of impending terror" but of "lawlessness" as well.[112] He told us that burning a cross has been considered an "un-American act"[113] and cited former FBI agent and Virginia governor Mills E. Godwin, Jr., who asserted that "law and order in the State were impossible if organized groups could *create fear by intimidation*."[114] Justice Scalia expressed concern for the traditionally conservative value of judicial modesty, criticizing the plurality for potentially "ced[ing] an enormous measure of power over state law to trial judges."[115]

Nonetheless, a casual reader of *Virginia v. Black*—without recognizing what the Court did *not* do—might risk being swept away by what the Court *appeared* to do through its powerful rhetoric, language that seemed to narrow, if not discredit, its hard line against hate-speech legislation in *R.A.V.* The truth is, the plurality's dubious determination that the Virginia law would satisfy *R.A.V.*'s three-tier exception is mere dicta. Having struck down the law on the basis of the prima facie evidence provision, there was quite simply no reason for the Court to engage in the *R.A.V.* analysis. The Court thus escaped the responsibility of making the very difficult determination of when a "true threat" becomes *truly threatening* for First Amendment purposes. Clearly *any* "intent to intimidate" will not suffice. Words are frequently intimidating, whether they occur on the stage of a presidential debate, in a corporate boardroom, or during a heated philosophical discussion in a college seminar. Sharp words can be intended to cause profound discomfort in a listener—and often have this effect. They may even result in feelings of physical discomfort and vulnerability.

Yet, the Court is clearly not telling us that *all* such words would be unprotected speech because they are "intended to intimidate." Indeed, any rudimentary student of First Amendment law could recount the half-century-long process of trial and error by which the Court—addressing a variety of factual scenarios primarily in the area of subversive speech—eventually settled on a difficult-to-satisfy variant of Justice Holmes's "clear and present danger" test. The earliest Supreme Court cases to seriously engage the First Amendment addressed the question of at what point expression that incites, persuades, or even mildly encourages unlawful conduct may be punished.[116] The Court and others who grappled with this question considered a wide range of tests: from a mere "bad tendency" of speech to inspire illicit behavior regardless of whether there was actual intent to cause this impact;[117] to words that expressly incite illegal acts;[118] to a "clear and present danger" test that would balance the gravity of the potential harm against its improbability to determine on a case-by-case basis whether or not the speech is protected.[119] It settled finally on a "clear and present danger" test *with teeth* that would only permit the curtailment of expression where "advocacy is directed to inciting or producing imminent lawless action and is likely to incite or produce such action."[120]

The last test is derived from one of the most important and well-known First Amendment cases decided by the Court: *Brandenburg v. Ohio*.[121] While rarely characterized in this manner, *Brandenburg* was, in a matter of speaking, a cross-burning case. Granted, the fact of the cross burning was not central to the Court's analysis. The wooden cross burned *in the background*, as twelve

Klansmen in hooded regalia spewed forth a range of derogatory remarks aimed primarily at African Americans.[122] However, the symbolic impact of the incendiary act—as well as the visible firearms and traditional Klan uniforms—implicitly contributed to the overall message conveyed. This was, without a doubt, a message that today would be readily classified as hate speech. The eight justices who participated in the case—writing a short unanimous (per curiam) decision—comprised what was arguably the most liberal Supreme Court in the tribunal's history. The liberal Warren Court minced no words. The Ohio Criminal Syndicalism statute was unconstitutional:[123]

> [W]e are here confronted with a statute which, by its own words and as applied, purports to punish mere advocacy and to forbid, on pain of criminal punishment, assembly with others merely to advocate the described type of action. Such a statute falls within the condemnation of the First and Fourteenth Amendments.[124]

The case itself was arguably distinguishable from the facts of *Black* in a number of ways. In *Brandenburg* the Court considered the Ohio law's constitutionality not as a proscription of a categorically unprotected "true threat," nor as "fighting words" as in *R.A.V.*, but as "subversive advocacy," also historically considered a "low-value" category of speech. Additionally, in *Brandenburg* the focus was on speech rather than symbolic expression. Yes, the words spoken by the Klansmen in *Brandenburg* advocated criminal behavior—including the suggestion that "revengeance [sic]" be taken against the President, Congress, and Supreme Court if they continued "to suppress the white, Caucasian race."[125] And as mentioned above, under what would come to be understood as a particularly forceful version of the "clear and present danger" test, punishing "mere advocacy" of unlawful action, without "imminence" and "likelihood" of such action, would be held to be constitutionally impermissible.[126]

However, what the Court in *Brandenburg* failed to consider was whether the same words spoken could have been construed as an unprotected "true threat" and, if so, whether the bar for determining whether a true threat in fact exists is lower than the bar for subversive advocacy. Not only did the words used by the Klansmen in *Brandenburg* suggest that revenge might be taken against the three federal branches of the U.S. government, but the following highly threatening words, among others, could be heard: "This is what we are going to do to the niggers"; "Let's give them back to the dark garden"; "Bury the niggers"; and "We intend to do our part."[127] Yet, there was no mention, by this very politically liberal Court, of the possibility that these words, in combination with the menacing symbolism used in the rally, might comprise a constitutionally proscribable threat.

What should we make of this omission? Certainly, if we were to place *Brandenburg* and *Black* side by side, it would be hard to avoid the conclusion that the explicit language in conjunction with the frightening symbolism in *Brandenberg* was *at minimum* as threatening as the purely symbolic act in *Black*. Yet, there was no mention of the "true threat" rubric in *Brandenberg*. Why? One answer lies in the fact that the Supreme Court's doctrinal categorical "true threat" exception was remarkably underdeveloped at the time of *Brandenberg* (and remains so to this day).[128] Indeed, the only significant First Amendment decision by the Supreme Court on threats when *Brandenberg* was decided was a thin opinion that had been handed down less than two months earlier, *Watts v. United States*.[129] This sparse, five-paragraph decision merely acknowledged the existence of the low-value "true threats" category, while summarily rejecting the position that a hyperbolic claim by an 18-year-old Vietnam War protestor constituted unprotected speech.[130] In *Watts*, the petitioner had sarcastically asserted that he would get President "L.B.J." in his "sights" if he were ever forced by the government to "carry a rifle."[131] Thus, one possible interpretation of the *Brandenburg* Court's failure to address threats is that it implicitly assumes that what distinguishes a "true threat" from a lower-grade constitutionally protected threat should parallel the significant gulf between "mere advocacy" and advocacy that meets the rigorous "clear and present danger" standard set out in *Brandenburg*. In other words, the bar is set equally high.

Despite appearances, it is important to observe that the *Black* plurality did not necessarily lower that bar. By striking down the law on overbreadth grounds, it avoided having to *apply* its hypothetically permissible but loosely constructed notion of a "true threat" to actual facts. Granted, the *Black* Court's rationale does seem to accept a conception of what might constitute a true threat that is broader than what Schauer has referred to as the "archetypal threat."[132] Under this traditional conception, a threat is typically face-to-face, aimed at a particular individual, and designed to provoke a real and substantial fear in that individual by communicating that the threatener "actually intends to wreak physical (or perhaps financial or reputational) harm on the target."[133] In other words, without explicitly acknowledging that it was doing so, the *Black* plurality seemed to be suggesting that one variant of a proscribable "true threat," a category that had been assumed to be quite narrow, may in fact include "group threats"—threats that apply not to specific individuals but to large swaths of the population. However, like the *Beauharnais* Court's short-lived experiment in stretching the traditionally target-specific understanding of libel into the questionable notion of "group libel," there is reason to predict that the *Black* Court's bark might ultimately prove much more daunting than its bite.

In practice, it is likely that a group threat would prove just as slippery as the group-libel concept in *Beauharnais*. We might question whether, without effectively undoing a half century of First Amendment doctrine, courts could realistically formulate a principled and consistent method of cabining the concept of "group threat." An enormous amount of political and other rhetoric could conceivably fall within this category. How would one decide what groups might permissibly be considered to be intimidated? What standard would apply when determining what intimidation must tangibly mean for each member of such a group? One could easily imagine the doctrinal concept of group threats degenerating into the kind of ad hoc balancing found in the Court's notorious Red Scare–era *Dennis* decision—a standard that has been roundly repudiated. Elevating the *Black* plurality's dicta from the level of theory to the level of application presents clear practical obstacles.

It is thus conceivable that the Court's powerfully compelling but jurisprudentially superfluous historical account of cross burnings in America may ultimately amount to nothing more than political grandstanding. It would certainly not be the first time justices on the Supreme Court utilized dicta as a vehicle for communicating a political or ideological message that is not essential, if at times utterly irrelevant, to the jurisprudential task at hand. At the same time, such dicta can be illuminating. It can draw attention to justices' internal ideological ambivalence about ruling in a particular way. There is a long history of justices using dicta to say, "I personally do not care for this law. I think it is silly, perhaps even repugnant, but that doesn't make it unconstitutional." It was the great First Amendment absolutist Justice Black, who, when confronted with a sympathetic claim that privacy had been infringed, famously proclaimed: "I like my privacy as well as the next one, but I am nevertheless compelled to admit that government has a right to invade it unless prohibited by some specific constitutional provision."[134] Although as precedent such pronouncements may not be terribly relevant to practitioners attempting to understand the legal import of a particular case, such expressions do provide insight into the justices' thinking.

So, what might explain the tenuous, if purely symbolic, return to a less speech-protective approach in *Black*, when it is looking at a set of facts that is in reality quite familiar to the Court? Why, in turn, were the political alignments of the justices in *Black* ideologically scrambled, whereas in *Beauharnais, Brandenburg*, and even *R.A.V.* they were neatly tilted in accordance with political proclivities? In addition to the explanations offered above—Justice Thomas's unique role and influence, for example—one cannot ignore the historical-ideological context. In the era of *Beauharnais* and *Brandenburg*, speech suppression was firmly associated with the effort to thwart communism. Although the facts of these two cases had little to do with the Red Scare, the vestigial ideological alignments and associations from this era remained—indeed, in the case of *Beauharnais*, they were not vestigial at all, as McCarthyism was at the time in full swing. As discussed in the Introduction, political conservatives generally supported the aggressive efforts to weed communism out of American life, while political liberals were much more skeptical of perceived abusive tactics used to combat communism. And these positions were firmly associated, respectively, with either a loose First Amendment jurisprudence or a strict, speech-protective one. This explains why—startling as it may seem in today's political context—in *Brandenburg*, an opinion delivered by the most staunchly liberal Supreme Court in history, there was scarcely a hint of ambivalence in the decision to unequivocally, perhaps even callously, reject a government's power to penalize noxious hate speech (in today's vernacular). It also explains why conservatives in *Beauharnais* seemed so eager to do precisely the opposite, without any of the implicit political concerns reflected in Justice Scalia's *R.A.V.* majority opinion.

As discussed above, *R.A.V.* was decided at a time when politically driven ideological opposition to perceived political correctness was at or near its peak. However, by 2003, the time of *Virginia v. Black*, much of the furor had subsided on the right, at the same time that the negative liberal associations of speech-punitive policies with the Red Scare began to fade. In their place arose a growing chorus of scholars who argued that there was a compelling need to revisit the traditional liberal "absolutist" positions on the First Amendment and replace them with a more balanced approach that better accommodates equality concerns.[135] Although, as I have argued, the right had been moving toward a more speech-protective conservative libertarian view of the First Amendment, the ideological and political passions of the time that urged the Court's conservatives to lash out at political correctness in 1992 were less apparent when *Black* was decided in 2003.

First Amendment Legal Mobilization: Post–Political Correctness Indictment

All of the above leads us to the curious case of FIRE, the Foundation for Individual Rights in Education. Regardless of how one stands on the debate over whether judges are indeed political, or in what sense they may be said to be liberal or conservative, few would contest the importance of legal mobilization by activists on both the right and left—and FIRE certainly qualifies as just such an organization. However, as we shall see, where FIRE fits on the ideological spectrum is a much more debatable question. Politics invariably plays out in many areas external to judging itself, including strategic advocacy intended to promote particular ideological ends and legal idea entrepreneurship. Understanding constitutional politics involves much more than parsing the decisions of courts in search of ideologically driven judicial activism and reviewing the words of political pundits, commentators, and scholars; it also requires an understanding of influential organizations such as the NAACP and the Federalist Society. To truly understand, for example, the constitutional liberalism of the civil rights era in America, a close reading of *Brown v. Board of Education* will not suffice. Scholars and other observers have long acknowledged the critical role of the NAACP in combating racial segregation in American schools through various strategies, including bringing to the courts the litigation that led to the *Brown* decision.[136]

Political scientist Steven Teles, in a much-lauded study, took an in-depth look at the rising influence of the liberal network's counterpart, the conservative legal network.[137] There are clearly variations within the liberal and conservative legal movements, just as there are variations among purely political liberal or conservative actors. And while it would be a gross oversimplification to paint such actors with a single broad brush, these "networks" act as an important link between the political and the legal worlds. Legal activists advocate using the law to promote a political agenda, an agenda that is intimately connected to the ideological objectives of liberals and conservatives outside of the legal sphere. An early document produced by the Federalist Society—an influential legal organization born in the early 1980s out of the frustration of a perceived liberal hegemony in the legal academy—"emphasized the Society's intellectual mission to 'stimulate thought and discussion about applications of conservative principles to the law.'"[138] Members of respective ideological legal networks quite naturally gravitate to particular legal causes or positions. For conservatives, this might mean supporting states rights through a robust reading of the Tenth Amendment and a concomitant narrow interpretation of the Necessary and Proper Clause. It might likewise mean supporting a revival of the Contracts Clause or economic substantive due process, in order to promote economic freedom and the interests of business.

The most celebrated members of the liberal legal network, on the other hand, such as Thurgood Marshall in his role as NAACP advocate, successfully argued for a broad inclusive reading of the Equal Protection Clause. Teles, however, traces the origins of the liberal legal network to well before the civil rights era of the 1950s. It was the ACLU, taking shape in the early twentieth century, with its focus on then–liberally dominated First Amendment advocacy, that marked the most prominent early entrant.[139] By the latter end of that very same century, however, the proverbial tables were turning. Conservative organizations began to take notice—from both a substantive and strategic angle. In 1991, an internal discussion at the conservative public interest firm, the Center for Individual Rights, acknowledged the resultant opportunities. Founder Michael Greve advocated the expansion of the organization's activities into the First Amendment area. He explained that "the 'PC' movement is a genuine menace, and the protection afforded to conservative and middle-of-the-roadish students and academics by organizations such as the ACLU and the AAUP is insufficient and, shall we say, unreliable."[140] At the same time, he pointed to the way the movement has "split the Left on campus," which Greve described as an "opportunity [that] should be exploited: the more of a wedge we can drive between heretofore closely aligned leftist constituencies, the better."[141]

Enter the Foundation for Individual Rights in Education. FIRE was founded by conservative libertarian University of Pennsylvania history professor Alan Charles Kors and attorney Harvey A. Silverglate in 1999, just one year after they published their influential critique of pervasive political correctness on college campuses, *The Shadow University*, discussed in Chapter 3.[142] The organization describes its mission as "defend[ing] and sustain[ing] individual rights at America's colleges and universities."[143] A key focus is promoting free speech and First Amendment values on campus, and litigation is one, but not its only tool for achieving these ends.

Through its Speech Code Litigation Project, attorneys affiliated with FIRE's legal network have been responsible for legal victories against speech codes at numerous colleges and universities.[144] Much of its work simply involves contacting administrators at individual schools to inform them that a particular university policy inhibits free speech.[145] According to representatives of the organization, this approach often garners results. However, where the school fails to agree to alter its policies, FIRE will frequently take the next step of publicizing the infringement to apply public pressure on the college.[146]

Many university actions that lead to intervention by FIRE are handled internally and non-transparently by universities and involve administrative decisions FIRE claims would "shock the conscience" of the non-college community. One of the many examples cited by FIRE includes a school finding that a student was guilty of "racial harassment" for reading a critical history of the Ku Klux Klan in public, because the cover of the book included a black-and-white photograph of a Klan rally.[147] Another involved a student who was determined by a major state university to be guilty of harassment, disorderly conduct, and an affirmative action violation for posting a sign in his high-rise dormitory suggesting that students on the lower floors take the stairs, implying, perhaps in bad taste, that it would be a way for "freshman girls" to do something proactive about the "10–15 pounds" they gain, on average.[148] For this act, he was kicked out of the dormitory, required to attend psychological counseling, placed on probation for two years, and required to write a lengthy reflection paper about the incident.[149]

In a 2012 report published by the organization, FIRE found that 65 percent of the top 392 colleges have policies in place that substantially restrict speech protected by the First Amendment.[150] The political and pop cultural focus on so-called political correctness that dominated the national conversation in the late 1980s and early 1990s may have subsided in the new millennium. However, according to FIRE, the related First Amendment concerns remain.

FIRE is an organization that regularly positions itself as a direct opponent of the politically liberal policies instituted by American universities, many of which openly subscribe to the views advocated by critical theorists. It would thus be no surprise that a *National Review* article by deputy managing editor Robert VerBruggen readily agreed that FIRE is "typically considered a conservative group."[151] Yet, when one looks deeper one finds an organization that largely defies political pigeonholing. Despite FIRE's frequent defense of conservative students allegedly silenced by university speech codes, the organization professes not to have a "particular political agenda."[152] Indeed, the president of FIRE, Greg Lukianoff, appears at times to be on a passionate mission to dispel the pervasive notion that his organization is a strictly conservative one. He expresses a palpable frustration that campus free speech has been conceptualized as "a conservative niche issue" and that this has encouraged many to write off such concerns as illegitimate.[153] Although his 2012 book *Unlearning Liberty: Campus Censorship and the End of American Debate* was published by right-leaning Encounter Books, within the first few pages Lukianoff emphasizes his status as a "lifelong Democrat" who passionately supports "gay marriage, abortion rights, legalizing marijuana, and universal health care."[154]

FIRE touts the fact that it has worked in support of free-speech rights with organizations that run the political gamut, from the ACLU on the left to the Alliance Defense Fund on the right.[155] These two exemplar legal organizations do not just have sharply divergent political allegiances. Ironically, the president of the recently renamed Alliance Defense Fund—now known as Alliance Defending Freedom—describes the inspiration for his "legal ministry" as "the critical need to protect religious freedom from repeated attacks by the American Civil Liberties Union."[156] FIRE's status as a bridge between organizations—not merely with differing ideological viewpoints but in this case with an overtly adversarial relationship—speaks to the dramatic ideological shifts that have occurred in First Amendment politics. It is symptomatic of the phenomenon explored in this study: a partial untethering of free-speech advocacy from liberalism and its targeted adoption by conservatism.

The range of individuals who choose to affiliate themselves with FIRE exemplifies the curious ideological breadth of the organization. On the board of advisors sits former Clinton Treasury Secretary Lawrence Summers, conservative American Enterprise Institute Fellow Christina Hoff Sommers, and the prolific Harvard cognitive scientist Steven Pinker.[157] Lukianoff celebrates the unique political diversity of FIRE. He recounts how, when he first began at the Philadelphia-based advocacy group, he suddenly found himself "in an office where people didn't even vote for the same candidates."[158] According to Lukianoff, surrounding himself with others who had a shared mission with regard to the First Amendment, but otherwise disagreed, resulted in frequent debates and was "tremendously fun."[159] David French, a former president of FIRE whose ideology rests on the opposite end of the political spectrum as his successor Lukianoff, expresses similar sentiments: "We live in a country that is divided red and blue—there's all this talk about the red states and the blue states and how were increasingly polarized. One of the nice things about doing consistent civil liberties work is that it's actually a unifying exercise."[160]

Why then, is an organization like FIRE, which is ostensibly dedicated to many of the same goals as the politically liberal ACLU, commonly perceived to be politically conservative? There are two possible explanations: its posture as an advocate and its association with the anti–political correctness movement. First, as an advocacy organization for student rights, FIRE takes positions that are critical of, and adverse to, the policies of American colleges and universities. Because the academic community has long been perceived to be dominated by political liberalism, FIRE might appear antagonistic to the liberal enterprise. As seen above, there are many examples of conservative commentators in the mainstream political press expressing harsh critiques of university policies—particularly those that seem to punish or disadvantage students merely because they have unpopular conservative viewpoints. And indeed, FIRE's president acknowledges that many of the students and groups FIRE represents *are* conservatives whose views are particularly offensive to the liberal zeitgeist dominant on many campuses—perhaps making them more likely targets of the often vague speech-code regulations that allow for selective enforcement by university administrators.[161]

However, the organization has also represented the interests of many who do not fall within the politically conservative category, including an environmental-activist student who was kicked off campus for registering his opposition to a planned university parking garage[162] and an art professor at a university in the American South whose work was censored because it was critical of the Confederate flag.[163]FIRE's association with and advocacy for conservatives thus cannot provide a full explanation for the popular conception that FIRE itself is a politically conservative organization. After all, for much of the ACLU's history, this famously liberal organization rushed with great fanfare to the defense of politically illiberal groups and individuals—defending the "speech we hate" even where it advocated racism, sexism, or bigotry; yet its credentials as a politically liberal organization remained unquestioned.

The second explanation perhaps is a better way of understanding the common view that FIRE is "conservative." The historical association between so-called political correctness and political liberalism that was so dominant in the 1990s still firmly resides in the American memory. Because FIRE's activities may be seen combating all that is PC, the organization might be perceived to be indistinguishable from the previous generation of conservative critics. This is a political era that remains captured, and perhaps caricatured, in the popular imagination as one of conservatives scrutinizing liberals for their culture of excessive sensitivity. It is a recent political and social history that, rightfully or wrongfully, instilled a series of indelible images of PC run amok in the American mind—images that were firmly associated with ideological warfare. The judicial manifestation of this ideological battle was the *R.A.V.* decision.

If the ACLU's history of defending the free-speech rights of communists cemented its alignment with the liberal team, so might FIRE's defense of politically incorrect students at America's universities stamp the organization with a badge of conservatism. However, while many political conservatives have indeed reverted to a brand of libertarian conservatism similar to the views of late-nineteenth-century legal scholars, the moralistic and authoritarian strains remain. The same can be said of political liberalism: No longer solidly associated with free-speech advocacy the way it had been up until the 1980s and the emergence of critical legal studies, significant portions of the liberal establishment remain committed to a civil-libertarian vision of the First Amendment.

FIRE thus perhaps represents the new portrait of First Amendment advocacy for the twenty-first century. Untethered from historic political associations, many of today's advocates of free expression see the need to operate free from the influence of instrumentalist politics. Indeed, Lukianoff recounts how, after more than a decade of defending student rights, at times the speech-restrictive left and the speech-restrictive right begin to look quite a bit alike.[164] Today it is not uncommon for speech codes and broadly drawn harassment policies on college campuses to target behavior that, on its face, would appear more objectionable to moralistic conservatism than egalitarian liberalism. Barnard College, for example, enumerates an explicit list of the prohibited swear words in the body of its speech code.[165] As Lukianoff explains, "Swearing, profanity, or cussing still retains what is, to First Amendment lawyers like me, a puzzling power to provoke outrage and calls for censorship. When it comes to cussing, some liberals and conservatives start sounding an awful lot like each other in calling for 'decency' and 'civility.'"[166] The liberal moral foundation of "avoiding hurt" has come full circle; and its destination is where moralistic conservatives have long resided.

Perhaps the most important legacy of the anti–political correctness era is that it freed political conservatism from the previously held conventional wisdom that to adopt a free-speech position is to be politically liberal. Standing for free speech, even outside of a circumstance in which a conservative has been ostensibly victimized, has evolved into a respectable, if not universally accepted, conservative position. In sum, politics influenced constitutional principle, and in turn, this constitutional principle influenced what is understood to constitute conservative politics.

By the time *Snyder v. Phelps* was decided in 2011, what could be considered the Court's most recent hate-speech decision, none of the culture war politics that informed so much of the Court's rhetoric in *R.A.V.* was apparent. There was simply principled agreement across the Court's sometimes-intractable ideological lines that even obnoxious, hurtful speech is deserving of First Amendment protection. And in *Snyder*, it was not as if there would not have been ideological benefits to ruling against robust speech protection. Had the members of the *Snyder* Court been inclined to act on political instrumentalism rather than constitutional principle, there would have been much to gain for the liberals and conservatives alike. For political liberals, *Snyder* could have provided the opportunity to carve out a new categorical hate-speech exception to the First Amendment. While the Court did not choose to frame this "intentional infliction of emotional distress" case as one that was centrally about something called hate speech, there can be little question that the signs carried by picketers outside of Matthew Snyder's funeral—including "God Hates Fags," "You're Going to Hell," and "God Hates You"[167]—would qualify.

Many political liberals would presumably welcome the opportunity to strike a blow against homophobia and bullying by making explicitly constitutional the kinds of policies that are now the norm at colleges and universities—policies that penalize hurtful and stigmatizing speech targeting sexual orientation. On the other hand, many patriotic political conservatives would have cheered the opportunity to dial back protections afforded to the sort of blasphemy to national pride facilitated by, for example, the Court's protective flag-burning cases.[168] Indeed, the fact that the protests at issue in *Snyder* took place outside of the funeral of a fallen soldier who made the ultimate sacrifice for his country—and that his family had to endure the sight of placards reading "God Hates the USA/Thank God for 9/11," "Don't Pray for the USA," and "Thank God for Dead Soldiers"[169]—might have made this an even more compelling case for limiting free expression.

Justice Alito, the lone dissenting justice and sole conservative to disagree that such speech is protected, exhibited just such a willingness to carve out exceptions to First Amendment principle in the face of ideological concerns. Here the concern was the sacred nature of the funeral. "Funerals," Alito argues, "are unique events at which special protection against emotional assaults is in order."[170] When in 1985 Alito applied for a Reagan Justice Department job, he included "an essay asserting that as a teenager in the 1960s, 'the greatest influences on my views were the writings of William F. Buckley, Jr., [and] the *National Review*."[171] Alito's brand of First Amendment conservatism, however, once the norm both on and off the Court, is now more of an outlier.

Many liberals, particularly the critical theorists discussed in the previous chapter, would likely find similarly ideological justifications for curtailing free expression, but in their case equality and sensitivity to the plight of the disempowered would motivate the call for reduced speech protection. Yet, in *Snyder* a coalition of four liberals and four conservatives held fast to First Amendment values, resisting the temptation to dilute constitutional principle in favor of political instrumentalism. The majority opinion ruled *explicitly* that "we cannot react to pain by punishing the speaker";[172] *implicitly*, the Court's alignment tells us that it does not matter whether the pain is felt by conservatives, with profound respect for the sacred and the nationalistic, or by liberals, with deep compassion for a subjugated minority.

This is not just a triumphant story of principle over politics. For many on the right, principle has become politics; conservative libertarianism on the First Amendment has once again become an accepted and respectable conservative position even in the face of conflicting interests—just as liberal civil libertarians have long accepted the inevitable tensions between speech protection and other liberal values. The *Snyder* majority explained, in unified voice, that "[a]s a nation we have chosen a different course—to protect even hurtful speech."[173]

5 The Rise of Free-Market Conservatism

UNWANTED PREGNANCY—LET US HELP YOU
Abortions are now legal in New York.
There are no residency requirements.
FOR IMMEDIATE PLACEMENT IN ACCREDITED HOSPITALS AND
CLINICS AT LOW COST
Contact
WOMEN'S PAVILION . . .[1]

In 1971, it would have been difficult to imagine conservatives rushing to the defense of this speech. Consider that, at the time, the above message would have firmly fallen under an unprotected category of expression—commercial speech[2]—and combine this fact with an appreciation of the inherent repugnance such a message likely carried for most anti-abortion moralistic conservatives. There would be little reason to believe that such tradition-minded individuals would give a second thought to the possibility of altering the narrow jurisprudential status quo on commercial speech. And indeed, in the year the Supreme Court decided the fate of the above advertisement, which appeared in a weekly newspaper aimed at a college community in Virginia, it was the most conservative justice—William Rehnquist—who authored the dissent rejecting broader protection for this commercial expression.[3] However, in the 1970s and 1980s free-market and libertarian conservatives—joined in many cases by liberals—would begin to reframe the First Amendment debate under the rubric of commercial speech. In just a few short decades, conservatives would shift from unabashed skepticism and First Amendment minimalism to a passionate libertarianism and free-speech free-marketism.

Strikingly, as we shall explore in the next chapter, moralistic conservatives would also eventually join the fray and find themselves on the speech-protective side of the ledger. Admittedly, this support would be qualified. However, at least with regard to the freedom to make the very opposite argument—using aggressive expressive tactics to *discourage* abortions[4]—moralistic conservatives would become strident advocates of free-speech principles. Leading up to and arguably undergirding this shift was the rising salience of commercial speech.

The End of an Era

In 1969, *National Review* looked back disapprovingly on the legacy of the Warren Court: "We live in a stormy society and age, lashed by revolution, racial conflicts, subversion and alienation, ravaged by crime. The Warren Court carried through a unilateral disarmament of much of our defensive system. That was its most distinctive, and its most iniquitous, achievement."[5]

However, the close of the 1960s marked another deeply significant change for conservatives who had been critical of the Court's First Amendment jurisprudence: hope. The Warren Court came to an end in 1969, and with Chief Justice Warren's retirement, and a Republican in the White House determined to fill seats on the Supreme Court with more conservative justices, the prospect of a rightward slide on First Amendment issues was a very real possibility. As noted in the *National Review Bulletin* in 1970, "with the departure of Chief Justice Earl Warren and Abe Fortas—taken in the context of the advanced age of three other Justices . . . it seems very likely that President Nixon will sooner or later replace a majority of the bench. He will become the first President since Franklin D. Roosevelt to have that opportunity."[6]

While Nixon would ultimately fall one justice short of this dream, Nixon's appointments to the high court without a doubt offered conservatives the chance to radically realign its jurisprudential trajectory. In *National Review*'s highly critical summation of the Warren Court's jurisprudential philosophy, pro–First Amendment decisions such as one protecting a "topless 'walking the dog' dance" on free-expression grounds, implicitly fell within the Court's larger, purportedly misguided, approach to constitutional interpretation. The Warren Court justices, an editorial opined, "seem to have set themselves to guarantee a totality of all possible rights to every defendant, above all the poor and 'disadvantaged,' and to every dissident no matter how revolutionary or distasteful his dissidence."[7] To conservative eyes, First Amendment jurisprudence was one tool among many utilized by the Warren Court to further a liberal agenda—an agenda that consistently favored groups and interests preferred by the left.

In a 1974 *National Review* article, the preeminent economist R. H. Coase questioned the presumed dichotomy between "the market for goods and services" and the "market for ideas."[8] Coase asked, skeptically, why it was that the government is assumed to be competent to regulate the former but not the latter. In the process of posing this question, although approached from an economic point of view, Coase in fact foreshadowed (or perhaps indirectly influenced) what would be a major shift in the Supreme Court's First Amendment jurisprudence—a reversal on the status of commercial speech. Coase proclaimed:

> It is an odd feature . . . that commercial advertising, which is often merely an expression of opinion and might therefore be thought to be protected by the First Amendment, is considered to be part of the market for goods. The result is that government action is regarded as desirable to regulate (or even suppress) the expression of an opinion when it appears in an advertisement, which, if expressed in a book or article, would be completely beyond the reach of government regulation.[9]

Why, in other words, are there presumed to be two separate boxes for two markets that are fundamentally similar (ideas and goods), and why, when these two markets overlap in the area of commercial advertising, does the Court put certain speech—commercial speech—in the box that is regulable? Such advertising, after all, looks quite similar to speech that is offered full protection. This latter incisive question would largely become moot in just two years, when the Supreme Court would broadly declare, for the first time, that commercial speech is protected by the First Amendment.[10]

Nonetheless, as to the first question, Coase found it curious that free speech "is 'the only area where laissez-faire is still respectable.'"[11] And it is not merely those adorned in black robes who held this "unjustified" paradoxical view; "intellectuals [also] have shown a tendency to exalt the market for ideas and depreciate the market for goods."[12] What explained this inconsistency? To Coase, the best answer had to do with "self-interest and self-esteem."[13] Intellectuals not only believe deeply in the profound value of their profession—which is at heart the search for truth—but they understand that allowing government regulation of expression would hamper their ability to freely pursue their calling.[14] Coase also found a persuasive explanation for robust support of the First Amendment in "the press"—an industry with a vested interest in free expression. He cited John Milton's classic 1644 *Areopagitica*, "probably the most celebrated defense of the doctrine of freedom of press ever written," as an example of how "self-interest" and "intellectual pride" often figure prominently among those who take a strong pro–free-expression stance.[15]

Coase readily acknowledged that there are many instances in which governmental intervention was required and appropriate in the economic market—for example, "when the market does not operate properly."[16] However, "we should use the same *approach* for all markets when deciding on public policy" including the marketplace of ideas.[17] Coase did not explain precisely what this would mean for free speech. However, what is clear to Coase is that where "market failure" is determined to exist, we should be no more reluctant about government intervention in the sphere of free expression than we should be about regulation of the economic realm. We live in a world where a double standard is widely accepted. Coase reasoned:

> It would be difficult to deny that newspaper articles and the speeches of politicians contain a large number of false and misleading statements—indeed, sometimes they seem to consist of little else. Government action to control false and misleading advertising is considered highly desirable. Yet a proposal to set up a Federal Press Commission or Federal Political Commission modeled on the Federal Trade Commission would be dismissed out of hand.[18]

Coase's argument for consistency was concededly rooted in the belief that there is no meaningful distinction, from an economic point of view, between a market of goods and a market of ideas. This was not an argument explicitly based on constitutional law, where there is unequivocally no precise parallel to the First Amendment in the economic realm—for example, language barring Congress from "abridging the freedom to buy and sell goods." Indeed, the explicit power granted by the Commerce Clause of Article I, Section 8, suggests the very opposite. Coase's plea was nonetheless one for principled consistency. It was a position that harkened back to familiar conservative claims of hypocrisy on the part of liberals who were quick to applaud big government *except* when it came to certain *preferred* rights.

Perhaps most consequentially, Coase would have required that the two markets be tethered to each other as far as government regulation is concerned.

> We have to decide whether the government is as incompetent as is generally assumed in the market for ideas, in which case we would want to decrease government intervention in the market for goods, or whether it is as efficient as it is generally assumed to be in the market for goods, in which case we would want to increase the government regulation in the market for ideas.[19]

The implications of this approach would be dramatic indeed. Under this approach, government incompetence in one sphere would necessitate extracting government from all spheres (or, at least those involving speech regulation). Under this rubric—and especially in today's political climate in which hostility toward government among conservatives is at an all-time high[20]—it becomes all the more understandable to hear conservatives taking on the role of First Amendment defender.

Thus, in the 1970s, as the composition of the Court itself began to change, conservative commentators did not merely focus their hope on the days when Warren Court–style liberal jurisprudence would become a distant memory. Something else happened as well. Conservatives began to see that some of the very same tools utilized by the left to achieve their instrumentalist goals might be useful to promote their free-market political objectives. Commenting on the improving "judicial climate" that seemed to be accompanying Chief Justice Warren's replacement with Warren Burger, Donald Waterford observed:

> that better feeling springs from the fact that all of the Chief Justice's decisions involving labor and management have thus far come down squarely on management's side. It seems he believes the "right to work" also gives individuals a First Amendment right not to join a union if that's the way they want it.[21]

Thus far, broad grants of free expression were largely perceived as a boon to those with liberal political interests—whether it be the freedom of those with alternative political beliefs to advocate an unpopular viewpoint, the right to criticize the segregated status quo in the Jim Crow South, or the freedom to deviate from traditional moral conventions against open sexuality.

There may appear to be something unseemly about viewing the principled fundamental rights spelled out in the Constitution's amendments as mere opportunities for political gain. However, it must be remembered that there is an entire political realm outside of the Supreme Court's sacred Marble Palace, and this realm is made up of real people with real political interests. African American parents who rallied to give their children the opportunity to attend integrated schools and ambitious entrepreneurs who seek to advertise their wares without governmental constraint are all stakeholders in constitutional decision making. Favorable Supreme Court decisions have the power to change lives; it is thoroughly unsurprising that concrete objectives—rather than theoretical constitutional ideals—are often the primary drivers of constitutional advocacy.

There is nothing inherently unprincipled about acknowledging that a broad interpretation of a particular constitutional provision might serve political interests, even where, in other contexts, it has been one's ideological adversaries who have taken a like approach to constitutional interpretation. Instrumental goals are legitimate goals in the political sphere. For those less focused on the consistent application of constitutional principles, the ends may justify the means, even where those very same means were formerly condemned. Thus, it may be perfectly defensible for a political activist on either end of the political spectrum to see constitutional doctrine, and law generally, as a tool to achieve political ends. A political activist, after all, strives to affect *political* change (or maintain an advantageous status quo) to achieve a desirable *political* outcome.

However, this "results-oriented" approach that may apply with unassailable logic to *political* operatives—untainted by principled jurisprudential ambivalence—may be highly suspect when applied by *judicial* operatives. The mission of the judiciary is, unlike political activists and legislators, not to achieve particular results but to achieve *justice.*[22] On the margins, particularly in "hard" cases, ideology can certainly make a difference. And as discussed in Chapter 2, the fact that a judge's ideological worldview colors her interpretation is hardly surprising. But a rule of law, not of men, often means applying the law with principled consistency *despite*—not because of—the political results.

Thus, it is one thing for political observers to reverse their position on a legal principle abruptly—for example, when it becomes increasingly understood that a key conservative constituency, business interests, will benefit from a broad First Amendment interpretation. It is quite another for ideologically motivated members of the judiciary who formerly adopted a contrary interpretive view to follow suit. Judges risk diminishment of credibility and self-respect.[23] And because precedent can open doors that call for an apolitical application going forward, results-oriented judging can backfire in unanticipated ways. The case of the speech-protected abortion advertisement, *Bigelow v. Virginia*, presents one illustration.

Bigelow and Big Change

If any case must be analyzed in light of its broader sociopolitical and jurisprudential context, it is *Bigelow v. Virginia.*[24] The decision set the stage for the seminal commercial speech case *Virginia State Board of Pharmacy v. Virginia Citizens Consumer Council* the following year, the holding that fundamentally reshaped the Court's approach to commercial speech. Although there was no question that *Bigelow* was primarily a First Amendment case, the dynamics underlying the decision cannot be appreciated without considering its historical context: The facts and ultimate disposition of the Supreme Court decision temporally bookended *Roe v. Wade*.[25] None other than Justice Harry Blackmun, the author of the *Roe* decision, delivered the *Bigelow* majority opinion. *Roe* was, in fact, pending at the time Bigelow's appeal arrived at the Supreme Court. Although it did not ultimately affect the state court's non–speech-protective posture, upon deciding *Roe* the Court remanded the case to the Virginia Supreme Court to reconsider newspaper editor Bigelow's fate in light of the new precedent.

In the 1974 term, Blackmun was a relatively moderate conservative justice; but over time, this Nixon appointee would move to the left, with votes that ultimately aligned him with the more liberal members of the Court.[26] In addition, as the author of *Roe*—the ambitious and novel decision that would become a lightning rod for both criticism and praise—Blackmun was deeply wedded to the opinion and the associated right to abortion.[27] It is perhaps therefore unsurprising that his majority opinion agreed, with little apparent ambivalence, that an abortion-related advertisement in Virginia was protected First Amendment speech.[28]

The newspaper ad was for an abortion referral service that offered to provide placements (and access) to abortion services in other states where the procedure was readily available. Even though Court precedent had been quite clear up to this point that commercial speech was a largely unprotected category of expression,[29] Blackmun was instantly receptive to *Bigelow*'s First Amendment argument. He noted in a preargument memo that the case was "easy."[30] Although he ultimately won over much of the Court to his position—with exception of Justices Rehnquist and White, the same two dissenters in *Roe*—there is evidence that at least one majority justice expressed reservations about the broader implications of the decision.[31] Chief Justice Warren Burger, Blackmun's childhood friend and fellow Nixon appointee, described his "grave second thoughts" in a letter to Blackmun marked "PERSONAL."[32] Burger would eventually sign on to Blackmun's opinion. It is worth noting that Burger was among the most conservative members of the Court that term, next only to dissenting author Rehnquist.[33]

Roe v. Wade would, of course, prove to be one of the most politically consequential and polarizing decisions in Court history. Linda Greenhouse, upon reviewing the extensive personal papers of Harry Blackmun, opined that Blackmun's approach to *Bigelow* was motivated "by its connection to abortion" and that there was "no indication that he was thinking ahead to the next case."[34] From the perspective of constitutional *law*, the First Amendment questions that were at issue in *Bigelow* and the Fourteenth Amendment right to privacy concerns in *Roe* were distinct constitutional interests. However, as we see here, from an *ideological* perspective, the application of largely discrete constitutional interests can overlap. An ideological nudge can lead to a doctrinal shift in constitutional principle. In the early 1970s, free-speech issues still appeared to be the domain of political liberalism, and although there were occasional suggestions that there may be practical benefits for conservatives who adopt a more robust First Amendment view, this stance remained a distinctly minority position for conservatives both on and off the Court. In *Bigelow*, however, the stars were aligned for an ideological nudge by those on the more liberal side of the political spectrum, urged on by the momentum of *Roe* and the issue of abortion, as well as the longstanding association between the First Amendment and liberal politics. Resistance, as we see, came from the more conservative members of the Court.

There is significant irony here. At the time *Bigelow* was decided, the 1942 decision *Valentine v. Chrestensen* had been the leading commercial speech case. In a short unanimous opinion, the Court had summarily rejected that a handbill advertising a submarine exhibit was protected speech.[35] The *Valentine* Court also blithely dismissed the relevance of a clearly noncommercial political statement written on the opposite side of the handbill, reasoning that if "that evasion were successful, every merchant who desires to broadcast advertising leaflets in the streets need only append a civic appeal, or a moral platitude, to achieve immunity from the law's command."[36] It was clear that for the nine justices on the *Valentine* Court, not only was commercial speech not protected speech, it was not even a close question. The minimalist opinion attested to just how cavalierly the *Valentine* Court brushed aside the possibility that commercial advertising should be constitutionally protected speech. Indeed, Justice Douglas would years later renounce his position in *Valentine*, describing the decision as one that was "casual, almost offhand [that] has not survived reflection."[37]

In *Bigelow* the majority implicitly overruled the *Valentine* decision.[38] The *Bigelow* majority attached an exceedingly narrow interpretation to *Valentine* and then proceeded to cite instances in which justices had cast doubt on its "continuing validity" as precedent.[39] At the same time, however, *Bigelow v. Virginia* was drafted in a highly qualified manner; the majority seemed unwilling to commit to a broadening of commercial speech rights yet was obviously convinced that under the factually bounded circumstances of abortion-service advertising, expanded speech rights were appropriate. In one protracted footnote, the majority explicitly refused to spell out "the precise extent to which the First Amendment permits regulation of advertising that is related to activities the State may legitimately regulate or even prohibit."[40] These included: "advertising in readily distinguishable fact situations" where "there usually existed a clear relationship between the advertising in question and an activity that the government was legitimately regulating"; "legislative prohibitions of certain kinds of advertising in electronic media"; and continued adherence with "holdings in the Fourteenth Amendment cases that concern the regulation of professional activity."[41]

As we shall see, the ideological nudge that inspired this decision would ultimately result in a relatively broad principled adoption of commercial speech as protected expression. However, at the time, the list of caveats in the *Bigelow* majority opinion had the distinct flavor of results-oriented judging. This left a bad taste in the dissenters' mouths. It was Justices Rehnquist and White—the familiar dissenting duo from *Roe*—who expressed alarm about the larger policy implications of the precedent the Court was setting. The dissenters enumerated worries associated with a broad protection of commercial speech that would have been much more at home with traditionally liberal political thinkers, such as "preventing commercial exploitation" and a regression to "the — lowest common denominator for commercial ethics and business conduct."[42]

It is also worth noting that just two years before *Bigelow*, when the Court was confronted with a case in which liberal ideological interests were decidedly *not* in sync with commercial speech protection, the Court resolved a dispute in the opposite direction. In *Pittsburgh Press v. Pittsburgh Commission on Human Relations*, the two dissenters in *Bigelow* had been joined by three other justices to form a close 5–4 decision upholding a Pennsylvania antidiscrimination law that outlawed newspaper help-wanted advertisements separating jobs on the basis of the gender of the applicant sought.[43] It is striking that a Court with precisely the same composition as in *Bigelow* addressing such a similar issue would decide a case so differently. However, a closer look at *who* switched positions provides a possible explanation.

With the feminist movement gaining significant currency—and a Court that was still relatively liberal even after four Nixon appointments—the *Pittsburgh Press* Court took care from the very beginning of its opinion to make clear that it was *not* taking the issues at stake lightly. This case brought to the fore the two sets of interests that were both comfortably within the liberal political domain: first, the interests in equality raised by a growing chorus of feminists who had been increasingly successful in lobbying for gender-equality measures such as the law at issue and, second, the freedom of the press. In *Pittsburgh Press,* one of these two interests would have to take a backseat. Thus, it becomes easier to see why, for Justices Brennan and Marshall (the two most liberal justices on the Court during that period aside from Douglas),[44] what was a "hard case" in *Pittsburgh Press* would become an "easy case" in *Bigelow* two years later.

These two justices moved from a position that allowed for an incursion into editorial judgment—preventing a newspaper from configuring its help-wanted page in three separate "Male Interest," "Female Interest," "Male-Female" columns[45]—to one that rejected an arguably similar prohibition on abortion advertising. This observation of inconsistency is not intended to impugn the integrity of these two justices. There are certainly fact-based, non-ideological distinctions between these cases that arguably justified the change in disposition. However, wherever balancing, rather than a form of nuanced absolutism,[46] is adopted as the preferred method of First Amendment interpretation, there is the possibility that a justice will give determinative weight to a countervailing social interest that he finds ideologically compelling and less and ultimately non-determinative weight to interests he finds less compelling. Balancing can push the camel's nose under the categorical tent, and it seems to have done so in *Bigelow.* Today, a more categorical (and thus more absolutist) approach to the First Amendment has come to dominate much First Amendment jurisprudence. Thus, what began as a tentative, somewhat reluctant, and highly qualified holding in *Bigelow* would rapidly evolve into a more clear-cut categorical rule that gives commercial speech almost the same degree of protection as is afforded noncommercial speech.

Where a particular categorical protection comes to be associated with a certain set of ideological interests—as partisan First Amendment dogma—the category can take on a life of its own. We saw this in the incitement cases discussed earlier, in which the liberal Warren Court moved as close as it would to absolutism with regard to a category of speech whose suppression was associated with rightwing, Red Scare–era fear-mongering. Liberals on the Court were so wedded to this association that the Court's celebrated speech-protective incitement decision in *Brandenburg* occurred without notice in a setting replete with racist hate speech.[47] As we saw in Chapters 3 and 4, as the political bonds between incitement protection and liberalism weakened with the rise of critical legal studies, the principled liberal commitment to free speech concomitantly deteriorated—at least in the area of so-called hate speech. Although both *Pittsburgh Press* and *Bigelow* addressed the doctrinal category of commercial speech, the interest in deregulating the economic sphere through the First Amendment had yet to become a widely held conservative political objective. This was quite unlike the liberal relationship with the speech category of "incitement," which by this time had come to be firmly associated with protecting political nonconformists from persecution. In due time, these relationships would change. Perhaps aided by the liberal ideological nudge in *Bigelow*, conservatives would come around and eventually see the profound deregulatory power of robust commercial speech protection and, by extension, protection for so-called corporate speech.

William F. Buckley, Jr.: Free-Speech Champion?

The gradual conservative conversion from moralistic free-speech minimalism to libertarian expressive maximalism was assisted by a number of tangible conservative grievances that increasingly seemed to call out for First Amendment retorts. In 1971 the very real-world implications of First Amendment interpretation became clear to none other than William F. Buckley, Jr. His confrontation with free-speech concerns placed Buckley in the unlikely position of enthusiastically "invit[ing] the American Civil Liberties Union to declare its solidarity with" his effort to challenge the constitutionality of a compulsory union membership law.[48] In his capacity as host of the long-running public affairs program *Firing Line*, Buckley had been informed that he was required to join the American Federation of Television and Radio Artists, the union representing those who appear on television or radio. In Buckley's view, the interpretation of the National Labor Relations Act allowing that he be required to join and pay dues to a designated union for the privilege of expressing ideas "over the public airways" was a violation of his First Amendment rights.[49]

Although the practical implications of the issue for Buckley were hard to ignore—if he failed to join the union, his program would no longer be broadcast on television—he was not shy about declaring that the rights he was asserting had import far beyond its ramifications in his individual case:

> What is involved here is a fundamental civil and human right. And unless this country has lost hold of its reason, the Supreme Court will acknowledge, as I am confident it will, that right of the individual to exercise his rights as guaranteed under the First Amendment, even if he declines to join a union.[50]

Here, Buckley's prescience proved inadequate. Although a federal trial court initially ruled in his favor, his claim was rejected on appeal, and the Supreme Court ultimately refused his petition for review.[51] The Appeals Court for the Second Circuit reasoned that mandatory dues prevent free-rider problems and enable unions to bargain effectively.[52] Because "minimizing industrial strife and thereby insuring the unimpeded flow of commerce" is a permissible congressional purpose, the Court concluded that the mandatory dues serve a "substantial public interest" and are therefore constitutional.[53]

Nevertheless, Buckley's adamantly pro–First Amendment posture was striking. Three years prior to the case's ultimate disposition, Buckley lavished uncommon praise upon his intellectual adversaries, requesting that "liberals" join him in his quest to vindicate First Amendment principles typically associated with the left:

> Many of the people in the country labeled as "liberals" eloquently object to any compromise of the individual rights of the citizen against the government—particularly free speech and privacy. I think it is time they join me in demanding that the individual have a right to join or not join, to pay dues or not pay dues to a private organization without surrendering his right to speak.[54]

Did this entreaty suggest an enduring move to the left on the issue of free speech and expression by the iconic conservative opinion leader? Or would it prove to be fleeting—perhaps explained by the narrow labor-related issues involved and the self-interest of a man who quite simply wanted to remain unaffiliated with an organization he did not support? This was, after all, a rarity. At this point in its history, there had been very few major pieces in *National Review* strongly advocating a pro–free-speech position.

An article Buckley penned just four years later would suggest that Buckley's position was short-lived, or at least narrowly cabined to the facts of his case. In 1978, Buckley echoed the commonsense conservatism of the magazine's past, a time when *National Review* frequently emphasized the need to relax First Amendment principles when needed to combat the perceived communist threat. In discussing the right of Nazis to march and hold rallies in major city centers, Buckley agreed with the critics of the marketplace metaphor:

> [T]he notion that all ideas have a right to compete in the marketplace presupposes that any one idea has the right to win. Therefore if the Nazis have the right to argue, they have the right to assume power. But if they assume power, intolerable results follow. These results contradict the bases of the Declaration

of Independence, namely that there are "self-evident" truths. If there is one self-evident truth, it is surely that genocide cannot be tolerated.[55]

Buckley likened a parade of Nazis through predominantly Jewish Skokie, Illinois, or a march through predominantly African American Harlem by the KKK, to "an obscene phone call" inappropriately seeking shelter "under the umbrella of the First Amendment."[56]

Today, as discussed in Chapter 4, such rallies would be referred to as hate speech, and ironically it is political liberals who are most readily associated with the battle to eradicate them. But conservatives who shared Buckley's view were drawing from the conservative well of anticommunism—rather than the liberal fountain of racial and gender equality—to justify the very same limited conception of the First Amendment. Buckley explained: "Against the consideration that the pragmatic experience suggests we indulge the little tyrants, there is that other consideration that little tyrants sometimes—overnight—become big tyrants. The moral is that little boys / Should not be given dangerous toys."[57] The "dangerous toys" Buckley was, of course, referring to were the expressive freedoms provided by the First Amendment.

Commercial Speech Comes of Age

The seminal 1976 commercial speech decision *Virginia State Board of Pharmacy v. Virginia Citizens Consumer Council* largely adhered to the expected conservative–liberal cleavage that had become familiar in the First Amendment context. Close on the heels of *Bigelow*, *Virginia State Board of Pharmacy* carried forward a full-throated variant of the implicit, yet tentative, principle spelled out just two years earlier. Commercial speech—defined as expression that does "no more than propose a commercial transaction"—does not lack First Amendment protection.[58] As in *Bigelow*, the decision was centered in the state of Virginia, was authored by Justice Blackmun, and was opposed (or qualified in concurrences) by more conservative justices.[59] The suit, brought by two consumer groups, challenged a state law prohibiting price advertisements of prescription drugs by pharmacists.[60] The Court ultimately struck down the law as an infringement on the free "flow of prescription drug price information."[61]

At first glance, the decision might appear to be a paradigmatic example of how, like *Brandenburg* discussed in the previous chapter, an ideological interest not directly related to a constitutional principle can catalyze principled constitutional change. Here, even in the absence of a politically liberal impetus—

like the abortion-related advertisement in *Bigelow*—the Court's liberals were propelled forward by *Bigelow's* doctrinal momentum. Indeed, in *Virginia State Board of Pharmacy*, like in *Pittsburgh Press*, there would seem to be a countervailing ideological weight that might make this a "hard" decision for the liberals on the Court. Here it was the interest in regulating economic activity; there it was the interest in promoting gender equality. Indeed, *Virginia State Board of Pharmacy* was laced with language that would put a smile on the face of even the most impertinent free-market conservative. The fact that the advertiser's interest is "purely economic," the Court told us, "hardly disqualifies him from protection by the First Amendment."[62] Adopting the model of the rational economic actor, the Court reasoned that in a "predominantly free enterprise system," there is a powerful public interest in a "free flow of commercial information."[63] The Court drew an analogy between the informed democratic decision making that had long anchored philosophical justifications for freedom of speech and informed consumerism—even hinting that in today's world the latter may be necessary for the former.[64] Thus, it might be logical to conclude that this paean to the free market, wholeheartedly supported by the Court's most liberal members and challenged by its most conservative ones, was an example of constitutional consistency trumping ideology.

This narrative, however, does not tell the whole story. For, at the same time the Court was singing the praises of unbridled capitalism, it emphasized traditionally liberal values and the tangible benefits that arguably accrue to liberal constituencies as a result of expansive commercial speech protection. Not only, as we saw in *Bigelow*, might broad commercial speech rights promote the availability of legal and safe abortions, but we were told that they may: protect endangered animals by allowing manufacturers of artificial furs to compete with those who market products made with genuine fur;[65] defend American jobs by permitting domestic producers to advertise their American-made products;[66] prevent excessive profits from accruing to professionals who otherwise might be insulated from competition for lack of advertising;[67] and, most central to its argument here, provide invaluable information to the poor, the sick, and the aged regarding the lowest prices available for the drugs upon which they so desperately depend.[68] Liberal critics of robust commercial speech protection have since pointed out that while certain advertising may indeed carry some social benefits, many corporations are legally obligated to seek profit in the interest of their shareholders, and thus produce advertising messages without regard to the public benefit.

One could quite easily turn the illustrations provided by the majority on their heads. Imagine, for example, an exploitative advertisement by a for-profit adoption agency inaccurately implying that large sums of money might be available to the vulnerable women who agree to put their children up for adoption. Or, envision a manipulative commercial portraying an unhealthy over-population of a fur-producing species that is in fact endangered, or depicting workers in what appears to be a small American factory manufacturing products that are in fact produced abroad. It would have taken but a small amount of reflection to imagine how easily the rosy portrait provided by the majority could degenerate into something much darker. One might foresee, for example, aggressive marketing designed to convince those sympathetic indigent prescription drug consumers that they need, and should spend their hard-earned money on, drugs that at best provide marginal health benefits and at worst are risky and overpriced. This nuance was notably absent from the majority's opinion, one that repeatedly (and selectively) emphasized the politically liberal benefits of combining free speech with free-market principles.

The Court majority attempted to allay concern by asserting that "[u]ntruthful speech, commercial or otherwise, has never been protected for its own sake."[69] However, it glossed over the difficult doctrinal challenges that inevitably follow the need to draw jurisprudential lines between advertisements that are unprotected because they are considered to be deceptive or misleading and those that are deemed to be sufficiently truthful. Although price advertising might be a comparatively easy case, commercial persuasion typically involves evoking a positive emotion and associating this emotion with whatever is being sold rather than a straightforward recitation of factual information about a product or service.[70] The majority casually speculated in a footnote that when it comes to commercial speech, truth "may be more easily verifiable by its disseminator than, let us say, news reporting or political commentary, in that ordinarily the advertiser seeks to disseminate information about a specific product or service that he himself provides and presumably knows more about than anyone else."[71] Regardless of whether or not one feels that the costs of robust speech protection in the commercial sphere are worth the benefits, such an assessment appears stunningly naïve in the light of today's sophisticated, multibillion-dollar advertising industry machinery. Much, if not most, advertising today has little if anything to do with communicating an elusive "truth" about the product or service being sold.[72]

Ironically, it was the dissent by the most conservative member of the Court at the time, Justice Rehnquist,[73] that saw through the unduly sanguine portrait offered by the Court's more liberal members. Indeed, in a clever tribute to the famous *Lochner* dissent by liberal jurisprudential hero Oliver Wendell Holmes, Rehnquist coopts the progressive critique of inappropriately deciding constitutional law in accordance with economic theory. Rehnquist opines, "there is certainly nothing in the United States Constitution which requires the Virginia Legislature to hew to the teachings of Adam Smith in its legislative decisions regulating the pharmacy profession."[74] How might we make sense of this surreal scene: a deeply conservative justice calling out the more liberal wing of the Court for being far too optimistic about, of all things, free-market capitalism? The answer has to do not only with the aforementioned liberal loyalty to a robust First Amendment, but to the fact that Rehnquist was speaking in the mode of a moralistic and commonsense conservative—not as one of the free-market or libertarian conservatives we have grown accustomed to on today's Court.

Moralistic conservatives, of course, are not only more comfortable with intrusions into individual autonomy, but they may feel that such intrusions are necessary for social stability and moral order. Such conservatives are generally less hesitant to attach moral judgment to individual behavior, even when purportedly "immoral" behavior has little if any direct impact on others. Even where a particular "immoral act" is not itself thought to be a candidate for legal prohibition, moralistic conservatives look to other forms of social pressure—such as shame, displays of disapproval, non-legal behavioral codes—to rein in deviant social conduct. Rehnquist is deeply troubled that "[u]nder the Court's opinion the way will be open . . . for active promotion of prescription drugs, liquor, cigarettes, and other products the use of which it has previously been thought desirable to discourage."[75] In other words, this decision—presented as a narrow ruling addressing the mere advertisement of pharmaceutical drug prices—is a wolf in sheep's clothing. The constitutional principle espoused may prevent legislatures from exerting control over the moral climate of their jurisdictions and open the advertising floodgates for a range of immoral activities, products, and services.

Moralistic conservatives also carry an abiding concern for the endurance of established social roles thought to anchor society, as well as principles such as honor and respect. To Rehnquist, and also Chief Justice Burger in concurrence, the thought that the *Virginia State Board of Pharmacy* decision would ultimately allow for distasteful advertising by dignified professionals was profoundly unsettling. The majority asserted that the case would "not automatically" apply to professional advertising in law and medicine, but Rehnquist found little comfort in what he characterized as "a bone [tossed] to the traditionalists."[76] While the conservative chief justice was less focused on the future implications of what he seemed to see as a factually bounded decision, he was clear in his concurrence that the principle should not extend to attorney and physician advertising.[77] In characteristically moralistic terms he described the community's concern for "providing safeguards not only against deception, but against practices which would tend to demoralize the profession by forcing its members into an unseemly rivalry."[78] Chief Justice Burger would lose this battle just one year later. In *Bates v. State Bar of Arizona*—another Blackmun-authored decision—the Court would strike down restrictions on lawyer advertising.[79] This time, the three most conservative justices on the Court—Burger, Rehnquist, and Powell[80]—along with the moderately conservative Justice Stewart would all dissent.[81]

Justice Rehnquist's dissent in *Virginia State Board of Pharmacy* is perhaps best known for its biting, anti-consumerist wit injected near the end of the opinion. He famously mocked the perversity of equating consumer choice over hair-care products with the heady dialogue that contributes to public decision making. To Rehnquist, it was quite clearly "political, social, and other public issues" that were on the minds of the framers when they drafted the First Amendment, not trivial consumerism.[82] Rehnquist's commonsense conservatism was on full sardonic display: "It is undoubtedly arguable that many people in the country regard the choice of shampoo as just as important as who may be elected to local, state, or national political office, but that does not automatically bring information about competing shampoos within the protection of the First Amendment."[83]

Rehnquist provided a memorably snide parade of hypothetical horribles that would accompany such an absurd constitutional outcome. He imagined objectionable ads such as "Pain getting you down? Insist that your physician prescribe Demerol" and "Don't spend another sleepless night. Ask your doctor to prescribe Seconal without delay."[84] Such advertisements would, of course, not only become commonplace to most Americans, but they would seem remarkably tame compared to the intimate, sexually oriented prescription drug ads that are pervasive today. Conservatism, by definition, is aversion to change. Commonsense conservatism looks to the status quo—current norms of behavior rooted in tradition—as intuitively correct. To a commonsense conservative, the prospect of diverging from the status quo is often worthy of ridicule—for it is so clearly understood to be eccentric. The traditionalist feels confident that equating shampoo choice with democratic deliberation is downright silly.

During the latter half of the 1970s, the period in which commercial speech had just been revived as a protected form of expression, the Court struggled to work out the contours of its new doctrinal rule. At times it upheld commercial speech protection,[85] and other times it accepted its curtailment.[86] However, the moralistic and commonsense views that marked the conservative reaction to the early commercial speech cases often resulted in a predictable ideological alignment.[87] In *Carey v. Population Services International*, decided within days of *Bates*, the Court struck down a prohibition by New York of any advertising or display of contraceptives.[88] The two most conservative justices, Chief Justice Burger and Justice Rehnquist, dissented.

Rehnquist expressed dismay and disbelief at the degrading notion that the framers of the First Amendment could have imagined its use to protect "the right of commercial vendors of contraceptives to peddle them to unmarried minors through such means as window displays and vending machines located in the men's room of truck stops."[89] In his *Carey* dissent, Rehnquist lamented that constitutional principles, once established, have the power to become vehicles for perverse results. "There comes a point when endless and ill-considered extension of principles originally formulated in quite different cases produces such an indefensible result that no logic chopping can possible make the fallacy of the result more obvious."[90] As we shall see, in the coming decades these very same sentiments would become a familiar refrain in the commercial speech (and related corporate speech) area, but one made by the more liberal justices objecting to conservative protective overreach in the commercial sphere.

Emerging Tensions: Libertarians Versus Moralists

Outside of the confines of the conservative cadre on the Supreme Court, in the 1970s rightwing commentators would express similar skepticism about robust First Amendment coverage. *National Review* would remain largely hostile to notions of expansive free-speech rights during this period. Yet, exceptions to this rule would gradually grow more and more frequent. In this decade the magazine would begin to directly confront the increasingly visible tensions between moralistic conservatism and libertarianism and their very different views on First Amendment interpretation.

In a 1971 review of two formerly suppressed books by the late Theodore Schroeder—the founder of the Free Speech League, a precursor of the ACLU—David Brudnoy highlighted the sharp distinction between Schroeder's libertarian vision and that of Anthony Comstock, who "reigned supreme as the outstanding opponent of vice."[91] Brudnoy described the conflict thusly:

> The ultra-libertarian, like Schroeder, demands only freedom, while the super-moralist, like Comstock, recognizes only restraint and limitation. The libertarian believes the First Amendment prohibits any censorship of obscenity and that obscenity is not harmful to most people. The moralist retorts that the First Amendment was not intended to protect obscenity, and that obscenity is an objective reality, an insidious evil.[92]

Brudnoy was not shy about exposing his own libertarian leanings, nor in predicting that a "Schroeder Renaissance" was likely on its way.

Nevertheless, just two years after Brudnoy's review appeared, Gary North wrote a pro-censorship piece falling firmly on the other side of the libertarian/moralist divide.[93] Unlike Brudnoy, North was dismissive of the First Amendment argument that pornography should be considered protected speech. North made an argument right from the playbook of judicial conservative icon, Robert Bork. For moralistic conservatives, the conclusion that the First Amendment only applies to expressly "political" speech allowed for an appropriate level of control over society—one that, according to North, "is necessary in any system of social order."[94] Like Bork, North was no fan of libertarian conservatism. He argued that the "libertarian shibboleth, 'laws cannot make men moral; you cannot legislate morality,' is a silly half-truth. Are we to conclude that laws are to be totally neutral, abstracted from any system of morality? . . . All law is legislated morality; each law will infringe on somebody."[95]

North saw, in other words, an explicitly and vitally active role for government, particularly at the local level. He invited government regulation as a method of social engineering, as a means of shaping moral attitudes. Notably, the government intervention North so vigorously promoted was not action presumed to be taken "in the face of overwhelming public opinion."[96] To North it was particularly important for government to act when the public *didn't* directly request it. "[I]n those often wide zones of public confusion or indifference, law can be used as a means of upgrading community standards."[97] North envisioned a proactive government that embraced its role as a moral leader and architect for the greater good. For North, it is the job of government to use law to instill "distinct value systems" implicitly, even where the bulk of the public does not know what is good for them, where they are "confused" or "indifferent."[98]

This view ran directly contrary to the dominant conservative perspective in the economic sphere—but North limited his zealous advocacy of governmental action to the realm of morality. Drawing on Durkheim and Freud, North argued that the governmental role in morality serves an important instrumentalist function: Defining and roundly condemning social deviance with clarity and the force of law binds communities together.[99] This was of no minor concern. To North, the cost of not acting to censor pornography, for example, would be potentially catastrophic. He described how, in the novel *Tropic of Cancer*, Henry Miller celebrated a "deliberate attempt to convert others" to a worldview that embraced the obscene. To North, this constituted nothing short of "full-scale intellectual warfare" in which the stakes were extremely high.[100] Indeed, the urgency and intensity of North's argument for a narrow First Amendment was quite reminiscent of the conservative justification for communist suppression. It was essentially a claim that society as we know it is at risk. "To deny the right of a local community to defend itself from this kind of literary propaganda is to invite suicide. It symbolizes the triumph of the nihilists through a novel, the absolute rout of the community by the ideology of radical relativism."[101]

Moralistic, commonsense conservatism was again on bold display in a laudatory 1977 review of a "remarkable and magnificent book" by Walter Berns entitled *The First Amendment and the Future of American Democracy*.[102] Here, once again, re-emergent libertarian conservatism was nowhere to be found. George W. Carey's book review heaped only praise upon a book that was deeply critical of the Supreme Court's First Amendment jurisprudence, which was, according to the author, increasingly dominated by "the relativism of Justice Holmes."[103] Carey readily agreed that "decent republican government depends on the moral character and virtue of the people. The political and social institutions of a republic thus bear a very special responsibility for constantly reinforcing and nourishing those values essential to its moral health."[104] Supreme Court decisions protecting profane language, all but "the rankest forms of pornography," and "the Communist Party" thwart the government's ability to fulfill its critical job of maintaining a virtuous society.[105] Such decisions require that the First Amendment "operates in a moral vacuum."[106] Under this reading, principles of tradition were to trump a principled adherence to First Amendment ideals—ideals that place freedom above moral judgment. Carey's critique of the high court was unequivocal: Its "relativism has no place for guidelines or principles, the Court has abandoned established rules of decency, civility, and common sense which have emerged in the course of Western civilization."[107]

Perhaps most significant to this chapter's focus on commercial speech was the striking fact that Carey's indictment of the Court's First Amendment jurisprudence reached beyond the ostensible harm imposed by standard morality villains such as pornographers and social deviants. It targeted laissez-faire capitalism itself. Carey explained that America, from the very beginning, was "destined to be a large commercial republic wherein there would flourish a distinct tendency to place great emphasis on materialistic goods and values with a corresponding de-emphasis of the necessary moral underpinnings."[108]

Carey was effectively arguing that capitalism must be tempered in order to promote morality—and that the Court had mischievously prevented governments from doing so. A claim such as this—coming from the premier conservative periodical—would be unfathomable today. Without directly acknowledging the reemergence of libertarian conservatism, Carey implicitly critiqued it. It was not just the hedonists on the left who were subject to criticism. It was also the instrumentalists on the right who would utilize the First Amendment to promote economic interests: "Properly understood, these provisions [in the First Amendment] in no conceivable way embody the extreme libertarian sentiments attributed to them by our modern courts."[109]

The 1980s: Unlocking a Pandora's Box—
A Conservative's Prescient Warning to Liberals

The contrasts between the moralistic views explicated by North and the libertarianism advocated by Brudnoy were not merely subtly distinctive variants of a fundamentally similar worldview. For First Amendment purposes, there would seem to be very little middle ground between these two strains of thinking. Yet, as America clawed its way out of the political and economic doldrums of the 1970s and moved into the optimistic 1980s, some reconciliation seemed due. For conservatives, as the iconic political advertisement professed, the 1980s were "Morning in America." This was the decade of Ronald Reagan, with its emphasis on *both* free markets and moralism.

This tension would play out in 1980, in what is one of the most doctrinally significant commercial speech cases to date, *Central Hudson v. Public Service Commission of New York*.[110] The case would stake out a middle ground between the most vociferous commercial speech advocates, perhaps best represented by Justice Blackmun, and those who would accord commercial speech little if any protection, most emblematic of the views expressed by Justice Rehnquist. The facts of *Central Hudson* were more *Pittsburgh Press* than *Bigelow*. From an ideological perspective, liberals who agreed that a regulation by the New York Public Service Commission barring all advertising promoting the use of electricity was unconstitutional had only the left's historical alliance with the First Amendment as support.[111] Absent were the independent and not free speech–related policy interests that nudged liberals toward the speech-protective position in previous cases, bolstering their conviction that expanded commercial speech rights were justified. To the contrary, like in *Pittsburgh Press*, the restraint on the targeted advertising served an interest dear to the hearts of progressives. In *Pittsburgh Press*, gender equality was the policy goal; this time it was environmental conservationism. Yet, illustrating the power of constitutional interpretation to—at times—trump politics and ideology, unlike in *Pittsburgh Press* the Court struck down the regulation.

The Court's new four-part test would frustrate partisans on both ends of the First Amendment spectrum; of the eight justices who voted to strike down the law, only five would agree with the majority's rationale. The new *Central Hudson* test put doctrinal flesh on the bones of *Virginia State Board of Pharmacy*, clarifying that as a baseline, commercial speech could be neither misleading nor related to illegal activity to be protected.[112] Furthermore, to curtail commercial speech a government's interest must be substantial, must directly advance that interest, and must not be more extensive than necessary.[113] Rehnquist, still the most conservative justice on the Court,[114] dissented, maintaining his distinctive skepticism of commercial speech protection. Justices Blackmun, Brennan, and Stevens, the three most liberal justices (with the exception of Justice Marshall),[115] concurred but were troubled that the majority opinion was not protective enough.[116] In the moderate-conservative center emerged a coalition of justices, led by Justice Powell, which seemed to find its comfortable equilibrium on commercial speech.

Justice Lewis Powell, as the author of the legendary "Powell Memo," is perhaps the most potent representative of the changing sentiment that would characterize the rightwing of the Court with regard to the First Amendment. The now-famous 1971 memo, penned by then corporate lawyer Powell shortly before being placed on the high court, outlined a strategic response to what he titled "An Attack on the American Free Enterprise System" by the left.[117] Today many progressives view the Powell Memo as having enormous significance; it is "routinely invoked as the blueprint for virtually all of the conservative intellectual infrastructure built in the 1970s and 1980s—'a memo that changed the course of history.'"[118] Although the true influence and import of this confidential memorandum directed to the U.S. Chamber of Commerce remains a contested matter,[119] it tells us quite a lot about Powell's orientation and perspective.

Powell was no conservative firebrand. His memo was a practical proposal to address what he saw as an ideological imbalance of power. His emphasis was not on moralistic social issues, but rather the "assault" upon the American "enterprise system" by well-financed "extremists of the left."[120] Although according to Powell these extremists represented just a "small minority" of the population, their influence was permeating "perfectly respectful elements of society"—such as the college campus, the mainstream media, and other institutions.[121] For Powell there was significant irony in the fact that the business community was not only tolerating, but effectively participating in, "its own destruction" through the view communicated by the corporate-owned (and controlled) media and corporate infusions of financial support to, and leadership of, American colleges and universities.[122]

Powell expressed dire concern about the pervasive influence of Marxist thought, but he did not home in on the purported threat to national security that was the focus of many of the early *National Review* pieces highlighted in the Introduction. Instead, Powell emphasized how Marxist doctrine, which "has a wide following among Americans," contributed to the "near-contempt" with which business interests were held by much of the public.[123] A significant portion of the Powell Memo addressed the purported need of the business community to engineer a counteroffensive in order to effectively have *its* voice heard. With regard to college campuses where Powell found the imbalance favoring liberal critics of capitalism to be particularly acute, he suggested that the Chamber employ a staff of academic speakers and "insist upon equal time on the college speaking circuit."[124] Textbooks, Powell instructed, should be evaluated to ensure that they provide fair and equal treatment for the free-market perspective and should not shy away from highlighting capitalism's positive accomplishments.[125] A cadre of respected scholars sympathetic to free-market ideals should be responsible for communication aimed directly at the public, and these scholars should disseminate their views on television and the radio, and through scholarly journals, books, pamphlets, and paid advertisements.[126]

The fact that Powell would go on to author the majority opinion in *Central Hudson*, leading a coalition of moderate-conservative justices (with the exception of the liberal Marshall, who also joined with the majority's rationale), is particularly significant considering the substance of the memo Powell drafted nine years earlier. He broke with the moralistic conservatism of Rehnquist, his more conservative colleague, to strike a balance that would at the same time decline to go as far as the more liberal members of the Court; Justices Blackmun and Brennan proposed applying strict scrutiny to most commercial speech restrictions, essentially putting commercial speech in the same category as other fully protected expression.[127] Powell's middle position in *Central Hudson* fit remarkably well with the pragmatic free-market conservatism on display in his politically astute memo. Indeed, if we placed his *Central Hudson* majority opinion back to back with his famous memo, we might come to the cynical conclusion that he was following his own strategic advice.

Powell noted in his memo that a conservative Chamber of Commerce speaker, eager to share the gospel of free enterprise, would be understandably skeptical about the prospect of receiving invitations to share her ideas on progressive college campuses. Powell even claimed in his memo—decades before the advent of FIRE, discussed in the previous chapter—that "[o]n many campuses freedom of speech has been denied to all who express moderate or conservative viewpoints.[128] Powell, however, was politically savvy and proposed using liberal principles to conservative advantage. He recommended that conservative representatives of business interests make robust claims for "equal time": "University administrators and the great majority of student groups and committees would not welcome being put in the position publically of refusing a forum to diverse views, indeed, this is the classic excuse for allowing Communists to speak."[129] It is thus hard to ignore the possibility that Powell was effectively utilizing a similar strategy himself in *Central Hudson*, adopting a middle-ground position that coopted liberal ideological commitments to free speech to justify a decision that provided profound instrumentalist benefits to the business community. The decision freed even public utilities, by necessity highly regulated monopolistic businesses, from most regulations on advertising.

It is also worth noting that Powell, in his influential memo, explicitly suggested that business use *paid advertisements* to get their free-market message out to the world. He explained:

> Business pays hundreds of millions of dollars to the media for advertising. Most of this supports specific products; much of it supports institutional image making; and some fraction of it does support the system [of free enterprise]. But the latter has been more or less tangential, and rarely part of a sustained, major effort to inform and enlighten the American people. If American business de-

voted only 10% of its total annual advertising budget to this overall purpose, it would be a statesman-like expenditure.[130]

Powell, the former corporate lawyer and chair of the Education Committee of the U.S. Chamber of Commerce, was now in a position to judge the constitutional status of the very advertising he had suggested businesses utilize to promote their free-market goals.[131] And judge he did. In the 1980s, a political era personified by Ronald Reagan and the potent fusion of free-market conservatism with moralistic conservatism, it was understandable that jurists with a free-market orientation like Powell would attempt to moderate—by staking out a middle ground—their move toward a libertarian First Amendment to avoid alienating moralistic allies.

Justice Rehnquist, however, was not fooled by this gesture. He, unlike other conservative justices on the Court, refused to budge from the narrow conception of commercial speech protection he elucidated in *Virginia Pharmacy*. Indeed, in *Central Hudson*, Rehnquist stepped up his rhetoric, explicitly arguing what was only implicit in *Virginia Pharmacy*. At same time, Rehnquist appeared to be declaring a sort of covert civil war on the First Amendment approach taken by his free-market and libertarian conservative compatriots. Rehnquist's lengthy dissenting opinion in *Central Hudson* was packed with metaphorical military language. As we shall see, it was to be a long and bumpy war—and one that moralists in the Rehnquist mold would eventually lose. Rehnquist, however, put up quite a good fight.

To Rehnquist, "the Court unlocked a Pandora's Box when it 'elevated' commercial speech to the level of traditional speech."[132] As in the cautionary Greek myth, opening new doctrinal boxes through constitutional interpretation can have undesirable and unpredictable effects, and Rehnquist took pains to outline the litany of evils that had, and would likely follow from, this still relatively recent unsealing. Interestingly, his illustrative examples seemed designed to appeal to anxieties that had been primarily the province of modern liberalism. He cited approvingly the New York Court of Appeals decision upholding the advertising restriction and its rationale emphasizing "environmental values and the conservation of natural resources."[133] He noted that even the great liberal First Amendment absolutist Justice Black readily agreed with what Rehnquist characterized as a commonsense traditional distinction between ideas conveyed "in the realm of business transactions" and those appropriately protected by free-speech principles.[134] Rehnquist reminded us that Black, after all, signed on to the unanimous decision in *Valentine*, unequivocally denying commercial advertising First Amendment protection.[135]

Throughout his dissent, Rehnquist showed little concern for the business interests that were so clearly front and center to a jurist like Lewis Powell. Indeed, this deeply conservative justice seemed to be issuing a warning to his liberal colleagues—one that would ultimately fall on deaf ears. Placing commercial speech within the ambit of the First Amendment was in truth, Rehnquist implied, a profoundly reactionary move, one that turned back the clock on almost half a century of jurisprudence rejecting *Lochner v. New York*.[136] As we shall see in Chapter 7, liberals both on and off the Court would eventually see the wisdom in this characterization—particularly in the era of *Citizens United*, in which a sharply ideologically divided Court would grant full First Amendment rights to non-human for-profit corporations. However, at the time these words were written, the First Amendment had a liberal wind at its back, and the notion of a "Constitution in Exile"—in which a critical mass of influential conservatives would indeed argue for a return to *Lochner*-era jurisprudence (including even one sitting Supreme Court justice)—would have been difficult to foresee.

Ironically, only Justice Rehnquist would foreshadow what was to come: that applying the First Amendment to commercial speech, and later corporations generally, was a doctrinal shift that had the potential, by judicial fiat, to deregulate large swaths of the American economy and frustrate legislative efforts to promote the political and social good. In strong words, Rehnquist asserted that "the Court errs here in failing to recognize that the state law is most accurately viewed as an economic regulation. . . . [It] ignores the fact that the monopoly here is entirely state-created and subject to an extensive state regulatory scheme from which it derives benefits as well as burdens."[137] Aside from Rehnquist's emphasis on the fact that the corporation here was a monopoly, these words might read like a modern dissent from the liberals on today's Court. He reminds us of a fact that contemporary conservatives are likely to ignore: that the supposed First Amendment incursion of such a regulation falls upon "an entity that could not exist in corporate form" but for the state's laws.[138]

Yet, Rehnquist's dissent is still a conservative one. Like the progressives of the early twentieth century—a very different breed from today's liberals in that they embraced moralistic justifications for their progressive goals—Rehnquist's views were grounded in moralistic conservatism. He questioned the relativistic assumption that "truth" can only be judged through a competition of the market—particularly when it is commercial speech that is competing. To a moralist, absolutes exist; subjecting them to popularity contests is neither appropriate nor socially beneficial. Rehnquist's dissent was also grounded in common sense and tradition from which the Court diverged, Rehnquist argued, in *Virginia Pharmacy*.[139] "[I]n a democracy, the economic is subordinate to the political, a lesson that our ancestors learned long ago, and that our descendants will undoubtedly have to relearn many years hence."[140]

Powell's View Takes Hold Outside the Court

In the 1980s the speech-protective free-market conservatism on the Court was increasingly mirrored in the pages of *National Review*. In 1983, Richard McKenzie, then a senior fellow at the conservative Heritage Foundation, made a libertarian argument that recalled the one made by Coase almost a decade earlier; however, this time the argument had a more explicitly pro–free-speech orientation.

McKenzie's goal was to convince his readers of the close analogy between free speech and a free economic market. His argument targeted the press and sought to persuade journalists that the same rationales they cited in support of their zealous belief in a free press applied to the free market as well. He asked rhetorically: "Is there any reason why ideas inked on newsprint should qualify for any greater protection from government controls than the ideas incorporated into the structure of a garment, a bicycle, or a home?"[141] McKenzie took on the classically liberal arguments in favor of robust First Amendment rights—not to cast doubt on them but to broaden their application to cover economic rights. One such argument is that freedom of speech empowers not just the speaker but the rest of society—the potential listeners. He explained that "[a]lmost all supporters of free speech see its suppression as a denial of valuable information that people need to conduct their daily lives effectively. It can be argued with equal vigor, however, that the suppression of market forces by government controls also muffles valuable information."[142]

Importantly, in taking on the traditional arguments for free expression, McKenzie breezed past views typically propounded by moralistic conservatives like Rehnquist. He told his readers, for example, that "[o]ne of the strongest arguments of proponents of basic First Amendment rights is: 'We do not know which ideas are 'right' when any issue is first discussed. Indeed, we do not even know what issues, out of the whole ranges of issues, warrant public consideration."[143] A moralistic conservative would likely respond to these assertions with dismay, claiming that we *do indeed* know what ideas are "right" or "wrong" and that we should look to traditional faith-based sources, not secular Platonic dialogue, to reach these conclusions. McKenzie's concern lay, however, not with moral certitude but with efficient competitive market mechanisms. "We must allow an individual the freedom to test his ideas in order that he may learn what goods and services—are actually preferred. In short, a free market is, like free speech, a competitive process in ideas. We need both freedoms for essentially similar reasons."[144]

At the same time that McKenzie seemingly ignored concerns that would be at the forefront for moralistic conservatives, he glossed over what would likely be the view held by commonsense conservatism. While a commonsense conservative might be quick to abbreviate First Amendment rights where conventional wisdom suggested that free expression went "too far," McKenzie placed principles about practicalities. He readily acknowledged that free speech may be abused and that, in light of these potential abuses, free speech can never truly be "unlimited."[145] However, these should be limitations of necessity, to be construed as narrowly as possible, under the same logic that an ardent free-marketeer would accept the inevitable necessity of some narrowly circumscribed controls over the economy. "In the case of free speech, unlimited freedom for all would make the world resemble a Tower of Babel, with no one able to communicate effectively with anyone else. In the case of free markets, unlimited freedom would mean nonexistent property rights and nonexistent markets."[146]

Nonetheless, when it comes to the First Amendment, McKenzie was no commonsense conservative—at least as I have defined this admittedly simplified archetype. The fact that some regulation was required in both free speech and free-market regimes would not justify letting down one's guard and allowing more government intervention than is absolutely necessary. Even in the face of "abuse," McKenzie argued that government involvement should only occur with "extraordinary caution."[147] With both markets there should be "a predisposition, a social proclivity, toward freedom and against control."[148]

The libertarian right, however, was not so quick to assume that liberals could be trusted to consistently be on the speech-protective side of the ledger. Indeed, during the 1980s, *National Review* frequently targeted instances in which free expression was restricted in order to achieve liberal political aims. Thus, for example, in 1982 the magazine criticized a Federal Home Loan Bank Board policy that prohibited real-estate appraisers from using certain words or phrases in their property value reports. "Among them are 'church,' 'synagogue,' 'pride of ownership,' 'declining neighborhood,' 'prestigious neighborhood,' 'homogeneous,' and 'poor schools.' The agency thinks that appraisers who use these dirty words and phrases are violating the Civil Rights Act of 1968."[149] Coded language had long been used in the real estate industry to send messages about race and religion that may not have been palatable through more direct means. Here, however, *National Review*'s editors aligned themselves with the "[d]efenders of free speech."[150] The rules were a wrongheaded attempt to manipulate the market for residential property. The assumption that a "prestigious neighborhood" was code for one that "excludes racial or religious minorities" was both "insulting" and "wrong," the editorial argued.[151] It was also troubling to the magazine that appraisals were prohibited from reflecting the true market value of a home, incorporating relevant attributes such as the perceived quality of the local schools in the district where the home was situated.[152] The editorial raised concerns that were, in other words, directly relevant to the Supreme Court's "commercial speech" doctrine. One key justification for robust commercial speech protection is the adverse impact such restrictions purportedly have on the consumer/listener—thwarting knowledge, transparency, and the ability to make the most informed consumer decisions possible.[153]

In sum, the two-decade span from the point at which the Court began to dramatically realign its commercial speech jurisprudence in 1971 through the end of the 1980s was a period of change both on and off the Court. What began as a doctrinal shift largely instigated and supported by ideological liberals, long characterized by their strong support for robust free-speech rights, was gradually embraced and expanded upon by conservatives. Although deep tensions remained—with many moralistic conservatives holding fast to a more constrained vision of First Amendment freedoms and remaining sharply opposed to the changing doctrinal landscape—there was no question that mainstream conservatives were changing their tune on free speech. As we shall see in the next chapter, this shift would only grow more pronounced in the coming decades.

6   Commercial Speech in the Modern Era

In this chapter, we move toward and into the new millennium, arriving at a period in which the conservative position on commercial speech would become remarkably unified. As we saw in the previous chapter, the 1980s were characterized by conservative support for an expanded view of free commercial speech, yet that approval was still contingent upon context.

In the 1990s, some of this inconsistency lingered. *National Review* editor John O'Sullivan took on the issue of solicitations by the homeless—a perfect vehicle for illustrating the vestigial ambivalence that remained. When the "commercial speaker" was not a middle-class home seller standing up against "the word police" for the right to present all relevant information on a home appraisal, but instead a panhandler on a New York subway platform, support for robust commercial speech protection softened considerably. O'Sullivan's 1990 piece critically reflected on a federal district court judge's conclusion that begging was protected speech under the First Amendment.[1] To O'Sullivan, if this action was understood to be "harassment," begging should fall "outside the First Amendment."[2] He did concede that in some instances, where begging is "neither supported by intimidation nor vitiated by fraud," such behavior might be appropriately considered "commercial speech."[3] However, in the process, O'Sullivan misstated— or, at minimum, severely understated—the rule that evolved under the Supreme Court's commercial speech doctrine. He told his readers that commercial speech

does not enjoy the full protection of the First Amendment; government may regulate it in the public interest. And since it is plainly in the public interest that the public should not be subjected to unwelcome intrusion as it travels about the city, the MTA is well within its rights to ban begging in the subway.[4]

The Supreme Court's *Central Hudson* test, however, requires much more than a mere "public interest." The interest must be "substantial," and this interest must not be able to be "served as well by a more limited restriction."[5] So there is much reason to doubt O'Sullivan's matter-of-fact dismissal of a commercial speech argument protecting panhandling.

As we shall see, in just over a decade, a number of conservative Supreme Court justices would argue not merely that the *Central Hudson* test should be applied with rigor, but that the test *did not go far enough* to protect commercial speech. In *Thompson v. Western States Medical Center*, Justice O'Connor would point out that "several members of the Court have expressed doubts" about the sufficiency of the *Central Hudson* test to protect First Amendment Interests.[6] Justice Thomas would go as far as to argue that the *Central Hudson* test should be eliminated entirely and that commercial speech should be treated as indistinguishable from noncommercial speech for First Amendment purposes.[7]

O'Sullivan's editorial, however, addressed an issue that was politically loaded. The right–left divide on how to balance quality-of-life concerns in an urban environment against the civil rights of those who were thought to impinge on this quality of life was as sharp as ever. Indeed, the early 1990s was a time in which pragmatic commonsense conservatism—in the form of high-profile New York City Mayor Rudolph Giuliani's aggressive and controversial efforts to tame a chaotic urban environment—became a prominent part of the national conversation. Just a few years after O'Sullivan penned his editorial, Giuliani agreed to take a "harder line" on the homeless in the New York City subway system, supporting a public relations campaign urging riders to refuse to give money to panhandlers and imposing harsh new sentences on those caught begging repeatedly.[8]

Skepticism of a broad First Amendment still loomed large in some conservative circles. When Robert Bork was nominated by President Reagan to sit on the high court just a few years earlier, Bork's conservative supporters celebrated his exceedingly narrow view of the First Amendment, as discussed earlier. In a lengthy 1987 article, Richard Vigilante detailed with approval Bork's judicial philosophy, including his view that "the First Amendment protects only political speech."[9] Vigilante, like Bork, saw a sharp distinction between the "conservative" and "liberal" approaches to interpreting the First Amendment.[10] "The liberal method is to peel off a favorite proposition from the Constitution and, contemplating it in the resulting isolation, to use it as a justification for some highly abstract claim of right."[11] The consequence of this approach was "to defeat common sense."[12]

In 1990, D. Keith Mano authored a satirical article that subtly illustrated the underlying internal tension between laissez-faire libertarian conservatism and moralistic or commonsense conservatism.[13] Mano recounted his travails sorting through the onslaught of "charitable junk mail" he received in his mailbox on a regular basis. "Give any philanthropic org $5, and you'll be on the whole world's sucker list tomorrow afternoon."[14] The full-page article was largely devoted to lambasting the method by which charities "*package* wretchedness and pain," as well as decrying the adverse impact such frequent mailings have on the recipients:

> Should I feed one homeless man in New York ($25 available NOW at Holy Apostles' soup kitchen) or a whole Ethiopian family for $21? The choices are so dreadful that they end up being absurd—ultimately they trivialize suffering and put a scab on sentiment. Yet charitable mail seems to proliferate.[15]

Notably, Mano does *not* suggest that the law should intervene. He does briefly observe, with a hint of sarcasm, that the "First Amendment apparently guarantees free speech and a captive audience as well."[16] However, he does not suggest that this interpretation is incorrect. Was this because he aligned himself with First Amendment absolutism, or the views of the ACLU? Presumably not. More likely, it had something to do with his admission that he was "a free-market man."[17]

Granted, moralist conservatism was also in evidence throughout the piece. Mano mourned the "modern charity market" as a product of "social collapse."[18] With regret, he described a nostalgic past in which "churches were a mediator between giver and recipient. But that social tissue is rotten now: the sense of community sustained by religion has left us. Individualism, even in woe, is predominant. Famine and pestilence seek celebrity."[19] Yet, as distressed as Mano may have been about this phenomenon, he was compelled to conclude that the charitable solicitations he received in his mailbox were ultimately no different from the for-profit free-market behavior conservatives routinely lionize: They are competitive attempts to convince Americans to part with their hard-earned dollars. Begrudgingly, in other words, conservatives seemed to be accepting that free-marketism must trump moralism on the First Amendment.

Sin and Commerce—A Conservative Transformation

On the Court, the most dramatic transformation with regard to commercial speech would occur with the change in membership from the mid-1980s to the mid-1990s. Considering the direction the Court had been taking, by the 1980s a prediction that moralistic conservatives on the Court would succeed in turning back the clock on commercial speech protection seemed unlikely. But this is precisely what happened in 1986. Rehnquist would have his victory, but it would be short-lived. The Court would look quite different from the 1986 case *Posadas De Puerto Rico v. Tourism Company of Puerto Rico*, which upheld a restriction on advertising of casino gambling by a closely divided 5–4 margin, and the 1996 case *44 Liquormart v. Rhode Island*, in which a unanimous Court struck down—with highly fractured reasoning—a prohibition on price advertising of alcoholic beverages. Only three of the nine justices on the bench during the 1985 term remained in the 1995 term. Along with this shift would come a very different vision of conservatism.

As discussed in the previous chapter, the doctrinal test crafted by Powell in *Central Hudson* might be seen as a compromise between free-market and moralistic conservatism. Free-market conservatives like Powell, whether out of genuine philosophical conviction, jurisprudential strategy, or a combination of both, were not ready to completely abandon the concerns of moralistic conservatives in favor of a fully libertarian commercial speech doctrine. Indeed, it might have been much more difficult, if not impossible, to bring along moralistic conservatives like Chief Justice Burger and Justice White had Powell not fashioned a test that allowed for the possibility of curtailing certain commercial speech where the interests of the government were "substantial" and the restriction not "more extensive than necessary."[20] A more speech-protective test, such as the one favored by Justices Blackmun and Brennan, was unacceptable to moralistic conservatives, many of whom still viewed the First Amendment though the lens of the 1960s counterculture—as a liberal cause célèbre in the service of amoral, if not hedonistic, relativism.

As we have seen in many contexts, free-speech interests do not always align neatly with other outstanding ideological commitments. A principled consistency in the realm of the First Amendment invariably involves some holding of the nose. It becomes easier for one ideological "side" or the other to do this when free-speech values become deeply embedded in the self-conception of that political "side." ACLU-style liberalism had this effect on political liberals for many decades, encouraging them to make hard calls in the interest of free expression. Conservatives had yet to make this leap—but they were clearly moving in an analogous direction. It is the transitional stages, however, that exhibit the greatest variability. Utilizing the inherent flexibility in the *Central Hudson* balancing test, the *Posadas* case would offer one last hurrah for the moralistic position.

Instead of striking down the Puerto Rican law prohibiting casino advertising directed at local residents, a classically divided 5–4 Court—in which the most conservative justices were on one side and the most liberal were on the other[21]—upheld it. It was one thing to strike down a law intended to serve the politically liberal interest of environmental conservation as the Court had done in *Central Hudson*; but the Court's five most conservative members would put their collective foot down when the interest at stake was thwarting a classic immoral vice such as gambling.[22] Rehnquist authored the opinion that would at last seem to vindicate his more restrictive view of commercial speech.[23] Utilizing a test that he rejected just six years earlier, the rationale seemed on its face to be unassailable.

Under the first prong of the *Central Hudson* test, a Court must begin by asking the threshold question of whether the commercial speech at issue relates to a legal activity.[24] If it does not, that expression—as it advocates illegality—is in all likelihood not protected speech under the First Amendment. The Puerto Rican government, like the vast majority of American states at the time, had the clear option to keep casino gambling illegal and thus constitutionally prohibit any advertising thereof. To the *Posadas* majority it was constitutional common sense to conclude that if the government had the power to prohibit an activity altogether and, thus, under *Central Hudson*, ban advertising of such activity, it surely may opt to do only the latter. Banning an entire activity would seem on its face to be a more intrusive act than merely prohibiting the marketing of such activity. It would be counterintuitive, perhaps even irrational, to confidently point to two restrictions a government may constitutionally impose and then deny such authority where only one of the two restrictions is chosen. Four liberal justices, however, disagreed. The closely divided Court was perhaps more a sign of the *Central Hudson* test's ultimate frailty than a persuasive challenge to the majority's logic. Ideological compromise on the Court often takes the form of a flexible balancing test like the one found in *Central Hudson*; while such tests may not always represent the best of constitutional law, they preserve the ability of ambivalent justices to change their mind in the future. In *Posadas* the conservatives took up this invitation.

The facts of *Posadas* were a conservative mirror image of *Pittsburgh Press.* Like the liberal goal of gender equality promoted by the newspaper ad restriction in *Pittsburgh Press*, the interests served by the Puerto Rican legislation restricting casino advertising read like a standard to-do list for moralistic conservative politicians. The legislation was aimed at preventing "the disruption of moral and cultural patterns, the increase in local crime, the fostering of prostitution, the development of corruption, and the infiltration of organized crime."[25] With little hesitation, the five conservative justices on the Court concluded that such governmental interests were "substantial," as required under the *Central Hudson* test.[26] Indeed, the majority's application of the test showed remarkable deference to the legislature in Puerto Rico and little appetite for close scrutiny. The majority was willing to take on its word the conclusion that the law would "directly advance" the interests of the legislature—dismissing in one paragraph the objection that the restriction did not apply to other forms of gambling and was thus "underinclusive."[27]

On the fourth prong of *Central Hudson*—whether the limitations on speech are "no more extensive than necessary to serve the government's interest," the prong *Central Hudson* itself failed—the majority likewise accepted the legislature's judgment, even in the face of the claim that a "counter speech" approach to discouraging casino gambling would have been just as effective.[28] It is indeed hard to avoid the conclusion, as the dissenters suggest, that the majority was effectively treating *Central Hudson* as a rational basis test. To the dissenters, *Central Hudson* placed a much higher burden on a government seeking to restrain commercial speech: "[A] court may not, as the Court implies today, simply speculate about the valid reasons that the government might have for enacting such restrictions."[29]

Strikingly, this placed the liberal dissenters including Justices Brennan and Marshall in a position comparable to the free-market conservatives who, in the post-*Lochner* era, continued to express deep skepticism, not only about the benefits of economic regulations, but about the motivation of the legislators who drafted them. Brennan's dissent echoes critics of decisions such as *Williams v. Lee Optical*—in which the Court upheld regulations that on their face seemed to serve the goals of a self-interested professional lobby rather than the interests of the public at-large.[30] Inverting the traditional relationship between ideology and suspicion of economic regulations, here it was the liberal dissenters who painted the Puerto Rican government with a cynical brush. They speculated that it "is surely not farfetched to suppose that the legislature chose to restrict casino advertising not because of the 'evils' of casino gambling, but because it preferred that Puerto Ricans spend their gambling dollars on the Puerto Rico lottery."[31]

This peculiar alignment would not last. It would take just ten years—perhaps acknowledging the inevitable, perhaps just tiring of his role as the lone holdout conservative on the issue of commercial speech—for Justice Rehnquist, by then *Chief* Justice Rehnquist, to relent in the case of *44 Liquormart*. The parallels between *44 Liquormart* and *Posadas* were striking. Like Puerto Rico, Rhode Island sought to temper what was perceived by many to be a moral vice. To address problems associated with excessive alcohol consumption, Rhode Island *could have* taken the rather dramatic step of prohibiting the sale of alcohol entirely, and alongside this prohibition, banning price advertising of such beverages. It did not do this. Like Puerto Rico, it chose the seemingly less-draconian option: It limited itself to a ban on advertising. Yet, *unlike Posadas*, the Court would declare Rhode Island's restriction to be an infringement on the freedom of commercial speech. Indeed, the Court moved from a 5–4 decision upholding a commercial speech restriction to a unanimous decision striking one down.

Chief Justice Rehnquist would himself sign on to a concurring opinion that would directly place the continuing validity of the approach taken in *Posadas* in doubt. This concurrence explained that since *Posadas* the Court had been less willing to take legislative explanations "at face value" and that this greater level of scrutiny "comports better" with the test spelled out in *Central Hudson*.[32] While it is impossible to know precisely why Rehnquist was persuaded to change his mind, it was clear that he was now surrounded on the Court by a new breed of conservatives. In the time between *Posadas* and *44 Liquormart*, Rehnquist saw the departure of Warren Burger, Lewis Powell, and Byron White and the ascension of Anthony Kennedy, Antonin Scalia, and Clarence Thomas. While it would not be accurate to claim that these new conservative justices lacked a moralistic ideology, Kennedy and Thomas both exhibited strong libertarian leanings on the First Amendment. Scalia is a vehement proponent of free-market conservatism—even if he is a bit more reticent than Kennedy or Thomas about adopting a full-throated libertarian position.

Scalia's brief concurrence in *44 Liquormart* did express some ambivalence about criticizing the paternalistic stifling of commercial speech for the good of the people, when the Court itself was arguably behaving "paternalistically" toward a state that was exercising *its* moral judgment.[33] Yet, drawing upon a loose originalism—also characteristic of the new wave of conservatives on the Court—he begrudgingly accepted one form of paternalism (the one ostensibly mandated by the First Amendment) over the other. The libertarian tone of the decision is hard to ignore. The words "paternalism," "paternalistic," and "antipaternalistic" appear nine times throughout the opinions of *44 Liquormart*.[34] Whereas Justice Blackmun's commercial speech decisions might have emphasized—in the long tradition of liberal First Amendment advocacy—the impact of speech restrictions on vulnerable minorities, this was a new era. This was the era of the anti–nanny state First Amendment.

Rhode Island—betting on the remaining influence of moralistic conservatism—put forth one argument that seemed tailor-made for the traditionalists on the Court. If all else failed, and the Court was ready to throw out its restriction on advertising as a violation of free speech, the state had prepared a last-ditch argument that would likely have succeeded just a few years earlier. It maintained that deference to a legislature is *at least* appropriate where certain "vice" products are at issue.[35] After all, just three years before *44 Liquormart*, the Court had upheld a federal lottery-advertising restriction.[36] In *United States v. Edge Broadcasting*, the Court cited *Posadas* favorably.[37] Those in the majority seemed thoroughly comfortable implying that the laws supporting a state's regulation of "vice" activities—activities that could themselves be, and frequently are, banned—constitute a per se "substantial interest."[38] Regulation of morality, after all, is a traditional function of the state. The ten-year period between *Posadas* and *44 Liquormart*, however, was very bumpy, as both the Court's membership and the conservative position on commercial speech continued to evolve.

By 1995, just two years after *Edge Broadcasting*, the Court appeared poised for an about-face. In a case addressing the constitutionality of a federal law that prohibited beer labels from revealing their alcohol content, the Court rejected the premise that socially harmful "vice" activities should be treated any differently when it comes to commercial speech regulation.[39] By the time *44 Liquormart* was decided, the state's claim that excessive alcohol consumption was morally objectionable—and thus arguably within a legislature's traditional police powers to restrain—was of no avail. Both Justices Kennedy and Thomas signed on to a portion of the opinion explicitly rejecting a "vice products" exception to commercial speech protection.[40] Pointing to the Court's precedent just a few years earlier in *R.A.V.*, these justices were clear that just because a broader set of immoral action (or in *R.A.V.*, speech) is constitutionally proscribable, that does not suggest that a narrower regulation targeting speech *will be* constitutional.[41]

Although Scalia was uncomfortable with the doctrinal status quo established by *Central Hudson*, he made clear in his concurrence that he did not feel ready to disrupt the test—yet.[42] Thomas's proposed approach, however, was another matter. Never the incrementalist, Thomas was ahead of the conservative commercial speech curve, advocating an almost complete dismantling of the separate standards that applied to its regulation.[43] "I do not see a philosophical or historical basis for asserting that 'commercial' speech is of 'lower value' then 'noncommercial' speech," Thomas forthrightly professed.[44] Relying upon "some historical materials"—consistent with the new conservative fashion of jurisprudential originalism—Thomas even suggested that, considering the centrality of advertising and commercial activity in colonial America, such expression might fall on the high-value end of the First Amendment spectrum.[45] Justice Thomas's concurrence reads as a paean to the rational individual; he repeatedly scolds legislatures and courts for even entertaining the idea that a policy of keeping people "ignorant" could ever be justified under a free-speech regime. Thomas seemed intent on closing the chapter of conservative First Amendment ambivalence on commercial speech.

Ironically, this would mean that conservatives would adopt the position held by the most liberal justices in the 1970s and early 1980s—represented by Justice Blackmun's opinion in *Virginia Pharmacy* and his concurrence in *Central Hudson*.[46] From a libertarian perspective, this was all quite sensible. But the implications of this stance for traditional conservatives were arguably dire. Taken to its logical conclusion, a judge with morally conservative inclinations would be foreclosed from ratifying a conservative legislature's decision to limit advertising of immoral (but legal) activities. That splashy billboard promoting a resort specializing in the pagan, gay, free love lifestyle? Protected. That condom advertisement utilizing lovable cartoon creatures on the back of a cereal box? Protected. Conservatism had come a long way, baby.

At the same time Thomas was effectively arguing for a new conservative status quo on commercial speech, the First Amendment libertarianism on the Court was increasingly cheered on from the non-judicial conservative sidelines. Numerous *National Review* articles advocated the continued expansion of commercial speech rights. In "The Court's Mr. Right," Daniel E. Troy heaped ample praise on the *conservative* jurisprudence of Clarence Thomas during his first five years on the high court.[47] Strikingly, as evidence that Justice Thomas may surpass even the conservatism of Justice Scalia, the author cited the assessment that he is "among the most ardent advocates of free-speech rights on the Court."[48] On its own, this suggestion that conservatism and First Amendment advocacy are obvious corollaries might strike many as surprising, especially considering the history of the Warren Court's "liberal" expansion of free speech and its subsequent denouncement by a generation of conservatives. This characterization was emblematic of how ideological perceptions of the First Amendment had indeed shifted. However, it is also important to note that the First Amendment advocacy that Thomas was approvingly said to so assertively support was a very particular brand of free speech: speech that invites commerce. Troy admiringly described how "Thomas reaffirmed his commitment to the view that advertising . . . should not be treated, as it is now, as the poor stepchild of political, artistic, and scientific speech. . . . Thomas is, accordingly, now the Court's strongest advocate of the right to advertise."[49]

Other examples of *National Review* lauding free commercial speech in the 1990s—and condemning those who would make it *un*free—abound. In "Pack It In," Robert A. Levy of the Cato Institute skewered proposed legislation regulating the tobacco industry.[50] Levy characterized the bill as

> an outrageous violation of the industry's First Amendment right to advertise a legal product. It would ban outdoor and Internet ads, characters like the Marlboro Man and Joe Camel, tobacco logos on non-tobacco merchandise, sponsorship of sporting events, even color ads on the back cover of adult magazines; and it would restrict the placement, color, and size of point-of-sale displays. It doesn't take a constitutional scholar to realize that the proposed rules are ridiculous.[51]

In other words, conservative common sense tells us that such legislation is a flagrant violation of the First Amendment and an unnecessary and paternalistic incursion on the free market.

In 1997, constitutional scholar Alexander Volokh registered a similar complaint about "overzealous regulation" by the Food and Drug Administration.[52] The complaint centered on restrictions imposed by the FDA on manufacturers who sought to tout the purported beneficial health effects of their products directly on the label. To Volokh, the standout example that most egregiously violated tenets of common sense was the FDA prohibition on prune juice manufacturers from printing directly on the label the claim that consumption of the product "may relieve constipation."[53] And while this arguably trivial illustration may have served to drive home Volokh's point, he asserted that other instances of FDA oppression cause genuine harm to consumers and society alike—such as that aspirin manufacturers were for decades prohibited from publicizing the well-documented protective effect of a low-dose regimen of aspirin against heart attacks or that the health benefits of many dietary supplements may not appear on the label.[54]

The process and speed by which the FDA determines whether a particular health claim has enough support in the scientific community to merit use in advertising is a public policy issue of genuine significance. However, for Volokh, this was much more than a mere issue to be addressed by the legislature and executive branches of government. It was a constitutional question appropriate for the courts. Volokh described, with implicit approval, increased judicial intervention in the areas of commercial speech. He celebrated the fact that "the FDA reversed its position" on a particular prohibition as perhaps a "political reaction" to a pending lawsuit.[55] "Given the FDA's traditional inflexibility, even this small victory for free speech and free choice calls for a toast."[56]

Free speech, in other words, is a vehicle for the free market; the First Amendment is a method of facilitating free consumer choice. As we have seen, this perception appears to be a distinctly modern innovation—a product perhaps of a dominant consumer culture. Although conservative libertarianism has always been about freedom *from* government generally,[57] the metaphor of a free market of ideas first popularized by philosopher John Stuart Mill was always just that: a *metaphor*. The free-market conservatives that emerged in the last few decades, however, would ultimately argue that the First Amendment is *about* the economic market—a view that conservatives as recently as Chief Justice Rehnquist had mocked with scorn.

A Brief Tangent:
Moralistic Movement on the First Amendment

Over the same period that the conservative position on commercial speech was being reshaped by the increasing dominance of libertarian and free-market conservatives, it is worth noting that moralistic conservatives were being urged to come along for the ride. To a growing chorus on the right, conservatives were being portrayed as the true stewards of free speech, and no conservative need be left behind.

In 1994, in the pages of *National Review*, Michael Greve condemned political liberals not merely for hypocrisy on the First Amendment, a common critique going back to the earliest days of the publication, but to genuinely lament "a sad truth: liberalism no longer stands unequivocally for free speech."[58] Greve attributed the left's waning interest in speech protection to the liberal weakness for egalitarianism, not unlike the dichotomy identified by Kathleen Sullivan discussed previously.[59] He was troubled that "the civil libertarian ranks have grown alarmingly thin, and they are confronted with an army of partisan agitators— on everything from racial justice to sexual equality to homosexual rights—who are far more ambitious."[60] Greve cited the Supreme Court decisions *Wisconsin v. Mitchell*[61] and *Madsen v. Women's Health Center*[62] to illustrate his point that the Court has been influenced by the regrettable tendency to loosen First Amendment constraints. Both cases upheld laws—at least in significant part— that were challenged on free-speech grounds. *Mitchell*, in which the Court declined to strike down a hate-crime penalty enhancement statute that ratcheted up punishments for those whose crimes were motivated by racial animus, was a unanimous decision bringing together the Court's conservatives and liberals.[63] Whereas *Madsen*—a case that upheld in significant part an injunction prohibiting certain protesters from a buffer zone around abortion clinics—split the conservatives, with only O'Connor and Rehnquist in the majority.[64]

Interestingly, the majority opinions in both *Mitchell* and *Madsen* were written by Chief Justice Rehnquist. As we know, this solidly conservative chief justice was, relatively speaking, not terribly speech protective. However, as discussed, Rehnquist's justifications for adopting a minimalist First Amendment posture were typically rooted in commonsense and moralistic conservatism, not equality-based liberalism. If there was any silver lining to these decisions, to Greve it was the "grudging pragmatism" that seemed to inform the holdings.[65] Greve observed that while these two cases regrettably narrowed First Amendment freedom, the majority opinions did "not embrace the egalitarian agenda; rather, they read like tactical concessions to shrill constituencies, intended to lower the temperature of overheated controversies."[66]

Nevertheless, Greve used this observation about creeping egalitarianism to make palatable what was effectively an impassioned pro–free-speech argument to a conservative audience with a history of supporting speech regulation. It was as if Greve was tasked with the challenge of standing in front of an auditorium full of moralistic and commonsense conservatives and convincing them of the merits of the libertarian view of the First Amendment, knowing full well that this was an audience that in the past had not been responsive to such arguments.

It might be tempting to think, then, that the damage [from *Mitchell* and *Madsen*] has been limited. One might even be inclined to welcome the demise of

First Amendment absolutism and liberalism's newfound concern with the harmful effects of certain forms of speech. . . . But dismissing this as judicial pragmatism and tactical games fails to recognize that the egalitarian agenda is the most serious and thoroughgoing assault on free speech in decades. . . . And unlike the Religious Right—which, far from being able to censor anybody, has to suffer the expulsion of *its* speech from many a public forum where it might make a difference—the egalitarian censors occupy the command posts of government, universities, and other elite institutions. They are already well positioned to suppress speech.[67]

This was a call to arms. Greve was imploring conservatives to unite. Was this call for unity among moralistic conservatives and libertarian conservatives motivated primarily by an authentic desire to uphold First Amendment values? At first glance, Greve seemed primarily concerned about the perceived "assault" on "free speech." Greve acknowledged the historical rift between conservatisms, noting that the moralistic conservative vision of the First Amendment "has struck libertarians as unduly narrow."[68]

However, looking a bit closer, it would seem that there was an ample dose of political expediency behind Greve's passionate plea for First Amendment adherence. To Greve, egalitarianism was a creeping threat that had to be addressed. Greve was effectively telling his conservative brethren on the religious right that their previous attempts to censor for the moralistic good had been rebuked and that *they* had instead become the targets of liberal attempts at suppression. We must fight back, Greve seemed to be suggesting; uniting behind the First Amendment was the most effective route to doing so.

After railing against the vast societal terrain the liberal equality ethic had invaded, Greve warned that speech suppression may be next and "soon become an integral part of the welfare state's agenda."[69] He observed the way egalitarianism insidiously affected attitudes toward the First Amendment. "Like the Supreme Court, the ACLU has made tactical concessions to the egalitarian agenda, while still trying to maintain its historic commitment to free speech."[70] These concessions, however, had meant not only that the First Amendment had become less protective of free expression, but it had selectively become so, favoring voices preferred by the left. Greve contrasted the way liberals rushed to defend "raucous" and implicitly distasteful public displays of homosexual pride against their eagerness to suppress insensitive, politically incorrect speech on college campuses. He concluded that "the animating principle of egalitarianism is not moderation or civility; it is thought control and coerced sensitivity toward professional victims."[71] Implicitly, he was suggesting that while he may perhaps not count himself among them, moralistic conservatives are the true victims of this coerced sensitivity. Joining with libertarian conservatives to reframe the First Amendment as a conservative value would be in their political interests.

There was perhaps no better case than *Madsen* to help rally the moralistic right to the side of the First Amendment. Almost twenty years after *Bigelow*, in which the Court found speech protection in the commercial speech setting where it was formerly absent—seemingly nudged along by the abortion-rights implications of shielding expressive advertisements for safe, legal abortion services—the tables had completely turned. According to Scalia, in his scathing *Madsen* dissent, the Court was now effectively *failing* to protect speech *just because* abortion was implicated.[72] Granted, in this case it was abortion *protestors*—not advertisers seeking to make abortion more readily available—whose speech was at issue. To Scalia, however, the Court had created a special, less stringent First Amendment test, especially designed for, and only for, abortion-related decisions.[73] Citing the precise language of a previous dissent from the two conservative justices who *did not* join his dissent in *Madsen*, Scalia decried the impression that "no legal rule or doctrine is safe from ad hoc nullification by this Court when an occasion for its application arises in a case involving state regulation of abortion."[74] As we shall explore soon, *Madsen* was in fact the first of a series of cases spanning two decades involving abortion clinic buffer zones.

Madsen was also just one example of the way moralistic conservatives were perceived as victims of the left. This theme of outrage from the right would recur, and perhaps more than any other influence contribute to the continued, albeit still inconsistent, joining of forces between moralism and libertarianism. Thus, for example, in 1994 G. Robert Blakey, one of the authors of the federal anti-racketeering statute known as RICO, wrote a piece condemning what he saw as an inappropriate use of the law to target and thwart anti-abortion demonstrators.[75] Blakey explained that when the RICO statute was drafted, it was intentionally tailored to address the fear that its application might expand well beyond organized crime; the most prevalent worry was that RICO might be used to prosecute those involved in unpopular protests, such as anti-war demonstrators.[76] And while the ACLU was apparently one of the most vocal original opponents of the legislation—along with the National Organization for Women (NOW)—Blakey pointed out that, ironically, the ACLU was now one of the parties involved in bringing RICO complaints against anti-abortion demonstrators. "Until the applicability of RICO to demonstrators is definitely rejected, the success of the [NOW president, Patricia] Ireland strategy in the Supreme Court will chill political and social protest of all types. Such a weapon of terror against First Amendment freedoms was not what I was told to design."[77]

In a five-page "Statement of Pro-Life Principle and Concern" published by *National Review* in 1996, the many signatories likewise opined that the

> Supreme Court's insistence on a "right" to abortion has had other disturbing effects on our public life. This "right" has been used to justify the abridgement of First Amendment free-speech rights, as when sidewalk counselors are threatened with legal penalties for proposing protection and care to women in crisis at the crucial moment of decision outside an abortion clinic.[78]

In 1997 *National Review* published an article criticizing a high school principal's decision to prohibit a student from disseminating "pledge cards" inviting her peers to "commit themselves to sexual chastity until marriage" on the grounds that the pledge movement was affiliated with a Christian organization.[79] The piece applauded a district court holding "that by forbidding the pledge solicitation the principal was depriving the Say No movement of its First Amendment right to free speech."[80]

In another piece critiquing federal bureaucratic overreach, Stuart Creque reported on the alleged free-speech misdeeds of the U.S. Department of Housing and Urban Development (HUD), which had participated in the early stages of a discrimination suit against a few residents of Berkeley, California.[81] The residents, who challenged a proposed conversion of a local motel to a residence for the homeless, voiced their opposition through public hearings, the distribution of flyers, and op-ed pieces in newspapers.[82] Since the occupants "were to include drug addicts and alcoholics, whom federal law deems 'handicapped,' the Berkeley Three stood accused of illegal discrimination."[83] Even though HUD, under intense pressure due to media exposure, eventually relented, ultimately concluding that the residents' activities constituted protected speech under the First Amendment, according to Creque, the damage was done.[84] "[O]rdinary citizens were investigated by the Federal Government because their vocal opposition to a housing project spurred its advocates to take action to save it."[85]

Creque's message was primarily a libertarian one: We must always be on guard against an over-zealous federal government. Yet, the author also took the opportunity to throw moralistic conservatism into the mix. He explained that the "Bel Air Motel is near two liquor stores and a nightclub, hardly an appropriate locale for people with alcohol problems."[86] The First Amendment is framed not as it historically had been by moralistic conservatives—as a get-out-of-jail-free pass for hedonists and amoral relativists—but as a defensive weapon of choice for traditional-values conservatives who increasingly felt themselves the victims of overly ambitious liberal legislation.

The new millennium brought greater First Amendment consistency among conservatives. Indeed, as discussed above, by this point a clear majority of *National Review* articles addressing the First Amendment and free speech presented the pro–free-speech stance as *a*, if not *the*, conservative position of choice. Indeed, the few substantial pro–speech-regulation pieces in *National Review* after 2000 were primarily written by members of the old conservative guard, such as Robert Bork[87] and William F. Buckley[88] himself. Bork, unlike many of his compatriots, had steadfastly refused to drink the new conservative First Amendment Kool-Aid. But by 2007, Bork felt compelled to acknowledge that his views on the First Amendment were no longer representative of the conservative status quo. He conceded: "[T]hose hybrids known as libertarians generally favor the further expansion of the category of protected utterances. Conservatives can be found on both sides."[89]

Bork made his feelings known in unequivocal language, critiquing the outcome of a Ninth Circuit free-speech decision as emblematic of "the lunacies of America's rights-crazed culture."[90] The case itself, *Frederick v. Morse*,[91] was indeed colorful and ultimately led to a Supreme Court holding that does, on its face, seem contrary to the narrative of a conservative Court broadly sympathetic to free-speech concerns. The *Morse* decision centered on a high school student who unfurled a large banner that read "Bong Hits 4 Jesus" during a school-authorized fieldtrip to the 2002 Olympic torch relay.[92] The student, in what would become known as the Bong-Hits-For-Jesus-Case,[93] challenged his subsequent punishment as a violation of his First Amendment rights. At first blush, it would seem that the conservatives on the Supreme Court, who would decide the case shortly after Bork wrote his *National Review* piece—and who would vote in a 5–4 ideological alignment in favor of the school's right to punish a student for his speech—agreed with Bork. But this would be wrong. Indeed, *Morse* presents an excellent illustration of the previously discussed limitations of attitudinal political science—an approach to understanding judicial ideology that whitewashes nuance in favor of a pure, up-or-down assessment of whether or not a "liberal" vote or a "conservative" vote was cast. In free-speech cases, context can be everything,

Granted, *Morse* was not a speech-protective decision. In this respect it might be said to be one of the few modern decisions that counter the narrative of emergent libertarian conservatism. However, a closer look reveals an opinion that has little in common with the speech-restrictive conservatism of old. Indeed, the majority opinion written by Chief Justice Roberts possesses an almost apologetic, defensive quality. Roberts was deeply troubled by the charge of the dissenters that the majority was doing "violence to the First Amendment" and sought to make clear that there was, in actuality, very little distance between the perspective of the majority and that of the dissent. The majority repeatedly and emphatically stressed both the narrowness of its holding and its nominal significance from the perspective of First Amendment doctrine.[94] Justices Kennedy and Alito expressed suspicion of government power, acknowledging that "[m]ost parents, realistically, have no choice but to send their children to a public school and little ability to influence what occurs in the school."[95]

Most significantly, the conservatives did not use *Morse* as an opportunity to uproot *Tinker v. Des Moines*, the celebrated Warren Court–era decision that famously asserted that students do not "shed their constitutional rights to freedom of speech or expression at the schoolhouse gate."[96] The controversial 1969 decision, upholding the right of public school students to wear black armbands signifying their opposition to the war in Vietnam, seemed to take sides in what was perhaps the most pronounced political fissure between liberals and conservatives of the era—the war in Vietnam and the propriety of political protests against it. Yet all of the conservative justices (with the exception of Justice Thomas), far from replicating Bork's view that *Tinker* represented a "wrong turn," would go out of their way to reaffirm *Tinker*'s continuing validity.

It may appear ironic that it was Justice Thomas—lauded by *National Review* as the Court's most speech-protective justice[97]—who was willing to take the narrowest First Amendment road. He stood out as the single contemporary conservative on the Court who, like Bork, outright rejected the soundness of *Tinker* as precedent. In his concurrence, he propounded the notion that public schools govern under the traditional legal doctrine of *in loco parentis*, a conclusion conservatives Kennedy and Alito, also in concurrence, identified as "a dangerous fiction."[98] Thomas's view drew heavily on traditionally conservative moral foundations lionizing hierarchy, authority, loyalty, and obedience. For Thomas, the First Amendment quite simply "does not protect student speech in public schools."[99] And while such a view may not appear consistent with a broadly speech-protective approach to the First Amendment, it might be

recalled that even the most ardent First Amendment advocates have historically placed rigid boundaries on what is, or is not, within the ambit of First
Amendment "speech." It was, after all, Justice Hugo Black, the famed liberal
"free-speech absolutist," who wrote a dissent in *Tinker*.[100]

In the hands of moralistic conservatives, the First Amendment was under-
going an extreme makeover. Freedom *from* discrimination—the abiding clarion
call among political liberals in America—was becoming freedom *to* discriminate. Of course, it was not framed in this manner; it was understood as a sort
of conscientious objector status for traditional moralistic conservatives—those
whose beliefs and practices were being encroached upon by rapidly changing
social norms. Moralistic conservatives saw themselves as the victims of an increasingly irreverent society. Making matters worse, an enlightened mainstream
conservative press was becoming less vehemently moralistic on issues such as
gay rights. Thus, after a California court legalized gay marriage in 2008, *National
Review* published a piece focusing not on the inherent moral outrage of vali-
dating homosexuality, but on the secondary "oppressive" effects of the ruling.[101]
Mark Hemingway critically observed that there had "been an effort in the courts
not just to legalize gay marriage but to force acceptance of it as a matter of conscience and religious practice."[102] He cited the example of a wedding photogra-
pher who might be legally prohibited from declining to photograph homosexual
marriage ceremonies.[103] Here the envisioned artist/protagonist was no longer
the "subversive" Robert Mapplethorpe type demonized by conservatives of the
1990s, but a traditional community member who had "close relationships with
specific churches" and relied on "word-of mouth and referrals" for business.[104] To
Hemingway, the implications were deeply troubling. "Photography is considered
a form of artistic expression, . . . putting a seal of approval on same-sex marriage
might end up requiring a legal definition of what is art and what is a service, aside
from the question of whether a person can be compelled to produce either."[105]

From an instrumentalist political perspective, Hemingway's posture was
brilliant. Instead of arriving at an indelible and incurable contradiction between libertarian and moralistic conservatism, the argument bound the two
views. It championed the interests of traditionalists, while refusing to alien-
ate libertarians who may have a more progressive view on sexual freedom. It
said to libertarians, you have permission to oppose gay marriage—not because
you are Stone Age conservatives who willingly defy modernity, but because you
believe in *freedom*. And hey, even if you do support same-sex marriage, your
respect for the First Amendment should mean, at minimum, that freethinking

individuals and associations should have the right to discriminate against those gay couples *if they so choose.* In one fell swoop, moralistic and libertarian conservatives were brought together under the banner of the First Amendment.

Claims of religious oppression were no longer exclusively tied to the most intuitive constitutional provision, the First Amendment's Free Exercise Clause. In a 2005 column William F. Buckley, Jr. addressed a controversy at Dartmouth College in which the president of the Dartmouth Student Assembly gave a speech to the freshman class extolling Jesus as an aspirational role model.[106] Outrage among the student body ensued from what Buckley described as a perceived "violation of secularist decorum."[107] As the student-antagonist described it, the problem was "that Dartmouth has a speech culture, where some topics are off limits and some perspectives shouldn't be uttered."[108] Free-speech values, in other words, are a friend of moralistic conservatives, who must fend off the persistent and unrelenting effort to shut out their voices.

In the 2014 case of *McCullen v. Coakley,* this impression would be fully vindicated by a unanimous Supreme Court.[109] In *McCullen* the Court struck down, as a violation of the First Amendment, a Massachusetts law establishing a 35-foot fixed buffer zone around abortion clinics. Over the course of the previous two decades, the Court had upheld, beginning with *Madsen,* components of similar buffer zones—some in the form of injunctions.[110] The law at issue in *McCullen,* however, effectively halted all anti-abortion counseling or protests on public sidewalks abutting abortion facilities, and for all members of the Court, on the left and the right, the law went too far. Granted, the Court could have gone further than it did in *McCullen.* It had been asked to reverse its 2000 holding in *Hill v. Colorado,* in which it upheld a similar—but arguably less speech-restrictive buffer zone law that made it a crime to approach within 8 feet a person in the vicinity of a healthcare facility. In *McCullen* the majority failed to explicitly overrule *Hill,* instead striking a balance that would potentially allow narrowly tailored speech-restrictive abortion clinic measures to stand in the future. A concurrence joined by three conservative justices called for more robust First Amendment protection and harshly criticized the majority for this approach.[111]

The Commercial Speech Doctrine in the 2000s— A New Ideological Status Quo

The conservative free-market perspective that played out on the pages of *National Review* in the 1990s, with regard to tobacco advertising and food and drug regulations, would be front and center in two prominent Supreme Court

commercial speech cases in 2001 and 2002. Justice Thomas would use the opportunity to flesh out with even greater detail his proposed approach to commercial
speech, one that would replace the *Central Hudson* test with even more speech-
protective strict scrutiny.[112] While refusing to go quite so far, the other conservatives eagerly moved in Thomas's direction. The liberals, at the same time, began
to head for the exits, showing less and less comfort with the conservatives' increasingly vigorous and inflexible free-market posture on commercial speech.

In 2001, the Court decided *Lorillard Tobacco v. Reilly*, once again seeming to
pit morality against free expression. The opinion, addressing a complex regime
of regulations governing the advertising and sale of tobacco products, is a con-
fusing one, particularly for an analyst attempting to disaggregate the positions
of the various justices. The body of the Court's main opinion contains more
than a dozen subsections, with various configurations of justices either signing
on, or refusing to sign on, to portions of the decision. It also included a number
of concurrences and partial dissents. While the liberal and conservative justices
continued to agree—with the exception of Justice Thomas—that commercial
speech should be evaluated under the four-prong *Central Hudson* test, it was
now three of the four most liberal justices, rather than the conservative coalition in *Posadas*, who argued for a more forgiving and deferential application.

In resolving the constitutional fate of a prohibition of advertising for smokeless tobacco and cigars within a 1,000-foot radius of a school or playground,
the Court explained that only the final two prongs of *Central Hudson* were at
issue.[113] By looking closely at the Court's application of these two prongs, we
see the widening gap between the liberals and conservatives on the Court. The
third *Central Hudson* prong asks "whether the regulation directly advances the
governmental interest asserted."[114] On this question, the five most liberal justices
(relatively speaking)—which included Stevens, Ginsburg, Breyer, Souter, and
the moderate-conservative O'Connor[115]—joined with Chief Justice Rehnquist
to conclude that there was ample evidence that underage use of smokeless tobacco and cigars was a problem and that a regulatory regime limiting exposure
to advertisements for the products would decrease their use.[116] This portion of
the opinion presented the administrative and legislative process in a positive
light, portraying what would seem to be a rational regulatory apparatus. The
Court cited with approval the many studies relied upon by the government
showing that "advertising plays a crucial role" in the decision of minors to begin
using tobacco products.[117] The cynical tone that often accompanies a conservative free-market perspective on governmental regulation was notably absent.

However, as the Court moved on to the fourth prong, the four most liberal justices dropped out of the picture and refused to sign on. In their stead were Kennedy, Scalia, and Thomas, meaning that this portion of the opinion represented the view of just the five conservative justices. The five ultimately struck down the outdoor advertising regulation under the fourth prong of *Central Hudson*, concluding that the "fit" between the means and ends of the regulation was simply not reasonable.[118] The liberals on the Court were sympathetic with the concern that the regulation may have been overly broad—because it would, for example, have effectively banned outdoor advertising of certain tobacco products in 87 to 91 percent of Boston.[119] The liberals, however—in this case Stevens, Ginsburg, and Breyer—would instead have remanded that issue so that the question could be reassessed in light of qualitative and quantitative evidence that was, at the time, lacking.[120]

On its face, the distinction between the liberals and the conservatives may not seem terribly significant. But it is illustrative of the growing ideological divide on commercial speech cases in which the conservatives, consistent with Justice Thomas's formal position, were increasingly intolerant of the regulatory interests of the government in a First Amendment "balance." It is also notable that Chief Justice Rehnquist, in his final years on the bench, maintained some of his trademark ambivalence on commercial speech, dating back to the very earliest commercial speech cases. He positioned himself with the liberals on the third prong of *Central Hudson* but with the conservatives on the fourth prong—ultimately agreeing to strike down the regulation. The following year, in what would be his final opportunity to lend his voice to a commercial speech case, Rehnquist would come full circle, returning to where he started and dissenting as he did in *Virginia Pharmacy*, but this time alongside the Court's most liberal members.

Thompson v. Western States Medical Center was a 5–4 decision, and with the exception of Justices Souter and Rehnquist, it divided along clear ideological lines. *Thompson* would return the Court to the very issue that brought new life to the commercial speech doctrine in the 1970s: the question of pharmaceutical marketing. Here the Court was asked whether the legality of compounded drugs may be contingent upon an absence of advertising and promotion.[121] Compounded drugs are not subjected to the rigorous testing normally required by the FDA, but are tailored to the unique needs of an individual patient. Under the government's logic, drug compounding allowed pharmacists to serve customers with distinctive needs where safety and efficacy testing were not economically feasible.[122] Establishing advertising as a "trigger" for requiring FDA approval ensured that safety and efficacy goals would not be undermined by pharmacists who market compounded drugs to a larger, and perhaps inappropriate, population of consumers.[123] The conservative majority, however, was not convinced. To the Court's conservatives (minus Rehnquist), the restrictions were another example of paternalism run amok: The government had not adequately accounted for the possibility that non–speech-related alternative measures would suffice to prevent the drug approval process from being undermined.[124] As the Court's conservatives continued to ratchet up the stringency of the *Central Hudson* test, free speech and the free market were increasingly difficult to disaggregate.

The Commerce Clause in the original body of the Constitution expressly contemplated governmental regulation of the commercial sphere—and the contested breadth of this grant, of course, has fueled more than two centuries of ideological controversy. Commerce, however, has always required expression. This is not a new insight. A willing consumer must be made aware that there are things to consume—otherwise, there would be no commerce. In other words, the "demand" side of the "supply and demand" equation is largely premised upon expression. Remove the ability to regulate the expressive component of commerce, and government's ability to intervene in economic affairs takes a huge hit.

The pharmaceutical industry—the target of the Court's initial "switch in time" on commercial speech—is illustrative. The impetus for regulating this industry is self-evident. Most would readily agree that the intensive expertise, education, and training required to make informed decisions about pharmaceutical drug availability and consumption, and the high-stakes risks and rewards inherent in drug use or misuse, mean that some form of regulation is necessary. Complete deregulation—removing drugs entirely from the ambit of the law—is not a position one generally observes in mainstream political discourse. This, however, is where the agreement ends. Although most libertarians do not advocate an anarchic view with regard to "supply"—drug legalization advocacy for certain limited classes of illegal drugs notwithstanding—regulation of "demand" is another matter entirely.

Government regulation of supply remains a widely accepted practice—for example, requiring a doctor's prescription or simply criminalizing certain drugs. However, under the Court's commercial speech jurisprudence post–*Virginia Board of Pharmacy*, governments are losing the ability to regulate demand. Arguing the need for this latter form of regulation, Justice Breyer, in dissent, explained that here, the "restrictions try to assure that demand is generated doctor-to-patient-to-pharmacist, not pharmacist-to-advertisement-to-patient-to-doctor. And they do so in order to diminish the likelihood that those who do not genuinely need untested compounded drugs will not receive them."[125] In a line of argument that implicitly throws into question not just the restriction on compounded drug advertising at issue in *Western States Medical Center* but the entire deregulatory thrust of the Court's modern commercial speech jurisprudence, Breyer points to the "considerable evidence that consumer oriented advertising will create strong consumer-driven demand for a particular drug [and] that doctors will often respond affirmatively to a patient's request for a specific drug that the patient has seen advertised."[126] To the conservative majority, this affirmation of demand is unobjectionable—even beneficial. It is the free market at work—empowering individuals to make their own decisions rather than keeping them "in the dark for what the government perceives to be their own good."[127] However, where the majority sees empowerment, the dissent sees circumvention of critical consumer protections. Breyer points out, "71% of the active members of the American Academy of Family Physicians 'believe that direct-to-consumer advertising pressures physicians into prescribing drugs that they would not ordinarily prescribe.'"[128]

The *Lochner* Volley

Ever since Chief Justice Rehnquist first alluded to *Lochner*-era judicial overreach in his *Virginia Board of Pharmacy* dissent, the bogeyman of economic substantive due process would make frequent reappearances in the commercial speech context. *Western States Medical Center* was no exception. Justice Breyer, like Rehnquist before him, compared the majority's holding to the "tragic constitutional misunderstanding" in the due process arena that for a protracted period during the Great Depression prevented "the legislature from enacting necessary protections."[129] Almost a decade later, in *Sorrell v. IMS Health*, a decision that would take the deregulatory possibilities of the First Amendment to a new level, Chief Justice Roberts had the foresight to preempt the inevitable *Lochner* reference.

In *IMS Health*, the five most conservative members of the Court—plus Justice Sotomayor—struck down the Vermont Prescription Confidentiality Law. The law prohibited pharmacies and others from selling or using prescriber-identifying information for marketing purposes without the prescriber's consent. At first glance, one might struggle to see the First Amendment issue—

regulating the sale or distribution of personal medical data would not appear on its face to implicate any standard free-speech interests. This information is not speech in the traditional sense; it is raw data and does not convey any identifiable idea or ideas. Justice Breyer framed the stakes thusly: "The Vermont statute before us adversely affects expression in one, and only one, way. It deprives pharmaceutical and data-mining companies of data, collected pursuant to the government's regulatory mandate, that could help pharmaceutical companies create better sales messages."[130] The majority, however, was deeply troubled by the content-based and speaker-based nature of the law.[131] The law not only targeted specific content, but it applied differently to different speakers. Under the Vermont law, the same information that is prohibited from purchase by those who would use it for marketing may be purchased or acquired by others who would use the information for non-marketing purposes—for example, academic organizations.[132]

In a breathtaking rhetorical inversion, Chief Justice Roberts cites Justice Holmes—not in his role as steadfast free-speech champion, but as dissenter against the activist free-market conservative Court of *Lochner v. New York*.[133] Roberts tells us, in Holmes's famous words, that the "Constitution 'does not enact Mr. Herbert Spencer's Social Statics.'"[134] Roberts would seem to be suggesting that if the Court were to uphold the Vermont law, it would effectively be conceding a First Amendment that takes sides in economic debates—in this instance, singling out for special disfavored treatment commercial speech and market-based interests.

However, placed in context, it is clear that Holmes's *Lochner* dissent was excoriating not a democratically elected legislature's choices, but the majority of the Supreme Court for using *its* raw *judicial* power to strike down a law simply because *it* did not agree with the law's economic, not legal, premises. It was the *Lochner* Court's choice to override the democratic will of the people and impose its own "economic theory which a large part of the country does not entertain"[135] that Holmes found so objectionable. In other words, contrary to the chief justice's suggestion, critics of the majority *IMS Health* decision would have cause to make the very same claim.

7 Citizens United and the Paradox of Associational Speech

Citizens United v. FEC has proven to be one of the most controversial, contested, and ideologically divisive decisions of the modern Supreme Court.[1] No discussion of conservatism and the First Amendment could be complete without an exploration of this 2010 5–4 opinion, which overturned significant Court precedent, reshaping political campaigning in America.[2] In *Citizens United*, the Court struck down a federal law prohibiting independent expenditures by unions and corporations "in connection with any election to any political office, or in connection with any primary election or political convention or caucus held to select candidates for any political office."[3] Heightening the perception by critics that the Court had taken a sharp reactionary turn,[4] the Court reversed and substantially eroded its own precedent.[5]

However, there is another way of viewing this decision. In providing corporations with a constitutional right to spend unlimited sums of money on political communications—what the Court and others dub "corporate speech"—the Court's conservatives were merely tracking their trajectory on free speech, now decades in the making. In subsequent years *Citizens United* would be followed by similarly ideologically divided First Amendment decisions addressing campaign finance law, such as *Arizona Free Enterprise Club v. Bennett*[6] and *McCutcheon v. FEC*,[7] in which the Court's five conservatives would once again

This chapter has been adapted from an article that was published in 2012. Wayne Batchis, Citizens United *and the Paradox of "Corporate Speech"* From Freedom of Association to Freedom of the *Association,* 36 N.Y.U. REV. L. & SOC. CHANGE 5 (2012).

unite to strike down laws on free-speech grounds in the face of dissents from the Court's four liberals.

However, *Citizens United* was different from these cases in that it also emanated from the Court's freedom of association jurisprudence, a doctrinal line of cases that was historically championed by the Court's liberals. Over the past seventy-five years, the Court has moved from recognizing a non-textual freedom of an individual to associate with others—understanding this right to be a "medium"[8] by which individuals express their textual freedom of speech—to offering constitutional protection to "speech" by the association itself. Thus, a shift originating with the Court's liberals marks what is perhaps the most pronounced First Amendment ideological split today. In a few short decades, the freedom of association became a freedom of *the* association; it has been divorced from the individual right—and political ideology—from which it was begotten.

This chapter takes a rather different form and tone from earlier portions of this study. In this chapter, I make a normative argument about the freedom of association as a discrete area of First Amendment doctrine. It is a critique that recognizes the profound influence ideology can have in spurring doctrinal change. Like a decorative weed planted with good intentions, a new doctrinal constitutional interpretation can grow in unexpected directions, sometimes with undesirable consequences. Both political liberals and political conservatives on the Supreme Court have been guilty of innovative First Amendment interpretation. Expanding the application of a constitutional principle to new or unanticipated factual contexts is, of course, neither inherently good nor bad. Indeed, it is the stuff of normative legal analysis, filling the pages of law reviews and many a dissent on the Supreme Court. In this chapter, I merge a critical analysis of the evolution of a particular First Amendment doctrine with an examination of ideology both on and off the Court.

The opinions in *Citizens United*—majority, concurrences, and dissents—take for granted the constitutional existence of something called "corporate speech." Perhaps a testament to the independent power of doctrine, legal interpretation, and precedent, the liberals and conservatives were in this regard unified. It is true that Justice Stevens, who was at the time the most liberal member on the Court,[9] issued a remarkably lengthy and comprehensive dissent writing for himself and the three other liberal justices.[10] However, when Justice Stevens reached the question of corporate speech, his powerful voice of dissent was tempered. He tepidly explained: "Given that corporations were conceived of as artificial entities and do not have the technical capacity to 'speak,' the burden of establishing that the Framers and ratifiers understood 'the freedom of speech' to encompass corporate speech is, I believe, far heavier than the majority acknowledges."[11] He relegated this point—perhaps his strongest and most persuasive critique—to a mere footnote. Throughout his dissent, Stevens conceded that corporations themselves are "speakers," implicitly accepting the default position that they are potentially eligible for protections clearly designed for human beings by the amendment's framers.

Without the baseline foundation that corporate communications somehow constitute "speech," the conservative majority's opinion would have stood on nothing but ether. With it, the conservatives on the Court were able to craft a decision that even the adamant dissenters admitted had "rhetorical appeal."[12] Why did it have such appeal? Because the *Citizens United* majority won the jurisprudential language war. Stevens used the term "corporate speech" fourteen times throughout his dissent.[13] Scholars and journalists of all stripes have likewise blithely accepted the assumption that there is something called "corporate speech."[14]

In doing so, the dissenters—and others who find the *Citizens United* decision troubling—have ceded unnecessary ground. By reifying corporations and imbuing them with the sympathetic qualities of citizens seeking to assert their fundamental First Amendment freedoms, the majority opinion resembled constitutional common sense. It became the liberal dissenters who seemed to be sidestepping "ancient"[15] constitutional principles, at the same time appearing to violate the liberal tradition of robust support for free-speech values. The result was that the dubious underlying assumptions of the majority were validated.

The Decision

For over a century, the United States has struggled to establish a regime of effective campaign finance laws to address myriad concerns about the influence of money on politics. Congress passed the first significant federal campaign finance law, the Tillman Act, in 1907, at the urging of President Theodore Roosevelt.[16] However, it was not until 1976, in *Buckley v. Valeo*, that the Supreme Court held that restrictions on campaign spending may constitute a restraint on protected political speech in violation of the First Amendment.[17]

In *Buckley*, the Court famously split the baby, leaving only half of the ambitious Federal Election Campaign Act of 1972 (FECA) and its amendments intact.[18] Opposition to this early wave of comprehensive campaign finance reform produced strange ideological bedfellows—liberals with their strong attachment to First Amendment principles aligned with free-market and libertarian conservatives who objected to attempts to quell the influence of money through more aggressive government regulation. Conservative Republican James L. Buckley and liberal Democrat Eugene McCarthy joined forces to lead the First Amendment legal challenge against FECA.[19]

The decision was remarkably complex and addressed a wide range of constitutional questions. Ultimately, the Court issued a per curiam opinion that brought together the most liberal justice on the Court at the time, Justice Brennan, with its most conservative, Justice Rehnquist.[20] The *Buckley* Court struck down spending restrictions on political communications but upheld restrictions on political contributions to candidates or campaigns.[21] However, the litigants never asked the Court to address the constitutionality of the bar on *corporate* contributions and expenditures.[22] According to Justice Stevens, the *Buckley* Court's "silence on corporations only reinforced the understanding that corporate expenditures could be treated differently from individual expenditures."[23]

The View from *Review*

Shortly before the new campaign finance reform legislation that was the focus of *Buckley* was on the table, *National Review* anticipated the likely constitutional questions and adopted a pro–free-speech posture. The legislation would lead to a many-decades-long cascade of critical First Amendment decisions addressing the relationship between campaign spending and free speech. Discussing the prospect of campaign finance legislation, a 1973 editorial opined: "Financing a candidate to one's heart's content is presumably among the activities the First Amendment protects. Free speech has some limitations, but the evidence disclosed to date is not convincing on the point that giving more than $3,000 to a candidate is like crying 'fire' in a crowded theater."[24]

What explains this instinctive rush to defend First Amendment values— bolstered by a reference to the famed language of liberal jurisprudential hero Oliver Wendell Holmes, Jr.—even in the absence of actual legislation that would purportedly pose a threat? The final two paragraphs of this brief editorial suggest an answer. First, the editorial implied that corporate influence in government, and the influence of those with money generally, is a social good. The magazine asked: "[W]hat to do about corporations that influence public officials by promising them employment after they leave government service?"[25] And answered: "Any legislation that precluded such employment after government service would likely keep the best qualified people out of government."[26] The piece also reflected the suspicion that any proposed campaign finance reform legislation would likely be structured to favor liberal interests: "And then there are the labor unions. If they are omitted from the campaign financing regulation, the reforms will be biased and half-baked."[27] Thus, from an instrumentalist perspective, we see an early awareness that in this setting the First Amendment could be used as a tool to thwart a liberal political agenda.

Less than two years later, when the U.S. Court of Appeals for the District of Columbia initially upheld the campaign finance reform legislation that eventually did materialize, the magazine opined that "the First Amendment has become a ball of silly putty."[28] Although the editorial did not expressly retract the largely narrow vision of the First Amendment advocated by the magazine in other contexts, it was quick to point out what it saw as liberal hypocrisy.[29] The magazine contemptuously argued that the same supposed First Amendment advocates who rushed to defend as free speech the publication of government secrets, pornography, "flag-burnings and blood-pourings" readily dismissed the First Amendment concerns about "a law that restricts candidates from spending their own money to get out their political messages."[30] On the Supreme Court at that time, this would turn out not to be true, at least with regard to the Court's most liberal justice, Brennan,[31] who would vote to strike down the spending limits in *Buckley*.[32] The editorial cited with approval words of a dissenting judge on the circuit court, applauding his conclusion that the law represented a form of "paternalism" that is "completely alien to our system of democratic government."[33] For a publication with a long record, at the time, of First Amendment minimalism, this editorial seemed to take pride in its posture as a free-speech champion, lamenting the "beating" the First Amendment was given by the circuit court majority.[34]

In the 1980s, as we saw with commercial speech in the last chapter, mainstream political conservatives began to take on the role of First Amendment advocates in discrete areas. Campaign finance reform was one such area—and in writing about the issue, *National Review* repeatedly adhered to a strongly speech-protective stance. Thus, in a lengthy 1980 piece addressing the challenges inherent in attempting to legislatively reform political campaigns, journalist Ida Walters alluded to *Buckley* and concluded: "Perhaps the best solution is to do what the Supreme Court almost did in 1976: throw out the whole bundle of campaign-reform laws on the ground that they violate the constitutional right of free speech."[35]

In 2002, Congress passed the Bipartisan Campaign Reform Act (BCRA), which intended to comprehensively address the perceived regulatory gaps left behind in *Buckley*'s wake.[36] It represented the most significant attempt at reforming campaign finance since the passage of FECA and its amendments. Like FECA before it, BCRA was comprehensively challenged on First Amendment grounds. In the politically momentous decision *McConnell v. FEC*, the Court upheld the vast majority of BCRA, including the provision that prohibited corporate use of "general treasury funds to finance electioneering activity."[37] Strikingly, in the decades since *Buckley*, the Court had grown much more ideologically polarized on the First Amendment implications of campaign finance reform. The core issues in *McConnell* were resolved in a 5–4 ideological split, in which the most liberal justices at the time—Justices Stevens, Ginsburg, Souter, Breyer—and the moderate-conservative O'Connor[38] formed a bloc to uphold the law's key provisions.[39]

Just over six years after *McConnell*, the Court handed down *Citizens United*. In the interim, Justice O'Connor, the lone remaining conservative justice who generally voted to uphold campaign restrictions under the First Amendment, retired from the Court. If any question remained after *McConnell* of the correlation between ideology and a justice's view of campaign spending and the First Amendment, the sharp 5–4 breakdown in *Citizens United* (and indeed, in a number of subsequent cases[40]) would dispel such doubts. *Citizens United* was not a mere a refutation of *McConnell*.

McConnell's focus was on the many dramatic changes BCRA made to campaign finance law, including a ban on soft money contributions and new disclosure requirements, among other changes.[41] In *McConnell*, the basic principle that corporations and unions may be prohibited from using their treasury funds for express political advocacy appeared beyond question. The *McConnell* Court characterized this understanding as "firmly embedded in our law."[42] It explained that the formation and administration of PACs—separate organizations allowing corporations to solicit individual contributions used for political expenditures—"has provided corporations and unions with a constitutionally sufficient opportunity to engage in express advocacy. This has been the Court's unanimous view, and it [was] not challenged in [the *McConnell*] litigation."[43]

In *Citizens United*, however, the conservative majority reached beyond *McConnell* and took specific aim at *Austin v. Michigan Chamber of Commerce*, the 1990 decision that had "firmly embedded" the principle that banning corporations and unions from using their treasury funds for political advocacy was constitutionally valid.[44] It did so despite the fact that—as the *Citizens United* dissenters would point out—the notion that campaign spending by corporations may be treated differently than individual spending had largely gone unquestioned for over a hundred years.[45] Notably, *Austin* was decided before ideological positions on the issue had fully solidified. In 1990, Chief Justice Rehnquist, at the time the most conservative justice on the Court,[46] had signed on to the 6–3 decision upholding the ban.[47]

In the aftermath of *Citizens United*, *National Review* articles addressing the constitutionality of campaign finance reform leave to the dustpan of history any lingering perception that free speech might have at one time been thought to be an exclusively "liberal" value. In 2010 Shannen Coffin celebrated the *Citizens United* decision by heaping praise on the Court for affirming "a longstanding principle—anathema to the Left—that 'political speech does not lose First Amendment protection 'simply because its source is a corporation.'"[48] The same year, Bradley Smith wrote a piece tarring Democrats in Congress for supporting the DISCLOSE Act, a piece of legislation that ultimately failed to become law but was intended to address the perceived harm done to the American electoral process by *Citizens United*.[49]

On its face, the law was designed to increase transparency by requiring extensive disclosure of those—both individuals and corporations—who make expenditures intended to influence elections. Smith, however, argued that the law, if passed, would be unconstitutional, drawing upon a celebrated 1958 civil rights decision, *NAACP v. Alabama*—discussed in the coming pages—to make his case.[50] The decision addressed narrow circumstances in which complying with a membership disclosure law in civil rights–era Alabama would have placed members at significant risk. It thus struck down this application of the law as a violation of the First Amendment's implicit freedom of association.[51] Smith omits any sense of how narrow and factually bound this case was, asserting that the Court simply "held that the government cannot compel groups to reveal their member lists and financial supporters."[52]

However, perhaps even more damning than what Smith saw as the DISCLOSE Act's constitutional infirmity was that this proposed legislation—as well as all campaign finance reform generally—had an inherently nefarious purpose. Smith asserted that "[a] key goal of every 'reform' bill has been partisan gain."[53] He cited as evidence a memorandum of Elena Kagan, then an aide to President Bill Clinton, describing the anticipated partisan impact of the McCain–Feingold legislation. The proposed law was not merely a misguided attempt to address an issue that did not truly need addressing, which along the way would adversely inhibit free speech; for Smith, the legislation's "real purpose" was to "burden speech."[54]

In the following section, I trace the gradual emergence of a First Amendment freedom of *the* association. As we shall see, without this jurisprudential wrong turn, *Citizens United* would not have been possible.

The Constitutional History of Associational Rights
A Funny Thing Happened on the Way to Citizens United

The question of whether organizational membership for expression-related purposes is afforded First Amendment protection was first posed to the Supreme Court in the 1927 case *Whitney v. California.*[55] Although the Court rejected the defendant's claim of First Amendment immunity, it implicitly accepted, with minimal explanation, the view that "association" is to be included alongside the textual protections of "speech" and "assembly."[56] As discussed in the Introduction, it was the liberal Justice Brandeis, with his famously impassioned concurrence, who would have gone much further in protecting First Amendment interests. Nonetheless, *Whitney* can be read to support the proposition that the freedom of speech may in some circumstances encompass an individual's right to join an association—albeit in language that was arguably just dicta.[57] At root, this early articulation of a freedom of association remained centered within a discourse of individual rights.[58] Gradually, however, in the decades ahead, the freedom of association would gradually morph into something very different—culminating, of course, in the stunning leap for associational rights in *Citizens United.*

This evolution began in the civil rights era of the 1950s. In *NAACP v. Alabama* ex rel. *Patterson*, the liberal Warren Court firmly and explicitly established that a freedom of association is included among the protections provided by the Constitution.[59] *Patterson* may be the most recognizable doctrinal starting point demarcating an unequivocal right to association. However, the constitutional underpinnings of the opinion are, in many respects, enigmatic. While the *Patterson* Court took care to limit freedom of association to the adjudication of an association member's individual rights, the Court did not elucidate this point as thoroughly as it could have. As a result, *Patterson* added association to the Court's jurisprudential arsenal in a manner that would contribute to more than half a century of troubling ambiguity as to the source and scope of this right.

John D. Inazu speculates that the vague language of the opinion was perhaps a way for its author, Justice Harlan, to achieve a unanimous opinion.

According to Inazu, disputes within the Court eventually led Harlan to strip his draft of language explicitly grounding the associational right in the First Amendment. "Justice Douglas and Frankfurter were both troubled by the draft language, but for opposite reasons. Frankfurter pushed for Harlan to rely expressly on the liberty argument and avoid any mention of the First Amendment."[60] It was the exceedingly liberal Justice "Douglas, on the other hand, [who] feared that Harlan's due process analysis diluted the First Amendment as applied to the states."[61] Although the liberal First Amendment absolutist Justice Black eventually relented, he "thought that the opinion . . . read 'as though the First Amendment did not exist'" and thus intended to file a concurring opinion clarifying his view.[62] Initial reaction to *Patterson* by legal scholars mirrored the lack of clarity in the opinion; there was great disagreement within the community of legal commentators regarding the constitutional source of this newly identified right of association.[63]

In *Patterson*, a very liberal Court unanimously struck down, as applied to the NAACP, an Alabama law that required the association to publicly disclose a list of its members.[64] The association itself, as an entity, was deemed an appropriate party to bring the constitutional claim.[65] The Court reasoned that the disclosure required by the Alabama law would have a "deterrent effect" on speech-related freedoms in the Jim Crow South.[66] The Court explained that there was an "uncontroverted showing that on past occasions revelation of the identity of [the NAACP's] rank-and-file members has exposed these members to economic reprisal, loss of employment, threat of physical coercion, and other manifestations of public hostility."[67]

As in *Whitney*, the Court in *Patterson* tossed "association" into the mix alongside the explicit textual rights provided by the First Amendment; here, the Court referred to "indispensible liberties . . . of speech, press or association."[68] Unlike *Whitney*, the Court proceeded to explain specifically how and why an associational right can and should be derived from these other liberties. Wrote Justice Harlan for the majority, "Effective advocacy of both public and private points of view, particularly controversial ones, is undeniably enhanced by group association . . . [t]his Court has more than once recognized [this] by remarking upon the close nexus between the freedoms of speech and assembly."[69]

While Justice Harlan acknowledged the logical relationship between association and speech, a close reading of the decision shows that he also took care to state that the constitutional implications of this relationship were limited to the adjudication of an association member's individual rights. Here, the

NAACP was granted standing because it "assert[ed], on behalf of its members, *a right personal to them*."[70] To the Court, the association was a mere "medium through which its individual members" were able to express their ideas.[71] In other words, at this point in the Court's jurisprudential history, the "freedom of association" had not yet become synonymous with "freedom of *the* association." There was no suggestion in the opinion that associations qua associations may assert First Amendment rights.[72] Indeed, as I shall argue, to claim that they could is to carve out an entirely new set of rights, rights nowhere to be found in the Constitution itself. As is exemplified by *Citizens United*, such associational rights may even be in tension with the actual individual rights enumerated in the Constitution.

A quarter of a century after *Patterson*, the Court revisited the so-called freedom of association in *Roberts v. United States Jaycees*.[73] By this time, the Court had issued numerous decisions addressing associational rights through the prism of substantive due process, without addressing the communication of ideas.[74] In *Roberts*, the Court drew a clear distinction between the due process and communicative lines of association cases.[75] The Court reasoned that, while at times these classes of associational rights may overlap, the liberty interest of "maintain[ing] certain intimate relationships" implicates fundamentally different concerns than the right to join together with others in order to participate "in those activities protected by the First Amendment—speech, assembly, petition for the redress of grievances, and the exercise of religion."[76] Thus, in *Roberts*, the Court for the first time used the phrase "expressive association," a fresh term of art that would help solidify this relatively new concept in constitutional adjudication.[77] Indeed, the Court used the term in twelve additional cases in the twenty-six years between *Roberts*, decided in 1984, and *Citizens United*, decided in 2010. During this period, "expressive association" evolved from verb to noun—from an individual right to an entity itself purportedly deserving of First Amendment rights.

In *Roberts*, the freedoms of *both* "intimate association" *and* "expressive association" were at issue. The respondent claimed that its members' freedom of association had been violated by the application of a Minnesota antidiscrimination statute.[78] Under the law, the Jaycees, an organization with a policy of denying full membership to women, was required to admit women as regular members.[79]

After disposing of the intimate association question—and holding that a "large" and "unselective" group such as the Jaycees may not exclude particular members under the constitutional shelter of a right of intimate association[80]—the Court proceeded to explore whether expressive association was implicated. The majority opinion, penned by Justice Brennan, stated clearly that the "[f]reedom of association . . . plainly presupposes a freedom not to associate."[81] Requiring an association to include members it would otherwise exclude would "interfere with the internal organization . . . of the group" and potentially intrude upon the associational freedoms of individual members.[82]

However, the Court explained that it must balance any asserted adverse impact on associational rights against the compelling interests of the state—here, combating gender discrimination and promoting public access.[83] Like in *Pittsburgh Press*, discussed in Chapter 5, *Roberts* was presumably a case in which the liberals on the Court felt some degree of internal conflict: on one hand, their commitment to a continued expansion of a freedom of association doctrine informed by a history of highly speech-protective liberal First Amendment jurisprudence and, on the other hand, their progressive goal of gender equality. Using its balancing formulation, the Court—including all of the liberal justices—ultimately upheld the Minnesota law, despite the First Amendment concerns.[84]

Upon first glance, it might appear that little had changed since *Patterson*—aside, of course, from the added complexity that accompanies the newly articulated dual-track analysis for associational freedom. As for the nature of so-called expressive association, however, it still appeared from much of the language of the decision to be a quintessential *individual* right. Justice Brennan repeatedly referred to the relevant alleged infringement as one that occurred against the "male members" of the organization.[85] In other words, the rights at stake were the rights of the association's individual members, not the association itself. Indeed, the complaint itself stated the claim in these terms, alleging that "application of the Act would violate the *male members'* constitutional rights of free speech and association."[86] The members of the Jaycees were simply bringing suit on behalf of *their* individual right to freely associate. Or were they?

Reading a bit closer, one notices certain points in the *Roberts* opinion in which the lines begin to blur, and it becomes somewhat less clear that the Court was protecting a purely individual right. Justice Brennan inserted language in his opinion that clouded the issue—for example, where he conceded that "enforcement of the Act causes some incidental abridgement *of the Jaycees'* protected speech."[87] Whatever it may mean for an organization without vocal chords, penmanship, or a brain to "speak," the Jaycees' purported speech is not necessarily synonymous with the interests of individual "male members" to associate with a likeminded group of individuals for the purpose of "speaking." Yet, the Court did not address this troubling, perhaps subtle, conundrum. In fact, the Court failed to acknowledge that it interchangeably referred to what are really two distinct interests.

Quite simply, the expressive interests of an organization are distinguishable from—if not at odds with—the expressive interests of many of its individual members. This is particularly true in the case of sizable general-interest organizations such as the Jaycees. Associations that serve a wide array of goals, and are large enough in size to accommodate a broad range of members, most of whom do not even know one another, are bound to include individuals with a diversity of viewpoints. Members participate in associations for a wide variety of reasons, particularly when such organizations have loosely defined objectives and engage in a broad range of activities. Indeed, one could easily imagine a member of the Jaycees remaining affiliated with the organization despite, rather than because of, its ostensibly male-centric message.

When focus shifts from the constitutional rights of individual members to those of the organization itself, constitutional tensions such as this one become increasingly apparent. Just whose right to "speak" was being infringed upon by Minnesota? Who was the "speaker" in *Roberts*, considering that the organization served many goals and contained a diversity of viewpoints? If the organization itself is eligible for First Amendment protection, should this "right" be treated any differently if only 51 percent of the members individually share the desire to speak a particular message? What if the number is only 5 percent?

Admittedly, an organization such as the Jaycees is a voluntary one; members who are disgruntled with a particular organizational message may revoke their membership at any time. However, voluntary resignation is not necessarily a reasonable expectation where the expression of certain disagreeable ideas represents just a small fraction of an organization's overall activities. On balance, an individual member might understandably determine that the benefits of continued membership outweigh the costs of being a disgruntled accomplice to unwanted speech. In the alternative, a member may neither find the time nor have the inclination to learn of the "speech" propagated by the organization in the first place.

Once we acknowledge the inherent tension between individual free speech and so-called associational speech, vexing questions arise. For example, are there any circumstances under which conflicting interests of particular members who wish to assert their right *not* to speak would trump the association's right? This issue is particularly germane in the case of organizations so large and diverse that it would not be reasonable to expect each individual member take the time to vet all official organizational speech.

In a perfect world, the right of the association itself *would* correlate directly with the right of the individuals who comprise the association. In the case of a small association that is 100 percent devoted to speech, the choice of individual members to remain affiliated with that association would presumably—again, in a perfect world—be entirely rooted in each individual's continued support for that association's speech. In such a scenario, it might be said that the association's speech is an unequivocal proxy for individual speech. Individuals in this perfect world would either become members or revoke their membership, entirely on the basis of whether or not they want to utilize the association as a First Amendment conduit.

Justice O'Connor's concurrence in *Roberts* acknowledged some of the complications that become inevitable when the *individual* right of free speech morphs into a *collective* right. By contrasting a hypothetical organization "engaged exclusively in protected expression" with a commercial association engaged in a limited amount of "incidental" speech, Justice O'Connor obliquely addressed this definitional challenge.[88] For Justice O'Connor, this is the crux of the problem:

> Many associations cannot readily be described as purely expressive or purely commercial. No association is likely ever to be exclusively engaged in expressive activities, if only because it will collect dues from its members or purchase printing materials or rent lecture halls or serve coffee and cakes at its meetings.[89]

Furthermore, even an ostensibly pure expressive association will presumably propagate a range of communication, and with associations of significant size, it would be the rare case that absolute agreement was reached among all members as to each expressive idea conveyed.[90] Collective action typically involves some degree of compromise, even among highly cohesive groups.

Catalyzed by quintessential liberal political interests—the civil rights movement of the 1950s and 1960s—the Court had opened the door to an associational right of expression in *Patterson*, and the moderate O'Connor, ever the pragmatist, was seeking a workable middle-ground standard that could be applied going forward. While Justice O'Connor is to be commended as an outlier justice who acknowledged the doctrinal conundrum, her proposed solution is unsatisfying. O'Connor's framework would require the construction of artificial doctrinal categories for each association asserting a claim to this new constitutional right of expressive association.[91] O'Connor's test would require an assessment of whether a particular "association is predominantly engaged in protected expression," which even O'Connor herself conceded would be "difficult" to "determine."[92] Only if this question is answered in the affirmative would "state regulation of its membership [be determined to] affect, change, dilute, or silence one collective voice that would otherwise be heard."[93]

This framework is problematic. It is questionable that it is possible to determine with principled consistency what constitutes "predominant engagement" in expression by an association. O'Connor stated that the "proper approach to analysis of First Amendment claims of associational freedom is . . . to distinguish nonexpressive from expressive associations and to recognize that the former lack the full constitutional protections possessed by the latter."[94] But courts are poorly equipped to quantify the activities and purposes of organizations in a manner that would avoid claims of unconstitutional vagueness. Under this framework, laws regulating associations would cast a shadow of constitutional uncertainty on all organizations that might—but also might not—be determined to be an "expressive association." More critically, this proposed test would further the misconception that the First Amendment should confer a right to associations per se, rather than a right to the individuals who may or may not choose to exercise *their* rights *through* an association.

O'Connor is not the only one to have struggled with this question of freedom of association. Many scholars, in numerous disciplines, have devoted considerable effort to unpacking the meaning and import of freedom of association.[95] Ashutosh Bhagwat argues that the Supreme Court went astray, not by acknowledging a First Amendment associational right, but by linking it to speech.[96] He points to the similarities between the textual right to "assembly" found in the First Amendment and the concept of association.[97] However, it takes quite a logical leap to conclude that because there is a textual right to assemble, and an assembly is related in form and purpose to an association, that we should extend First Amendment rights to associations, qua associations. Indeed, Bhagwat acknowledges that there is historical "ambiguity about whether the assembly and petition clauses were understood by (some of) the Framing generation to protect permanent associations."[98]

While Bhagwat agrees that the O'Connor formulation is flawed—affording free-speech rights to associations based on a nebulous assessment of whether or not a particular association is "expressive"—his proposed alternative is perhaps even more problematic.[99] To Bhagwat, the

> better distinction is one drawn based on the primary *goals* of the association at issue. Protected associations are those whose primary goals are relevant to the democratic process. These include not only expression but also political organization, value formation, and the cultivation of skills relevant to participation in the democratic process.[100]

However, asking courts to draw such lines—effectively picking and choosing which associations are deserving of First Amendment protection—would on its face appear to demand wildly subjective decision making. There are likely as many views on what "skills" are "relevant to participation in the democratic process," and how to effectively "cultivate" those skills, as there are judges.

The Court's confused constitutional jurisprudence in *Roberts*, originating with the ideologically inspired doctrinal nudge in *Patterson*, laid the groundwork for the unfortunate *Boy Scouts of America v. Dale* decision and, ultimately, for *Citizens United*. These are cases in which the Court's conservatives grabbed the reins of the First Amendment and reversed the traditional ideological alignment in a subset of associational free-speech cases.

The right of association as a First Amendment protection was still taking shape throughout the late 1980s. It was clear that the ability to choose one's associates was deserving of First Amendment protection on the theory that individual association leads to a more dynamic exchange of ideas both within that group and to the outside world.[101] It was also well settled that associating with others had a close relationship with the ability to speak freely and assemble.[102] However, the contours of the right to associate—as a First Amendment claim in itself—were far from clear. Many questions remained regarding the extent to which a government could regulate the membership of an organization. The Court stated that "effective advocacy . . . is undeniably enhanced by group association,"[103] while at the same time conceding that an association is "but the medium though which its individual members seek to make more effective the expression of their own views."[104] Although the Court had yet to fully embrace the view that associations are, for First Amendment purposes, distinct from the individuals who comprise them, its opinions left open the possibility that it might eventually be willing to untether the associational right from the individual right.

A New Century, a New Constitution

Going forward, the challenge for the Court was to determine precisely *how* to establish the boundaries of the freedom of association. Free association is quite simply, in many circumstances, a speech facilitator. This does not mean, however, that this ancillary or derivative right should, or must, become an *equivalent* to the initial right. The Court had elaborated, beginning in *Roberts*, that this qualified freedom of association comes in two varieties: expressive and intimate. Both are *subsets* of association. Association does not necessarily fall into one of these categories, but in order to be constitutionally protected, the association at issue should presumably have a concrete connection to an actual constitutional right.

At the turn of the twenty-first century, a range of questions still confronted the Court regarding associational rights. The weakness of categorizing association into expressive and intimate varieties was that the categories themselves begged the most important questions. Just how are courts to determine when an association is expressive or intimate in nature? Are such categories dichotomous or do they exist on a continuum? Of course, the latter answer might be more reflective of reality—instances of expressive or intimate action are likely to be found in almost every human exchange. Such an acknowledgment, however, makes the task of constitutional adjudication more daunting.

Indeed, a range of difficult questions emerges from the Court's evolving doctrinal framework surrounding the freedom of association. How should the Court treat an association that is "just a little bit" expressive or "somewhat" intimate? Should it allocate constitutional rights on a sliding scale, or should the freedom of association be an all-or-nothing proposition? Finally, and of central concern here, what of the relationship between the individual and the association? Should a constitutional right *to join* an association suggest a concomitant constitutional right *of the association* to determine *its* membership? If so, how do we go about determining the true, unified voice of that association? An association, like any collective body, contains a range of views and desires. While it may make sense to impute, for some purposes, "a single voice" to an association, particularly for corporations and other entities provided with a unique legal status, this unified voice is ultimately something of a convenient fiction.

A critical turning point for the freedom of *the* association came in 2000, when, in *Boy Scouts of America v. Dale*, an ideologically fractured Supreme Court confronted many of these lingering questions.[105] In *Boy Scouts*, the Court for the first time held a state antidiscrimination law unconstitutional as applied against an association's exclusionary membership policy.[106] Cobbling together disparate elements from the Court's confused precedents addressing the so-called right of expressive association—minted less than two decades earlier—a five-member majority composed of the most conservative member of the Court at the time[107] struck down the application of a New Jersey public accommodations statute.[108] The law would have required the reinstatement of an adult Boy Scout leader whose membership had been revoked based on his sexual orientation.[109]

Justice Rehnquist wrote the majority opinion. Here Rehnquist was outside of the commercial speech context, where, as discussed in the previous chapters, the changing world of First Amendment conservatism had transformed him from a status quo conservative critical of expansive speech rights into a conservative outlier, out of sync with the new libertarian and free-market conservative norm. In *Boy Scouts*, Rehnquist was comfortably within a factual setting in which a speech-protective holding would be well aligned with his moralistic worldview. He was quick to adopt, with minimal explanation, what had been a perspective articulated only by Justice O'Connor. In so doing, he was able to convert an after-the-fact policy statement against homosexuality by a "representative" of an organization composed of over 1 million members into a tool for unprecedented and potentially limitless constitutional immunity.

The Court acknowledged that "the Scout Oath and Law do not expressly mention sexuality or sexual orientation" and conceded that "[d]ifferent people would attribute . . . very different meanings" to Scout Oath and Law terms such as "morally straight" and "clean."[110] However, under the guise of judicial modesty, the Court professed, "it is not the role of the courts to reject a group's expressed values because they disagree with those values or find them internally inconsistent."[111] To support this claim, the Court cited the well-established principle that First Amendment freedoms are not to be interfered with "on the ground that [a Court] view[s] a particular expression as unwise or irrational."[112]

However, the Court did not acknowledge the perverse consequences of applying this commonsense First Amendment principle to an entity to which it was simply not intended to apply. It is uncontroversial that the First Amendment protects individuals who make absurd or foolish statements and individuals whose speech is socially unpopular or broadly unaccepted.[113] However, there is simply no logical relationship between the goals behind this principle—promoting free and uninhibited expression of ideas by individuals—and the Court's refusal to apply scrutiny to an association's purported statement of its expressive values. The "unwisdom" or "irrationality" that Rehnquist rightfully argued is traditionally protected by the First Amendment is a protection intended for individuals. Yet he used it to immunize associations against claims of internal inconsistency—claims, in other words, that the ostensible expressive goals of the association do not authentically represent the views of the individuals who compose it. This deferential posture would afford immunity to any association that professes to be in some respect "expressive," exempting it from any regulation that might be said to even marginally or tangentially impact its "expressive message"—which, of course, can be defined however that organization decides to define it. This application of First Amendment principles where they do not belong—to associations themselves with a strained and insufficiently justified "group speech" theory—can only produce circular and potentially illimitable results.

The breadth with which the *Boy Scouts* Court defined what it means to be an expressive association has exacerbated this confusion. The conservative *Boy Scouts* Court seemed intent on establishing a bright-line rule that would do away with much of the nuance that consumed the Court in previous expressive association cases.[114] Rehnquist explained, quite succinctly: "To determine whether a group is protected by the First Amendment's expressive associational right, we must determine whether the group engages in 'expressive association.'"[115] This protection "is not reserved for advocacy groups."[116] To enjoy First Amendment protection, the association simply "must engage in some form of expression, whether it be public or private."[117] Under such a definition, it is difficult to imagine any group that would not qualify as an expressive association.

Beyond the initial inquiry, the *Boy Scouts* majority constructed a second threshold issue that must be answered in order to claim a right of expressive association. According to the Court, this next hurdle was to "determine whether the forced inclusion of Dale as an assistant scoutmaster would significantly affect the Boy Scouts' ability to advocate public or private viewpoints."[118] Once again, the Court asked a question with an answer that was effectively preordained. To answer it, we must "explore, to a limited extent, the nature of the Boy Scouts' *view* of homosexuality."[119] But the Court had already set up a dramatically deferential approach to determining an association's "view."[120] Putting aside the highly dubious proposition that a large and diverse general-interest organization such as the Boy Scouts even has a single, definable viewpoint, the Court told us that it would essentially take the association at its word, even in the face of contradictory evidence.[121] In other words, the viewpoint of an association is defined as whatever the anointed representative—for the purposes of the particular litigation—says it is.

The majority did not deny or refute the New Jersey Supreme Court's finding that the organization "includes sponsors and members who subscribe to different views in respect of homosexuality."[122] Rather, it dismissed the significance of this fact by concluding that "the First Amendment simply does not require that every member of a group agree on every issue in order for the group's policy to be 'expressive association.' The Boy Scouts takes an official position with respect to homosexual conduct, and that is sufficient for First Amendment purposes."[123]

This is a radical reconception of the First Amendment. One might even argue that such a conclusion turns the original reasoning for recognizing a First Amendment right to associate on its head. Under this conception, not only is the right to associate no longer primarily about acknowledging the link between associating with a group and facilitating individual speech, but here, the majority seems to be telling us that an association's speech may *trump* the speech of the individuals who comprise it. The Court strays unrecognizably far from the most common understanding of the First Amendment. Not only is the Court not protecting individual speech, but it is asserting that—by way of one "official statement" by a "representative" of a membership organization the size of Chicago[124]—a group may circumvent laws intended to protect individual liberties. At the same time the Court is carving out an unprecedented associational right, it is disregarding the fact that a sizable percentage of that association's members likely disagree with this "official" statement.[125]

As the exasperated liberal dissenters exclaimed, "We have never held . . . that a group can throw together any mixture of contradictory positions and then invoke the right to associate to defend any one of those views."[126] Yet the dissenters themselves contributed to the doctrinal confusion by conceding that "[a]t a minimum, a group . . . must adhere to a clear and unequivocal view."[127] Inspired by the critical civil rights issues at stake in *Patterson* and their ideological commitment to free-speech values that encouraged further expansive readings in subsequent cases, the liberals had backed themselves into a doctrinal corner. Their concession implicitly validated the fundamentally misguided approach to the First Amendment that enabled the majority to arrive at its holding. It accepted the underlying assumption that "group views" can somehow be determined with a requisite degree of certainty, such that any law that might indirectly interfere with that group's supposedly expressive actions may be struck down as unconstitutional. However, unless it is explicitly and closely tied to each individual's freedom of expression, such a formulation offers nothing other than a license for judicial activism akin to the economic substantive due process of the *Lochner* era.

Group rights are often at odds with the individual rights the First Amendment was intended to protect. The framers feared a tyranny of the majority, and the First Amendment was intended to protect individuals from oppressive government officials who might use their position to suppress unpopular speech.[128] The *Boy Scouts* majority inverted this principle, utilizing the First Amendment as a tool for oppression rather than as a remedy. Large organizations, particularly those the size of the Boy Scouts, are in many respects analogous to representative democratic states. As with a citizen of a representative democracy, a member of a large voluntary organization does not typically agree with all of the official positions taken by that organization's leadership.[129] Indeed, one takes for granted the existence of significant diversity, changing or revolving representational leadership, and sizable groups of minorities with positions on many issues that are utterly distinct from current "official" views.[130]

The liberal dissenters' alternative suggestion—that sufficient evidence should first demonstrate significant group unity with regard to that group's viewpoint—while preferable to the majority's approach, is also problematic. Once the right of free speech is construed as a right possessed by the association itself—divorced from the individuals it was intended to protect—constitutional contradictions are inevitable. How would a judge determine what it means for an organization with more than a million members to have, in the dissenters' words, a "clear and unequivocal view?"[131] What would be an appropriate and manageably applicable threshold? Suppose it is determined that 90 percent of the members of an organization agree with a particular position statement and that this ratio is deemed to be sufficient to grant that organization constitutional immunity from any law that might adversely impede the pursuance of expressive goals related to that purpose. This would leave 10 percent of the association's members unable to avail themselves of laws passed by their democratically elected officials simply because of their membership in an "expressive association."

The Court was thus arguably subverting the democratic process: distorting the First Amendment to endow associations, entities the framers characterized as dangerous factions, with a constitutionally protected status.[132] One possible rejoinder is that a membership organization such as the Boy Scouts is purely voluntary, and if one has sufficient disagreement with an official position of that organization, one can simply revoke one's membership. This is of course true. It is also true that American citizens may voluntarily revoke *their* citizenship. This theoretical "choice" did not change the framers' belief that minority interests still require protection. Any theoretical freedom of exit should not carry that implication today. It would be repugnant to republican ideals to propose that an American whose ideas are detested by 90 percent of the population must revoke her citizenship in order to speak freely. Should a similar principle, mandated by the Constitution, apply to private associations?

National Review *Weighs In*

In 2000, the preeminent conservative legal scholar Richard Epstein brought together both moralistic and free-market justifications for a broad reading of the First Amendment, a reading even Epstein conceded was "activist."[133] If any decision was to convince moralistic conservatives of the political and ideological benefits of adopting a pro–free-speech position, it was *Boy Scouts v. Dale*.[134] The decision effectively ensured that conservative associations have a constitutional right to remain true to their conservative moral values, even if this means violating a state policy intended to foster inclusion, tolerance, and equality. Epstein was confident that freedom of association is "a derivative right of freedom of speech."[135] The fact that association was nowhere mentioned in the language of the First Amendment, and that the Court had "flexed its activist muscles"[136] to reach its result, did not appear to bother Epstein. If anything, Epstein was troubled by the fact that the Court did not go far enough. In Epstein's view, the narrow conservative majority erred in limiting its opinion to so-called expressive associations. "The law would be better off not trying to draw any line at all between expressive and nonexpressive associations. It should hew to the simpler line that freedom of speech protects the rights of association for *all* voluntary groups."[137]

The implications of such a reading would be quite profound—not only would moralistic conservatives be handed a powerful weapon against perceived liberal incursions into the internal governance of organizations promoting conservative morality, but free-market and libertarian conservatives would be ceded the freedom *from* government they had long desired. Epstein argued that, interpreted correctly, well-established prohibitions on discrimination by private employers under the Civil Rights Act of 1964 would be suspect under the First Amendment. It would be "flatly unconstitutional for the U.S. to force any private organization to adopt a color-blind or sex-blind policy in hiring or admission to membership."[138] This was a vision that fit well with Epstein's well-known libertarian and free-market conservatism. Under its logic, the market would be expected to self-correct: "[P]eople who are offended by the Boy Scouts or the Jaycees can go elsewhere. Vigorous competition keeps these organizations in line, so there is no public reason to second-guess their policies."[139]

Indeed, rather than joining the long line of conservative commentators who had singled out Justice Oliver Wendell Holmes as a target of disdain—as a source of regrettable relativistic thinking on the Court—Epstein cited with approval Holmes's aphorism that "the best test of truth in ideas is competition in the marketplace."[140] And while this message had historically run contrary to the vision held by moralistic conservatives, the growth of the narrative of the tradition-minded social conservative as victim of government intervention meant that the political First Amendment alliance between libertarianism and moralism was in fact growing stronger.

The Lead-Up to Citizens United

Words matter. In 2010, two words redefined First Amendment jurisprudence and political campaigning in one fell swoop: "corporate speech." This paradoxical phrase was not entirely new to the Supreme Court's lexicon—the Court had previously used this combination of words in seven cases, beginning in 1978. However, it was not until *Citizens United* that these words would be used to fundamentally reshape American politics and the conventional understanding of the First Amendment.[141] Not long ago it would have been equally preposterous to refer to "corporate emotions" or "corporate arthritis" as it would have been to posit that there is something called "corporate speech." But today, there is no doubt that, at least from a legal perspective, the fiction of corporate speech has become doctrinal fact. The non-human has become human.

A corporation (if it is composed of more than one individual), of course, is a particular kind of association. The cases discussed thus far in this chapter have been concerned primarily with the free-speech benefits derived from association. In some contexts, the ability of an individual to speak is assisted by her associations. However, it is one thing to acknowledge that associating with others may carry important advantages for individuals; it is quite another to treat associations as if they are *themselves* individuals. As we saw, the right to enhance or make possible individual expression through association gradually, and without acknowledgment, evolved into a right of the association itself.[142] One layer of free-speech rights became two.

This new layer of free speech comes with a wide range of challenges. Defining the association for First Amendment purposes has proven difficult. In *Boy Scouts*, the conservative majority ultimately allowed an association to define itself on its own terms through a litigant representative in an adversarial setting. Yet, as discussed, identifying the true unified "voice" or "viewpoint" of an association is a nearly impossible task unless a Court simply defers to the words of whoever the association's designated spokesperson happens to be for purposes of the litigation.[143]

Such blind adherence to a spokesperson's words becomes even easier with the assistance of state law. If "speech" is deemed to exist wherever state law creates an artificial "person," then the entire question of whether or not a particular organization is a so-called expressive association falls away. Indeed, at the same time that the Court was fleshing out the meaning of "expressive association," quietly transforming an individual's right into a group right, it was wrestling with the inevitably knotty issues that accompany corporate "personhood" for First Amendment purposes. Although the mid-1980s Court was not yet ready to take the startling leap it would in 2010—essentially declaring *all* corporations to be the equivalent of individuals for First Amendment purposes—the Court was unevenly moving in that direction.

Just two years after *Roberts* was decided, the Court decided *FEC v. Massachusetts Citizens for Life (MCFL)*.[144] In *MCFL*, a majority of the Court, led by the liberal champion Justice Brennan, embarked on the precarious and misguided adventure of handpicking *which* incorporated associations were worthy of the First Amendment's protections. On the basis of a highly case-specific analysis, the majority in *MCFL* declared that it was unconstitutional to restrict independent political expenditures by particular nonprofit, non-stock corporations.[145] Ironically, it was Justice Rehnquist, along with three other dissenters, who chastised the majority for taking "a well-defined prohibition [on corporate political spending, and adding] a vague and barely adumbrated exception certain to result in confusion and costly litigation."[146] Such "confusion" could have been avoided had the Court simply rested on the quite logical conclusion that "free speech" applies only to individual "speakers." Instead, the Court's most liberal member inadvertently paved the way for the decision that would politically empower moneyed corporations to an extent that would have been unimaginable in previous generations. Attempting to craft principled doctrinal lines may have been the motivation, but from an ideological perspective, the liberals were sealing their fate.

Unlike in *Citizens United*, the majority in *MCFL* did not cavalierly dismiss federal election law's allowance for the establishment of political action committees (PACs).[147] The Court explained that "corporation[s] remain free to establish a separate segregated fund, composed of contributions earmarked for that purpose by the donors, that may be used for unlimited campaign spending."[148] PACs, of course, make the very distinction to which the Supreme Court in *Citizens United* was willfully blind—that is, the fundamental difference between individual speech and corporate communications. By design, PACs simply provide a mechanism to more closely correlate what might be characterized as corporate speech with *actual* speech. By strictly segregating and earmarking funds contributed by *individuals* to further the expressive goals of those *individuals*, a PAC's activities are more directly linked to individual speech.[149] Although the *MCFL* Court ultimately relied upon the presence of the segregated fund provision to find the application of the Massachusetts law unconstitutional, it still maintained that that there had not been "an absolute restriction on speech."[150]

In stark contrast, the *Citizens United* majority characterized the law prohibiting corporate political expenditures as "an outright ban . . . notwithstanding the fact that a PAC created by a corporation can still speak."[151] The Court reasoned that a "PAC is a separate association from the corporation. So the PAC exemption . . . does not allow corporations to speak."[152] Unlike *Citizens United*, the *MCFL* Court showed an appreciation for the individual speech-facilitating function of PACs.[153] Yet, at the same time, as applied to organizations "formed to disseminate political ideas, not amass capital," the *MCFL* Court concluded that the PAC requirement was a *hindrance* to speech.[154] Establishing a segregated fund involves compliance with a range of administrative requirements that may prove costly.[155] Thus, the *MCFL* Court concluded that these "regulations may create a disincentive for such organizations to engage in political speech."[156]

Defined correctly, PACs have nothing whatsoever to do with impeding speech. Instead, PACs are designed to facilitate speech; they create a legal mechanism by which a fictional legal entity may act as a true conduit for individual speech. As the *MCFL* dissenters explained, the Court had previously "declined the invitation to modify [a] statute to account for the characteristics of different corporations. . . . We saw no reason why the governmental interest in preventing both actual corruption and the appearance of corruption could not 'be accomplished by treating unions, corporations, and similar organizations differently from individuals.'"[157]

With *Citizens United*, the Court has returned to an unambiguous view of corporations and other associations. However, the Court's consistency has taken the form of an absolute reification of the corporation for First Amendment purposes. The Court's equivocation and dubious balancing in *MCFL*, in a majority opinion written by the Court's most liberal justice, William Brenan, allowed for misplaced certitude twenty-four years later in *Citizens United*. In the following section, I explore the inherent contradictions in the approach taken by the *Citizens United* majority.

The Concept of Association in *Citizens United*

It is difficult to imagine how the *Citizens United* Court, in addressing whether and to what extent corporations are protected by the First Amendment, could avoid addressing the vexing question of what it means for an association to "speak."[158] One might expect that the question of associational rights would preoccupy the Court. As discussed previously, the Court has been forced to confront the question "What is speech?" in a number of contexts. Although the Court's analysis in the expressive association line of cases, beginning with *Roberts*, left much to be desired, these decisions did spend considerable time questioning what it means for an association to speak for First Amendment purposes. The Court in *Citizens United* did not focus primarily on how constraints imposed on a corporation might adversely affect First Amendment rights of shareholders. Nor did the Court adopt the approach of O'Connor's concurrence in *Roberts*, which would require an assessment of whether Citizens United, as an association, was "predominantly engaged in protected expression" as opposed to "commercial activity."[159] Instead, the Court simply sidestepped the issue, no doubt aided by the term of art "corporate speech" that covertly answered the question for them.[160]

In fact, this most vexing of questions is addressed only as an aside in Justice Scalia's concurrence.[161] Scalia acknowledged "that when the Framers 'constitutionalized the right to free speech in the First Amendment, it was the free speech of individual Americans that they had in mind.'"[162] Yet he went on to assert, with a striking absence of support, that this "individual person's right to speak includes the right to speak *in association with other individual persons*."[163]

On its face, this might sound like a reasonable proposition; but on its own, it means very little. Does an individual have a right to speak among or in the presence of her associates? Of course. Does someone attending a rally with a large group of similarly minded individuals have a First Amendment right to hold up a sign, next to others doing the same, detailing a political position? This is classic freedom of expression.[164] Could a member of this association, at this same public rally, repeatedly chant that her organization supports the repeal of anti-polygamy laws across the nation, if she is entirely aware that two members strongly disagree with this position? This presents a different question. Her words, if maliciously uttered, could be construed as slander, leaving her exposed to a potential legal penalty.[165] Would the result be different if this potentially slanderous member declared herself to be the official spokesperson of the group? How about if there was some dispute within the group as to who was in fact the designated spokesman? Would using these words still constitute, in Scalia's words, "the right to speak in association with other individual persons?"[166] How much disagreement among the group would suffice to remove such speech from this category? The answers to all of these questions are far from clear. While a right to speak for oneself is firmly established First Amendment orthodoxy, the right to speak for others has clear limits—illustrated by the Court's well-established libel exception to the First Amendment.[167] Yet Scalia presents his claim as if it were simple common sense, no nuance involved.

Scalia derides as "sophistry" the argument that corporations are not protected by the First Amendment because they are non-humans and incapable of oral speech.[168] He explains that "[t]he authorized spokesman of a corporation is a human being, who speaks on behalf of the human beings who have formed that association—just as the spokesman of an unincorporated association speaks on behalf of its members."[169] If only matters were this simple.

"Authorization" to represent a group, whether it is a corporation or informal association, comes in many forms. And while the types of statements that are made by official authorization are likely as vast and diverse in number as there are associations, one thing is clear: Authorization has its limits. The word "authorized" implies that much remains "unauthorized" and that even an officially designated spokesperson is limited to a circumscribed role. This spokesperson may be allowed to speak for the association only on particular topics, or only following a vote among association members to determine its official views, but certainly this "representative" speech, coming from a spokesperson, shares little resemblance to uninhibited individual speech. As an individual, this spokesperson is generally free to say whatever she likes. It is her speech. If she exceeds the limits of her authorized role, she, as an individual, must deal with the consequences. If her statement purports to be the official position of the organization but does not comport with association or legal guidelines governing such statements, she may be reprimanded or ejected from the organization. Like a private employer who may freely penalize an employee for her words while on the job, this spokesperson is responsible for her own speech whether it is false, misleading, libelous, or even just inconsistent with the views of some in the organization.[170]

In other words, so-called associational speech is a matter internal to each association, governed by that association's internal processes. As Daniel A. Farber suggests, "[W]e do well to remember that associations are in the end merely groups of people, and that it is their rights (and ours)—not those of abstract entities called expressive associations—which the Constitution ultimately seeks to protect."[171] Official or designated speech of an association or corporation may reflect a hard-fought compromise during a business meeting, a majority vote among various proposed official policy positions, or an internal political power play among members, but it *is not*, by any means, the equivalent of the individual speech the framers intended to protect in the First Amendment.

Yet, well before *Citizens United* the Court began conflating these concepts. As far back as 1981, an ideologically pluralistic Court struck down a Wisconsin law that would have bound the national Democratic Party, in contravention of party rules, to honor results from "open" primaries that included non-Democrats.[172] The Court took care to use the *language* of individual rights, concluding that "the interests advanced by the State do not justify its substantial intrusion into the *associational freedom of members* of the National Party."[173] At the same time, the Court explained that "the members of the National Party, speaking through their rules, chose to define their associational rights by limiting those who could participate in the process leading to the selection of delegates to their National Convention."[174] This justification begs this question: Just what kind of "rules" did the Democratic Party "speak" through? The Court did not ask whether these associational rules merit constitutional protection; it simply assumed that by virtue of the existence of rules purporting to speak for the members of the party, the members and the party should be treated as one and the same for First Amendment purposes. In making this assumption, the Court failed to acknowledge ways in which individual speech is fundamentally distinct from the ultimate product of associational rules and procedures. Individual speech reflects thoughts or desires derived from a single human brain.

It is especially ironic that Justice Scalia, of all members of the Court, took the view in *Citizens United* that an "individual person's right to speak includes the right to speak *in association with other individual persons*."[175] Scalia is well known for being particularly hostile to the use of legislative history.[176] He is primarily concerned that judges not be encouraged to cherry-pick among a wide array of statements of intent in order to produce a results-oriented holding—one that comports with the judge's desired outcome rather than what the law itself demands.[177] He states: "Legislative history provides . . . a uniquely broad playing field. In any major piece of legislation, the legislative history is extensive, and there is something for everybody."[178] The rationale behind Scalia's position on the utility of legislative history is both quite lucid and related to the way that Congress functions as an association: An individual is inescapably distinct from a collective. The sum is not a simple reflection of each individual part.

Under such an understanding, claiming that an associational right of free speech naturally flows from the framers' intent establishing an individual right to speak—and, of course, the textual original meaning of the Constitution—is a non sequitur. As Chief Justice Marshall explained in 1819, a "corporation is an artificial being, invisible, intangible, and existing only in contemplation of law. Being the mere creature of law, it possesses only those properties which the charter of its creation confers upon it, either expressly, or as incidental to its very existence."[179] Given the temporal proximity of this statement to the founding and the close relationship of Marshall with the framers, it is difficult to conclude that Scalia's footnote 7—declaring that the voice of a spokesman for a corporation and the voice of individual human speakers may be treated as equivalent—is tied to anything remotely resembling his standard criterion: original understanding. It would be exceedingly difficult to square Marshall's understanding of a corporation with Scalia's view. If Marshall was correct that corporations exist "only in contemplation of law"—with a character that is defined and constricted by what is provided in their charter—Scalia's conception would afford an astounding and untenable grant of power to the authors of corporate charters. With the mere stroke of a pen, drafters could endow their "artificial," "invisible," and "intangible" creation with whatever constitutionally protected characteristics they choose.

As the previous review of associational rights jurisprudence reveals, it is not simply the conservative justices in the *Citizens United* majority who stray far from the framers' original intent with respect to the First Amendment. Although many of Scalia's predecessors on the Court would likely have disagreed with the outcome of *Citizens United*,[180] justices on both the right and left either implicitly or explicitly accepted the claim that associations may somehow claim speech rights separable and distinct from, and inevitably at times adverse to, the claims of individuals. A quarter of a century of confused expressive association decisions—many of which were joined, if not drafted, by politically liberal justices—certainly clouded the issue and contributed to the majority's ultimate disposition. Indeed, in his *Citizens United* dissent, Justice Stevens acknowledged, "[i]n fairness, our campaign finance jurisprudence has never attended very closely to the views of the Framers, whose political universe differed profoundly from that of today."[181]

Core First Amendment Values and Corporations

It is thus clear that the word "speech" in the First Amendment contemplated communications by individuals, and that, in most settings, equating associational speech with an individual's speech—especially when that association is a corporation—requires a sustained exercise in jurisprudential gymnastics. The campaign finance jurisprudence—and the debate in the United States over campaign finance laws generally—has been shaped not only by arguments grounded in legal doctrine but also by arguments grounded in the values the First Amendment was intended to protect. Although scholars have long been frustrated by the lack of evidence regarding original intent,[182] philosophical arguments generally recognize three widely accepted purposes of the First Amendment: "truth, democracy, and self-realization."[183] Of these three, the *Citizens United* majority understandably spends little time on the third value, for there is, as we have seen, no "self" involved in corporate expression. Instead the Court devotes much of its energy on the first and second of these values.[184] In the following discussion, I argue that neither of these two goals—democracy promotion nor truth seeking—are served by the Court's holding in *Citizens United*.

Democracy

With regard to the claim that corporate expenditures during political campaigns are beneficial to the health of American democracy, the *Citizens United* Court explains that "[s]peech is an essential mechanism of democracy, for it is the means to hold officials accountable to the people."[185] This is true. But what the Court fails to acknowledge is the inseparable relationship between the first and last words of this quotation. The veracity of the statement is premised on an accurate reading of the word "speech." "Speech" is beneficial to a political process made up of "people" because it is "of the people."

While the concept of accountability is consistent with a thoughtful evaluation of the impact political behavior has had on the economic interests of entities, individuals, and the country as a whole, true political accountability is much broader than this. When an individual engages in political speech to demand accountability of her political leaders, she presumably does so based on a cumulative assessment of that representative's performance. Yes, political leaders must be accountable for the way their actions might be thought to impact the economic fortunes of that individual. But concomitantly, political speech by individuals may reflect assessments of a candidate's trustworthiness, approach to foreign policy, political party, or views on everything from family values to global warming. Individual speech in opposition or support of a particular candidate may be informed by the speaker's perceptions of how ethical that candidate is, how that candidate's policies might affect generations to come, or whether or not the candidate is a persuasive speaker.

In other words, as most social scientists would surely attest, human beings are complex multivariate decision-makers—corporations, much less so.[186] The limited goals of a corporation are right there for all to see, spelled out in their articles of incorporation and the applicable laws that narrowly construe their permissible objectives. Although modern civilization has yet to fully grasp the true complexity of human nature, in a democracy intended to represent "We the People," human beings, confounding and multifaceted as we may be, must be the primary participants. By inappropriately attaching the label "speech" to nonhuman corporations, we dilute the effectiveness of true speech coming from the American people.

The analogy between American government and corporate governance is particularly apt. Collective action—whether in government, business, or any other endeavor—is a challenging proposition.[187] The framers understood this just as well as those who draft corporate laws and articles of incorporation. At the time of America's founding, rule by "We the People" was hardly assured. In the eighteenth century, autocracy was the dominant system of government. To avoid this fate, the framers established what would prove to be a remarkably enduring governmental structure with highly defined rules.[188] Madison describes the "great object" of constitutional government as "secur[ing] the public good, and private rights, against the danger of [a majority] faction, and at the same time . . . preserv[ing] the spirit and the form of popular government."[189] While the Court's freedom of association cases focus almost exclusively on the benefits of association, Madison's concerns about the power of "factions" reveal a different strain of thinking—one highly suspicious of group power.

In *Citizens United*, the majority mischaracterizes and distorts Madison's argument. Citing Madison, the Court argues that "[f]actions will necessarily form in our Republic, but the remedy of 'destroying the liberty' of some factions is 'worse than the disease.'"[190] Madison however, writes not of the liberty of the factions *themselves*. Rather, he warns of the danger of "destroying the liberty which is essential to [the factions'] existence"—that is, individual liberty.[191] In an eloquent metaphor, Madison argues: "[I]t could not be less folly to abolish liberty, which is essential to political life, because it nourishes faction, than it would be to wish the annihilation of air, which is essential to animal life, because it imparts to fire its destructive agency."[192] The Court spins Madison's assertion that taking away individual liberties is not an acceptable solution to the problem of factions into an argument for affirmatively empowering factions by providing them with rights intended for individuals. As Farber explains, there is a

> venerable American tradition that takes a more jaundiced view of associations. This view was reflected in George Washington's Farewell Address, which condemned "all combinations and associations, under whatever plausible character, with the real design to direct, control, counteract, or awe the regular deliberation and action of the constituted authorities."[193]

The Supreme Court's confused, if not revisionist, perspective on the framers' view of political associations is on full view in its decisions addressing the rights of political parties to exclude non–party member voters. For example, in *California Democratic Party v. Jones,* the Court struck down a so-called blanket primary law because it would have required that all primary ballots "list[] every candidate regardless of party affiliation and allow[] the voter to choose freely among them."[194]

To justify its holding, Justice Scalia sought to highlight the foundational importance of parties, observing that "[t]he formation of national political parties was almost concurrent with the formation of the Republic itself."[195] This is most certainly true, but "almost" is the key word here. Many of the framers did not intend American politics to be dominated by political parties and in fact warned of their dangers.[196] In *The Federalist* No. 1, Hamilton cautioned that "nothing could be more ill-judged than that intolerant spirit, which has, at times, characterized political parties. For, in politics as in religion, it is equally absurd to aim at making proselytes by fire and sword."[197] However, the *Jones* 7–2 majority opinion—which included all of the Court's most conservative members and two liberals—ignored this side of the equation. Indeed, at the same time that it emphasized "a political party's associational freedom,"[198] it cavalierly dismissed the dissent's suggestion that there might be "'First Amendment associational interests' of citizens to participate in the primary of a party to which they do not belong, and [a] 'fundamental right' of citizens 'to cast a meaningful vote for the candidate of their choice.'"[199]

The majority thus perversely seemed to favor a conception of the First Amendment that sanctifies the rights of parties (or factions) while at the same time denying rights to the individual voters. This posture is confounding, particularly in light of the fact that the dominant party duopoly in the United States risks completely locking out those individuals who choose not to affiliate with the two major parties—effectively preventing them from having a voice in all relevant political contests leading up to a general election.[200]

Understanding that democratic governments are themselves associations of individuals with certain shared interests and values, the framers not only warned of factions external to the government, but they allocated and divided power within government with great caution.[201] To prevent the people's government from itself becoming an oppressor, the framers established a governmental structure imbued with ceaseless—perhaps maddening—internal conflict. Madison famously declares that "[a]mbition must be made to counteract ambition."[202] And to Madison, this concern is by no means limited to the governmental sphere:

> This policy of supplying by opposite and rival interests, the defect of better motives, might be traced through the whole system of human affairs, private as well as public. We see it particularly displayed in all the subordinate distributions of power; where the constant aim is to divide and arrange the several offices in such a manner as that each may be a check on the other; that the private interest of every individual, may be a sentinel over the public rights.[203]

Of course, to many framers, even this conflictual structure was not sufficient.[204] A bill of rights carving out individual rights, in the face of a powerful association (here, the federal government), was necessary to seal the deal.[205] As Jefferson emphatically argues in a letter to Madison, "a bill of rights is what the people are entitled to against every government on earth, general or particular, and what no just government should refuse, or rest on inference."[206]

These debates over the structure of American government occurred, in part, because there is no perfect representation of a collectivity, no precise algorithm for determining the voice of a people. Indeed, except in the case of autocratic rule, it is difficult to conceive of an instance in which the "collective view" in a representative association would ever replicate with precision the perspective of any single represented individual, let alone all individuals at the same time. In the context of democratic rule, strict majority voting on every issue of concern by members of a collective might risk fatally weakening the whole, as it does not allow an effective leader to take the reins. A majority vote will also inevitably leave behind an unhappy minority. Thus, in order to ensure stability, durability, and governability, America's framers granted an executive the power to lead for a designated period of time, while delegating the authority to make law to a majoritarian legislature. Concomitantly, regardless of majority sentiment, certain individual rights were constitutionally guaranteed, indelibly carved into our system of representative government.

Similar principles and needs apply to nongovernmental associations. However, such associations may opt to afford greater or lesser power to leadership and increased or decreased protection for the individual members, in accordance with their goals and mission. Individual guarantees might be perceived to be more essential where individual members face greater barriers of exit—for example, in the case of corporate shareholders whose economic stake in the association may require a long-term investment. Durability of leadership might be of greater importance in a politically driven organization that strives to promote a consistent message, even in the face of significant differences of opinion among its membership.

Systems of collective decision making invariably come in many forms, governed by idiosyncratic rules intended to achieve particular ends or promote a particular vision of the good. As artificial legal entities, corporations, just like representative governments, must have a set of procedural rules to produce something that might be said to roughly resemble collective goals. Ultimately, any official viewpoint or voice of the whole is merely a useful construct. Having a reliable system of rules to establish an institutional voice simply allows an association—whether for the purposes of civil government, commerce, or advocacy—to function effectively in its legally prescribed role. Yet, what is useful if not essential in one setting may be counterproductive if not dangerous in another.

Electoral politics is ideally a fierce contest of individual ideas: The battle to make sure that it remains so has been an important and difficult challenge since the Constitution was ratified over two centuries ago. *Citizens United*, the logical conclusion of an ideologically inspired doctrinal wrong turn that arguably began more than a half century earlier, perverts the framers' rulebook for fair and effective collective action in the electoral setting. The Court converts an individual right—one intended to carve out and protect individual speech even in the face of a hostile majority—into a collective one. The majority takes the critical defense of the individual built into American constitutional government—a system that by necessity allows enormous power to accrue to those with majority support—and turns it into a bludgeon to be used *against* individuals. From a political perspective, the liberals on the Court were clearly alarmed by the implications. Justice Stevens warned that, "Corporations have 'special advantages—such as limited liability, perpetual life, and favorable treatment of the accumulation and distribution of assets'—that allow them to spend prodigious general treasury sums on campaign messages that have 'little or no correlation' with the beliefs held by actual persons."[207] Yet the dissenters were seemingly blind to that fact that it was a doctrinal innovation championed by their ideological predecessors that led the Court down this road.

Few would argue against the claim that the corporate form has been a valuable, if not essential, ingredient in promoting economic advancement and prosperity in the United States. However, to equate an individual's economically rational choice to associate in the corporate form—and the economic benefits that accrue as a result—with the freedom and benefits that attach to the individual speech right protected by the framers is to strain credulity. Corporations only began to resemble their contemporary form during the early waves of industrial development, when the benefits of being able to raise large amounts of capital from a large number of investors, while at the same time maintaining centralized control, became increasingly apparent.[208]

Presumably, the corporate structure was perceived to be in the economic interest of both the individuals who sought to establish corporations and the states whose laws made them possible. If corporations were simply replicating the legal, economic, and ideational interests of the individuals involved, there would have been neither need nor impetus for the corporate form. In effect, corporations allowed individuals to join together in order to extract and concentrate one particular aspect of their individuality: their economic interests. Corporations "are legally required to represent not a group of people but a legally defined set of interests—the interests of a fictional creature called a shareholder that has no associations, economic incentives, or political views other than a desire to profit from its connection with this particular corporation."[209] It is quite rational for individuals to join in and become members of this kind of association, because corporations allow such individuals to leave behind certain less desirable aspects of their personhood, such as legal and financial liability.[210] However, in exchange for the potential economic benefit, investors must largely cede decision-making authority over how their funds are used unless they are majority shareholders.[211]

The *Citizens United* decision converts a single decision by a shareholder to purchase and hold an interest in a particular company—a choice that in the case of publicly held for-profit corporations is typically limited to one's economic interests as an investor—into a proxy for that individual's political speech. As previously explored, it is infeasible enough to attempt to correlate the supposed "viewpoint" of an association with its members in the case of so-called expressive associations such as the Jaycees and the Boy Scouts. In the case of large, publicly held, profit-making corporate associations, the claim is downright ludicrous. Not only does one's choice to invest in a company as a stockholder represent a *de minimis* aspect of an individual who might otherwise exercise her right to free speech in the context of a political campaign, but it may be a stretch to even call it a choice. For much of the American population, mutual funds—investment vehicles that compile interests in hundreds if not thousands of stocks—have become an essential component of a secure retirement.[212]

After *Citizens United*, the fiction of the "associational corporate speaker" has taken on a new identity as a potent player in political contests intended for individual citizens. It does so at the expense of both (a) those individuals outside the corporation whose voices will be potentially overwhelmed by the collective and concentrated power accrued as a result of legal grants by the state, and (b) shareholders within the corporation, who either disagree, do not have knowledge of, or do not wish to convey the message corporations now have a constitutional right to express. The spurious doctrinal First Amendment innovation that "speech" can somehow be divorced from an actual "speaker" is responsible for this perverse outcome. Troublingly, this blind spot has obscured the vision of not only the members of the majority and dissent in *Citizens United*, but of one of the preeminent scholars of the First Amendment.

Writing in the *Harvard Law Review*, Kathleen Sullivan characterizes the dissenting and majority opinions in *Citizens United* by asserting that the former represents an egalitarian vision of free speech and the latter a libertarian vision.[213] Implicitly, one represents today's political liberalism, which has ostensibly abandoned its pure speech-protective stance in favor of equality interests, and the latter opinion is the emergent conservative libertarianism that has been the focus of this study. In other doctrinal settings, such as hate speech discussed in Chapters 3 and 4, it may be true that many liberals have moved from a libertarian to a more egalitarian perspective on free speech. But the difference between liberals and conservatives, when it comes to the line of precedent establishing a freedom of *the* association, is not a question of "if" but of "how." Although sharply divided in *Citizens United*, justices on both sides of the ideological spectrum remain loyal to the initial doctrinal misstep that treated associations as if they were individuals.

Sullivan praises the libertarian approach in the context of her analysis of the *Citizens United* decision. However, in doing so, she perpetuates the logical fallacy that has informed much of the Court's freedom of association jurisprudence. She begins by explaining that the "view of free speech as liberty starts from a textual interpretation of the Free Speech Clause as written in terms of speech, not speakers."[214] She then mentions some of the implications of accepting this notion that the First Amendment is "indifferent to a speaker's identity or qualities," one of which is the claim that the First Amendment might apply to "inanimate" objects.[215] Perhaps implicitly acknowledging the lunacy of a First Amendment for rocks, two sentences later Sullivan backpedals, conceding that "[i]f this interpretation requires an ultimate foundation in the rights of individuals, corporations enable individuals to 'speak in association with other individual persons,' banding together in a 'common cause.'"[216] Of course, this caveat does not merely qualify the premise of a First Amendment "indifferent" to the "identity" of a "speaker"—*that is*, whether or not a speaker is a real-life person—it *contradicts* it. Sullivan seems to support the ideal of a First Amendment that protects speech without regard to "speaker" yet is unable to avoid acknowledging that such a conception is just a conceit.

The nature of this paradox comes into high relief when Sullivan explains the "speech as liberty" response to the claim that prohibiting corporate spending protects dissenting shareholders.[217] Sullivan suggests that Justice Kennedy rejects the shareholder protection justification as "impermissibly paternalistic" because there are "other means" for protecting dissenting shareholders.[218] Sullivan sees Kennedy as mandating that "government . . . leave speakers and listeners in the private order to their own devices in sorting out the relative influence of speech."[219] However, the "other means" that Kennedy offers for protecting the dissenting shareholder is "changing state corporate governance laws to increase the opportunities for shareholders to control whether and in what amounts and to what ends corporate political expenditures will be made."[220] This alternative approach to protecting the shareholder, implicitly endorsed by Sullivan, blatantly violates the ideal that "speakers . . . in the private order" should be left "to their own devices."[221]

In the same breath that advocates of the "speech as liberty" model make a "keep government out" argument, they concede that this is workable only with significant state governmental involvement. This is the paradox of decrying government suppression of what we now call corporate speech: There can be no such thing as corporate speech without government. State governments define its very meaning by defining the parameters of what it means to be a corporation.

Truth and the Marketplace of Ideas

The *Citizens United* majority claims that allowing for unlimited spending on corporate political expression contributes to the key First Amendment goal of seeking truth by those who might listen.[222] Even if corporate spending serves as a proxy for individual speech, the freedom to disseminate a political message through corporate spending is said to contribute to the marketplace of ideas.[223] According to the majority, "[t]he Government may not by these means deprive the public of the right and privilege to determine for itself what speech and speakers are worthy of consideration."[224] However, all of the true speakers who have ties to the corporation, as well as all of the individuals who are collectively responsible for the corporations' actions—whether they be employees, shareholders, or members of the board of directors—retain their First Amendment rights. They remain free to speak, and the public remains free to listen.

The establishment of the corporate form is an act of legislative grace—premised upon the belief that allowing individuals to structure certain narrowly defined economic affairs through a particular legal vehicle will be beneficial to society at large. By restricting corporate communications, the government is not depriving anyone of anything; it is merely declining to extend to a particular affirmative legal benefit (the corporate form) all aspects of individual civic membership. The Court has long held that "[t]he Government can, without violating the Constitution, selectively fund a program to encourage certain activities it believes to be in the public interest, without at the same time funding an alternative program which seeks to deal with the problem in another way."[225] Corporations, just like any other government-subsidized program, are mere creatures of law. Corporate tax benefits and limited liability encourage particular activities because the government designed the corporate form to achieve limited goals. As the Court acknowledges in *Rust v. Sullivan*, "[t]he Government has no constitutional duty to subsidize an activity merely because the activity is constitutionally protected."[226] In deciding to join a corporation, individual members are not required to forfeit their constitutional rights. As they were in the past, they are free to speak at will.

The *Citizens United* majority asserts that "[c]orporations, like individuals, do not have monolithic views. On certain topics corporations may possess valuable expertise, leaving them best equipped to point out errors or fallacies in speech of all sorts, including the speech of candidates and elected officials."[227] However, the majority reifies an artificial entity, imbuing it with human characteristics where none are to be found. It is certainly true that the individuals who make up a corporation typically accrue expertise and that the knowledge that accompanies such expertise is of value. But corporations do not have "views," let alone "monolithic" ones. Thus, any decision to "point out errors or fallacies in speech" of others will be made in a truth-neutral manner. A corporation may aggressively and publicly point out falsehoods when such whistleblowing serves its economic interests. However, if this falsehood is coming from a politician who promotes deregulatory policies that are an economic boon for the corporation, it becomes increasingly unlikely that the corporation will "point out" the politician's "errors." Indeed, a corporation may very well be inclined to leverage its perceived expertise to "point out . . . fallacies" where they do not exist, especially when the source of the speech is a candidate whose policies impede that corporation's economic interests.

There are, of course, limits to how far this truth-neutral "speech" may be utilized. Malice and commercial misrepresentation are well-established exceptions to the First Amendment's protections.[228] However, for those associations with adequate resources, highly sophisticated advertising has meant that blatant misrepresentations are no longer necessary to achieve one's ends.[229] Political messages can be conveyed through a wide variety of high-production formats, propagating powerful imagery intended to provoke emotional reactions that ultimately promote or deter desired outcomes.[230] At this level, communication is merely a tool to achieve narrow ends.

The belief that increased corporate spending on political advertising somehow equals a greater contribution to the marketplace of ideas has never been substantiated; it is simply "assumed to be" by the majority.[231] Because of the distortion of incentives built into the design of the corporate structure, there is reason to believe not only that extending the freedom of expression to corporations *does not* contribute to the marketplace of ideas and the search for truth but, rather, that it actively, and mischievously, subverts this goal. After

Citizens United, what has been dubbed "corporate speech" in the political process will be used freely as a tool of economic advancement. Truthfulness will have minimal bearing on the words or images conveyed. Truth is irrelevant for an artificial entity with a legal obligation to narrowly pursue its economic interests, except to the extent that truth bears a positive correlation with those interests—for example, where truthfulness is necessary to work within the confines of the law in order to avoid financial or other penalties.[232]

Corporations lack fundamental human traits; they possess neither a conscience, nor a multiplicity of motivations, nor an appreciation for the complex ramifications that accompany taking hard positions on nuanced issues. In contrast, individuals may have ambivalence about speaking on a particular issue or in favor of a particular political candidate; for any major public policy debate or political election, innumerable human concerns are at stake all at once. These diverse interests and apprehensions push in various directions simultaneously—consciously and unconsciously.[233] For example, would a speech deemphasizing the adverse consequences of a particular law, when the benefits would clearly accrue to the speaker, feel morally correct to that speaker? Would such a speech be felt to manipulate the truth in an inappropriate way and risk tarnishing the speaker's reputation or sense of self? Would the speaker feel comfortable with the internal conflict that might result from speaking to promote his interests without regard to the truth? An individual's internal moral compass might help answer these questions—and a so-called moral compass is just one of limitless intangible forces that shape human speech.

As artificial entities, corporations do not share in the subtle, if not subconscious, internal balancing all human beings must by necessity engage in when they speak. Nor do they have to deal with the moral, spiritual, ethical, or personal accountability that is central to being human. Due to mechanisms such as limited liability, the individuals who make up these associations are sheltered, not only from the inevitable human trade-offs of real speech but also from adverse financial or legal consequences beyond the amount invested. In sum, corporate political spending contributes to the human marketplace of ideas only in the way counterfeit currency might be said to contribute to the economic marketplace: Its presence simply manipulates and distorts the ultimate goal of the system. The ongoing quest for truth is in no way served by applying an individual's right to free speech to a legal artifice.

Although the liberal dissenters in *Citizens United* are highly critical of the majority's claims regarding corporate political spending, no member of the current Court seems willing to accept this core tenet. The fault lies with a Supreme Court doctrine that over the course of many years subtly began to conflate the individual and the group. Then, in 1978, the Court used the unfortunate phrase "corporate speech" for the first time.[234] The *Citizens United* dissent would have benefited from a clear line between that which falls under the logical category of speech—expressive activity that has, at its source, the attributes of an individual speaker—and that which is simply too distant to qualify. Instead, the liberal dissenters contend with (and perpetuate) a mushy, qualified argument that makes for an easy target.

The *Austin* Mistake and an Alternative Way Forward

The liberal Justice Marshall's majority opinion in the now-overturned decision *Austin v. Michigan State Chamber of Commerce* rightfully emphasized the "special advantages" granted under state law to corporations "such as limited liability, perpetual life, and favorable treatment of the accumulation and distribution of assets."[235] However, instead of utilizing these and other facts to argue the obvious—that corporate political expenditures simply do not fall within the concept of speech the framers intended to protect—Marshall referred to such spending as "corporate speech."[236] The Court's liberals, joined by Chief Justice Rehnquist, thus gave the impression that they were carving out selective exceptions to the First Amendment rather than simply applying a straightforward reading rooted in its textual meaning. In doing so the *Austin* majority effectively ceded the high ground to the *Austin* dissenters, creating the false impression that *they* were the First Amendment purists.

Nothing could have been further from the truth. Yet, Scalia, empowered by this concession, began his *Austin* dissent with this alarming allusion: "Attention all citizens. To assure the fairness of elections by preventing disproportionate expression of the views of any single powerful group, your Government has decided that the following associations of persons shall be prohibited from speaking or writing in support of any candidate . . . "[237] The only reason Scalia could have read the majority opinion as an "endorse[ment of] the principle that too much speech is an evil that the democratic majority can proscribe"[238] is because the majority made the fatal error of recognizing speech where it does not exist.

Accepting that "corporate speech" is a misnomer raises the question of whether communications disseminated by other types of associations, such as nonprofit advocacy groups, should be denied classification as speech for First

Amendment purposes. Many nonprofits ostensibly represent mere groups of individuals who seek to come together in order to facilitate, and perhaps amplify, their own voices. The suggestion that the First Amendment would not protect a reputable organization with a primary goal of contributing to the marketplace of ideas to promote a particular view of truth might strike some as deeply troubling. In *Austin* the majority addressed just such a claim. The respondent argued that "even if the Campaign Finance Act [prohibiting the use of corporate treasury funds to support or oppose political candidates] is constitutional with respect to for-profit corporations, it nonetheless cannot be applied to a nonprofit ideological corporation like a chamber of commerce."[239] The *Austin* Court rejected this argument with respect to the Michigan State Chamber of Commerce[240] but continued to accept the premise of "corporate speech," therefore necessitating that courts pick and choose which speech is deserving of protection.

In *Austin*, the Court distinguished the Michigan State Chamber of Commerce from Massachusetts Citizens for Life, Inc. (MCFL), a non-profit corporation that it had, in 1986, concluded *was* protected by the First Amendment.[241] It delved into a case-specific analysis of the respective associations, pointing to three characteristics of MCFL that purportedly qualified *it* for First Amendment protection but *not* the Chamber of Commerce.[242] Specifically, the Court identified "MCFL's narrow political focus,"[243] its "absence of shareholders,"[244] and its "independence from the influence of business corporations."[245] The majority concluded that the Chamber lacked two of these three attributes.[246] The two corporations did have an "absence of shareholders" in common. However, the Court explained that the intent of focusing on this attribute was to ensure

> that persons connected with the organization will have no economic disincentive for disassociating with it if they disagree with its political activity. Although the Chamber also lacks shareholders, many of its members may be similarly reluctant to withdraw as members even if they disagree with the Chamber's political expression, because they wish to benefit from the Chamber's nonpolitical programs and to establish contacts with other members of the business community.[247]

The attributes that distinguished the Michigan State Chamber of Commerce from MCFL were enough for the Court; it upheld the Michigan law as applied to the Chamber. While these are certainly legitimate distinctions, by engaging in this hair-splitting exercise the Court obscured the simple fact that all corporations, regardless of their attributes, are fundamentally distinct from the individuals who are the intended beneficiaries of the First Amendment.

It is true that individual members of the Chamber of Commerce may remain members because they have other reasons for doing so, despite that corporation's expression. Yet, while this concern may be more evident in the case of businesses (or shareholders) that are economically motivated, it is no less a possibility for members of associations that have goals that are not primarily economic. For example, a member of the KKK in the Jim Crow South might have remained a member because of the political and social connections membership provided, despite disagreeing with the association's message. Indeed, the iconic First Amendment absolutist Justice Black infamously joined the Klan as a way of capitalizing on its political influence in early twentieth-century Alabama.[248] According to Noah Feldman, "The decision was motivated primarily by Black's political ambition. . . . He was not greatly concerned about the Klan's views."[249] Likewise, a member of the NRA may remain a member because she is an avid gun enthusiast, even if she disagrees with the organization's political opposition to gun control in particularly violent urban areas.

The decision to remain a member in these examples—and countless others—may not be economically motivated, but it has much in common with an oil company shareholder, who, despite disagreeing with the corporation's position on the regulation of offshore drilling, continues to hold that company's stock because it provides ample dividends. There is simply no constitutionally principled way of distinguishing between associations that deserve constitutional rights and those that do not. The First Amendment protects *individuals*. But under the Court's misguided jurisprudence, these same individuals are essentially asked to give up their First Amendment right *not* to speak unless they make the requisite sacrifice of withdrawing from membership in an organization from which they derive significant, non–speech-related benefits.

What is the alternative then? Would the argument I am making relegate influential political advocacy organizations to irrelevancy and impede the free flow of critical political dialogue? Certainly not. There is no reason to believe that individuals would have to sacrifice the ability to associate for speech-related purposes. On the contrary, they would continue to do so and continue to derive expressive benefits from such association. It would simply be made clear that the *constitutionally* protected right belongs to them, as individuals. If people seek to pool their resources with others, rather than utilizing a corporate form or establishing some other artificial entity, they would contractually join together with others in partnership. But without individual accountability for the communications made, and a clear intent on the part of the individuals to "speak" the message conveyed, the First Amendment's protections would not be implicated. Rather than engaging in the tortured analysis that the Court has used in the past, under this formulation there is only one threshold question: whether the speech at issue is legally equivalent to individual speech.

Furthermore, for associations with the singular mission of contributing to the marketplace of ideas, the literal text of the Constitution provides a reprieve: the Freedom of the Press Clause of the First Amendment, which states that "Congress shall make no law . . . abridging the freedom . . . of the press."[250] The Press Clause can be read to provide First Amendment protection where the Speech Clause would not—to a narrow class of associations dedicated to the propagation of ideas. As Justice Stevens argues in his dissenting opinion in *Citizens United*, "The text and history [of the First Amendment] suggests why one type of corporation, those that are part of the press, might be able to claim special First Amendment status."[251] Unlike the word "speech," "press" does not necessarily imply, or require, the existence of an individual speaker. As Justice Potter Stewart observed, "the Free Press Clause extends protection to an institution. The publishing business is, in short, the only organized private business that is given explicit constitutional protection."[252] Ironically, as the *Citizens United* dissent pointed out, Justice Scalia "emphasizes the unqualified nature of the First Amendment" while at the same time "seemingly read[ing] out the Free Press Clause."[253] However, if one goal of constitutional interpretation is to best apply the law in accordance with the document's original spirit, the Press Clause would appear to be a much more rational route to protecting communications of a certain narrow class of associations.[254] Adapted to today's world, the word "press" might reasonably be expanded to include a range of corporations singularly dedicated to the propagation of ideas.

In sum, *Citizens United* marks an understandable but troubling development in the Court's First Amendment jurisprudence, particularly when one closely examines the gradual shift that has occurred in the Court's treatment of associational freedom since the 1950s. It was a doctrinal expansion that was instigated in a time when a robust reading of the free speech guaranteed by the First Amendment was seen as a politically liberal value. This quiet revolution has had radical implications. With little notice from scholars, the Court has subtly converted the quintessentially individual right of free speech into a collective right. This new group right is not "more of a good thing"—an expansion of rights consistent with the Supreme Court's grand tradition of broadening the Constitution's applicability. On the contrary, there is reason to believe that the fiction of the "corporate speaker" runs counter to foundational First Amendment principles. While this jurisprudential wrong turn did not begin—nor will it likely end—with *Citizens United*, in ruling as it did the Court's conservatives, with ample support from liberal justices on the Court now and in the past, has subverted the very goals the First Amendment was intended to promote. Honestly confronting this regrettable mistake is the first step toward repairing the damage it has done.

Conclusion

As I argued in Chapter 7, the right's First Amendment is sometimes *wrong*. This, however, is an equal opportunity critique. The left must also be held responsible for being an accessory to what I have posited is quite simply bad constitutional interpretation. As we have seen, there is good reason to believe that the inspiration for this and other First Amendment doctrinal change— whether one agrees that it is bad or good—was at least in part ideological. We have also seen, however, that the relationship between ideology and doctrine is far from straightforward. It is rich and complex. Influence flows in both directions. Ideology and doctrine are both distinct and overlapping, independent and interdependent. Ideological modeling of judicial decision making may in some ways serve to clarify but in other important ways obscure the nature of the relationship.

In this study I have explored the vigorous debates as to how we understand the intersection of ideology and First Amendment interpretation—debates that are far from resolved. We have seen how the conservative libertarian view of the late nineteenth century was coopted by the liberal civil libertarians of the early twentieth century. Claiming the First Amendment as their own, liberals both on and off the Court celebrated their alignment with free speech and eagerly contrasted themselves with their conservative ideological opponents, who had grown deeply skeptical of robust First Amendment freedom. In the 1960s, at the height of this marriage between First Amendment values and liberalism, intense allegiance to speech-protective doctrine propelled ideology—so much so that there was nary a hint of liberal ambivalence in the celebrated *Branden-burg* decision, upholding a broad expressive guarantee in the face of noxious racism and bigotry. In contrast, the constrained conservative position on free speech was intensified by the conservative enthusiasm for stamping out communist subversion in America's two Red Scare eras.

However, two social fissures would eventually help shake up this alignment between conservatism and a narrow reading of the First Amendment, culminating in what would appear to be an almost complete reversal. Just two decades after *Brandenburg*, with the right increasingly consumed by feelings of victimization and resentment rooted in perceived liberal political correctness on college campuses and elsewhere, ideology inspired a new wave of doctrinal development. In outcome, *R.A.V. v. St. Paul* may have appeared to be just another speech-protective decision by the Supreme Court; just under the surface, however, we find a majority opinion that was inspired by, and crafted in response to, the rightwing zeitgeist of the early 1990s. As with the liberals of the *Brandenburg* era, the proverbial doctrinal cart would shortly begin to push the conservative ideological horse. In recent cases such as *Snyder v. Phelps* and *Brown v. Entertainment Merchants Association*, conservative justices would put to the side traditional conservative concerns such as patriotism, loyalty, authority, and parental hierarchy in favor of an increasingly solidified doctrinal commitment to a robust First Amendment.

In Chapters 5 and 6 I traced a similar pattern in the sphere of commercial speech. Conservative skepticism over a freedom of commercial speech was once the norm—and was given voice by a wide range of luminaries on the right, from William Rehnquist and Robert Bork to William F. Buckley. Once liberals opened the door to commercial speech protection, however—nudged along in a narrow case in which an abortion advertisement hung in the balance—conservatives rushed in, adopting the commercial speech cause as their own. Initial resistance informed by decades of communist subversion cases would give way to a pragmatic awareness that protecting commercial speech would aid in the conservative free-market cause. In the process, robust free expression rights in the commercial sphere morphed into *the* conservative position—so much so that the conservative justices' pro-speech views in this area are now frequently at odds with the approach of many of their liberal colleagues. The result has been a series of strained First Amendment opinions that would have been unimaginable in previous generations—such as a recent decision to strike down, on free expression grounds, a prescription confidentiality law that would have merely prevented pharmacies from selling prescriber-identifying information without that prescriber's consent.

In the final chapter, I examined how ideological catalysts for doctrinal change can sometimes lead to less than ideal outcomes—using the example of associational speech as a representative case study. As with the other areas focused on in this study, we see how a commitment to liberal values, such as the admirable concern for the civil rights of NAACP members in 1950s Alabama, sparked an unfortunate doctrinal transformation that spanned more than a half century. As a consequence, a First Amendment right intended for individuals was quietly transformed into a right for collectives. I argue that this transformation has had the perverse effect of diminishing the very individual rights the Amendment was originally intended to protect. Underlying this normative claim, however, is a complex tale of how ideology and doctrine interact over time.

Doctrinal choices, motivated in part by ideological commitments on the left, were, in fits and starts, gradually adopted by the right. While adherence to the principle of *stare decisis* may at times be in tension with a justice's ideology, it also sometimes works in tandem with political preferences. As we saw in the *Boy Scouts* decision—in which the Court's conservatives identified a First Amendment right of associations to discriminate against homosexuals—such synergy spurred continued doctrinal movement in a direction originally championed by the conservatives' ideological adversaries. Ultimately, the Supreme Court—with outright opposition from the high court's liberal wing—would shock the country with their *Citizens United* decision. But a close examination of the Court's doctrinal trajectory over many decades exposes "shock" to be an inappropriate emotion. *Citizens United* was decades in the making.

We have seen that legal doctrine is path dependent. The principle of *stare decisis* has a life of its own. An ideological pebble placed on one side of an otherwise balanced scale not only helps resolve the issue at hand but sets a lasting precedent. And it is not merely the Supreme Court that must adhere to the principles spelled out in its decisions. A new doctrinal path is an invitation—indeed, an order—for a multitude of lower courts to deeply embed the high court's interpretation of the Constitution in America's broader legal and ideological culture. Legal precedents have the capacity to alter our understanding of constitutional principles long after that single ideological pebble is forgotten.

Does this mean that the attitudinalists are correct—that "ideology is destiny" in constitutional decision making? Certainly, in those rare cases where the scales of justice are otherwise in perfect symmetry, one ideological pebble *may* conceivably make all the difference. And it just so happens that the Supreme Court is tasked with resolving some of the most "well-balanced" cases in the land, controversies in which the finest legal minds who sit on America's prestigious circuit courts simply do not agree. Especially with "hard" cases, an ideological nudge may not merely make or break a particular constitutional decision; it may—like the flap of a butterfly's wings—indelibly alter the future of constitutional meaning.

As critical consumers and analysts of the law, it is legitimate to question whether that ideological pebble set us on the wrong doctrinal course. As long as courts of justice produce winners and losers, there will inevitably be tension between constitutional principles and ideological interests. From a normative perspective, it is fully appropriate to challenge the substance of one or another ideological worldview and question the extent to which—and the way in which—it has influenced a particular judicial decision. One might, in retrospect, be thankful for that ideological influence. Ideological interests and impulses might be the impetus for a renewed respect for important constitutional principles. Free-speech advocates—regardless of their own ideological orientation—might feel that this was the case with the conservative response to perceived political correctness on college campuses and the renewed appreciation among conservatives for the economic benefits of free commercial speech.

It is no doubt easier for someone who sees himself as a victim—as an oppressed and misunderstood minority—to appreciate the value of unbending free expression. The universal principles behind the First Amendment are perhaps best appreciated, and more likely to endure, in societies in which all sectors of the population have, at one point or another, had a turn at feeling themselves to be "the victim." Yet it is an abiding hope—and from judges *an expectation*—that once appreciated, constitutional principles will have a life beyond self-service. First Amendment principles will live on—rightly or wrongly—to apply to the speech that hurts one's political party, to the expression that thwarts one's instrumental goals, and to the speech one hates.

Notes

Preface

1. Linda Greenhouse, for example, rightfully points out in a *New York Times* op-ed that for the first time in history, all Republican-appointed justices are to the right of all Democratic appointees. Linda Greenhouse, Op-Ed., *Polar Vision*, N.Y. TIMES, May 28, 2014, http://www.nytimes.com/2014/05/29/opinion/greenhouse-polar-vision.html.

2. See, for example, Adam Liptak, Sidebar, *In Justices' Votes, Free Speech Often Means "Speech I Agree With*," N.Y. TIMES, May 6, 2014, at A15.

Introduction

1. Robert H. Bork, *An End to Political Judging?*, NATIONAL REVIEW, December 31, 1990, at 30.

2. *Id.*

3. *Id.*

4. *Id.*

5. The full question reads: "Consider a person who advocates doing away with elections and letting the military run the country. a. If such a person wanted to make a speech in your community, should he be allowed to speak, or not?" National Data Program for the Social Sciences, *http://sda.berkeley.edu/quicktables/quickoptions.do.*

6. National Data Program for the Social Sciences, *http://sda.berkeley.edu/quicktables/quickoptions.do.*

7. The full question reads: "There are always some people whose ideas are considered bad or dangerous by other people. For instance, somebody who is against churches and religion. . . . a. If such a person wanted to make a speech in your (city/town/community) against churches and religion, should he be allowed to speak, or not?" National Data Program for the Social Sciences, *http://sda.berkeley.edu/quicktables/quickoptions.do.*

8. JOHN W. DEAN, THE REHNQUIST CHOICE: THE UNTOLD STORY OF THE NIXON APPOINTMENT THAT REDEFINED THE SUPREME COURT 1 (2001).

9. Miller v. California, 413 U.S. 15, 23 (1973).

10. GEOFFREY R. STONE, LOUIS M. SEIDMAN, CASS SUNSTEIN, PAMELA S. KARLAN, & MARK V. TUSHNET, CONSTITUTIONAL LAW 1181 (6th ed. 2009).

11. *Id.*

12. Roth v. U.S., 354 U.S. 476 (1957).

13. LEE EPSTEIN, JEFFREY A. SEGAL, HAROLD J. SPAETH, & THOMAS G. WALKER, THE SUPREME COURT COMPENDIUM 553 (5th ed. 2012).

14. Roth v. U.S., 354 U.S. 476 (1957).

15. Paris Adult Theatre v. Slaton, 413 U.S. 49, 73 (1973).

16. *Id.* at 84.

17. LEE EPSTEIN, JEFFREY A. SEGAL, HAROLD J. SPAETH, & THOMAS G. WALKER, THE SUPREME COURT COMPENDIUM 553 (5th ed. 2012).

18. Paris Adult Theatre v. Slaton, 413 U.S. 49, 97 (1973).

19. These included, in order of conservatism according to the justices' Martin-Quinn scores that term: Rehnquist, Burger, Blackmun, Powell, and White. LEE EPSTEIN, JEFFREY A. SEGAL, HAROLD J. SPAETH, & THOMAS G. WALKER, THE SUPREME COURT COMPENDIUM 553 (5th ed. 2012).

20. Paris Adult Theatre v. Slaton, 413 U.S. 49, 63 (1973).

21. *Id.* at 61.

22. *Id.* at 64, 69.

23. Miller v. California, 413 U.S. 15, 33 (1973).

24. Paris Adult Theatre v. Slaton, 413 U.S. 49, 63 (1973).

25. *Id.*

26. Lee Epstein & Jeffrey A. Segal, *The Rehnquist Court and the First Amendment: Trumping the First Amendment?*, 21 WASH. U. J.L. & POL'Y 81, 87–88 (2006).

27. Brown v. Entertainment Merchants Association, 2011 U.S. LEXIS 4802 (2011).

28. *Id.* at 31.

29. *Id.* at 5–6.

30. *Id.* at 5.

31. *Id.*

32. *Id.* at 16.

33. *Id.*

34. *Id.* at 82–83.

35. *Id.* at 57.

36. *Id.* at 62.

37. *Id.* at 65.

38. United States v. Stevens, 130 S. Ct. 1577, 1582 (2010).

39. Snyder v. Phelps, 131 S. Ct. 1207, 1219 (2011).

40. *Id.* at 1213.

41. United States v. Stevens, 130 S. Ct. 1577, 1589 (2010).

42. *Id.*

43. *Id.* at 1592.

44. *Id.* at 1601.

45. Snyder v. Phelps, 131 S. Ct. 1207, 1222 (2011).

46. Jonathan Haidt & Selin Kesebir, *Morality, in* HANDBOOK OF SOCIAL PSYCHOLOGY 822 (S. Fiske, D. Gilbert, & G. Lindzey eds., 5th ed. 2010).

47. Snyder v. Phelps, 131 S. Ct. 1207, 1227 (2011).

48. *Id.* at 1222.

49. Kathleen M. Sullivan, *Two Concepts of Freedom of Speech*, 124 HARV. L. REV. 143, 144 (2010).

50. *Id.*

51. David M. Rabban, *Free Speech in Progressive Social Thought*, 74 TEX. L. REV. 951, 952–953 (1996).

52. *Id.*

53. *Id.* at 1030.

54. *Id.* at 1031.

55. CASS R. SUNSTEIN, DEMOCRACY AND THE PROBLEM OF FREE SPEECH 17–51 (1995).

56. Lee Epstein, Christopher M. Parker, & Jeffrey A. Segal, *Do Justices Defend the Speech They Hate? In-Group Bias, Opportunism, and the First Amendment*, Revised version of a paper presented at the 2013 Annual Meeting of the American Political Science Association, Chicago, IL, http://epstein.wustl.edu/research/InGroupBias.pdf.

57. Frederick Schauer, *The Political Incidence of the Free Speech Principle*, U. COLO. L. REV. 935, 938 (1993).

58. *Id.*

59. Kathleen M. Sullivan, *Two Concepts of Freedom of Speech*, 124 HARV. L. REV. 143, 146 (2010).

60. *Id.* at 144.

61. Garcetti v. Ceballos, 547 U.S. 410 (2006).

62. Morse v. Frederick, 551 U.S. 393, 409 (2007).

63. Holder v. Humanitarian Law Project, 130 S. Ct. 2705 (2010).

64. BRUCE ACKERMAN, WE THE PEOPLE: FOUNDATIONS 125 (vol. 1, 1991).

65. GEOFFREY R. STONE, LOUIS M. SEIDMAN, CASS SUNSTEIN, PAMELA S. KARLAN, & MARK V. TUSHNET, CONSTITUTIONAL LAW 749 (6th ed. 2009).

66. Lochner v. New York, 198 U.S. 45, 75 (1905).

67. James M. Weinstein, *The Story of* Masses Publishing Co. v. Patten: *Judge Learned Hand, First Amendment Prophet, in* FIRST AMENDMENT STORIES 65 (Richard W. Garnett & Andrew Koppelman eds., 2012).

68. *Id.* at 65 n.16.

69. RICHARD POLENBERG, FIGHTING FAITHS: THE ABRAMS CASE, THE SUPREME COURT, AND FREE SPEECH 207 (1987).

70. James M. Weinstein, *The Story of* Masses Publishing Co. v. Patten: *Judge Learned Hand, First Amendment Prophet, in* FIRST AMENDMENT STORIES 66 (Richard W. Garnett & Andrew Koppelman eds., 2012).

71. *Id.*

72. See The Prize Cases, 67 U.S. 635 (1863).

73. Korematsu v. United States, 323 U.S. 214 (1944).

74. Schenck v. United States, 249 U.S. 47 (1919).

75. James M. Weinstein, *The Story of* Masses Publishing Co. v. Patten: *Judge Learned Hand, First Amendment Profit, in* FIRST AMENDMENT STORIES 61–62 (Richard W. Garnett & Andrew Koppelman eds., 2012).

76. Schenck v. United States, 249 U.S. 47, 52 (1919).

77. Patterson v. Colorado, 205 U.S. 454, 462 (1907).

78. Schenck v. United States, 249 U.S. 47, 52 (1919).

79. *Id.*

80. James M. Weinstein, *The Story of* Masses Publishing Co. v. Patten: *Judge Learned Hand, First Amendment Profit, in* FIRST AMENDMENT STORIES 89 (Richard W. Garnett & Andrew Koppelman eds., 2012).

81. *Id.*

82. Abrams v. United States, 250 U.S. 616 (1919).

83. THOMAS HEALY, THE GREAT DISSENT: HOW OLIVER WENDELL HOLMES CHANGED HIS MIND—AND CHANGED THE HISTORY OF FREE SPEECH IN AMERICA 5 (2013).

84. See Debs v. United States, 249 U.S. 211 (1919).

85. Schenck v. United States, 249 U.S. 47, 52 (1919).

86. Abrams v. United States, 250 U.S. 616, 626 (1919).

87. *Id.*

88. *Id.* at 627.

89. *Id.*

90. *Id.* at 628.

91. *Id.*

92. *Id.*

93. *Id.*

94. *Id.* at 629.

95. *Id.* at 630.

96. *Id.* at 628.

97. THOMAS HEALY, THE GREAT DISSENT: HOW OLIVER WENDELL HOLMES CHANGED HIS MIND—AND CHANGED THE HISTORY OF FREE SPEECH IN AMERICA 198–210 (2013).

98. Abrams v. United States, 250 U.S. 616, 628 (1919).

99. *Id.* at 630.

100. Bradley C. S. Watson, *The Curious Constitution of Oliver Wendell Holmes Jr.*, NATIONAL REVIEW, December 31, 2009, at 41.

101. JONATHAN HAIDT, THE RIGHTEOUS MIND: WHY GOOD PEOPLE ARE DIVIDED BY POLITICS AND RELIGION 257 (2012).

102. *Id.*

103. Gitlow v. New York, 268 U.S. 652, 673 (1925).

104. *Id.*

105. William Wayne Justice, *A Relativistic Constitution, in* JUDGES ON JUDGING: VIEWS FROM THE BENCH 198 (David M. O'Brien ed., 2013).

106. Bradley C. S. Watson, *The Curious Constitution of Oliver Wendell Holmes Jr.*, NATIONAL REVIEW, December 31, 2009, at 40.

107. Buck v. Bell, 274 U.S. 200, 208 (1927).

108. William Wayne Justice, *A Relativistic Constitution, in* JUDGES ON JUDGING: VIEWS FROM THE BENCH 199 (David M. O'Brien ed., 2013).

109. Jonathan Haidt & Selin Kesebir, *Morality, in* HANDBOOK OF SOCIAL PSYCHOLOGY 822 (S. Fiske, D. Gilbert, & G. Lindzey eds., 5th ed. 2010).

110. Melvin I. Urofsky, *Brandeis, Louis Dembitz, in* THE OXFORD COMPANION TO THE SUPREME COURT OF THE UNITED STATES 83 (Kermit L. Hall ed., 1992).

111. *Id.*

112. Schaefer v. United States, 251 U.S. 466 (1920).

113. *Id.* at 486.

114. *Id.*

115. *Id.* at 494–495.

116. Whitney v. California, 274 U.S. 357, 377 (1927).

117. *Id.* at 376.

118. *Id.*

119. *Id.* at 378.

120. M. Stanton Evans, *Trends*, NATIONAL REVIEW BULLETIN, December 25, 1962, at 6.

121. *Id.*

122. *Id.*

123. *Id.*

124. M. Stanton Evans, *Trends*, NATIONAL REVIEW BULLETIN, March 19, 1960, at 6.

125. *Id.*

126. *Id.*

127. Forrest Davis, *The Court Reaches for Total Power*, NATIONAL REVIEW, July 6, 1957, at 33–36.

128. Watkins v. United States, 354 U.S. 178 (1957).

129. See Barenblatt v. United States, 360 U.S. 109 (1959).

130. Watkins v. United States, 354 U.S. 178, 197 (1957).

131. Forrest Davis, *The Court Reaches for Total Power*, NATIONAL REVIEW, July 6, 1957, at 33–36.

132. *Id.*

133. *Id.*

134. Editorial, *Let the Intellectuals Take It from Here*, NATIONAL REVIEW, June 17, 1961, at 371.

135. *Id.*

136. *Id.*

137. *Id.*

138. *Id.*

139. *Id.*

140. *Id.*

141. Dahlia Lithwick, *Justice Grover Versus Justice Oscar: Scalia and Breyer Sell Very Different Constitutional Worldviews*, SLATE, December 6, 2006, http://www.slate.com/articles/news_and_politics/jurisprudence/2006/12/justice_grover_versus_justice_oscar.html.

142. Editorial, *Let the Intellectuals Take It from Here*, NATIONAL REVIEW, June 17, 1961, at 371.

143. M. Stanton Evans, *Trends*, NATIONAL REVIEW BULLETIN, August 19, 1961, at 6.

144. *Id.*

145. *Id.*

146. William F. Buckley, Jr., *A New Look at a Controversial Committee*, NATIONAL REVIEW, January 16, 1962, at 15–21.

147. *Id.*

148. Willmoore Kendall, *Baloney and Free Speech*, NATIONAL REVIEW, May 22, 1962, at 367–368.

149. *Id.*

150. *Id.*

151. *Id.*

152. *Id.*

Chapter 1

1. THE AMERICAN HERITAGE DICTIONARY OF THE ENGLISH LANGUAGE, http://ahdictionary.com/.

2. *Id.*

3. Stephen M. Feldman, *Conservative Eras in Supreme Court Decision-Making:* Employment Division v. Smith, *Judicial Restraint, and Neoconservatism*, 32 CARDOZO L. REV. 1791, 1792 (2011).

4. David Brooks, Op-Ed., *The Conservative Mind*, N.Y. TIMES, September 25, 2012, at A23 (emphasis added).

5. *Id.*

6. GREGORY L. SCHNEIDER, CONSERVATISM IN AMERICA SINCE 1930, 169 (2003).

7. Frank S. Meyer, *Libertarianism or Libertinism?*, NATIONAL REVIEW, September 9, 1969, at 910.

8. GREGORY L. SCHNEIDER, CONSERVATISM IN AMERICA SINCE 1930, 170 (2003).

9. *Id.*

10. *National Review* media kit, *http://www.nationalreview.com/media-kit.*

11. Richard Lowry, *A Personal Retrospective: NR and Its Founder*, NATIONAL REVIEW, August 9, 2004, http://www.nationalreview.com/article/216012/personal-retrospective-rich-lowry.

12. Ken I. Kersch, *Ecumenicalism Through Constitutionalism: The Discursive Development of Constitutional Conservatism in* National Review, *1955–1980*, 25 STUDIES IN AMERICAN POLITICAL DEVELOPMENT 86, 87, 98 (2011).

13. *Id.* at 88.

14. ANN SOUTHWORTH, LAWYERS OF THE RIGHT: PROFESSIONALIZING THE CONSERVATIVE COALITION 41 (2008).

15. Richard Lowry, *A Personal Retrospective: NR and Its Founder*, NATIONAL REVIEW, August 9, 2004, http://www.nationalreview.com/article/216012/personal-retrospective-rich-lowry.

16. *Id.*

17. William F. Buckley, Jr., *Feeling One's Way on Finance Reform*, NATIONAL REVIEW, April 16, 2001, at 62–63.

18. *Id.*

19. *Id.*

20. Richard Lowry, *A Spoiler's Crusade: Senator John McCain and "the System,"* NATIONAL REVIEW, February 19, 2001, at 30–32.

21. *Id.*

22. *Id.*

23. See, for example, Shannen W. Coffin, *"Not True": With Its* Citizens United *Decision the Supreme Court Struck a Blow for Free Speech*, NATIONAL REVIEW DIGITAL, February 22, 2010, https://www.nationalreview.com/nrd/articles/339532/not-true; Bradley A. Smith, *Disclosed Partisanship: An Unfair and Unnecessary Campaign-Finance "Reform,"* NATIONAL REVIEW DIGITAL, June 7, 2010, https://www.nationalreview.com/nrd/articles/316311/disclosed-partisanship.

24. Richard Lowry, *A Personal Retrospective: NR and Its Founder*, NATIONAL REVIEW, August 9, 2004, http://www.nationalreview.com/article/216012/personal-retrospective-rich-lowry.

25. *National Review Changing Editor*, N.Y. TIMES, November 5, 1997, http://www.nytimes.com/1997/11/05/business/national-review-changing-editor.html.

26. I searched all issues of *National Review* since its inception (including *National Review Bulletin*). Using *Opinion Archives*, I searched for the terms "First Amendment" and "free speech." Although there have certainly been articles that address substantive issues surrounding either "free speech" or the "First Amendment" that do not include both of these search terms, for the sake of consistency and economy only search results that contained both terms, and included an unequivocal perspective on the issue, were included in the enumeration below. Letters to the editor and advertisements were excluded, as were articles that were neutral or expressed a mixed message

on free speech. Articles that expressed a clear point of view on freedom of speech were coded either "pro–free speech" or "pro–speech regulation."

27. The pro–speech-regulation articles include: "The Court Reaches for Total Power," Forrest Davis, July 6, 1957; "Do We Want an 'Open Society'?" Willmoore Kendall, January 31, 1959; "Common Sense, By a Nose" Editorial, March 11, 1961; "Let the Intellectuals Take It from Here" Editorial, June 17, 1961; "Trends," M. Stanton Evans, August 19, 1961; "Baloney and Free Speech," Willmoore Kendall, May 22, 1962; "The Week" Editorial, June 26, 1962; "Trends," M. Stanton Evans, December 25, 1962. The pro–free-speech articles include: "The Supreme Court's Doubtful Analogy," C. Dickerman Williams, September 29, 1956; "The New South and the Conservative Tradition," Donald Davidson, September 10, 1960; "The Heisters' Day in Court," James J. Leff, January 14, 1964.

28. The pro–speech-regulation articles include: "The Angelic Vision of the Warren Court" Editorial, February 7, 1967; "How Do We Get Out of It?" Richmond Crinkley, June 4, 1968; "On the Left" Editorial, December 23, 1969; "Mass Intimidation," Frank S. Meyer, June 1, 1971; "On the Right: The POWs and the Professor," William F. Buckley, Jr., July 27, 1971; "Pornography, Community, Law," Gary North, August 31, 1973; "The Market for Ideas," R. H. Coase, September 27, 1974. The pro–free-speech articles include: "Business & Briefs," Donald Waterford, November 10, 1970; "Notes & Asides," William F. Buckley, Jr., January 26, 1971; "Comstock's Nemesis," David Brudnoy, September 24, 1971; "Political Reforms" Editorial, December 21, 1973; "Joe Rauh's Counterattack," Ralph de Toledano, December 20, 1974.

29. The pro–speech-regulation articles include: "Free and Freer Speech" Editorial, March 14, 1975; "The Week" Editorial, October 15, 1976; "Toward a Republic of Pigs," George W. Carey, February 4, 1977; "Notes & Asides" Editorial, February 18, 1977; "Against Folk-Constitutionalism," M. J. Sobran, Jr., August 4, 1978; "Postmortem on the Nazis," William F. Buckley, Jr., August 18, 1978. The pro–free-speech articles include: "Free Speech and Spending" Editorial, September 12, 1975; "At the FCC, We Try . . . ," Stephen J. Chapman, September 17, 1976; "The Week" Editorial, February 18, 1977; "The Elusive Goal of Campaign Reform," Ida Walters, May 30, 1980; "Seven Dirty Words" Editorial, October 15, 1982; "The High Cost of Free Speech," Richard McKenzie, September 2, 1983.

30. The pro–speech-regulation articles include: "Why Free Speech?," Joseph Sobran, March 22, 1985; "Who's Afraid of Robert Bork?," Richard Vigilante, August 28, 1987; "The Court and the Flag Decision," William F. Buckley, Jr., August 4, 1989; "Hooray for the Amendment," William F. Buckley, Jr., August 4, 1989; "Justice Goes Begging," John O'Sullivan, February 19, 1990; "On with the Dance," John O'Sullivan, July 29, 1991; "Just a Song?," Charlton Heston, August 17, 1992. The pro–free-speech articles include: "First Sightings," Jeffrey Hart, September 26, 1986; "Remember Wayne Dick" Editorial, October 24, 1986, "Liberalism Versus Free Speech," Wilcomb E. Washburn, September 30, 1988; "PC in LA," Linda Seebach, July 19, 1993; "The RICO Racket," G. Robert Blakeley, May 16, 1994; "Brrr!," Stuart Creque, October 10, 1994; "Speech Impediments," Michael Greve, October 10, 1994.

31. The pro–speech-regulation articles include: "The Sex Wars," Maggie Gallagher, May 15, 1995; "Burn the Flag? Well, No," William F. Buckley, Jr., July 10, 1995; "Speaking in Tongues," Harold Johnson, November 6, 1995; "Freeway to Damascus," John O'Sullivan, February 24, 1997; "As I Was Saying," John O'Sullivan, January 26, 1998; "That's Entertainment" Editorial, July 12, 1999; "Feeling One's Way on Finance Reform," William F. Buckley, Jr., April 16, 2001; "The Week" Editorial, October 27, 2003. The pro–free-speech articles include: "Works in Progress," John O'Sullivan, July 31, 1995; "The America We Seek: A Statement of Pro-Life Principle and Concern," multiple authors, March 25, 1996; "Hustlers," John Simon, February 24, 1997; "Fight, God, Fight," William F. Buckley, Jr., March 24, 1997; "Pruning the FDA," Alexander Volokh, August 11, 1997; "Pack It In," Robert A. Levy, May 4, 1998; "The Court's Mr. Right," Daniel E. Troy, August 9, 1999; "Free Association," Richard A. Epstein, October 9, 2000; "A Spoiler's Crusade," Richard Lowry, February 19, 2001; "Veto"

Editorial, March 11, 2002; "Taking the Con Out of Con. Law," Richard A. Epstein, June 3, 2002; "Being Lee Bollinger," Matthew Continetti, October 14, 2002.

32. The pro–speech-regulation articles include: "The Week" Editorial, November 6, 2006; "Thanks a Lot," Robert Bork, April 16, 2007; "The Week" Editorial, May 5, 2008. The pro–free-speech articles include: "The Week" Editorial, March 28, 2005; "Church/State at Dartmouth," William F. Buckley, October 24, 2005; "Speech Impediment," Jonah Goldberg, February 27, 2006; "Filth Before Freedom," Jonah Goldberg, May 5, 2008; "Gay Abandon," Mark Hemingway, July 14, 2008; "Not True," Shannen W. Coffin, February 22, 2010; "Disclosed Partisanship," Bradley A. Smith, June 7, 2010; "Censorship as 'Tolerance,'" Jacob Mchangama, July 19, 2010; "Fatwa Against Free Speech," Nina Shea, October 15, 2012; "Media Matter," James Lileks, October 15, 2012; "Fighting for Words," Larry Alexander, December 17, 2012; "The Week" Editorial, September 16, 2013; "The Week" Editorial, October 14, 2013; "In to Win," Mark Steyn, January 27, 2014; "The Week," Editorial, April 7, 2014; "The Week" Editorial, April 21, 2014; "Restore the Religious Freedom Restoration Act," David French, April 21, 2014; "The Climate Inquisitor," Charles C. W. Cooke, May 5, 2014; "The Week" Editorial, June 2, 2014; "The Week" Editorial, October 6, 2014; "Democrats vs. the First Amendment" Editorial, October 6, 2014.

33. JONATHAN HAIDT, THE RIGHTEOUS MIND: WHY GOOD PEOPLE ARE DIVIDED BY POLITICS AND RELIGION 211 (2012).

34. *Id.* at 183.

35. See, for example, FCC v. Pacifica Foundation, 438 U.S. 726 (1978); City of Renton v. Playtime Theatres, 475 U.S. 41 (1986).

36. MARK A. GRABER, TRANSFORMING FREE SPEECH: THE AMBIGUOUS LEGACY OF CIVIL LIBERTARIANISM 8 (1991).

37. *Id.*

38. JONATHAN HAIDT, THE RIGHTEOUS MIND: WHY GOOD PEOPLE ARE DIVIDED BY POLITICS AND RELIGION 212 (2012).

39. *Id.*

40. See discussion in Chapter 5.

41. Virginia State Board of Pharmacy v. Virginia Citizens Consumer Council, 425 U.S. 748, 762 (1976).

42. See Valentine v. Chrestensen, 316 U.S. 532 (1942).

43. Citizens United v. FEC, 130 S. Ct. 876 (2010).

44. Richard Cohen, *Bush's War Against Nuance*, WASHINGTON POST, February 19, 2004, at A17.

45. See HOWARD GILLMAN, MARK A. GRABER, KEITH WITTINGTON, AMERICAN CONSTITUTIONALISM: VOLUME II RIGHTS AND LIBERTIES 10 (2013).

46. Dennis v. United States, 341 U.S. 494, 580 (1951) (Black, J., dissenting).

47. *Id.*

48. Frederick Schauer, *The Political Incidence of the Free Speech Principle*, 64 U. Colo. L. Rev. 935, 943 (1993).

49. MARK A. GRABER, TRANSFORMING FREE SPEECH: THE AMBIGUOUS LEGACY OF CIVIL LIBERTARIANISM 154 (1991).

50. *Id.*

51. *Id.* at 155.

52. ACLU.org, *ACLU History: Speaking Up for Freedom of Expression*, http://www.aclu.org.

53. David M. Rabban, *The Free Speech League, the ACLU, and Changing Conceptions of Free Speech in American History*, 45 STAN. L. REV. 47, 53 (1992).

54. STEVEN M. TELES, THE RISE OF THE CONSERVATIVE MOVEMENT: THE BATTLE FOR CONTROL OF THE LAW 28 (2008).

55. *Id.* at 22.

56. Gitlow v. New York, 268 U.S. 652, 655 (1925).

57. United States Presidential Election, 1988, http://en.wikipedia.org/wiki/United_States_presidential_election,_1988.

58. Lee Epstein & Jeffrey A. Segal, *The Rehnquist Court and the First Amendment: Trumping the First Amendment?*, 21 WASH. U. J.L. & POL'Y 81, 87–88 (2006).

59. *Id.*

60. *Id.* at 82.

61. *Id.*; Lee Epstein, Christopher M. Parker, & Jeffrey A. Segal, *Do Justices Defend the Speech They Hate? In-Group Bias, Opportunism, and the First Amendment*, Revised version of a paper presented at the 2013 Annual Meeting of the American Political Science Association, Chicago, IL, http://epstein.wustl.edu/research/InGroupBias.pdf.

62. Richard A. Posner, *Why Didn't Robert Bork Reach the Supreme Court?* SLATE, December 19, 2012, http://www.slate.com/articles/news_and_politics/view_from_chicago/2012/12/robert_bork_dead_why_didn_t_he_reach_the_supreme_court.html.

63. Joseph Sobran, *In Ted Kennedy's America*, NATIONAL REVIEW, October 13, 1989, at 48–51.

64. ACLU.org, *ACLU Opposes Nomination of Judge Alito*, http://web.archive.org/web/20070406173742/http://www.aclu.org/scotus/alito/.

65. See, for example, Joe Nocera, Op-Ed., *The Ugliness Started with Bork*, N.Y. TIMES, October 21, 2011, http://www.nytimes.com/2011/10/22/opinion/nocera-the-ugliness-all-started-with-bork.html.

66. John M. Broder, *Edward M. Kennedy, Senate Stalwart, Is Dead at 77*, N.Y. TIMES, August 27, 2009, *http://www.nytimes.com/2009/08/27/us/politics/27kennedy.html.*

67. ACLU.org, *ACLU Opposes Nomination of Judge Alito*, http://web.archive.org/web/20070406173742/http://www.aclu.org/scotus/alito/.

68. Robert H. Bork, *Neutral Principles and Some First Amendment Problems*, 47 IND. L.J. 1, 23 (1971).

69. ROBERT H. BORK, THE TEMPTING OF AMERICA 247 (1990).

70. Linda Greenhouse, Op-Ed., *Robert Bork's Tragedy*, N.Y TIMES, January 9, 2013, http://opinionator.blogs.nytimes.com/2013/01/09/robert-borks-tragedy/?hp.

71. *Id.*

72. MARK A. GRABER, TRANSFORMING FREE SPEECH: THE AMBIGUOUS LEGACY OF CIVIL LIBERTARIANISM (1991).

73. *Id.* at 52.

74. *Id.* at 24.

75. *Id.*

76. *Id.* at 44.

77. *Id.*

78. *Id.*

79. *Id.* at 44–49.

80. *Id.* at 48–49.

81. See, for example, Frank S. Meyer, *Confusion in the Court*, NATIONAL REVIEW, January 11, 1956, at 22–23; *Oyez!*, NATIONAL REVIEW, October 22, 1960, at 232; *The Week*, NATIONAL REVIEW BULLETIN, June 26, 1962, at 2; M. Stanton Evans, *Trends*, NATIONAL REVIEW BULLETIN, March 19, 1960, at 6.

82. Frank S. Meyer, *Confusion in the Court,* NATIONAL REVIEW, January 11, 1956, at 22–23.

83. *Id.*

84. *Id.*

85. M. Stanton Evans, *Trends,* NATIONAL REVIEW BULLETIN, March 19, 1960, at 6.

86. *Id.*

87. *Id.*

88. *Id.*

89. *The Week,* NATIONAL REVIEW BULLETIN, June 26, 1962, at 2.

90. *Id.* (emphasis added).

91. Of course, from a constitutional perspective, there is no reason to believe that the existence of First Amendment "liberty" necessarily suggests a precisely parallel degree of "individual freedom" for property or contract under the Takings Clause of the Fifth Amendment or the Due Process Clause of the Fourteenth Amendment. Equivalence between property rights and expressive rights is neither required by the text of the Constitution nor by Supreme Court precedent. Furthermore, from a substantive perspective, there are surely arguments that could fill volumes explicating practical, philosophical, and jurisprudential reasons for treating these broad categories of freedom differently. Yet, these split personalities nonetheless remain curious and potent attributes of the "conservative" and "liberal" mind in modern America.

Chapter 2

1. See, for example, Madsen v. Women's Health Center, 512 U.S. 753 (1994); McCullen v. Coakley, 134 S. Ct. 2518 (2014).

2. See, for example, Rust v. Sullivan, 500 U.S. 173 (1991).

3. Some examples include Burt Neuborn, New York University law professor, and Steve Simpson of the Institute for Justice: see Greg Stohr, *Freedom of Speech Is Buttressed as U.S. Supreme Court Concludes Term,* BLOOMBERG, June 28, 2011; prominent First Amendment lawyer Floyd Abrams: see Adam Liptak, *Study Challenges Supreme Court's Image as Defender of Free Speech,* N.Y. TIMES, January 8, 2012.

4. See infra, Introduction at xx–xx.

5. Kathleen M. Sullivan, *Two Concepts of Freedom of Speech,* 124 HARV. L. REV. 143, 144 (2010).

6. See Monica Youn, *The Roberts Court's Free Speech Double Standard,* American Constitution Society Blog, November 29, 2011, *http://www.acslaw.org/acsblog/the-roberts-court%E2%80%99s-free-speech-double-standard;* Lee Epstein & Jeffrey A. Segal, *A (Brief) Report on the Roberts Court and Free Speech,* December 22, 2011, *http://epstein.usc.edu/research/RobertsFreeSpeech.pdf;* Erwin Chemerinsky, *Not a Free Speech Court,* 53 ARIZ. L. REV. 723 (2011).

7. Lee Epstein, Christopher M. Parker, & Jeffrey A. Segal, *Do Justices Defend the Speech They Hate? In-Group Bias, Opportunism, and the First Amendment,* Revised version of a paper presented at the 2013 Annual Meeting of the American Political Science Association, Chicago, IL, at 4–5, http://epstein.wustl.edu/research/InGroupBias.pdf.

8. *Id.* at 3, 14.

9. Texas v. Johnson, 491 U.S. 397, 399 (1989).

10. Peter Hanson, *Flag Burning, in* PUBLIC OPINION AND CONSTITUTIONAL CONTROVERSY 189 (Nathaniel Persily, Jack Citrin, & Patrick J. Egan eds., 2008).

11. See BARRY FRIEDMAN, THE WILL OF THE PEOPLE: HOW PUBLIC OPINION HAS INFLUENCED THE SUPREME COURT AND SHAPED THE MEANING OF THE CONSTITUTION 16 (2009).

12. Peter Hanson, *Flag Burning, in* PUBLIC OPINION AND CONSTITUTIONAL CONTRO-VERSY 189 (Nathaniel Persily, Jack Citrin, & Patrick J. Egan eds., 2008).

13. William F. Buckley, Jr., *On the Right: The Court and the Flag Decision,* NATIONAL RE-VIEW, August 4, 1989, at 54 (emphasis in original).

14. *Id.*

15. *Id.*

16. Frederick Schauer, *The Political Incidence of the Free Speech Principle,* 64 U. COLO. L. REV. 935, 943 (1993).

17. See Steven M. Feldman, *The Rule of Law or the Rule of Politics? Harmonizing the Internal and External Views of Supreme Court Decision Making,* 30 L. & SOC. INQUIRY 89 (2005).

18. See discussion in Charles Gardner Geyh, *Introduction: So What Does Law Have to Do with It?, in* WHAT'S LAW GOT TO DO WITH IT? WHAT JUDGES DO, WHY THEY DO IT, WHAT'S AT STAKE 1–4 (Charles Gardner Geyh ed., 2011).

19. *Id.*

20. See Steven M. Feldman, *The Rule of Law or the Rule of Politics? Harmonizing the Internal and External Views of Supreme Court Decision Making,* 30 L. & SOC. INQUIRY 89 (2005).

21. See discussion in Charles Gardner Geyh, *Introduction: So What Does Law Have to Do with It?, in* WHAT'S LAW GOT TO DO WITH IT? WHAT JUDGES DO, WHY THEY DO IT, WHAT'S AT STAKE 3 (Charles Gardner Geyh ed., 2011).

22. See, generally, Wayne Batchis, *Constitutional Nihilism: Political Science and the Deconstruction of the Judiciary,* 6 RUTGERS J.L. & PUB. POL'Y 1, 10–14 (2008).

23. JEFFREY A. SEGAL, HAROLD J. SPAETH, & SARA C. BENESH, THE SUPREME COURT IN THE AMERICAN SYSTEM 16 (2005).

24. *Id.*

25. JEFFREY A. SEGAL & HAROLD J. SPAETH, THE SUPREME COURT AND THE ATTI-TUDINAL MODEL REVISITED 86 (2002).

26. Barry Friedman & Andrew D. Martin, *Looking for Law in All the Wrong Places, in* WHAT'S LAW GOT TO DO WITH IT? WHAT JUDGES DO, WHY THEY DO IT, WHAT'S AT STAKE 163 (Charles Gardner Geyh ed., 2011).

27. JEFFREY A. SEGAL & HAROLD J. SPAETH, THE SUPREME COURT AND THE ATTI-TUDINAL MODEL REVISITED 45 (2002).

28. *Id.* at 46.

29. JEFFREY A. SEGAL, HAROLD J. SPAETH, & SARA C. BENESH, THE SUPREME COURT IN THE AMERICAN SYSTEM 16 (2005).

30. *Id.* at 17.

31. Lawrence Baum, *Law and Policy: More and Less Than a Dichotomy, in* WHAT'S LAW GOT TO DO WITH IT? WHAT JUDGES DO, WHY THEY DO IT, WHAT'S AT STAKE 84 (Charles Gardner Geyh ed., 2011).

32. Keith E. Whittington, R. Daniel Kelemen, & Gregory A. Caldeira, *The Study of Law and Politics, in* THE OXFORD HANDBOOK OF LAW AND POLITICS 9 (Keith E. Whittington, R. Daniel Kelemen, & Gregory A. Caldeira eds., 2010).

33. Thomas M. Keck, *From Bakke to Grutter: The Rise of Rights-Based Conservatism, in* THE SUPREME COURT & AMERICAN POLITICAL DEVELOPMENT 414 (Ronald Kahn & Ken Kersch eds., 2006).

34. Ronald Kahn & Ken I. Kersch, *Introduction, in* THE SUPREME COURT & AMERICAN POLITICAL DEVELOPMENT 21 (Ronald Kahn & Ken I. Kersch eds., 2006).

35. Lawrence Baum, *Law and Policy: More and Less Than a Dichotomy, in* WHAT'S LAW GOT TO DO WITH IT? WHAT JUDGES DO, WHY THEY DO IT, WHAT'S AT STAKE 76 (Charles Gardner Geyh ed., 2011).

36. *Id.*

37. McCulloch v. Maryland, 17 U.S. 316, 407 (1819).

38. *Id.*

39. Keith E. Whittington, R. Daniel Kelemen, & Gregory A. Caldeira, *The Study of Law and Politics, in* THE OXFORD HANDBOOK OF LAW AND POLITICS 9 (Keith E. Whittington, R. Daniel Kelemen, & Gregory A. Caldeira eds., 2010).

40. *Id.* at 7.

41. Rogers M. Smith, *Historical Institutionalism and the Study of Law, in* THE OXFORD HANDBOOK OF LAW AND POLITICS 48 (Keith E. Whittington, R. Daniel Kelemen, & Gregory A. Caldeira eds., 2010).

42. Jeffrey A. Segal, *What's Law Got to Do with It: Thoughts from "the Realm of Political Science, in* WHAT'S LAW GOT TO DO WITH IT? WHAT JUDGES DO, WHY THEY DO IT, WHAT'S AT STAKE 26 (Charles Gardner Geyh ed., 2011).

43. Rogers M. Smith, *Historical Institutionalism and the Study of Law, in* THE OXFORD HANDBOOK OF LAW AND POLITICS 48 (Keith E. Whittington, R. Daniel Kelemen, & Gregory A. Caldeira eds., 2010).

44. *Id.*

45. Gerald N. Rosenberg, *Protecting Fundamental Political Liberties: The Constitution in Context,* Paper presented at the Annual Meeting of the American Political Science Association, Washington, DC, September 1–4, 1988, *cited in* Jon B. Gould, *Difference Through a New Lens: First Amendment Legal Realism and the Regulation of Hate Speech,* 33 L. & SOC'Y REV. 761 (1999).

46. See, for example, Peter Hanson, *Flag Burning, in* PUBLIC OPINION AND CONSTITUTIONAL CONTROVERSY 184 (Nathaniel Persily, Jack Citrin, & Patrick J. Egan eds., 2008).

47. Nathaniel Persily, *Introduction, in* PUBLIC OPINION AND CONSTITUTIONAL CONTROVERSY 8–9 (Nathaniel Persily, Jack Citrin, & Patrick J. Egan eds., 2008).

48. Keith J. Bybee, *The Rule of Law Is Dead! Long Live the Rule of Law!, in* WHAT'S LAW GOT TO DO WITH IT? WHAT JUDGES DO, WHY THEY DO IT, WHAT'S AT STAKE 312 (Charles Gardner Geyh ed., 2011).

49. *Id.*

50. HOWARD GILLMAN, MARK A. GRABER, & KEITH WITTINGTON, AMERICAN CONSTITUTIONALISM: VOLUME II RIGHTS AND LIBERTIES 6 (2013).

51. Nathaniel Persily, *Introduction, in* PUBLIC OPINION AND CONSTITUTIONAL CONTROVERSY 8–9 (Nathaniel Persily, Jack Citrin, & Patrick J. Egan eds., 2008).

52. *Id.* at 12–14.

53. *Id.*

54. LAWRENCE BAUM, THE SUPREME COURT 44 (9th ed. 2007).

55. See, for example, Neil Irwin, *Tax Policy: Paul Ryan's Proposal Hints at Change in Tone on Poverty,* N.Y. TIMES, July 24, 2014 (discussing how the Earned Income Tax Credit was "once a conservative idea," but it is now viewed skeptically by the right), http://www.nytimes.com/2014/07/25/upshot/paul-ryans-proposal-hints-at-change-in-tone-on-poverty.html?abt=0002&abg=0.

56. Lee Epstein & Jeffrey A. Segal, *The Rehnquist Court and the First Amendment: Trumping the First Amendment?,* 21 WASH. U. J.L. & POL'Y 81, 87–88 (2006). (There is no evidence, as of 2006, that political scientists have amended this assumption.)

57. *Id.* at 82.

58. Eugene Volokh, *How the Justices Voted in Free Speech Cases, 1994–2002, www.law.ucla.edu/ volokh/howvoted.htm* (updating Eugene Volokh, *How the Justices Voted in Free Speech Cases, 1994– 2000*, 48 UCLA L. REV. 1191 (2001)).

59. *Id.*

60. See J. M. Balkin, *Ideological Drift and the Struggle over Meaning*, 25 CONN. L. REV. 869 (1993); Kathleen Sullivan, *The Justices of Rules and Standards*, 106 HARV. L. REV. 22, 103–104 (1992).

61. Kathleen M. Sullivan, *Two Concepts of Freedom of Speech*, 124 HARV. L. REV. 143, 143–144 (2010).

62. Lee Epstein & Jeffrey A. Segal, *The Rehnquist Court and the First Amendment: Trumping the First Amendment?*, 21 WASH. U. J.L. & POL'Y 81 (2006).

63. *Id.* at 94 n.52.

64. Citizens United v. FEC, 130 S. Ct. 876, 898 (2010).

65. *Id.* at 899.

66. *Id.* at 914.

67. Supreme Court Database, http://supremecourtdatabase.org/documentation. php?var=decisionDirection.

68. Carolyn Shapiro, *Coding Complexity: Bringing Law to the Empirical Analysis of the Supreme Court*, 60 HASTINGS L.J. 477, 480 (2009).

69. Lee Epstein & Jeffrey A. Segal, *The Rehnquist Court and the First Amendment: Trumping the First Amendment?*, 21 Wash. U. J.L. & POL'Y 81, 94 n.52 (2006).

70. *Id.*

71. Boy Scouts v. Dale, 530 U.S. 640, 659 (2000).

72. Lee Epstein & Jeffrey A. Segal, *The Rehnquist Court and the First Amendment: Trumping the First Amendment?*, 21 Wash. U. J.L. & POL'Y 81, 94 n.52 (2006).

73. *Id.*

74. *Id.*

75. JEFFREY A. SEGAL & HAROLD J. SPAETH, THE SUPREME COURT AND THE ATTITUDINAL MODEL REVISITED 44 (2002).

76. *Id.*

77. Lee Epstein & Jeffrey A. Segal, *The Rehnquist Court and the First Amendment: Trumping the First Amendment?*, 21 WASH. U. J.L. & POL'Y 81, 94 n.52 (2006).

78. *Id.* at 106, fig. 6.

79. *Id.*

80. *Id.*

81. *Id.* at 93.

82. *Id.*

83. *Id.* at 93 n.49.

84. *Id.*

85. *Id.* at 104.

86. *Id.*

87. *Id.* at 93.

88. JEFFREY A. SEGAL & HAROLD J. SPAETH, THE SUPREME COURT AND THE ATTITUDINAL MODEL REVISITED 46 (2002).

89. *Id.* at 47.

90. Keith J. Bybee, *The Rule of Law Is Dead! Long Live the Rule of Law!*, *in* WHAT'S LAW GOT TO DO WITH IT? WHAT JUDGES DO, WHY THEY DO IT, WHAT'S AT STAKE 317 (Charles Gardner Geyh ed., 2011).

91. David A. Strauss, *Freedom of Speech and the Common-Law Constitution, in* ETERNALLY VIGILANT: FREE SPEECH IN THE MODERN ERA 33 (Lee C. Bollinger & Geoffrey R. Stone eds., 2002).

92. New York Times v. Sullivan, 376 U.S. 254 (1964).

93. Curtis Publishing Co. v. Butts, 388 U.S. 130 (1967).

94. Whitney v. California, 274 U.S. 357 (1927).

95. NAACP v. Alabama *ex rel.* Patterson, 357 U.S. 449 (1958).

96. Citizens United v. FEC, 130 S. Ct. 876 (2010).

97. Frederick Schauer, *First Amendment Opportunism, in* ETERNALLY VIGILANT: FREE SPEECH IN THE MODERN ERA 175 (Lee C. Bollinger & Geoffrey R. Stone eds., 2002).

98. Amalgamated Food Employees Union Local 590 v. Logan Valley Plaza, Inc., 391 U.S. 308, 331 (1968) (Black, J., dissenting).

99. Adderley v. Florida, 385 U.S. 39 (1966).

100. Frederick Schauer, *First Amendment Opportunism, in* ETERNALLY VIGILANT: FREE SPEECH IN THE MODERN ERA 175 (Lee C. Bollinger & Geoffrey R. Stone eds., 2002).

101. *Id.* at 177–190.

102. See Monica Youn, *The Roberts Court's Free Speech Double Standard,* American Constitution Society Blog, November 29, 2011, *http://www.acslaw.org/acsblog/the-roberts-court%E2%80%99s-free-speech-double-standard*; Lee Epstein & Jeffrey A. Segal, *A (Brief) Report on the Roberts Court and Free Speech,* December 22, 2011, *http://epstein.usc.edu/research/RobertsFreeSpeech.pdf*; Erwin Chemerinsky, *Not a Free Speech Court,* 53 ARIZ. L. REV. 723 (2011).

103. Monica Youn, *The Roberts Court's Free Speech Double Standard,* American Constitution Society Blog, November 29, 2011, *http://www.acslaw.org/acsblog/the-roberts-court%E2%80%99s-free -speech-double-standard.*

104. J. M. Balkin, *Ideological Drift and the Struggle over Meaning,* 25 CONN. L. REV. 869, 871 (1993).

105. R.A.V. v. City of St. Paul, 505 U.S. 377 (1992).

106. Virginia State Board of Pharmacy v. Virginia Citizens Consumer Council, 425 U.S. 748 (1976).

Chapter 3

1. Editorial, *Remember Wayne Dick,* NATIONAL REVIEW, October 24, 1986, at 19.

2. *Id.*

3. Kenneth Lasson, *Political Correctness Askew: Excesses in the Pursuit of Minds and Manners,* 63 TENN. L. REV. 689, 692 (1996).

4. ALAN CHARLES KORS & HARVEY A. SILVERGLATE, THE SHADOW UNIVERSITY: THE BETRAYAL OF LIBERTY ON AMERICA'S CAMPUSES (1998).

5. James Boyle, *The PC Harangue,* 45 STAN. L. REV. 1457, 1460 (1993).

6. *Id.,* citing Evan Carton, *The Self Besieged: American Identity On Campus and in the Gulf,* TIKKUN, July–August 1991, at 40.

7. James Boyle, *The PC Harangue,* 45 STAN. L. REV. 1457, 1458 (1993).

8. *Id.*

9. *Id.*

10. *Id.*

11. *Id.*

12. See, for example, Susan Gellman, *Hate Speech and a New View of the First Amendment,* 24 CAP. U.L. REV. 309 (1995).

13. Editorial, *Remember Wayne Dick,* NATIONAL REVIEW, October 24, 1986, at 19.

14. David D. Boaz, *Private Means Private,* NATIONAL REVIEW, September 16, 1988, at 6.

15. Editorial, *The Second Dartmouth College Case,* NATIONAL REVIEW, August 5, 1988, at 20.

16. *Id.*

17. David D. Boaz, *Private Means Private,* NATIONAL REVIEW, September 16, 1988, at 6.

18. Kenneth L. Karst, *Boundaries and Reasons: Freedom of Expression and the Subordination of Groups,* 1990 U. ILL. L. REV. 95 (1990).

19. Editorial, *Sensitivity Fascism,* NATIONAL REVIEW, November 10, 1989, at 19.

20. Sam Tanenhaus, *P.C. 101,* N.Y. TIMES, November 8, 1998, http://www.nytimes.com/1998/11/08/books/pc-101.html.

21. KATHLEEN M. SULLIVAN & GERALD GUNTHER, FIRST AMENDMENT LAW 91 (2d ed. 2003).

22. Jon B. Gould, *Look Who's (Not) Talking: The Real Triumph of Hate Speech Regulation,* 8 GREEN BAG 2d 367, 368 (2005).

23. Charles Fried, *Speech in the Welfare State: The New First Amendment Jurisprudence: A Threat to Liberty,* 59 U. CHI. L. REV. 225, 249 (1992).

24. ALAN CHARLES KORS & HARVEY A. SILVERGLATE, THE SHADOW UNIVERSITY: THE BETRAYAL OF LIBERTY ON AMERICA'S CAMPUSES 5 (1998).

25. *Id.*

26. *"Water Buffalo" Lawsuit Settled by Penn Graduate,* N.Y. TIMES, September 10, 1997, http://www.nytimes.com/1997/09/10/us/water-buffalo-lawsuit-settled-by-penn-graduate.html.

27. Kenneth Lasson, *Political Correctness Askew: Excesses in the Pursuit of Minds and Manners,* 63 TENN. L. REV. 689, 712 (1996).

28. *"Water Buffalo" Lawsuit Settled by Penn Graduate,* N.Y. TIMES, September 10, 1997, http://www.nytimes.com/1997/09/10/us/water-buffalo-lawsuit-settled-by-penn-graduate.html.

29. *Penn to Alter Harassment Rules to Balance Free Speech and Privacy,* N.Y. TIMES, November 17, 1993, http://www.nytimes.com/1993/11/17/us/penn-to-alter-harassment-rules-to-balance-free-speech-and-privacy.html.

30. See, for example, Editorial, *The Angelic Vision of the Warren Court,* NATIONAL REVIEW, February 7, 1967, at 122.

31. Frank S. Meyer, *The Real Constitutional Crisis,* NATIONAL REVIEW, June 2, 1970, at 571.

32. *Id.*

33. *Id.*

34. Frank S. Meyer, *Mass Intimidation,* NATIONAL REVIEW, June 1, 1971, at 594.

35. *Id.*

36. *Id.*

37. *Id.*

38. Richmond Crinkley, *How Do We Get Out of It?,* NATIONAL REVIEW, June 4, 1968, at 557–558.

39. *Id.*

40. *Id.*

41. *Id.*

42. *Id.*

43. *Id.*

44. See, for example, City of Ladue v. Gilleo, 512 U.S. 43 (1993).

45. Richmond Crinkley, *How Do We Get Out of It?,* NATIONAL REVIEW, June 4, 1968, at 557–558.

46. *Id.*

47. William F. Buckley, Jr., *What Johnny Doesn't Know*, NATIONAL REVIEW, January 14, 1964, at 14–15.

48. *Id.*

49. *Id.*

50. Snyder v. Phelps, 131 S. Ct. 1207 (2011).

51. LEE EPSTEIN, JEFFREY A. SEGAL, HAROLD J. SPAETH, & THOMAS G. WALKER, THE SUPREME COURT COMPENDIUM 552 (5th ed. 2012).

52. Keyishian v. Board of Regents of the University of the State of New York, 385 U.S. 589, 593 (1967).

53. *Id.* at 593–597.

54. *Id.*

55. *Id.* at 603.

56. *Id.*

57. *Id.* at 598–599.

58. *Id.* at 601.

59. *Id.* at 609.

60. See GEOFFREY R. STONE, LOUIS M. SEIDMAN, CASS SUNSTEIN, PAMELA S. KARLAN, & MARK V. TUSHNET, CONSTITUTIONAL LAW 1113 (6th ed. 2009).

61. Gooding v. Wilson, 405 U.S. 518, 521 (1972).

62. Keyishian v. Board of Regents of the University of the State of New York, 385 U.S. 589, 621 (1967).

63. *Id.* at 621–622.

64. Editorial, *The Angelic Vision of the Warren Court*, NATIONAL REVIEW, February 7, 1967, at 122.

65. *Id.*

66. *Id.*

67. THE FEDERALIST NO. 51, at 319 (James Madison) (Clinton Rossiter ed., 2003).

68. Editorial, *The Angelic Vision of the Warren Court*, NATIONAL REVIEW, February 7, 1967, at 122.

69. *Id.*

70. *Id.*

71. *Id.*

72. Keyishian v. Board of Regents of the University of the State of New York, 385 U.S. 589, 628 (1967).

73. See supra, Chapter 3, at xx–xx.

74. Beauharnais v. Illinois, 343 U.S. 250 (1952); LEE EPSTEIN, JEFFREY A. SEGAL, HAROLD J. SPAETH, & THOMAS G. WALKER, THE SUPREME COURT COMPENDIUM 550 (5th ed. 2012).

75. LEE EPSTEIN, JEFFREY A. SEGAL, HAROLD J. SPAETH, & THOMAS G. WALKER, THE SUPREME COURT COMPENDIUM 550 (5th ed. 2012).

76. *Id.*

77. Beauharnais v. Illinois, 343 U.S. 250, 252 (1952).

78. *Id.*

79. *Id.* at 251.

80. *Id.* at 251–252.

81. *Id.* at 263.

82. New York Times v. Sullivan, 376 U.S. 254 (1964).

83. KATHLEEN M. SULLIVAN & GERALD GUNTHER, FIRST AMENDMENT LAW 91 (2d ed. 2003).

84. HOWARD GILLMAN, MARK A. GRABER, & KEITH WITTINGTON, AMERICAN CONSTITUTIONALISM: VOLUME II RIGHTS AND LIBERTIES 12 (2013).

85. Jesse Graham, Jonathan Haidt, & Brian A. Sosek, *Liberals and Conservatives Rely on Different Sets of Moral Foundations*, 96 J. PERSONALITY & SOC. PSYCH. 1029, 1030 (2009).

86. Beauharnais v. Illinois, 343 U.S. 250, 262 (1952).

87. *Id.* at 286.

88. *Id.*

89. Jesse Graham, Jonathan Haidt, & Brian A. Sosek, *Liberals and Conservatives Rely on Different Sets of Moral Foundations*, 96 J. PERSONALITY & SOC. PSYCH. 1029, 1031 (2009).

90. Beauharnais v. Illinois, 343 U.S. 250, 252 (1952).

91. *Id.* at 263.

92. *Id.*

93. Michael Kent Curtis, *Critics of "Free Speech" and the Uses of the Past*, 12 CONST. COMMENT. 29, 46 (1995).

94. Jonathan Haidt & Selin Kesebir, *Morality*, *in* HANDBOOK OF SOCIAL PSYCHOLOGY 822 (S. Fiske, D. Gilbert, & G. Lindzey eds., 5th ed. 2010).

95. Beauharnais v. Illinois, 343 U.S. 250, 259 (1952).

96. *Id.* at 258–261.

97. *Id.* at 262.

98. Jesse Graham, Jonathan Haidt, & Brian A. Sosek, *Liberals and Conservatives Rely on Different Sets of Moral Foundations*, 96 J. PERSONALITY & SOC. PSYCHOL. 1029, 1029–1030 (2009).

99. Beauharnais v. Illinois, 343 U.S. 250, 274 (1952).

100. *Id.* at 263.

101. *Id.* at 283.

102. Editorial, *Free and Freer Speech*, NATIONAL REVIEW, March 14, 1975, at 263–266.

103. *Id.*

104. *Id.*

105. *Id.*

106. *Id.*

107. Alan Crawford, *Leading Man*, NATIONAL REVIEW, December 24, 1976, at 1411.

108. *Id.*

109. Editorial, *Free and Freer Speech*, NATIONAL REVIEW, March 14, 1975, at 263.

110. Wilcomb E. Washburn, *Liberalism Versus Free Speech*, NATIONAL REVIEW, September 30, 1988, at 39–42.

111. *Id.*

112. See, for example, Brandenburg v. Ohio, 395 U.S. 444 (1969).

113. Wilcomb E. Washburn, *Liberalism Versus Free Speech*, NATIONAL REVIEW, September 30, 1988, at 39–42.

114. *Id.*

115. Cohen v. California, 403 U.S. 15, 25 (1971).

116. Wilcomb E. Washburn, *Liberalism Versus Free Speech*, NATIONAL REVIEW, September 30, 1988, at 39–42.

117. *Id.*

118. *Id.*

119. *Id.*

120. *Id.*

121. *Id.*

122. *Id.*

123. Editorial, *Sensitivity Fascism*, NATIONAL REVIEW, November 10, 1989, at 19.

124. Charles R. Lawrence, III, *If He Hollers Let Him Go: Regulating Racist Speech on Campus*, 1990 DUKE L.J. 431 (1990).

125. *Id.* at 472.

126. *Id.* at 476–477.

127. *Id.* at 477.

128. *Id.* at 449–457.

129. *Id.* at 452.

130. See *R.A.V. v. St. Paul*, 505 U.S. 377 (1992).

131. Charles R. Lawrence, III, *If He Hollers Let Him Go: Regulating Racist Speech on Campus*, 1990 DUKE L.J. 431, 480 (1990).

132. *Id.*

133. *Id.* at 481.

134. Richard Delgado, *Campus Antiracism Rules: Constitutional Narratives in Collision*, 85 NW. U. L. REV. 343 (1991).

135. *Id.* at 384.

136. *Id.* at 383–384.

137. See, generally, Nadine Strossen, *Regulating Racist Speech on Campus: A Modest Proposal?*, 1990 DUKE L.J. 484 (1990).

138. Richard Delgado, *Campus Antiracism Rules: Constitutional Narratives in Collision*, 85 NW. U. L. REV. 343, 386 (1991).

139. Nadine Strossen, *Regulating Racist Speech on Campus: A Modest Proposal?*, 1990 DUKE L.J. 484, 512 (1990).

140. *Id.* at 559.

141. *Id.* at 561.

142. Kenneth L. Karst, *Boundaries and Reasons: Freedom of Expression and the Subordination of Groups*, 1990 U. ILL. L. REV. 95, 149 (1990).

143. Charles Fried, *Speech in the Welfare State: The New First Amendment Jurisprudence: A Threat to Liberty*, 59 U. CHI. L. REV. 225, 226 (1992).

144. *Id.* at 250.

145. *Id.* at 250.

146. Jesse Graham, Jonathan Haidt, & Brian A. Sosek, *Liberals and Conservatives Rely on Different Sets of Moral Foundations*, 96 J. PERSONALITY & SOC. PSYCHOL. 1029, 1030 (2009).

147. Charles Fried, *Speech in the Welfare State: The New First Amendment Jurisprudence: A Threat to Liberty*, 59 U. CHI. L. REV. 225, 246–250 (1992).

148. *Id.* at 247.

149. *Id.* at 248–249.

150. *Id.* at 250.

151. *Id.* at 246.

Chapter 4

1. R.A.V. v. St. Paul, 505 U.S. 377 (1992).

2. *Id.* at 380.

3. LEE EPSTEIN, JEFFREY A. SEGAL, HAROLD J. SPAETH, & THOMAS G. WALKER, THE SUPREME COURT COMPENDIUM 555 (5th ed. 2012).

4. *Id.* at 555–557.

5. R.A.V. v. St. Paul, 505 U.S. 377, 415–416 (1992).

6. *Id.* at 380–381.

7. Chaplinsky v. New Hampshire, 315 U.S. 568, 572 (1942).

8. R.A.V. v. St. Paul, 505 U.S. 377, 381 (1992).

9. *Id.*

10. *Id.* at 383–384.

11. *Id.*

12. *Id.* at 388.

13. *Id.* at 391.

14. *Id.* at 424.

15. *Id.*

16. See Stephen W. Gard, *Fighting Words as Free Speech*, 58 WASH. U. L.Q. 531, 536 (1980), cited in GEOFFREY R. STONE, LOUIS M. SEIDMAN, CASS SUNSTEIN, PAMELA S. KARLAN, & MARK V. TUSHNET, CONSTITUTIONAL LAW 1089 (6th ed. 2009).

17. R.A.V. v. St. Paul, 505 U.S. 377, 391 (1992).

18. See Editorial, *Remember Wayne Dick*, NATIONAL REVIEW, October 24, 1986, at 19.

19. R.A.V. v. St. Paul, 505 U.S. 377, 391 (1992).

20. Beauharnais v. Illinois, 343 U.S. 250, 262–263 (1952).

21. R.A.V. v. St. Paul, 505 U.S. 377, 392 (1992).

22. *Id.* at 391 (emphasis added).

23. *Id.*

24. *Id.* at 396.

25. See, for example, Mari J. Matsuda, *Legal Storytelling: Public Response to Racist Speech: Considering the Victim's Story*, 87 MICH. L. REV. 2320 (1989); Charles R. Lawrence, III, *If He Hollers Let Him Go: Regulating Racist Speech on Campus*, 1990 DUKE L.J. 431 (1990); Richard Delgado, *Campus Antiracism Rules: Constitutional Narratives in Collision*, 85 NW. U. L. REV. 343 (1991).

26. R.A.V. v. St. Paul, 505 U.S. 377, 381 (1992).

27. GEOFFREY R. STONE, LOUIS M. SEIDMAN, CASS SUNSTEIN, PAMELA S. KARLAN, & MARK V. TUSHNET, CONSTITUTIONAL LAW 1089 (6th ed. 2009).

28. See Burton Caine, *The Trouble with "Fighting Words":* Chaplinsky v. New Hampshire *Is a Threat to First Amendment Values and Should Be Overruled*, 88 MARQ. L. REV. 441 (2004).

29. R.A.V. v. St. Paul, 505 U.S. 377, 402 (1992).

30. Charlton Heston, *Just a Song?*, NATIONAL REVIEW, August 17, 1992, at 37.

31. *Id.*

32. See Miami Herald Publishing Co. v. Tornillo, 418 U.S. 241 (1974) (rejecting the constitutionality of a government-enforced right of access by private publishers).

33. Charlton Heston, *Just a Song?*, NATIONAL REVIEW August 17, 1992, at 37.

34. *Id.*

35. See Brandenburg v. Ohio, 395 U.S. 444 (1969); Watts v. United States, 394 U.S. 705 (1969).

36. Charlton Heston, *Just a Song?*, NATIONAL REVIEW, August 17, 1992, at 37.

37. JONATHAN HAIDT, THE RIGHTEOUS MIND: WHY GOOD PEOPLE ARE DIVIDED BY POLITICS AND RELIGION 158 (2012).

38. Linda Seebach, *PC in LA*, NATIONAL REVIEW, July 19, 1993, at 27–29.

39. *Id.*

40. Wendy McElroy, *Feminism and Porn: Fellow Travelers, in* BEFORE THE LAW: AN INTRO-DUCTION TO THE LEGAL PROCESS 255–262 (John J. Bonsignore, Ethan Katsh, Peter d'Errico, Ronald Pipkin, Stephen Arons, & Janet Rifkin eds., 2006).

41. Roger Scruton, *Kiss Me, Cate,* NATIONAL REVIEW, November 1, 1993, at 61.

42. *Id.*

43. *Id.*

44. *Id.*

45. *Id.*

46. John O'Sullivan, *On with the Dance,* NATIONAL REVIEW, July 29, 1991, at 6.

47. John O'Sullivan, *Freeway to Damascus,* NATIONAL REVIEW, February 24, 1997, at 4.

48. Maggie Gallagher, *The Sex Wars,* NATIONAL REVIEW, May 15, 1995, at 67.

49. *Id.*

50. *Id.*

51. Editorial, *That's Entertainment,* NATIONAL REVIEW, July 12, 1999, at 16.

52. *Id.*

53. *Id.*

54. *Id.*

55. *Id.*

56. *Id.*

57. Matthew Continetti, *Being Lee Bollinger: The Very Model of a Modern College President,* NATIONAL REVIEW, October 14, 2002, at 44–45.

58. *Id.*

59. *Id.*

60. *Id.*

61. *Id.*

62. *Id.*

63. Doe v. University of Michigan, 721 F. Supp. 852 (1989).

64. *Recent Case: First Amendment—Racist and Sexist Expression on Campus—Court Strikes Down University Limits on Hate Speech,* 103 HARV. L. REV. 1397 (1990).

65. Doe v. University of Michigan, 721 F. Supp. 852, 858 (1989).

66. *Id.*

67. *Id.*

68. *Recent Case: First Amendment—Racist and Sexist Expression on Campus—Court Strikes Down University Limits on Hate Speech,* 103 HARV. L. REV. 1397 (1990).

69. Doe v. University of Michigan, 721 F. Supp. 852, 868 (1989).

70. *Id.*

71. *Id.*

72. *Id.*

73. *Id.*

74. *Id.*

75. *Id.*

76. RICHARD J. HERRNSTEIN & CHARLES MURRAY, THE BELL CURVE: INTELLI-GENCE AND CLASS STRUCTURE IN AMERICAN LIFE (1994).

77. Jim Naureckas, *Racism Resurgent,* Fairness & Accuracy in Reporting, Extra! January/February 1995, http://fair.org/extra-online-articles/racism-resurgent/.

78. Ernest Van den Haag, *Not Hopeless,* NATIONAL REVIEW, December 5, 1994, at 38.

79. *Id.*

80. Abrams v. United States, 250 U.S. 616 (1919).

81. Whitney v. California, 274 U.S. 357 (1927).

82. *Id.*

83. Doe v. University of Michigan, 721 F. Supp. 852, 869 (1989).

84. See, for example, Guy-Uriel E. Charles, *Colored Speech: Cross Burnings, Epistemics, and the Triumph of the Crits?*, 93 GEO. L.J. 575 (2005).

85. Virginia v. Black, 538 U.S. 343, 360 (2003).

86. *Id.*

87. *Id.* at 347.

88. Guy-Uriel E. Charles, *Colored Speech: Cross Burnings, Epistemics, and the Triumph of the Crits?*, 93 Geo. L.J. 575, 632 (2005).

89. Virginia v. Black, 538 U.S. 343, 348 (2003).

90. LEE EPSTEIN, JEFFREY A. SEGAL, HAROLD J. SPAETH, & THOMAS G. WALKER, THE SUPREME COURT COMPENDIUM 557 (5th ed. 2012).

91. *Id.*

92. Virginia v. Black, 538 U.S. 343, 368 (2003).

93. LEE EPSTEIN, JEFFREY A. SEGAL, HAROLD J. SPAETH, & THOMAS G. WALKER, THE SUPREME COURT COMPENDIUM 557 (5th ed. 2012).

94. Virginia v. Black, 538 U.S. 343, 394 (2003).

95. LEE EPSTEIN, JEFFREY A. SEGAL, HAROLD J. SPAETH, & THOMAS G. WALKER, THE SUPREME COURT COMPENDIUM 557 (5th ed. 2012).

96. Guy-Uriel E. Charles, *Colored Speech: Cross Burnings, Epistemics, and the Triumph of the Crits?*, 93 GEO. L.J. 575, 628 (2005).

97. *Id.*

98. Virginia v. Black, 538 U.S. 343, 352–358 (2003).

99. *Id.* at 388–394.

100. *Id.* at 388.

101. *Id.* at 389.

102. *Id.* at 395.

103. Guy-Uriel E. Charles, *Colored Speech: Cross Burnings, Epistemics, and the Triumph of the Crits?*, 93 GEO. L.J. 575, 629 (2005).

104. Virginia v. Black, 538 U.S. 343, 363 (2003).

105. Guy-Uriel E. Charles, *Colored Speech: Cross Burnings, Epistemics, and the Triumph of the Crits?*, 93 GEO. L.J. 575, 610 (2005).

106. *Id.* at 611.

107. Alexander Tsesis, *The Boundaries of Free Speech: Understanding Words That Wound*, 8 HARV. LATINO L. REV. 141 (2005) (book review).

108. *Id.* at 141–142.

109. See Alexander Tsesis, *Burning Crosses on Campus: University Hate Speech Codes*, 43 CONN. L. REV. 617, 662–663 (2010).

110. Alexander Tsesis, *The Boundaries of Free Speech: Understanding Words That Wound*, 8 HARV. LATINO L. REV. 141, 152 (2005) (book review).

111. See Watts v. United States, 394 U.S. 705 (1969).

112. Virginia v. Black, 538 U.S. 343, 391 (2003).

113. *Id.* at 392.

114. *Id.* at 393 (emphasis in original).

115. *Id.* at 377.

116. See GEOFFREY R. STONE, LOUIS M. SEIDMAN, CASS SUNSTEIN, PAMELA S. KAR-LAN, & MARK V. TUSHNET, CONSTITUTIONAL LAW 1028 (6th ed. 2009).

117. See Schaffer v. United States, 255 F. 886 (9th Cir. 1919).

118. See Masses Publishing Co. v. Patten, 244 F. 535 (S.D.N.Y. 1971).

119. Dennis v. United States, 341 U.S. 494 (1951).

120. Brandenburg v. Ohio, 395 U.S. 444, 447 (1969).

121. *Id.* at 444.

122. *Id.* at 445–446.

123. *Id.* at 448.

124. *Id.* at 449.

125. *Id.* at 446.

126. *Id.* at 447–448.

127. *Id.* at 446 n.1.

128. See Frederick Schauer, *Intentions, Conventions, and the First Amendment: The Case of Cross-Burning*, 2003 SUP. CT. REV. 197, 211.

129. Watts v. United States 394 U.S. 705 (1969); see Frederick Schauer, *Intentions, Conventions, and the First Amendment: The Case of Cross-Burning*, 2003 SUP. CT. REV. 197, 211.

130. Watts v. United States 394 U.S. 705, 706–708 (1969).

131. *Id.* at 706.

132. Frederick Schauer, *Intentions, Conventions, and the First Amendment: The Case of Cross-Burning*, 2003 SUP. CT. REV. 197, 212.

133. *Id.*

134. Griswold v. Connecticut, 381 U.S. 479, 510 (1965).

135. See, for example, Alexander Tsesis, *The Boundaries of Free Speech: Understanding Words that Wound*, 8 HARV. LATINO L. REV. 141, 152 (2005) (book review).

136. MARK TUSHNET, SEGREGATED SCHOOLS AND LEGAL STRATEGY: THE NAACP'S CAMPAIGN AGAINST SEGREGATED EDUCATION, 1925–1950 (1987).

137. STEVEN M. TELES, THE RISE OF THE CONSERVATIVE MOVEMENT: THE BATTLE FOR CONTROL OF THE LAW (2008).

138. *Id.* at 142.

139. *Id.* at 24.

140. *Id.* at 233.

141. *Id.*

142. Clay Calvert & Robert D. Richards, *Lighting a FIRE on College Campuses: An Inside Perspective on Free Speech, Public Policy & Higher Education*, 3 GEO. J.L. & PUB. POL'Y 205, 212 (2005).

143. http://thefire.org/about/mission/.

144. http://thefire.org/about/programs/.

145. Clay Calvert & Robert D. Richards, *Lighting a FIRE on College Campuses: An Inside Perspective on Free Speech, Public Policy & Higher Education*, 3 GEO. J.L. & PUB. POL'Y 205, 238 (2005).

146. *Id.* at 229.

147. GREG LUKIANOFF, UNLEARNING LIBERTY: CAMPUS CENSORSHIP AND THE END OF AMERICAN DEBATE 48 (2012).

148. *Id.*

149. *Id.* at 49.

150. *Id.* at 40.

151. Robert VerBruggen, *Free Speech on FIRE*, NATIONAL REVIEW, November 10, 2012, http://www.nationalreview.com/article/333029/free-speech-fire-robert-verbruggen.

152. Clay Calvert & Robert D. Richards, *Lighting a FIRE on College Campuses: An Inside Perspective on Free Speech, Public Policy & Higher Education*, 3 Geo. J.L. & Pub. Pol'y 205, 221 (2005).

153. GREG LUKIANOFF, UNLEARNING LIBERTY: CAMPUS CENSORSHIP AND THE END OF AMERICAN DEBATE 7 (2012).

154. *Id.* at 6.

155. Clay Calvert & Robert D. Richards, *Lighting a FIRE on College Campuses: An Inside Perspective on Free Speech, Public Policy & Higher Education*, 3 GEO. J.L. & PUB. POL'Y 205, 221 (2005).

156. http://www.alliancedefendingfreedom.org/page/new-name?referral=I0712AW2.

157. http://thefire.org/people/advisors/.

158. Clay Calvert & Robert D. Richards, *Lighting a FIRE on College Campuses: An Inside Perspective on Free Speech, Public Policy & Higher Education*, 3 GEO. J.L. & PUB. POL'Y 205, 217 (2005).

159. *Id.*

160. *Id.* at 217–218.

161. GREG LUKIANOFF, UNLEARNING LIBERTY: CAMPUS CENSORSHIP AND THE END OF AMERICAN DEBATE 5, 46 (2012).

162. *Id.* at 1.

163. *Id.* at 210.

164. *Id.* at 151.

165. *Id.* at 149.

166. *Id.* at 152.

167. Snyder v. Phelps, 131 S. Ct. 1207, 1213 (2011).

168. See infra, Chapter 2 at 45–46.

169. Snyder v. Phelps, 131 S. Ct. 1207, 1213 (2011).

170. *Id.* at 1227.

171. Linda Greenhouse, Op-Ed., *It's All Right with Sam*, N.Y. TIMES, January 7, 2015, http://www.nytimes.com/2015/01/08/opinion/its-all-right-with-samuel-alito.html.

172. Snyder v. Phelps, 131 S. Ct. 1207, 1220 (2011).

173. *Id.*

Chapter 5

1. Bigelow v. Virginia, 421 U.S. 809, 812 (1975).

2. See Valentine v. Chrestensen, 316 U.S. 52 (1942).

3. Justice Rehnquist's Martin-Quinn score stood at 4.302 in the 1974 term. The median justice score was .741. LEE EPSTEIN, JEFFREY A. SEGAL, HAROLD J. SPAETH, & THOMAS G. WALKER, THE SUPREME COURT COMPENDIUM 553 (5th ed. 2012).

4. See Madsen v. Women's Health Center, 512 U.S. 753 (1994).

5. Editorial, *Warren Goes*, NATIONAL REVIEW BULLETIN, July 8, 1969, at B97.

6. Donald Waterford, *Business & Briefs*, NATIONAL REVIEW BULLETIN, November 10, 1970, at B16.

7. Editorial, *Warren Goes*, NATIONAL REVIEW BULLETIN, July 8, 1969, at B97.

8. R. H. Coase, *The Market for Ideas*, NATIONAL REVIEW, September 27, 1974, at 1095–1099.

9. *Id.*

10. Virginia State Board of Pharmacy v. Virginia Citizens Consumer Council, 425 U.S. 748 (1976).

11. R. H. Coase, *The Market for Ideas*, NATIONAL REVIEW, September 27, 1974, at 1095–1099.

12. *Id.*

13. *Id.*

14. *Id.*

15. *Id.*

16. *Id.*

17. *Id.*

18. *Id.*

19. *Id.*

20. See *Distrust, Discontent, Anger and Partisan Rancor: The People and Their Government*, Pew Research Center for the People and the Press, April 18, 2010, http://www.people-press .org/2010/04/18/distrust-discontent-anger-and-partisan-rancor/.

21. Donald Waterford, *Business & Briefs*, NATIONAL REVIEW BULLETIN, November 10, 1970, at B16.

22. See LIEF CARTER & THOMAS BURKE, REASON IN LAW (2009).

23. See Alex Kozinski, *What I Ate for Breakfast and Other Mysteries of Judicial Decision Making*, *in* JUDGES ON JUDGING: VIEWS FROM THE BENCH 98–99 (David M. O'Brien ed., 2009).

24. Bigelow v. Virginia, 421 U.S. 809 (1975).

25. Roe v. Wade, 410 U.S. 113 (1973).

26. LEE EPSTEIN, JEFFREY A. SEGAL, HAROLD J. SPAETH, & THOMAS G. WALKER, THE SUPREME COURT COMPENDIUM 553–556 (5th ed. 2012).

27. See, generally, LINDA GREENHOUSE, BECOMING JUSTICE BLACKMUN: HARRY BLACKMUN'S SUPREME COURT JOURNEY (2005).

28. Bigelow v. Virginia, 421 U.S. 809, 829 (1975).

29. See Valentine v. Chrestensen, 316 U.S. 52 (1942).

30. LINDA GREENHOUSE, BECOMING JUSTICE BLACKMUN: HARRY BLACKMUN'S SUPREME COURT JOURNEY 117 (2005).

31. *Id.* at 118.

32. *Id.*

33. LEE EPSTEIN, JEFFREY A. SEGAL, HAROLD J. SPAETH, & THOMAS G. WALKER, THE SUPREME COURT COMPENDIUM 553 (5th ed. 2012).

34. LINDA GREENHOUSE, BECOMING JUSTICE BLACKMUN: HARRY BLACKMUN'S SUPREME COURT JOURNEY 119 (2005).

35. Valentine v. Chrestensen, 316 U.S. 52, 55 (1942).

36. *Id.*

37. Pittsburgh Press v. Pittsburgh Commission on Human Relations, 413 U.S. 376, 401 n.6 (1973).

38. Bigelow v. Virginia, 421 U.S. 809, 820 n.6 (1975).

39. *Id.*

40. *Id.* at 825.

41. *Id.* at 825 n.10.

42. *Id.* at 835–836.

43. Pittsburgh Press v. Pittsburgh Commission on Human Relations, 413 U.S. 376 (1973).

44. LEE EPSTEIN, JEFFREY A. SEGAL, HAROLD J. SPAETH, & THOMAS G. WALKER, THE SUPREME COURT COMPENDIUM 553 (5th ed. 2012).

45. Pittsburgh Press v. Pittsburgh Commission on Human Relations, 413 U.S. 376, 379 (1973).

46. I credit Ronald K. L. Collins for coining this term. See RONALD K. L. COLLINS, NUANCED ABSOLUTISM: FLOYD ABRAMS AND THE FIRST AMENDMENT (2013).

47. As discussed, there is reason to doubt whether, particularly considering *Virginia v. Black*, the Court would decide similarly today. See discussion of *Brandenburg* in Chapter 4.

48. William F. Buckley, Jr., *Notes & Asides*, NATIONAL REVIEW, January 26, 1971, at 72–73.

49. *Id.*

50. *Id.*

51. Buckley v. American Federation of Television and Radio Artists, 496 F.2d 305 (1974).

52. *Id.* at 311.

53. *Id.*

54. William F. Buckley, Jr., *Notes & Asides*, NATIONAL REVIEW, January 26, 1971, at 72–73.

55. William F. Buckley, Jr., *Postmortem on the Nazis*, NATIONAL REVIEW, August 18, 1978, at 1040.

56. *Id.*

57. *Id.*

58. Virginia State Board of Pharmacy v. Virginia Citizens Consumer Council, 425 U.S. 748, 762 (1976), citing Pittsburgh Press v. Pittsburgh Commission on Human Relations, 413 U.S. 376, 385 (1973).

59. Justice Rehnquist dissented and Justices Burger and Stewart concurred. That year, Rehnquist, followed by Burger, ranked as the most conservative justices. Ideologically, Stewart, known as a moderate conservative, fell precisely in the middle of the pack. LEE EPSTEIN, JEFFREY A. SEGAL, HAROLD J. SPAETH, & THOMAS G. WALKER, THE SUPREME COURT COMPENDIUM 553 (5th ed. 2012).

60. Virginia State Board of Pharmacy v. Virginia Citizens Consumer Council, 425 U.S. 748, 753 (1976).

61. *Id.* at 770.

62. *Id.* at 762.

63. *Id.* at 765.

64. *Id.*

65. *Id.* at 764.

66. *Id.*

67. *Id.* at 769.

68. *Id.* at 763.

69. *Id.* at 771.

70. See TAMARA R. PIETY, BRANDISHING THE FIRST AMENDMENT: COMMERCIAL EXPRESSION IN AMERICA 112–114 (2012); R. COLLINS & D. SKOVER, THE DEATH OF DISCOURSE 77, 80, 105, 114 (1996).

71. Virginia State Board of Pharmacy v. Virginia Citizens Consumer Council, 425 U.S. 748, 772 n.24 (1976).

72. TAMARA R. PIETY, BRANDISHING THE FIRST AMENDMENT: COMMERCIAL EXPRESSION IN AMERICA 88–97 (2012).

73. LEE EPSTEIN, JEFFREY A. SEGAL, HAROLD J. SPAETH, & THOMAS G. WALKER, THE SUPREME COURT COMPENDIUM 553 (5th ed. 2012).

74. Virginia State Board of Pharmacy v. Virginia Citizens Consumer Council, 425 U.S. 748, 784 (1976).

75. *Id.* at 781.

76. *Id.* at 785.

77. *Id.* at 774.

78. *Id.* at 775.

79. Bates v. State Bar Association of Arizona, 433 U.S. 350, 382 (1977).

80. LEE EPSTEIN, JEFFREY A. SEGAL, HAROLD J. SPAETH, & THOMAS G. WALKER, THE SUPREME COURT COMPENDIUM 553 (5th ed. 2012).

81. Bates v. State Bar Association of Arizona, 433 U.S. 350, 385–405 (1977).

82. Virginia State Board of Pharmacy v. Virginia Citizens Consumer Council, 425 U.S. 748, 787 (1976).

83. *Id.*

84. *Id.* at 788.

85. See, for example, Carey v. Population Services International, 431 U.S. 678 (1977); Linmark Associates v. Township of Willingboro, 431 U.S. 85 (1977).

86. See, for example, Ohralik v. Ohio State Bar Association, 436 U.S. 447 (1978); Friedman v. Rogers, 440 U.S. 1 (1979).

87. A unanimous decision in *Linmark Associates v. Willingboro* struck down, as protected commercial speech, a municipal prohibition on posting "For Sale" or "Sold" outside of homes. Justice Rehnquist, however, took no part in the decision. Linmark Associates v. Township of Willingboro, 431 U.S. 85 (1977).

88. Carey v. Population Services International, 431 U.S. 678, 700 (1977).

89. *Id.* at 717.

90. *Id.* at 718.

91. David Brudnoy, *Comstock's Nemesis*, NATIONAL REVIEW, September 24, 1971, at 1064–1065.

92. *Id.*

93. Gary North, *Pornography, Community, Law*, NATIONAL REVIEW, August 31, 1973, at 943–944.

94. *Id.*

95. *Id.*

96. *Id.*

97. *Id.*

98. *Id.*

99. *Id.*

100. *Id.*

101. *Id.*

102. George W. Carey, *Toward a Republic of Pigs*, NATIONAL REVIEW, February 4, 1977, at 158–159 (book review).

103. *Id.*

104. *Id.*

105. *Id.*

106. *Id.*

107. *Id.*

108. *Id.*

109. *Id.*

110. Central Hudson Gas & Electric Corp. v. Public Service Commission of New York, 447 U.S. 557 (1980).

111. *Id.* at 558.

112. *Id.* at 566.

113. *Id.* at 566.

114. LEE EPSTEIN, JEFFREY A. SEGAL, HAROLD J. SPAETH, & THOMAS G. WALKER, THE SUPREME COURT COMPENDIUM 554 (5th ed. 2012).

115. *Id.*

116. Central Hudson Gas & Electric Corp. v. Public Service Commission of New York, 447 U.S. 557, 573–583 (1980).

117. The Lewis Powell Memo—A Corporate Blueprint to Dominate Democracy, available at *http://www.greenpeace.org/usa/en/campaigns/global-warming-and-energy/polluterwatch/The-Lewis -Powell-Memo/*.

118. Mark Schmitt, *The Legend of the Powell Memo*, THE AMERICAN PROSPECT, April 27, 2005, http://prospect.org/article/legend-powell-memo.

119. *Id.*

120. The Lewis Powell Memo at 2, *http://research.greenpeaceusa.org/?a=view&d=5971*.

121. *Id.*

122. *Id.* at 3.

123. *Id.* at 24–25.

124. *Id.* at 17–19.

125. *Id.* at 16–17.

126. *Id.* at 20–24.

127. Central Hudson Gas & Electric Corp. v. Public Service Commission of New York, 447 U.S. 557, 573 (1980).

128. The Lewis Powell Memo at 18, *http://research.greenpeaceusa.org/?a=view&d=5971*.

129. *Id.*

130. *Id.* at 23–24.

131. JACOB S. HACKER & PAUL PIERSON, WINNER-TAKE-ALL-POLITICS: HOW WASH-INGTON MADE THE RICH RICHER—AND TURNED ITS BACK ON THE MIDDLE CLASS 119 (2010).

132. Central Hudson Gas & Electric Corp. v. Public Service Commission of New York, 447 U.S. 557, 598 (1980).

133. *Id.* at 583 n.1.

134. *Id.* at 597.

135. *Id.*

136. *Id.* at 591.

137. *Id.* at 584.

138. *Id.* at 588.

139. *Id.* at 599.

140. *Id.*

141. Richard McKenzie, *The High Cost of Free Speech*, NATIONAL REVIEW, September 2, 1983, at 1064–1068.

142. *Id.*

143. *Id.*

144. *Id.*

145. *Id.*

146. *Id.*

147. *Id.*

148. *Id.*

149. Editorial, *Seven Dirty Words*, NATIONAL REVIEW, October 15, 1982, at 1262.

150. *Id.*

151. *Id.*

152. *Id.*

153. See Virginia State Board of Pharmacy v. Virginia Citizens Consumer Council, 425 U.S. 748 (1976).

Chapter 6

1. John O'Sullivan, *Justice Goes Begging*, NATIONAL REVIEW, February 19, 1990, at 8.

2. *Id.*

3. *Id.*

4. *Id.*

5. Central Hudson Gas & Electric Corp. v. Public Service Commission of New York, 447 U.S. 557, 564 (1980).

6. Thompson v. Western States Medical Center, 535 U.S. 357, 367 (2002).

7. Lorillard Tobacco Co. v. Reilly, 533 U.S. 525, 572–577 (2001).

8. Melinda Henneberger, *Subway Plan Asks Riders Not to Give Money to Beggars*, N.Y. TIMES, January 11, 1994, http://www.nytimes.com/1994/01/11/nyregion/subway-plan-asks-riders-not-to-give-money-to-beggars.html.

9. Richard Vigilante, *Who's Afraid of Robert Bork?*, NATIONAL REVIEW, August 28, 1987, at 25.

10. *Id.*

11. *Id.*

12. *Id.*

13. D. Keith Mano, *The Gimlet Eye: The Marketing of Misery*, NATIONAL REVIEW, July 23, 1990, at 50–52.

14. *Id.*

15. *Id.*

16. *Id.*

17. *Id.*

18. *Id.*

19. *Id.*

20. Central Hudson Gas & Electric Corp. v. Public Service Commission of New York, 447 U.S. 557, 566 (1980).

21. LEE EPSTEIN, JEFFREY A. SEGAL, HAROLD J. SPAETH, & THOMAS G. WALKER, THE SUPREME COURT COMPENDIUM 555 (5th ed. 2012). Rehnquist, Burger, White, Powell, and O'Connor would vote to uphold the law, while Brennan, Stevens, Marshall, and Blackmun would dissent.

22. Posadas De Puerto Rico v. Tourism Company of Puerto Rico, 478 U.S. 328 (1986).

23. *Id.*

24. Central Hudson Gas & Electric Corp. v. Public Service Commission of New York, 447 U.S. 557, 564 (1980).

25. Posadas De Puerto Rico v. Tourism Company of Puerto Rico, 478 U.S. 328, 341 (1986).

26. *Id.*

27. *Id.* at 342–343.

28. *Id.* at 343–344.

29. *Id.* at 355.

30. See discussion in GEOFFREY R. STONE, LOUIS M. SEIDMAN, CASS SUNSTEIN, PAMELA S. KARLAN, & MARK V. TUSHNET, CONSTITUTIONAL LAW 758 (6th ed. 2009).

31. Posadas De Puerto Rico v. Tourism Company of Puerto Rico, 478 U.S. 328, 353–354 (1986).

32. 44 Liquormart v. Rhode Island, 517 U.S. 484, 531–532 (1996).

33. *Id.* at 517.

34. *Id.* at 497, 507, 510, 517, 519, 520.

35. *Id.* at 508.

36. United States v. Edge Broadcasting Company, 509 U.S. 418 (1993).

37. *Id.* at 434.

38. *Id.* at 426.

39. Rubin v. Coors Brewing Company, 514 U.S. 476, 582 n.2 (1995).

40. 44 Liquormart v. Rhode Island, 517 U.S. 484, 508– 514 (1996).

41. *Id.* at 512 n.20.

42. *Id.* at 518.

43. *Id.* at 522.

44. *Id.*

45. *Id.*

46. *Id.* at 526.

47. Daniel E. Troy, *The Court's Mr. Right: Clarence Thomas Makes His Mark,* NATIONAL REVIEW, August 9, 1999, at 39.

48. *Id.*

49. *Id.*

50. Robert A. Levy, *Pack It In: Tobacco Industry Settlement,* NATIONAL REVIEW, May 4, 1998, at 36.

51. *Id.*

52. Alexander Volokh, *Pruning the FDA,* NATIONAL REVIEW, August 11, 1997, at 44.

53. *Id.*

54. *Id.*

55. *Id.*

56. *Id.*

57. See MARK A. GRABER, TRANSFORMING FREE SPEECH: THE AMBIGUOUS LEGACY OF CIVIL LIBERTARIANISM (1991).

58. Michael Greve, *Assault on the First Amendment: Speech Impediments,* NATIONAL REVIEW, October 10, 1994, at 36–39.

59. Discussed supra, Introduction at 11.

60. Michael Greve, *Assault on the First Amendment: Speech Impediments,* NATIONAL REVIEW, October 10, 1994, at 36–39.

61. Wisconsin v. Mitchell, 508 U.S. 476 (1993).

62. Madsen v. Women's Health Center, 512 U.S. 753 (1994).

63. Wisconsin v. Mitchell, 508 U.S. 476 (1993).

64. Madsen v. Women's Health Center, 512 U.S. 753 (1994).

65. Michael Greve, *Assault on the First Amendment: Speech Impediments,* NATIONAL REVIEW, October 10, 1994, at 36–39.

66. *Id.*

67. *Id.*

68. *Id.*

69. *Id.*

70. *Id.*

71. *Id.*

72. Madsen v. Women's Health Center, 512 U.S. 753, 785 (1994).

73. *Id.* at 791.

74. *Id.* at 785.

75. G. Robert Blakey, *The RICO Racket,* NATIONAL REVIEW, May 16, 1994, at 61.

76. *Id.*

77. *Id.*

78. Various authors, *The America We Seek: A Statement of Pro-Life Principle and Concern*, NATIONAL REVIEW, March 25, 1996, at 36–41.

79. William F. Buckley, Jr., *Fight, God, Fight*, NATIONAL REVIEW, March 24, 1997, at 63.

80. *Id.*

81. Stuart Creque, *Brrrr!*, NATIONAL REVIEW, October 10, 1994, at 40–45.

82. *Id.*

83. *Id.*

84. *Id.*

85. *Id.*

86. *Id.*

87. Robert H. Bork, *Thanks a Lot: Free Speech and High Schools*, NATIONAL REVIEW, April 16, 2007, at 24.

88. William F. Buckley, Jr., *Feeling One's Way on Finance Reform*, NATIONAL REVIEW, April 16, 2001, at 62.

89. Robert H. Bork, *Thanks a Lot: Free Speech and High Schools*, NATIONAL REVIEW, April 16, 2007, at 24.

90. *Id.*

91. Frederick v. Morse, 439 F.3d 1114 (9th Cir., 2006).

92. Robert H. Bork, *Thanks a Lot: Free Speech and High Schools*, NATIONAL REVIEW, April 16, 2007, at 24.

93. Morse v. Frederick, 551 U.S. 393 (2007).

94. *Id.* at 409.

95. Morse v. Frederick, 551 U.S. 393, 424 (2007).

96. Tinker v. Des Moines, 393 U.S. 503, 506 (1969).

97. Daniel E. Troy, *The Court's Mr. Right: Clarence Thomas Makes His Mark*, NATIONAL REVIEW, August 9, 1999, at 39.

98. Morse v. Frederick, 551 U.S. 393, 424 (2007).

99. *Id.* at 410–411.

100. Tinker v. Des Moines, 393 U.S. 503, 515 (1969).

101. Mark Hemingway, *Gay Abandon: Must We Give Up Our First Amendment Liberties?*, NATIONAL REVIEW, July 14, 2008, 26–27.

102. *Id.*

103. *Id.*

104. *Id.*

105. *Id.*

106. William F. Buckley, Jr., *Church/State at Dartmouth*, NATIONAL REVIEW, October 24, 2005, at 70.

107. *Id.*

108. *Id.*

109. McCullen v. Coakley, 134 S. Ct. 2518 (2014).

110. See Madsen v. Women's Health Center, 512 U.S. 753 (1994); Schenck v. Pro-Choice Network of Western New York, 519 U.S. 357 (1997); Hill v. Colorado, 530 U.S. 703 (2000).

111. McCullen v. Coakley, 134 S. Ct. 2518, 2541–2548 (2014).

112. Lorillard Tobacco Company v. Reilly, 533 U.S. 525, 572 (2001).

113. *Id.* at 555–556.

114. *Id.* at 554.

115. LEE EPSTEIN, JEFFREY A. SEGAL, HAROLD J. SPAETH, & THOMAS G. WALKER, THE SUPREME COURT COMPENDIUM 556 (5th ed. 2012).

116. Lorillard Tobacco Company v. Reilly, 533 U.S. 525, 561 (2001).

117. *Id.* at 557–561.

118. *Id.* at 561.

119. *Id.* at 601–602.

120. *Id.*

121. Thompson v. Western States Medical Center, 535 U.S. 357 (2002).

122. *Id.* at 369–370.

123. *Id.* at 370.

124. *Id.* at 372–373.

125. *Id.* at 382.

126. *Id.* at 383.

127. *Id.* at 375.

128. *Id.* at 384.

129. *Id.* at 389.

130. Sorrell v. IMS Health Inc., 131 S. Ct. 2653, 2673 (2011).

131. *Id.* at 2665.

132. *Id.* at 2663.

133. *Id.* at 2665.

134. *Id.* at 2665.

135. Lochner v. New York, 198 U.S. 45, 75 (1905).

Chapter 7

1. See Adam Liptak, *The Roberts Court Comes of Age,* N.Y. TIMES, June 29, 2010, http://www.nytimes.com/2010/06/30/us/30scotus.html (describing *Citizens United* as "the most controversial decision since the Rehnquist court handed the presidency to Mr. Bush a decade ago in Bush v. Gore, and . . . easily the most debated of the Roberts court era so far"). See also Tom Udall, *Amend the Constitution to Restore Public Trust in the Political System: A Practitioner's Perspective,* 29 YALE L. & POL'Y REV. 235 (2010) (arguing that the Constitution should be amended to overrule *Citizens United*).

2. Op-Ed., *The Court and the Next President,* N.Y. TIMES, October 28, 2011, http://www.nytimes.com/2011/10/29/opinion/the-supreme-court-and-the-next-president.html ("[S]weeping aside established precedents that had not been challenged and inserting itself into politics, the conservative majority unleashed unlimited corporate and other money into American politics and gave the Republican Party a large advantage in fund-raising."); Citizens United v. FEC, 130 S. Ct. 876, 913 (2010) (overruling Austin v. Michigan State Chamber of Commerce, 494 U.S. 652 (1990)). See also Richard L. Hasen, Citizens United *and the Illusion of Coherence,* 109 MICH. L. REV. 581, 621 (2011) (arguing that although "the Court's jurisprudence will vary within a ride range," it is "likely constrained at its edges more by political considerations than legal coherence").

3. 2 U.S.C. § 441b(a) (2006).

4. Op-Ed., *The Court and the Next President,* N.Y. TIMES, October 28, 2011, at A20 ("The Roberts court is closely divided but also the most conservative since the 1950s.").

5. Citizens United v. FEC, 130 S. Ct. 876, 913 (2010).

6. *Arizona Free Enterprise Club v. Bennett,* 131 S. Ct. 2806 (2011).

7. *McCutcheon v. FEC,* 134 S. Ct. 1434 (2014).

8. NAACP v. Alabama *ex rel.* Patterson, 357 U.S. 449, 459 (1958).

9. LEE EPSTEIN, JEFFREY A. SEGAL, HAROLD J. SPAETH, & THOMAS G. WALKER, THE SUPREME COURT COMPENDIUM 558 (5th ed. 2012).

10. Citizens United v. FEC, 130 S. Ct. 876, 929–979 (2010).

11. *Id.* at 950 n.55.

12. *Id.* at 930, 945.

13. *Id.* at 929–979.

14. See, for example, Ashutosh Bhagwat, *Associational Speech*, 120 YALE L.J. 978, 1022 (2011); Noah Feldman, *Equality: What a Liberal Court Should Be*, N.Y. TIMES, June 27, 2010, (Magazine), at 38; Op-Ed., *The Court and Free Speech*, N.Y. TIMES, April 23, 2010, at A18.

15. Citizens United v. FEC, 130 S. Ct. 876, 886 (2010).

16. Wayne Batchis, *Reconciling Campaign Finance Reform with the First Amendment: Looking Both Inside and Outside America's Borders*, 25 QUINNIPIAC L. REV. 27, 33 (2006).

17. Buckley v. Valeo, 424 U.S. 1, 19 (1976).

18. *Id.*

19. BOB WOODWARD & SCOTT ARMSTRONG, THE BRETHREN: INSIDE THE SUPREME COURT 395–396 (1979).

20. LEE EPSTEIN, JEFFREY A. SEGAL, HAROLD J. SPAETH, & THOMAS G. WALKER, THE SUPREME COURT COMPENDIUM 553 (5th ed. 2012).

21. Buckley v. Valeo, 424 U.S. 1, 19–21 (1976).

22. Citizens United v. FEC, 130 S. Ct. 876, 954 (2010) (Stevens, J., dissenting) ("[N]o one [in Buckley] even bothered to argue that the bar as such was unconstitutional.").

23. *Id.*

24. Editorial, *Political Reforms*, NATIONAL REVIEW, December 21, 1973, at 1396.

25. *Id.*

26. *Id.*

27. *Id.*

28. Editorial, *Free Speech and Spending*, NATIONAL REVIEW, September 12, 1975, at 980.

29. *Id.*

30. *Id.*

31. LEE EPSTEIN, JEFFREY A. SEGAL, HAROLD J. SPAETH, & THOMAS G. WALKER, THE SUPREME COURT COMPENDIUM 553 (5th ed. 2012).

32. Buckley v. Valeo, 424 U.S. 1 (1976).

33. Editorial, *Free Speech and Spending*, NATIONAL REVIEW, September 12, 1975, at 980.

34. *Id.*

35. Ida Walters, *The Elusive Goal of Campaign Reform*, NATIONAL REVIEW, May 30, 1980, at 663–664.

36. See J. Robert Abraham, *Saving Buckley: Creating a Stable Campaign Finance Framework*, 110 COLUM. L. REV. 1078, 1078 (2010) ("[The] passage of the Bipartisan Campaign Reform Act of 2002 . . . attempted to limit the influence of political money by banning 'soft money' contributions to party organizations and restricting the ability of corporations to fund electioneering communications.").

37. McConnell v. FEC, 540 U.S. 93, 204, 209 (2003) (upholding new FECA § 316(b)(2) as amended by BCRA § 203).

38. LEE EPSTEIN, JEFFREY A. SEGAL, HAROLD J. SPAETH, & THOMAS G. WALKER, THE SUPREME COURT COMPENDIUM 553 (5th ed. 2012).

39. See McConnell v. FEC, 540 U.S. 93 (2003).

40. See, for example, Arizona Free Enterprise Club's Freedom Club PAC v. Bennett, 131 S. Ct 2806 (2011); McCutcheon v. FEC 134 S. Ct. 1434 (2014).

41. See McConnell v. FEC, 540 U.S. 93 (2003).

42. *Id.* at 203.

43. *Id.*

44. See Austin v. Michigan Chamber of Commerce, 494 U.S. 652 (1990).

45. Citizens United v. FEC, 130 S. Ct. 876, 930 (2010) (Stevens, J., dissenting) ("The Court today rejects a century of history when it treats the distinction between corporate and individual campaign spending as an invidious novelty born of *Austin v. Michigan Chamber of Commerce.*").

46. LEE EPSTEIN, JEFFREY A. SEGAL, HAROLD J. SPAETH, & THOMAS G. WALKER, THE SUPREME COURT COMPENDIUM 555 (5th ed. 2012).

47. See Austin v. Michigan Chamber of Commerce, 494 U.S. 652 (1990).

48. Shannen W. Coffin, *"Not True": With Its* Citizens United *Decision the Supreme Court Struck a Blow for Free Speech*, NATIONAL REVIEW DIGITAL, February 22, 2010, https://www.nationalreview.com/nrd/articles/339532/not-true.

49. Bradley A. Smith, *Disclosed Partisanship: An Unfair and Unnecessary Campaign-Finance "Reform,"* NATIONAL REVIEW DIGITAL, June 7, 2010, https://www.nationalreview.com/nrd/articles/316311/disclosed-partisanship.

50. *Id.*

51. NAACP v. Alabama *ex rel.* Patterson, 357 U.S. 449, 460 (1958).

52. Bradley A. Smith, *Disclosed Partisanship: An Unfair and Unnecessary Campaign-Finance "Reform,"* NATIONAL REVIEW DIGITAL, June 7, 2010, https://www.nationalreview.com/nrd/articles/316311/disclosed-partisanship.

53. *Id.*

54. *Id.*

55. Whitney v. California, 274 U.S. 357 (1927).

56. See Ashutosh Bhagwat, *Associations and Forums: Situating* CLS v. Martinez, 38 HASTINGS CONST. L.Q. 543, 550–551 (2011) (describing *Whitney* as the first case to dedicate sustained attention to associational rights under the First Amendment).

57. *Id.*

58. In *Whitney*, the Court explained:

We cannot hold that, as here applied, the Act is an unreasonable or arbitrary exercise of the police power of the State, unwarrantably infringing any right of free speech, assembly or association, or that *those persons* are protected from punishment by the due process clause *who abuse such rights by joining and furthering* an organization thus menacing the peace and welfare of the State. (274 U.S. 371 (emphasis added))

59. NAACP v. Alabama *ex rel.* Patterson, 357 U.S. 449, 460 (1958).

60. John D. Inazu, *The Strange Origins of the Constitutional Right of Association*, 77 TENN. L. REV. 485, 514–517 (2010).

61. *Id.*

62. *Id.*

63. *Id.*

64. NAACP v. Alabama *ex rel.* Patterson, 357 U.S. 449, 466 (1958).

65. *Id.* at 458–459.

66. *Id.* at 466.

67. *Id.* at 462.

68. *Id.* at 461.

69. *Id.* at 460.

70. *Id.* at 458 (emphasis added).

71. *Id.* at 459.

72. See *id.* at 466 ("We hold that the immunity from state scrutiny of membership lists which the Association claims *on behalf of its members* is here *so related to the right of the members* to pursue *their* lawful *private interests* privately and to associate freely with others *in so doing* as to come within the protection of the Fourteenth Amendment.") (emphasis added).

73. Roberts v. United States Jaycees, 468 U.S. 609, 617–618 (1984).

74. See, for example, Zablocki v. Redhail, 434 U.S. 374, 384 (1978) (discussing associational rights in the context of marriage and the right to privacy); Moore v. City of East Cleveland, 431 U.S. 494, 510 (1977) (discussing associational rights with respect to family living arrangements) (Brennan, J., concurring); Griswold v. Connecticut, 381 U.S. 479, 483 (1965) (discussing intimate associational rights in marriage).

75. Roberts v. United States Jaycees, 468 U.S. 609, 617–618 (1984).

76. *Id.*

77. *Id.* at 618.

78. *Id.*

79. *Id.* at 615

80. *Id.* at 621.

81. *Id.* at 623.

82. *Id.*

83. *Id.* at 628.

84. *Id.* at 609, 612.

85. *Id.* at 615, 623, 626.

86. *Id.* at 615 (emphasis added).

87. *Id.* at 628 (emphasis added).

88. *Id.* at 633–635 (O'Connor, J., concurring).

89. *Id.* at 635.

90. See MANCUR OLSON, THE LOGIC OF COLLECTIVE ACTION: PUBLIC GOODS AND THE THEORY OF GROUPS (1965).

91. Roberts v. United States Jaycees, 468 U.S. 609, 638 (1984).

92. *Id.* at 635.

93. *Id.* 635–636.

94. *Id.* at 638.

95. See, for example, FREEDOM OF ASSOCIATION (Amy Gutmann ed., 1998) (exploring the importance of association in America from the perspective of political science); ROBERT PUTNAM, BOWLING ALONE: THE COLLAPSE AND REVIVAL OF AMERICAN COMMUNITY (2001) (arguing that Americans have become increasingly disconnected from one another and are less likely to be members of civic associations than they were in the past); THEDA SKOCPOL, DIMINISHED DEMOCRACY: FROM MEMBERSHIP TO MANAGEMENT IN AMERICAN CIVIC LIFE (2004) (contemplating the consequences for U.S. democracy if voluntary participation in civic associations continues to wither). *See also* Ashutosh Bhagwat, *Associational Speech*, 120 YALE L.J. 978, 981 (2011); John D. Inazu, *The Strange Origins of the Constitutional Right of Association*, 77 TENN. L. REV. 485 (2010).

96. Ashutosh Bhagwat, *Associational Speech*, 120 YALE L.J. 978, 981 n.16 (2011); ("the nontextual association right is best understood as a significant and distinct right, tied to the Assembly Clause and not (as the modern Supreme Court has suggested) derivative of the free speech guarantee.").

97. *Id.* at 990. ("Both [assemblies and associations] were seen as forums in which citizens could engage in the process of self-governance, with the difference being that assemblies were

probably understood as ad hoc groups gathered in public or private while associations constituted more permanent groupings of citizens.").

98. *Id.* (citing Jason Mazzone, *Freedom's Associations*, 77 WASH. L. REV. 639, 742–743 (2002)).

99. *Id.* at 991.

100. *Id.* at 999–1000.

101. See NAACP v. Alabama *ex rel.* Patterson, 357 U.S. 449, 459–460 (1958).

102. See *id.* at 460.

103. *Id.*

104. *Id.* at 459.

105. Boy Scouts of America v. Dale, 530 U.S. 640 (2000).

106. See *id.* at 657–661.

107. LEE EPSTEIN, JEFFREY A. SEGAL, HAROLD J. SPAETH, & THOMAS G. WALKER, THE SUPREME COURT COMPENDIUM 556 (5th ed. 2012).

108. Boy Scouts of America v. Dale, 530 U.S. 640, 659 (2000).

109. *Id.* at 644.

110. *Id.* at 650.

111. See *id.* at 651.

112. *Id.* at 651 (quoting Democratic Party of United States v. Wisconsin *ex rel.* La Follette, 450 U.S. 107, 124 (1981)).

113. See, for example, Hustler Magazine, Inc. v. Falwell, 485 U.S. 46 (1988); Watts v. United States, 394 U.S. 705 (1969); Terminiello v. City of Chicago, 337 U.S. 1 (1949); Cantwell v. Connecticut, 310 U.S. 296 (1940).

114. Boy Scouts of America v. Dale, 530 U.S. 640, 648 (2000).

115. *Id.*

116. *Id.*

117. *Id.*

118. *Id.* at 650.

119. *Id.* (emphasis added).

120. *Id.* at 651.

121. See *id.* at 651.

122. *Id.* at 654–655 (quoting Dale v. Boy Scouts of America, 734 A.2d 1196, 1223 (N.J. 1999)).

123. *Id.* at 655.

124. In 2000, the Boy Scouts of America had approximately 4.5 million members (approximately 3.3 million youth and 1.2 million adults). Boy Scouts of America Annual Membership Summary, *http://www.scouting.org/About/AnnualReports/PreviousYears/2000/11.aspx*. In 2000, Chicago had a population of approximately 2.9 million. U.S. Census Bureau, Cities with 100,000 or More Population in 2000, *http://www.census.gov/statab/ccdb/cit1020r.txt*.

125. There was significant evidence of internal dissent among members of the Boy Scouts. Devin Smith, *The Double Standard of the Boy Scouts' Honor*, CORNELL DAILY SUN, February 27, 2001, http://cornellsun.com/blog/2001/02/27/the-double-standard-of-the-boy-scouts-honor/ ("The New York City board of The Boy Scouts of America called the national leadership's policy banning homosexual scouts and troop leaders 'stupid' and 'repugnant.'"); Op-Ed., *Discrimination by the Scouts*, N.Y. TIMES, September 3, 2000, http://www.nytimes.com/2000/09/03/opinion/discrimination-by-the-scouts.html (noting that, in response to the *Boy Scouts* holding, "[i]n some areas, parents and local council leaders are mobilizing to change the national leadership's policy banning homosexuals").

126. Boy Scouts of America v. Dale, 530 U.S. 640, 676 (2000).

127. *Id.*

128. ZECHARIAH CHAFEE, FREE SPEECH IN THE UNITED STATES 18–20 (1941) (discussing the likely "fear" the framers had for the "danger" faced by "political writers and speakers" from the government).

129. See, for example, Dora C. Lau & J. Keith Murnighan, *Demographic Diversity and Faultlines: The Compositional Dynamic of Organizational Groups,* 23 ACAD. MGMT. REV. 2, 325–340 (1998) (addressing issues of diversity and the creation of fault lines within organizational groups).

130. *Id.*

131. Boy Scouts of America v. Dale, 530 U.S. 640, 676 (2000).

132. THE FEDERALIST NO. 10 (James Madison) (Garry Wills ed., 1982).

133. Richard A. Epstein, *Free Association: The Incoherence of Antidiscrimination Laws,* NATIONAL REVIEW, October 9, 2000, at 38–40.

134. Boy Scouts of America v. Dale, 530 U.S. 640 (2000).

135. Richard A. Epstein, *Free Association: The Incoherence of Antidiscrimination Laws,* NATIONAL REVIEW, October 9, 2000, at 38–40.

136. *Id.*

137. *Id.*

138. *Id.*

139. *Id.*

140. *Id.*

141. Citizens United v. FEC, 130 S. Ct. 876 (2010).

142. See Daniel A. Farber, *Speaking in the First Person Plural: Expressive Associations and the First Amendment,* 85 MINN. L. REV. 1483, 1494–1495 (2001).

143. *Id.*

144. FEC v. Massachusetts Citizens for Life, Inc., 479 U.S. 238 (1986).

145. *Id.* at 241.

146. *Id.* at 271.

147. *Id.* at 252.

148. *Id.*

149. *Id.* at 258.

150. *Id.*

151. Citizens United v. FEC, 130 S. Ct. 876, 897 (2010).

152. *Id.*

153. FEC v. Massachusetts Citizens for Life, Inc., 479 U.S. 258 (1986).

154. *Id.* at 255.

155. *Id.* at 254–255.

156. *Id.*

157. *Id.* at 269 (quoting FEC v. National Right to Work Committee, 459 U.S. 197, 210–211 (1982)).

158. Even under the so-called hearer-centered view of the First Amendment, the sounds the listener is said to have a right to hear must, at minimum, constitute "speech." Otherwise, the First Amendment would expand beyond recognition into a nonsensical generalized right to hear anything audible and to see anything visible.

159. Roberts v. United States Jaycees, 468 U.S. 609, 635 (1984) (O'Connor, J., concurring).

160. Citizens United v. FEC, 130 S. Ct. 876, 897 (2010).

161. *Id.* at 928 (Scalia, J., concurring) (citing Justice Stevens's dissenting opinion).

162. *Id.*

163. *Id.* (emphasis in original).

164. See Snyder v. Phelps, 131 S. Ct. 1207, 1216–1219 (2011) (holding that the First Amendment protects picketers at a funeral from tort liability).

165. See New York Times v. Sullivan, 376 U.S. 254, 280 (1964) (holding that a state cannot award damages for libel unless a plaintiff proves malice).

166. Citizens United v. FEC, 130 S. Ct. 876, 928 (2010).

167. Gertz v. Robert Welch, Inc., 418 U.S. 323, 345–346 (1974) ("States should retain substantial latitude in their efforts to enforce a legal remedy for defamatory falsehood injurious to the reputation of a private individual.").

168. Citizens United v. FEC, 130 S. Ct. 876, 928 n.7 (2010).

169. *Id.*

170. See, for example, ROBERT W. HAMILTON, THE LAW OF CORPORATIONS § 11.2 (4th ed. 1996).

171. Daniel A. Farber, *Speaking in the First Person Plural: Expressive Associations and the First Amendment*, 85 MINN. L. REV. 1483, 1513 (2001).

172. Democratic Party of United States v. Wisconsin *ex rel.* La Follette, 450 U.S. 107 (1981).

173. *Id.* at 125–126 (emphasis added).

174. *Id.* at 122.

175. Citizens United v. FEC, 130 S. Ct. 876, 928 (2010) (emphasis in original).

176. Scalia favors reliance upon the text of a law itself. ANTONIN SCALIA, A MATTER OF INTERPRETATION: FEDERAL COURTS AND THE LAW 38 (1997).

177. *Id.* at 17–18.

178. *Id.* at 36.

179. Trustees of Dartmouth College v. Woodward, 17 U.S. 518, 636 (1819).

180. There were six justices in the majority in *Austin*, the primary decision overruled by *Citizens United*. Austin v. Michigan State Chamber of Commerce, 494 U.S. 652, 654 (1990).

181. Citizens United v. FEC, 130 S. Ct. 876, 952 (2010) (Stevens, J., dissenting) (internal citations omitted).

182. See GEOFFREY R. STONE, LOUIS M. SEIDMAN, CASS SUNSTEIN, PAMELA S. KARLAN, & MARK V. TUSHNET, CONSTITUTIONAL LAW 1019 (6th ed. 2009); R. George Wright, *What Counts as "Speech" in the First Place?: Determining the Scope of the Free Speech Clause*, 37 PEPP. L. REV. 1217, 1221–1222 (2010).

183. R. George Wright, *What Counts as "Speech" in the First Place?: Determining the Scope of the Free Speech Clause*, 37 PEPP. L. REV. 1217, 1231 (2010).

184. Citizens United v. FEC, 130 S. Ct. 876, 899, 904 (2010).

185. *Id.* at 898.

186. See Richard R. Lau, *Models of Decision-Making, in* OXFORD HANDBOOK OF POLITICAL PSYCHOLOGY 19–59 (David O. Sears, Leonie Huddy, & Robert Jervis eds., 2003) (describing the differences between collective decision making and individual decision making and exploring various approaches political psychologists employ to understanding political decision making by individuals).

187. See MANCUR OLSON, THE LOGIC OF COLLECTIVE ACTION: PUBLIC GOODS AND THE THEORY OF GROUPS (1965) (exploring the difficulty of collective action, especially among large groups).

188. See THE FEDERALIST NO. 51, at 261 (James Madison) (Garry Wills ed., 1982).

189. THE FEDERALIST NO. 10, at 45 (James Madison) (Garry Wills ed., 1982).

190. Citizens United v. FEC, 130 S. Ct. 876, 907 (2010).

191. THE FEDERALIST NO. 10, at 45 (James Madison) (Garry Wills ed., 1982).

192. *Id.*

193. Daniel A. Farber, *Speaking in the First Person Plural: Expressive Associations and the First Amendment,* 85 MINN. L. REV. 1483, 1503 (2001), citing Nancy L. Rosenblum, *Compelled Association: Public Standing, Self-Respect, and the Dynamic of Exclusion,* in FREEDOM OF ASSOCIATION 100 (Amy Gutmann ed., 1998).

194. California Democratic Party v. Jones, 530 U.S. 567, 570 (2000).

195. *Id.* at 574.

196. *Id.* at 591 n.2 (Stevens, J., dissenting) (citing RICHARD HOFSTADTER, THE IDEA OF A PARTY SYSTEM: THE RISE OF LEGITIMATE OPPOSITION IN THE UNITED STATES 2–3 (1969)).

197. THE FEDERALIST NO. 1, at 3 (Alexander Hamilton) (Garry Wills ed., 1982).

198. California Democratic Party v. Jones, 530 U.S. 567, 582 (2000).

199. See *id.* at 573 n.5.

200. See LISA JANE DISCH, THE TYRANNY OF THE TWO-PARTY SYSTEM (2002) (arguing that the two-party system inhibits democracy).

201. THE FEDERALIST NO. 51, at 262 (James Madison) (Garry Wills ed., 1982).

202. *Id.*

203. *Id.* at 263.

204. See THE FEDERALIST NO. 84 (Alexander Hamilton) (Garry Wills ed., 1982)(responding to the most significant of the "'remaining objections' to the Constitution as proposed, that the plan of the convention contains no bill of rights").

205. LOUIS FISHER & DAVID GRAY ADLER, AMERICAN CONSTITUTIONAL LAW 389 (2007) (noting that, in supporting the first ten amendments, Madison "argued that a Bill of Rights would remove apprehensions that the people felt toward the new national government").

206. Letter from Thomas Jefferson to James Madison (December 20, 1787), *in* THE ORIGINS OF THE AMERICAN CONSTITUTION: A DOCUMENTARY HISTORY 91 (Michael Kammen ed., 1986).

207. Citizens United v. FEC, 130 S. Ct. 876, 956 (2010) (Stevens, J., dissenting; internal citations omitted) (quoting Austin v. Michigan State Chamber of Commerce, 494 U.S. 652 (1990)).

208. ROBERT W. HAMILTON, THE LAW OF CORPORATIONS § 1.4 (4th ed. 1996).

209. Anne Tucker, *Flawed Assumptions: A Corporate Law Analysis of Free Speech and Corporate Personhood in* Citizens United, 61 CASE W. RES. L. REV. 497, 521 (2010) (quoting Daniel J. H. Greenwood, *Essential Speech: Why Corporate Speech Is Not Free,* 83 IOWA L. REV. 995 (1998)).

210. ROBERT W. HAMILTON, THE LAW OF CORPORATIONS § 2.3 (4th ed. 1996).

211. *Id.* at § 8.2.

212. See, for example, Ron Lieber, *Seeking Investment Flexibility in a 401(k),* N.Y. TIMES, July 9, 2011, at B1.

213. Kathleen M. Sullivan, *The Supreme Court, 2009 Term: Two Concepts of Freedom of Speech,* 124 HARV. L. REV. 143, 145 (2010).

214. *Id.* at 155.

215. *Id.* at 156.

216. *Id.* (emphasis added).

217. *Id.* at 157.

218. *Id.*

219. *Id.*

220. *Id.*

221. *Id.*

222. Citizens United v. FEC, 130 S. Ct. 876, 899 (2010).

223. *Id.*

224. *Id.*

225. Rust v. Sullivan, 500 U.S. 173, 193 (1991) (addressing government-funded family planning that failed to allow counselors to discuss abortion as an option).

226. *Id.* at 201.

227. Citizens United v. FEC, 130 S. Ct. 876, 912 (2010).

228. See Virginia State Board of Pharmacy v. Virginia Citizens Consumer Council, 425 U.S. 748, 772 n.24 (1976) (concluding that commercial speech that is deceptive or misleading, even if it is not provably false, is not protected by the First Amendment); Gertz v. Robert Welch, Inc., 418 U.S. 323, 340 (1974) (holding that intentional lies are not protected by the First Amendment).

229. Benedict Carey, *Can Fear Win Undecided Voters? Psychologists Say Maybe Not,* N.Y. TIMES, October 5, 2004, http://www.nytimes.com/2004/10/05/science/05fear.html (discussing studies assessing the impact of emotional political advertisements on voting behavior).

230. *Id.*

231. Citizens United v. FEC, 130 S. Ct. 876, 906 (2010).

232. In the political context, such limits are narrowly construed, barring only blatantly fallacious and malicious messages. See New York Times v. Sullivan, 376 U.S. 254, 280 (1964) (protecting false speech not containing "actual malice" from liability).

233. See Richard R. Lau, *Models of Decision-Making, in* OXFORD HANDBOOK OF POLITICAL PSYCHOLOGY 19–59 (David O. Sears, Leonie Huddy, & Robert Jervis eds., 2003) (exploring various approaches to understanding political decision making by political actors).

234. First National Bank of Boston v. Bellotti, 435 U.S. 765, 777 (1978).

235. Austin v. Michigan State Chamber of Commerce, 494 U.S. 652, 658–659 (1990).

236. *Id.* at 658.

237. *Id.* at 679.

238. *Id.*

239. *Id.* at 661.

240. *Id.* at 662.

241. *Id.*

242. *Id.* at 662–665.

243. *Id.* at 662.

244. *Id.* at 663.

245. *Id.* at 664.

246. See *id.* at 662–664.

247. *Id.* at 663 (internal citations and quotation marks omitted).

248. NOAH FELDMAN, SCORPIONS: THE BATTLES AND TRIUMPHS OF FDR'S GREAT SUPREME COURT JUSTICES 57 (2010).

249. *Id.*

250. U.S. CONSTITUTION, FIRST AMENDMENT.

251. Citizens United v. FEC, 130 S. Ct. 876, 952 n.57 (2010).

252. Potter Stewart, *Or of the Press,* 26 HASTINGS L.J. 631, 633 (1975).

253. Citizens United v. FEC, 130 S. Ct. 876, 951 (2010) (Stevens, J., dissenting).

254. See Patrick Garry, *The First Amendment and Freedom of the Press: A Revised Approach to the Marketplace of Ideas Concept,* 72 MARQ. L. REV. 187, 233 (1989) ("[T]he press clause seems to protect a physical entity—the press. The language, along with the historical conditions of the press, seem to indicate that the framers of the first amendment sought to protect the press as a competitive industry within society.").

Index